Kuril Islands

Hokkaido

• Sapporo

Hakodate

North Pacific

Ocean

•Akita
Akita

*Dewa
Sanzan*

Sado

Yamagata

• Niigata

Niigata

Honshu

Nagano

• Tsukuba

• Fujimi

Mount Fuji   **Tokyo**   • Narita

•Yokohama

•Kamakura

Hakone

Shimoda

N

N

W   E

S

P

A

JAPAN

The Tokaido Road

JAPAN

JAPAN

A Reinterpretation

PATRICK SMITH

HarperCollins*PublishersLtd*

Certain passages of this book have appeared in very different form in the *International Herald Tribune*, *The New Yorker*, the *Economist Yearbook*, and *National Geographic*

http://www.harpercollins.com/canada

First edition

Canadian Cataloguing in Publication Data

Smith, Patrick (Patrick L.)
Japan : a reinterpretation

ISBN 0-00-255064-4

1. Japan - Social conditions - 1945–   2. Japan - Social life and customs - 1945–
I. Title.

DS822.5.S64 1997   952.04   C97-930223-4

97 98 99 ❖ HC 10 9 8 7 6 5 4 3 2 1

Printed and bound in the United States

Book design by Susan Thomas
Map design by Vikki Leib

Cara Caro,
for you.
And to the memory of Sean Gervasi,
honorable friend.

But the underlying strangeness of this world,—
the psychological strangeness,—is much more
startling than the visible and superficial.

— LAFCADIO HEARN,
Japan: An Interpretation, 1904

CONTENTS

A Note on Names

Because this book is written primarily for Western readers, I have rendered Japanese names according to Western practice. The given name is first, the family name follows. The Japanese are of many minds when naming themselves in international company, and my judgment is intended merely to avoid confusion. In a few cases, such as Soseki Natsume, people are known by their given (or chosen) names. He is Soseki in subsequent mentions, not Natsume. These instances are noted in the text.

—P.S.

PROLOGUE

The lid has been warped
And no longer fits on the chest.

— BONCHO, *The Summer Moon*, 1690

IN THE EARLY 1990s ten small machinery companies in Tokushima Prefecture, a rural district of Shikoku Island, unveiled an unusual product. They proposed using robots to perform plays from the old Japanese tradition of puppet theater. A prototype was produced, stock characters planned. Each would consist of more than five hundred parts. Tiny robots draped in traditional clothing would be programmed to make every required move for the full length of the old dramas.

Something in the Tokushima puppets intrigued me. A robotic geisha dressed in kimono or an electronic samurai with sword and topknot surely said something about the way Japan evolves, about the connection between its past and its future. They eventually reminded me of the opening passage in one of the century's great books on Asia, Joseph Levenson's *Confucian China and Its Modern Fate*. "During much of Chinese history," Levenson wrote in the 1950s, "new ideas, to be acceptable, had to be proved compatible with tradition; in more recent times, tradition, to be retainable, has had to seem compatible with new, independently persuasive ideas."

This is precisely Japan's predicament today—predicament because the traditional and the modern have never been easily united in Japan.

Instead, for more than a century the elements of each have been thrown together as in the weathered house where I lived during my last year in Tokyo: electric wires stapled to the old wooden posts and beams, a gas spigot poking through the tatami floor. The old and new have existed side by side, but rarely have they stood in harmonious combination.

Until now modern Japan has defined itself according to two historic changes of direction. With the Meiji Restoration of 1868 it began to build an industrial state. After the defeat in 1945 it adopted democracy *à l'américaine*—or at least its trappings. In each case the results were tangible: Meiji gave Japan steel plants, shipyards, cotton factories, railroads. The Americans brought universal suffrage, the emancipation of women, freedom of speech; landless peasants became farmers.

At century's end we witness a change of equal importance. Today the Japanese are re-creating themselves, making themselves anew. This is not so daring an observation as it may seem, for they have done so many times before. They now seek to alter the very thing that most people think sets the Japanese apart: the relationship between the individual and society—between belonging and social duty on the one hand, and on the other the perceiving ego, the individual and his inner self. It was precisely this conflict between personal autonomy and the great extended household known as Japan that both Meiji and 1945 left unresolved. That is why both of those earlier projects, despite their achievements, must finally be judged failures. The first ended in tragic extravagance, while the second remains a kind of secret failure that our accepted discourse does not yet allow us to consider as such.

After a century and a quarter, the Meiji dream was fulfilled during the 1980s: Japan caught up with the West and would have to find something else, some other ambition, to drive it forward. Then the Cold War ended, so shredding all the assumptions of the previous four decades: Japan would have to begin making decisions for itself in a more complicated world. Between these two momentous developments came a third: The emperor died. Hirohito had seen Japan through sixty-two years of militarization, conquest, war, defeat, resurrection, and, finally, affluence. And for many years his lingering presence had kept the Japanese locked in the past, unable to see it clearly, unable to put history and tradition in their proper places.

A palpable unease has settled over the Japanese. For nearly a century the emperor and the economy—and after 1945, the economy and a fixed place in the postwar order—were their ruling imperatives. Now, suddenly, nothing is imperative, nothing fixed, and both past and future come with question marks. For a newspaper correspondent, to run a bureau in Tokyo was long considered something of a nightmare—one was sent to cover the land of the nothing new. Then everything seemed to be changing. No one could predict even the very near future. No one could explain fully even what had happened the previous day. Something had begun that no one really understood. Shifting political and economic circumstances and the passing of an imperial era were important changes in themselves, certainly, but as time went on it was evident that they were best taken as either catalysts or reflections of a deeper change, a change in consciousness.

As I write, Japan is struggling to emerge from its deepest postwar recession. Its political and social systems are in turmoil. It wrestles with the many questions raised by the phenomenon we call "globalization." In these circumstances it would be easy to assume that Japan's moment in the sun has ended barely a decade after it began—that the influence the Japanese began to extend in the second half of the last decade is already a thing of the past. This is a mistake, commonly made. The Japan I describe in these pages, a Japan in transformation, is not destined to emerge with all its problems solved. Far from it. Its problems will merely be different. But it is likely to be a stabler country with a stabler system. It is likely to be stronger, more assertive, more of its own mind, for the simple reason that its people are likely to be all of these things. This is a positive prospect.

The struggle toward the open expression of individuality is an old one. It has been submerged for long stretches of history, so it is sometimes (as now) more evident than at other times. This is why it is both fascinating and frustrating to live among the Japanese. It is impossible not to come away with a sense of great expectation: They seem always on the edge of some immense breakthrough. And yet, even amid change, nothing ever seems to move forward, or moves forward at a painful pace. It is a sort of Gordian knot that has befuddled generations of outsiders—scholars, diplomats, trade negotiators, correspondents—and it makes the business of predictions a treacherous thing.

Earlier in this century a Japanese writer identified an unusual aspect of native aesthetic taste. He called it *bitai*, erotic allure. The Japanese prefer to remain in the realm of anticipation, he said, for the pleasure of *bitai* lies in drawing as close to a desired object as possible, savoring proximity to the fullest, without ever achieving fulfillment. Nothing is consummated; the other is eternally the other. To dream, it would seem, is better than to realize.

It is a disturbing notion. It suggests that the Japanese are content to suspend themselves in an eternal state of becoming, like the cresting waves caught forever aloft in a nineteenth-century woodblock print. But this comparison stands only if we liken the Japanese to the artifice, the representation, and not the thing represented. In life—in time and history— the cresting waves depicted in the woodblock prints were about to arrive on the shore.

PART 1

AMONG THEMSELVES

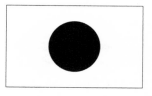

1

THE INVISIBLE
JAPANESE

She's like a quiet mountain lake whose waters are rushing
beneath the surface toward a waterfall. She's like the face on a
Noh mask, wrapped in her own secrets.

— FUMIKO ENCHI,
Masks, 1958

"IN FACT THE WHOLE OF JAPAN is a pure invention," Oscar Wilde wrote in
1889. "There is no such country, there are no such people."

Japan had opened to the West just thirty years before Wilde made this
observation. Europe was awash in what the French called *japonisme*.
Degas, Manet, Whistler, Pissaro—they were all fascinated by the imagery
of Japanese tradition. In 1887 Van Gogh decorated *Le Père Tanguy* with
prints of Mount Fuji and geisha in elaborate kimonos. Gauguin made
gouaches on paper cut in the shape of Japanese fans. This infatuation
permeated society. It was reflected on teapots and vases, in the fabric of
women's dresses, and in the way people arranged flowers.

But what did *japonisme* have to do with Japan as it was? The Japan of the
1880s was erecting factories and assembling steamships, conscripting an army,
and preparing a parliament. There were universities, offices, department

stores, banks. As Wilde elaborated, "The actual people who live in Japan are not unlike the general run of English people; that is to say, they are extremely commonplace, and have nothing curious or extraordinary about them."

Wilde was ahead of his time. We now have a word, albeit a contentious one, for the phenomenon he incidentally touched on in "The Decay of Lying." It is called Orientalism. Orientalism means "the eternal East." In his account of Japan Wilde left out only the quotation marks, for he was talking about the simple, serene, perfume-scented "Japan" of the Orientalist's imaginings.

Orientalism was made up of received notions and images of the people, cultures, and societies that stretch from the eastern Mediterranean to the Pacific. There was no dynamism or movement in Oriental society. The Orient was fixed in immutable patterns, discernible through the ages and eternally repeated, like the mosaics in Middle Eastern mosques. It did not, in a word, progress. Deprived of the Enlightenment, the East displayed no rational thought, no logic or science. The Oriental merely existed, a creature ruled by fate, timeless tradition, and an ever-present touch of sorrow. The Oriental was "exotic" rather than ordinary, "inscrutable" rather than comprehensible, "dusky" rather than light. The Orient was the "other" of the West, and the twain would never meet.

Japan, farthest east from the metropolitan capitals and least known among explorers, became the object of extreme Orientalist fantasies as soon as Europeans arrived, in 1542. The first Westerners to record their impressions were missionaries who took Japan and the Japanese to be a place and a people "beyond imagining," as an Italian Jesuit put it, "a world the reverse of Europe." Europeans were tall, Japanese were short. Churches were high, temples low. European women whitened their teeth, Japanese women blackened theirs. Japan was an antipodean universe, ever yielding, ever prostrate. "The people are incredibly resigned to their sufferings and hardships," the Jesuit wrote on another occasion, "yet they live quietly and contentedly in their misery and poverty." Francis Xavier, who arrived in 1549, asked why the Japanese did not write "in our way"—from left to write, across. His Japanese guide replied with a question that would have done Francis some good had he troubled with its implications: Why did Europeans not write in the Japanese way, from right to left, down?

The observations of sixteenth-century Europeans were not pure invention. By tradition Japanese women did blacken their teeth. An air of resignation is as evident among the Japanese today as it must have been then.

And Japanese locks—a peculiar obsession among these first visitors, noted again and again—are still opened by turning the key to the left, not as in the West to the right. But what makes these observations faintly ridiculous? Why did they produce the enduring idea of a place populated by mysterious gnomes? From our distant point of view it was a simple failure of perspective. The early travelers made no connections; the Japanese were not permitted, if that is the word, their own history, a past by which their great and small differences could be explained.

Orientalism grew from empire. One of its features was the position of the observer to the observed, the one always superior to the other. As Edward Said stresses in *Orientalism*, intellectual conventions reflect relationships based on power and material benefit. So Orientalism came into full flower in Britain and France, the great empire builders of the nineteenth century. Japan was never formally part of anyone's empire but it was hardly free of the Orientalism associated with imperial possessions. Its relations with Europe were based on the same material interests and marked by the same presumed superiority on the part of Europeans.

Today, of course, we call someone from India, Indonesia, Taiwan, or Japan an Asian rather than an Oriental. Our term is an acknowledgment of human complexity and diversity—even of equality. To call someone an Oriental would give at least mild offense because it would recall relations that no longer exist—at least not on maps. But this is not to say that the habits of Orientalism are not still with us, as any Asian can point out. Our Orientalism is remarkable for its fidelity to the ideas of centuries past: Japanese society is "vertical" while in the West social relations are "horizontal"; Westerners like competition, the Japanese compromise. When an earthquake struck Kobe in 1995 an American correspondent described the city as "an antipodean New York with more *sushi*." Asians stoically accept natural calamities as part of the timeless order of things, he explained, so that "the Japanese of Kobe are ideal disaster victims."

There was another notable aspect of Wilde's idea of Orientalism. He observed that the image of Japan abroad in the last century was partly a concoction of the Japanese themselves. Wilde called the Japanese "the deliberate self-conscious creation" of artists such as Hokusai, whose woodblock prints were much the fashion at the height of Europe's *japonisme*. This observation was exceptionally astute. We could easily make the same assertion about many of Japan's leaders and thinkers throughout history.

"Japan" has long been an act of the imagination among the Japanese, too. And to call some Japanese Orientalists is to stretch the term but slightly.

Along with Canada and numerous other countries, the United States did not much participate in Orientalism as a system of thought. Naturally enough, the former colonies had neither the economic need nor the inclination to colonize others. So America, even as it gained prominence among the industrialized countries, had no Eastern empire. It was a tagalong among the imperialists. In the nineteenth-century rush of flag-planting it possessed only the Philippines, and only briefly.

But what about the New World after 1945? In the postwar era "the American century" came into full flower, nowhere more than in the Pacific, and nowhere in the Pacific more than in Japan. The occupation of Japan from 1945 to 1952 was an allied exercise—but only nominally. Douglas MacArthur was called the Supreme Commander for the Allied Powers, S.C.A.P., but his general headquarters, G.H.Q., was an American outpost. Just as every Japanese alive today understands the old alphabet soup, so it is understood that it was the Americans who determined Japan's postwar course—and the West's understanding of it.

America developed its own version of Orientalism after the Second World War. It not only fixed Japan and the Japanese in its mind as a certain kind of country populated by a certain kind of people, it went on to create the country and the people it imagined. This was not accomplished alone, of course. America, without a trace of irony, enlisted the help of those who had led Japan into the war against allied soldiers. The British used to call this technique "indirect rule" and applied it chiefly in their African possessions. It was a neat fit for the Americans in Japan, for Tokyo's prewar conservatives were practiced Orientalists themselves and did much to assist America in its reinvention of their country.

The version of Japan America concocted after the war is still widely accepted. It is reflected in Washington's treatment of Tokyo, which resembles a colonial power's treatment of a dependency; more prevalently, it is evident in the way ordinary Americans think of Japan and the Japanese. But Americans are not alone in their view. Their Japan is also by and large the Japan taken to be genuine among Canadians, the British, the French, and others in the West. Our collective "Japan" has advanced somewhat beyond kimono and conical straw hats, though not entirely. We are still stuck with the quotation marks. In the 1970s, following the Americans' lead, we all took to calling our imagined Japan "Japan Inc."—an entire nation cast as a corporation, and its people as employees rather than citizens.

The novelist Kenzaburo Oe complains often about the two images of Japan the West now entertains. There is the old Japan of *samurai* and Zen gardens, and the new Japan of gadgets and efficiency. "Between the two," he once told me, "there is a blank, where the Japanese live." When he received the Nobel Prize for Literature in 1994, Oe said to an American writer who interviewed him in Stockholm:

> I am fascinated by Ralph Ellison's great book, *Invisible Man*, and it applies to us—us Japanese.... You can see Japanese technology in Europe, you know all about Japanese economic power, you know all about the quaint tea ceremony; but these are all images, masks of Japanese modesty or technological strength.... Even today, more than a hundred and twenty-five years after our great modernization,... we are inscrutable in the eyes of Europeans and Americans.... There is not much of a desire to understand the people who make all those Hondas. I don't know why. Perhaps we only imitate the West or are just silent in the face of European peoples.

INSCRUTABLE: KENZABURO OE is not alone in applying this tired term. It is true that the Japanese are a reserved people, ungiven to self-revelation even among themselves. It is also true, as it was a century ago, that Japan's image today is partly of its own making. But this does not explain the cloudy picture. The Japanese remain inscrutable because from the occupation onward—indeed, for a long time before the war—we in the West have never looked directly at them with a desire to understand who they are.

The postwar occupation of Japan began with an ambitious plan to remake the Japanese—to reinvent them in the American image—and ended by restoring the very things and the very people the allies had arrived intending to uproot and destroy. The initial effort was made of New Deal goodwill and the latter of Cold War calculation. But one trait united these two extremes: at no point did Japan's occupiers try to see the Japanese as anything other than a reflection of themselves.

The occupation's initial orders arrived from Washington in the autumn of 1945. They were remarkable for their sweep and idealism. MacArthur's G.H.Q. was to do nothing less than liberate the Japanese from the agony of their past and the absolutists who had used the vestiges of feudalism to lead Japan into tragedy. Politically, the occupation was to "democratize." Economically, it was to structure "a wide distribution of income and ownership of the means of production and trade." This was hardly the sort of language one would expect of Washington, but the era of Rooseveltian social crusades had carried over into the war years and its vocabulary suited the evangelists who staffed the G.H.Q. They wanted to change everything about the Japanese—their hearts, minds, and souls. Unofficially this extended to the introduction of pocket billiards, square-dancing, bowling, and big-band jazz. It would all make the Japanese better, happier people. "One trembles," an occupation memoirist noted, "at American presumption."

It is well known that the first soldiers to arrive in Japan after August 15, 1945, were shocked by their reception. People apparently prepared to die for the emperor a few days earlier greeted their conquerors with a relief approaching joy. Why was this? Because the Japanese have no morals, or honesty, or convictions? Or because, as a Japanese friend once told me, "Our only principle is that we have no principles"?

It would be hard to exaggerate the enthusiasm of ordinary Japanese for the occupation's original agenda. People old enough to recall the first post-surrender years are still deeply nostalgic about them, desperate as those years were. But no Japanese knew what was in store right after the surrender. No gift resembling democracy had yet been presented. A gift so large is always a problem, anyway. In the end, of course, no one can either give or receive it, as the Japanese soon learned. So it is fair to ask what precisely it was the Japanese appreciated as the allies arrived. All they knew was that the war was over, that they would not be dying for the emperor, and that the victors had no intention of slaughtering them: three surprises.

The occupation's greatest gift, the one the Japanese still remember with bittersweetness, was a smaller one. It was the prospect that they would have a chance to begin again, to find a new path forward. This gift lay in the limited extent to which the allies gave the Japanese nothing more than the room to make their own choices—to form political parties and labor unions, for instance, and to choose leaders by a method of their own making. It allowed the Japanese to question the norms and customs by which they had previously lived. Most of all, they were encouraged to think and make decisions as individuals for the first time in their long history. In all of this the Americans especially appeared to be something like gods. Accounts of this era often dwell with wonder upon the sheer physicality of the arriving G.I.s, who impressed the population not only with their size, their smiles, and their generosity but because in their very gestures they expressed a freedom, an autonomy, and a natural at-home-ness with themselves that the Japanese instantly recognized was absent in their own character.

Unfortunately, the occupation's generous gift—the gift of standing aside, one might say—was always attenuated and was quickly withdrawn altogether. In the autumn of 1946 American voters did to Harry Truman what they would do to Bill Clinton in 1994: They gave a Democratic president Republican majorities in both houses of Congress. America was never of one mind as to how Japan should be remade. There had long been a constituency for the idea that Japan was a "yellow peril" which, if it was not entertaining partnerships with European fascists, might as easily turn leftward toward communism. The 1946 elections tipped the scales, first in America, then in Tokyo. The Japanese refer to the events that followed as "the reverse course." As the shorthand implies, the change in the occupation's American priorities was fundamental.

The reverse course began in 1947 when the New Dealers at G.H.Q. were purged in favor of anticommunist ideologues and fiscal conservatives. A year later a policy directive written by George Kennan, the noted architect of Communist containment, brought the Cold War to Japan. The following year Mao took Beijing, and the year after that the Korean war began. These events sealed the fate of the original postwar reforms—and, for the next forty years, the fate of the Japanese.

Kennan's directive abandoned reform in favor of economic recovery and—grail of the Cold War era—stability. It called for "high exports through hard work," but the directive's language does not convey how profoundly it changed the work-in-progress called postwar Japan. Everything was to be sacrificed to containment. Purges of right-wing nationalists stopped and purges of those judged inimical to Western interests began. Efforts to disband the *zaibatsu*, family-led combines that had stood behind Japan's expansion on the Asian mainland and later supplied the war effort, were halted. Before 1948 was out the prewar industrialists were back in their offices and the old political elite was again running Japan.

Certain of the reforms lasted. No one can deny the importance of the civil rights Americans wrote into the postwar constitution (though these have often been abused). Land for landless farmers ended an old iniquity and remains a tribute to the early occupation (though land reform eventually produced new political inequalities). But most of the initial reforms were severely compromised—some fatally.

Consider the purge of the prewar order. It was extensive in the military, wiping out most of the nationalist fanatics the allies fought the war to defeat. G.H.Q. did not need the Japanese army—not until the early 1950s, anyway. Eighty percent of those eventually purged were militarists. But what about other areas: politics, the economy, and the powerful bureaucracy? Here the purge was sketchy at best. The restructured successors of the *zaibatsu* are still with us. Eight hundred and thirty bureaucrats—fewer than 2 percent of those screened—were purged. MacArthur used the prewar bureaucracy to run the country; the bureaucrats even ran the purge program. Politicians accounted for one in six of those barred from public life. A little more than a decade after the war, Japan had an accused war criminal as prime minister.

Japanese attitudes toward America have never recovered from the reverse course. Today the early period is recalled as a kind of Tokyo spring—a sentimental memory enhanced by the brevity of the season. Democracy came and went so quickly that the Japanese were soon debating whether they had ever had it. As early as 1950 the scholar Masao Maruyama declared Japanese democracy a fiction not worth defending. After the reverse course those who had looked up to Americans suddenly felt betrayed and distanced, while those who had so recently detested the victors found in them an ally in their quest to regain power. There are now few Japanese whose feelings about America are untinged with the ambivalence borne of this period: admiration and dislike, respect and mistrust.

Even America's closest allies, Britain and Canada, tend to hold at least a passably disinterested view of the occupation's performance. It is certainly detached and objective, to say the minimum, when compared with America's, for Americans spin many myths about the part they played in postwar Japan. "Considering what it might have been," an American analyst observed, "the American occupation proved to be, on balance, a surprisingly positive experience for both the victor and the vanquished." This was written in 1987; it is entirely typical of the American accounting of things since the occupation ended. But to consider "what it might have been" is a treacherous invitation. It is precisely when we accept it that the occupation of Japan is devalued for it could have been so much more than what it turned out to be. And what did it turn out to be? This question is easily answered, for the Japan before us today is the same one America created after the war: extravagantly corrupt, obsessed with market dominance, ecologically reckless, individually stifling, politically dysfunctional, leaderless, incapable of decisions.

How is it that Japan has remained frozen in such a state for five decades? The answer lies in two documents. One is the constitution written under General MacArthur and made law in 1947. Its most famous clause, Article 9, gives it the name by which it is commonly known—the peace constitution— because it bars Japan from raising an army and limits military activity to the defense of its natural borders. The other is the security treaty signed in 1951 and implemented the following year. It placed Japan under American military protection. Americans were responsible for both documents, and it is remarkable that they exist side by side for together they are a *tour de force* in political and diplomatic schizophrenia, the disease from which Japan still suffers.

The man who passed this affliction on to his countrymen was Shigeru Yoshida. It was Yoshida who, with American support, brought the prewar politicians back to power in 1948. The son of a Meiji-era liberal, Yoshida was a practiced diplomat before the war, an English-speaking bureaucrat who moved in peerage circles close to the throne. He was a nationalist but no militarist, and over several years of dexterous politicking, he and MacArthur cobbled together what can neatly be termed "the Yoshida deal."

The blunt but witty Yoshida famously held that Japan could win by peaceful means what it had lost in military adventure. It was Yoshida who placed Japan under the American security umbrella and turned the imperial army's lost crusade into the grinding war of attrition Americans track today with trade statistics. The Yoshida deal brought abundant benefits but it found shrill critics all around. Neither pacifists nor nationalists have ever quite digested one or another of its particulars. Coerced by John Foster Dulles, America's premier cold warrior, Yoshida oversaw Japan's undeclared rearmament: Japan today is the world's sixth most expensively armed country. He also let American military bases remain after the occupation ended—four decades on, they look like a permanent garrison. The price of this arrangement was nothing less than sovereignty, but Japan wasted no time proving Yoshida's point about making economic victory of military defeat.

Among the remarkable things about the Yoshida deal is that it was struck after Japan had already spent four years under the peace constitution, a document that also had its enemies. Rightists who favored rearmament detested it; the new Cold War establishment in Washington considered it a mistake as soon as it was written. Even pacifists balked before backing it since they disliked the idea of American domination. MacArthur never stopped defending the basic law he gave Japan, but that was simply MacArthur being MacArthur: He wanted a memorial to his administration modeled on the constitution he wrote for the Philippines in 1935.

There was a gaping contradiction between the peace constitution and Japan's Cold War assignment. But logically enough, MacArthur and Yoshida found the only way around it: They ignored it, so beginning Japan's postwar schizophrenia. Japan was pacifist by law but by treaty (and in practice) a spear carrier in the anticommunist crusade. Once the Japanese were drawn into the Cold War, the political center hollowed out. Voters either supported the constitution America gave them, which meant opposing America, or they supported the corruption of the constitution, so pleasing the nation that provided it. The Japanese call the political equation that fixed these polarities the "1955 system." In the autumn of that year the Socialists* reunited after several years of infighting. In response the two leading conservative parties joined to become the Liberal Democrats, who kept the rule of the old elite intact for the next thirty-eight years.

Through the 1955 system America exercised immense power over Japan after the occupation ended, as it continues to do today. Tokyo has articulated few foreign policy decisions without Washington's approval—none until the 1970s—and it usually supports American aims even when they run counter to Japanese interests. Americans pretend Japan is an independent country but fundamentally it is a military protectorate, as the Japanese, along with most people other than Americans, understand. America's power has also extended within. For roughly twenty years after the occupation, Washington did in Japan what it did in many Third World countries during the Cold War: It covertly but actively supported the political elite it had restored in

---

* Now renamed the Social Democrats.

1948. Then it invited Canada, Europe, and the rest of the world to pretend along with Americans that Japan was a working democracy.

And how did a small group of conservative politicians, closet xenophobes obsequious toward America but commanding no great enthusiasm among voters, hold power without serious challenge until 1993? This question has been asked often from the 1950s onward. And because Japan possesses the machinery of a democracy, the answer has not been simple. That there has been no credible alternative to the Liberal Democrats is true, but why? Because of corruption? Yes, but whose corruption? Why is Japan run by a system of patronage presided over by a succession of inept village headmen cast incongruously onto the world stage?

The answer lies in the nature of the reinstalled leaders from before the war. Rechristened Liberal Democrats, they prolonged traditional political customs— deference to authority, village identity, political clans, vote-purchasing—long after such practices ought to have died natural deaths. In short, the conservative elite self-perpetuated by discouraging democratic habits. And to what extent did the Americans assist in this endeavor? The answer is not altogether clear. But it has been a little clearer since 1994 when the *New York Times* revealed that the Central Intelligence Agency had been secretly passing funds to the governing party until well into the 1970s. With this money America manipulated elections, backed favorite premiers, and debilitated the political opposition. These funds numbered at least in the tens of millions of dollars, perhaps in the hundreds of millions. We do not know: the C.I.A. will not tell us.

America's concern was that of a Cold War commander. It feared for the loyalty of its troops. Specifically, Washington worried that a politically independent Japan would take the Switzerland-in-Asia route—that is, choose neutrality between East and West and opt out of the Cold War crusade. This was a possibility; we referred to it as a "danger." But it is reasonable, nonetheless, to take these secret events, along with the reverse course, as a measure of the importance America placed on a working democracy in Japan and the regard it had for the Japanese people. The logic was the same as during the Vietnam war when American soldiers burned villages to save them: Americans subverted democracy to save it.

AMERICANS DO NOT THINK of themselves as subverters of the democratic process in other countries. Destroying the choices of other people was what the Soviets were doing in Eastern Europe. This is an image Americans choose to obfuscate though most other nations, even its friends, have always been more polite about it than actually fooled. It will be difficult for Americans to face this aspect of its recent past but, with the Cold War over, sooner or later it will have to.

America's habit of dissembling reflected the essential Cold War bind: the chasm between the ideal and the real, the pretense and the actual. The space between the two is familiar to the Japanese. The Cold War produced only one more version of the gap between "Japan" and Japan, a distinction the Japanese have long lived with. Along with the millions in covert funds, this conditioned accommodation is why the Cold War, after some initial choking, seemed to go down smoothly despite its bitter taste. The Japanese have a phrase by which they learned long ago to live with their disappointments: *"Shiyo ga nai,"* they say, it can't be helped. It is true far less frequently than the Japanese believe but it expresses an emotion I place among their most basic: desire without hope. And it was desire without hope that the Japanese felt as they watched America destroy their postwar experiment.

It was not enough, though, that Japan was America's forward outpost in the Pacific, as George Kennan described it—an "unsinkable aircraft carrier," as a Japanese leader would later put it. Japan had to have a certain appearance, too. It had to *choose* the West. No other choice was possible, of course; Japan's entry into the Cold War was nothing more or less than a forced march. But Japan had to appear pristinely democratic in its decision to follow America's lead. And—no small thing—the Japanese had to be calm and happy with their lot. These matters were of supreme importance for Japan was to be a model in a region Washington viewed as one of teetering dominoes.

John Foster Dulles, as President Dwight Eisenhower's secretary of state, took an early and active interest in cultivating the proper image of Japan. During the decade after the war this concern grew in Washington and led Western scholars, primarily but not exclusively Americans, to conceive a new picture of the country the allies had recently defeated at great cost. This picture gradually advanced into the mainstream of American thought—first in scholarly papers and texts, then in popular books, and finally in films, newspapers, and advertising. It became, in short, the new paradigm. Establishing the paradigm was an American project, like the occupation. But the paradigm was accepted and supported, at least officially, by America's

Cold War allies—Canada included. The paradigm was, after all, a Cold War instrument.

The manipulation of history was of fundamental importance in this exercise for the paradigm rested largely on an image not of Japan after the war, and still less of the war itself, but of what came before the war. It was by recasting Japan's past that America's winning portrait of its Asian ally emerged. One could not pretend to alter the facts, Stalin-like. But they could be made to serve the emerging ideology nonetheless. History could be tailored with nips and tucks—by glossing over its unattractive parts and making much of minor matters. And with the past reshaped, the present would appear other than what it was.

Japan made itself modern, at least economically, with extraordinary speed after the Meiji restoration of 1868. But its people paid heavily for the course their leaders chose. There was no political freedom and much exploitation; feudal customs were preserved to prevent the development of democracy and modern social arrangements. The leadership suffused the nation with xenophobia and militarism to further its imperial ambitions. Above all, there was much dissent and conflict, and as much violence in its suppression. Until America took an interest in how Japan appeared to others, these were the ordinary facts of history. They were what the allies fought the war about. They had been established by a generation of scholars dedicated to understanding the complex, troubled path Japan followed as it modernized.

Then these facts were pushed to the margins so that America could justify its "Japan"—Japan as it had been reassembled from the past to suit new purposes. What had been so recently understood as burdensome feudal practices became "tradition." Tradition was embodied in the emperor, a good man who had opposed the war. Tradition explained the enviable work ethic of the Japanese, their patience with poor living conditions, their easy acquiescence to authority. Harmony and consensus prevailed, and strife was a foreign thing, for the Japanese were a modest people given to compromise in all matters. Nagatacho, Tokyo's political quarter, was not a hive of corrupt ultranationalists resurrected from wartime cliques; it was the home of East Asia's first up-and-running parliamentary democracy.

The new paradigm produced two essential conclusions, and whether we are aware of them or not they are the basis of what we assume to be true about Japan. The first was that the country's fifteen years of aggression were an aberration, a blip in an otherwise unbroken line. There was nothing really wrong with the Japanese system: it had swerved off course, but only briefly and the occupation fixed that. One need not come to terms with the Pacific War because it stood outside of Japan's progress toward liberal democracy. The second conclusion followed easily; not much was required by way of postwar reform. In one of the best-known books to argue this point, Edwin O. Reischauer asserted that "a slight readjustment of the rules" was all Japan needed to reverse the history of the 1930s and resume its westward stride.

This, in bare-bones outline, is the paradigm. Japan was responsible for one of the century's great tragedies, and its people subjected to many forms of degradation, but overnight these stark realities all but vanished—at least for most Americans. Reactions elsewhere to certain events—Hirohito's death in 1989, for instance—told a different story. On such occasions it becomes evident that the paradigm has not been a universal success, especially in countries that had made sacrifices during the war. But for the Americans the Japanese became no more or less than allies—hard-working, uncomplicated, compliant friends. Trade spats and bickering over security matters have frayed the basic conceit in recent years but this remains the image of Japan that Americans take to be true today. And establishing it so firmly was no small accomplishment. But those who created it often had the support of government agencies and private foundations—a point worth noting for there can be few other occasions, if any, when American scholarship was so thoroughly in the service of official ideology.

A number of the scholars who projected the new image taught at Harvard University. Prominent among them was Reischauer, a missionary's son who was born in Japan and whose life and career—scholar, Washington advisor, diplomat—remained intimately tied to the Japanese the whole of his life. Reischauer minced many words during his career but not all of them. Within a few years of the surrender he was urging Washington to recognize that scholarship could be useful as "propaganda work," as he put it, and that history rescripted could have "very profound practical results." Reischauer was hardly alone in these odd notions of the professor's task, but he was singularly keen on what we might call applied knowledge.

When the occupation ended Reischauer quickly pronounced it an unqualified success. The purges of wartime politicians and *zaibatsu* executives were completed, he declared. By his account there was no reverse course; there had been a "retrenchment" but only because the reforms were a thoroughgoing triumph. "What was now needed was for the Japanese themselves to adjust the new rules to Japanese realities," Reischauer wrote in 1953, "and to gain experience in living and governing themselves according to democratic processes." Consider the implications of this statement. Who would teach the Japanese these things? Who would show them how democracy works? Reinstalled officials from the 1930s dictatorship, the people who invented the thought police? This is what Reischauer must have meant, for they were back in charge.

These passages are from a single page in Reischauer's book, *The Japanese Today*.

> On the surface Japan gives all the appearances of a happy society and probably deserves this evaluation as much as any other country.

> Cultural schizophrenia, which may seem obvious to the untutored Western eye, simply does not exist for the Japanese, except possibly for some self-conscious intellectuals.

> The Japanese are clearly well satisfied with themselves both as individuals and nationally. Until only a few decades ago they tended to be painfully unsure of themselves, fearing that Westerners might be looking down on them, but in recent years such self-doubts have melted fast in the warmth of affluence and international acclaim.

First published in 1977 as *The Japanese* and brought up to date in 1988, *The Japanese Today*, Reischauer's most influential book, is packed with untruths, passages that bear no relation to Japanese reality, passages that can fairly be called propaganda passed off as history. The author's most remarkable assertion first occurred in the 1977 edition and is little altered in later printings. "Political corruption is not widespread in Japan," he notes in passing. Reischauer then observes that one does hear constant "cries of corruption" from the Japanese public. But he explains away such cries with the observation that foreigners do not understand what they mean.

Reischauer cast a spell. So did others with the same perspective. Among the best-known books of this genre was Ezra Vogel's *Japan as Number One,* published in 1979. This was one long invitation to learn the right lessons from the Japanese—lessons about consensus, the "higher interests" of politics, the excellence of Japanese schools, and the cooperative atmosphere in Japanese factories. Any wage-earner in a Western country who sings a company anthem, who belongs to a quality circle, or who accepts membership in a company union has been influenced by Reischauer, Vogel, and the scholars with whom they worked. So has anyone who believes Japan to be a country of adjusted, conflict-free followers. Or anyone who criticizes Japan's habits in international trade and security without troubling to understand the extent to which America is responsible for those habits.

The Japanese Today and its many companion volumes describe another "Japan"—the Orientalist "Japan" Americans conceived after the war. It is the "Japan" we all still read about in our newspapers. But it is not Japan.

THE REISCHAUER CIRCLE became known as the Chrysanthemum Club, named for the seal of the Japanese imperial house. The term was never meant to flatter. Chrysanthemum Club members were called *geisha.* They were considered uncritical apologists for Japan, a role they fulfilled on many occasions. Theirs was the perspective of results. They left out or glossed over the unattractive things about Japan so that "success" appeared to be the sanitary consequence of altogether agreeable arrangements. In *The Japanese Today* everyone wins, with the exception of intellectuals with whom the reader must not trouble himself. The appearance of "cultural schizophrenia" and corruption are put down to "the untutored Western eye."

In so simple a universe it is no wonder many in the West set off in the 1970s in search of the "secrets" behind Japan's economic "miracle." We found these just where we were supposed to, in Japan's synthetic "traditions": its respect for hierarchy and order, its sense of common purpose, its habit of company loyalty. A myth to match the cowboy emerged, the myth of the "corporate warrior," known in Japan as the ordinary *sarariman,* the salaryman, the employee tied to a major corporation for his entire career.

We are all familiar with the *samurai* who carries a briefcase. The Japanese worker, whether he is on the shop floor in a clean, white jumpsuit or behind a desk piled high with papers, is the key figure in the postwar economy. And he is so "satisfied with the way things are going" (Reischauer, *The Japanese Today*) that he has no interest in labor unions. Strikes are unwanted inconveniences; he prefers a consensus between labor and management. If he belongs to a union at all, it is one organized by his employers—a company union, otherwise known as a house, or "enterprise," union.

Let us consider briefly the history of Japanese labor. In it we find a fundamental lesson.

Even before the turn of the century, the rush to modernize prompted widespread strife in the nation's new factories. Conditions were horrendous and absenteeism chronic; job turnover was often more than 100 percent a year. Labor agents enticed farm girls into textile mills with false promises. People who "escaped" from factories were hunted down by private policemen. Wildcat strikes were more or less constant. Nobody could organize the first generation of industrial workers in Japanese history—not the new managers and not the first would-be unionists.

In 1912 a Christian activist named Bunji Suzuki founded a union called Yuaikai, the Friendly Society. Yuaikai had an interesting platform. It preached social reform and moderate unionism—it did not advocate strikes, for instance—but it encouraged members to assert themselves as individuals, a notion Suzuki called "self-revolution." Later unionists likened Yuaikai's founding document to "the pledge of a Sunday school club." The criticism is fair. But the society became Japan's first national union. In 1919 it changed both its name (to the Greater Japan Federation of Labor) and its political stance; it then became an important voice in a newly assertive labor movement.

The 1920s sounded a dissonant chord in the land of the dedicated corporate warrior. No year saw fewer than 250 major strikes. Violence was rife. During this decade employers began the first enterprise unions, structured not by trade or skill but by company affiliation. This arrangement led to a practice familiar today—the involvement of employers in all aspects of their employees' lives in the name of shared interests. What was public and what was private were thoroughly muddled. Over time a powerful group identity was imposed. House unions multiplied but they had nothing to do with harmonious sentiment. The cooperation of most employees was forced.

In 1938 the military dictatorship made all unions dissolve into the Industrial Patriotic Society, abbreviated in Japanese as Sanpo. Sanpo's name speaks for itself. Its aims were coerced calm in the workplace and, as the war escalated, higher production levels. Everyone from presidents to tea ladies had to belong. We can gauge Sanpo's popularity by what happened in 1945. Within four months of the surrender twelve hundred independent unions had nine hundred thousand members. At the end of the 1940s membership was 6.7 million—56 percent of the workforce.

The occupation was generous with the rights of workers. Union membership, strikes, and collective bargaining were all protected. Large labor federations formed. But freely organized labor was an early casualty of the reverse course. Displeased with the ties unions formed with political parties, the G.H.Q.'s cold warriors quickly opened the way to attacks on labor from the restored political and business elites, and it was the 1920s all over again. Seven hundred thousand workers were fired between 1949 and 1950; twelve thousand were labeled communists. House unions were rebuilt, often upon the remnants of Sanpo.

Gutted but standing, the independent unions of the post-surrender period hobbled on. Since 1955, labor's main event each year has been the *shunto*, or spring offensive, in which unions bargain for a nationwide wage settlement. The *shunto* has been more or less effective over the years, depending on economic conditions and what industry decides it is willing to give. It is less a negotiation than a ritual. It is as if employees are permitted to unite once a year to announce, "We are independent, and we are autonomous participants in the economy." Of course, they are neither.

It is true, as any Chrysanthemum Club scholar will assert, that the average employee does not care much about unions. Today less than a quarter of Japan's fifty million employees belong even to house unions. But this is so not because life is perfectly satisfying as it is; it is because unions have been rendered more or less useless. They are among Japan's many grand illusions—still there on the scene, still floating in and out of newspaper stories and so on, but entirely empty of purpose. If one could imagine such a thing, they are "virtual" unions.

What is at issue here? The above account touches on many contentious questions. There is acrimonious debate among scholars, writers, and journalists as to the prewar history of labor, the occupation, the reverse course, and the nature of the purges of the late 1940s. We should not be distracted by these matters. It is not important, not here, whether one favors unions, whether one believes that unions were subverted by "reds," or whether one accepts that ends justified means during the Cold War. The issue is omission.

The standard presentation of relations between labor and management gives us a placid image without accounting for how the placidity came to be. It leaves out the discord—indeed, the violence—that produced the apparent harmony we see today. It leaves out the possibility that the workplace consensus we are encouraged to admire has not been achieved happily or does not actually exist beneath the surface. In short, it leaves out history and human complexity, by which we could have learned something about the Japanese.

Most of all, standard accounts of Japan leave out evidence of the enduring desire of ordinary Japanese for individual autonomy, for an existence free of the humiliating paternalism that persists as a pervasive feature of Japanese life. It is a glaring omission for this desire and the suppression of it have been near the center of Japanese society from the beginning of the nation's modern era.

THE CHRYSANTHEMUM CLUB was high among the Cold War establishment's intellectual appendages, a major producer of the imagery that animated the American century. In the age of witchhunts its perspective prevailed without serious challenge, eclipsing the worthy work of entire generations. After a time it became dangerous to question the new orthodoxy. Scholars were inhibited from pursuing any analysis that conflicted with the paradigm; to dwell upon Japan's complexities, or the paradigm's inconsistencies, was to face that dreaded condemnation of the Cold War years: It was to be "political." The intellectual chicanery of the era discolored more than just America's understanding of Japan for there were also those elsewhere who, braving the prevailing wind, found themselves forced from jobs, institutions, and communities.

The most tragic case concerned the Canadian writer and diplomat E.H. Norman, surely the seminal Japan scholar of his generation. Norman more than anyone else was responsible for the understanding of Japan the Chrysanthemum Club was dedicated to erasing—a complex, altogether human Japan with no stock characters or easy notions of "tradition," a Japan with many serious problems, a Japan in need of the drastic change of course the Japanese wanted after the defeat. Norman's analysis rested on history; indeed, it was from his work before the war that much of Japan's authentic modern history was recovered. Norman's books, particularly

Japan's Emergence as a Modern State, are classics in the field. He was respected on both sides of the Pacific. Then his work was labeled, summarily and unfairly, "Marxist." In 1951 he was denounced in the American Senate as a communist. And as Reischauer and other scholars stood silently by, Norman was driven to suicide six years later. He was then serving as Ottawa's ambassador to Egypt.

There were always scholars, a beleaguered few, who wrote against the paradigm. Yet the single serious threat to it, at least until the Cold War ended, came not from Western professors but from ordinary Japanese. It occurred in the summer of 1960 when the treaty binding Japan to the American security system was to be renewed. The treaty is abbreviated in Japanese as AMPO. The events surrounding the renewal of AMPO are worth recalling for it was the anti-AMPO movement, which was immense, that implicitly challenged the paradigm in the simplest of ways: It showed how little the new imagery had to do with the Japanese as they really were.

The man at the center of the AMPO crisis was Nobusuke Kishi. Elected premier in 1957, Kishi seems to have been a prime recipient of the C.I.A.'s political funds. Who precisely was Kishi? The question is interesting because America's dealings with him were an insult not only to the Japanese but to every allied soldier who fought in the Pacific War and everyone who sacrificed for it at home. If Washington had purposely sought out an emblem of all that was repulsive in imperial Japan, it could not have made a better choice.

To put the matter simply, Kishi was a war criminal and a thug. During the 1930s, when Japan occupied Manchuria, Kishi was the second-ranked civilian in the colonial administration. In Hideki Tojo's wartime cabinet he held the industry portfolio and served as well as vice-minister for munitions. He was, nonetheless, described by Joseph Grew, Washington's prewar ambassador and a prominent figure in the Tokyo Lobby at the war's end, as "one of my highly valued friends in Japan." Kishi, it seems, let Grew out of prison to play golf in 1942, before Washington and Tokyo exchanged diplomats.

As an "A" list war criminal according to the international postwar classification, Kishi was held in Sugamo prison after the defeat, but the occupation released him (along with a number of others) at the end of 1948. No public explanation for this move was ever offered, though its place in the reverse course can hardly be disputed. Kishi then began a steady march toward the premiership, backed by postwar Japan's least-savory collection of unreconstructed fascists, Sugamo alumni, and *yakuza* crime bosses. Kishi brought many of his cronies into national politics with him. His administration, indeed, marked the consolidation of the prewar nationalists' future in Japanese politics. Kishi himself remained an influential figure in Nagatacho until his death in 1987.

In June of 1957, the just-elected Kishi visited the United States. He golfed with President Eisenhower and addressed both houses of Congress. He traveled to New York, met with senior Wall Street financiers, and tossed out a ball at a Yankee game. It was shortly after this visit, the scholar Michael Schaller wrote recently, that the C.I.A. appears to have begun sending Kishi covert funds. Three years later it was Kishi more than any other Japanese who made sure the AMPO treaty was renewed.

All of Japan knew the AMPO question was a crossroads. The country could either go on as it had since the war, under strict American tutelage, or it could declare the postwar era over and find its own way. In the Diet and among voters opposition to the AMPO treaty was widespread. The pacifism of the postwar constitution had sunk deep roots. People did not want Japan to continue as America's cold war partner; neither did they care to sacrifice sovereignty any longer to a victor that had brought back the prewar regime while pretending to purge it. Nonetheless, Kishi signed a new version of the treaty at the White House in January 1960, while Eisenhower looked happily on. By the following May, when the Diet was due to ratify the pact, the entire nation was absorbed by the AMPO issue—much of it mobilized against the treaty's extension.

Kishi brought the Diet to the brink of rioting, as he had a self-imposed deadline. He wanted the treaty signed into law before Eisenhower visited Japan in June. Impatient with lengthy debates, Kishi eventually ordered police to carry opposing politicians out of the legislative chamber. Then he railroaded through a renewal vote in his adversaries' absence. It was a messy, undignified scene all around. Kishi's forced vote was legal, but it sat badly with a population that knew him as a wartime bureaucrat imprisoned after the surrender. It also looked as if the Liberal Democrats were more concerned with pleasing Washington than with honoring the wishes of the electorate.

Kishi's vote prompted protests all over the country. Several hundred thousand people ringed the Diet building in Tokyo. Eleven days before

Eisenhower was to arrive, a military helicopter had to rescue his press secretary from demonstrators who surrounded his car as it made its way in from the airport. Soon after, amid violent clashes between demonstrators and rightists recruited by the government, Tokyo canceled Eisenhower's visit. It would have been an embarrassment for America, anyway. By then Kishi had organized security that would have made the president's visit look like a military maneuver. There were command posts, first-aid squads, aircraft units, eighteen thousand policemen, and twice that number of ultranationalists and *yakuza* goons.

How many of us today are even slightly familiar with these momentous events? And how should we understand them? What had begun as a fight over Japan's place in the Cold War order was changed by the forced vote. After Kishi rammed through the treaty, AMPO also became a struggle over the failure of democracy in Japan—the democracy Americans still congratulate themselves for giving the Japanese. The scholar Chalmers Johnson likens the anti-AMPO revolt to the Hungarian revolution of 1956, minus the troops and tanks. It is a provocative comparison. An American president unable to visit the happy capital of its closest ally in the Pacific—wasn't that, indeed, a scene from the Soviet satellites? Didn't the Liberal Democrats, in ignoring the will of their own people, behave just as the pro-Moscow communists in Budapest who crushed the uprising of ordinary Hungarians? Without meaning to, Johnson raises an even more compelling question. Why is it that Americans must resort to the history of Soviet misdeeds in Eastern Europe to understand their own postwar conduct elsewhere on the globe? If we reflect upon this even briefly, the answer does not seem as elusive as one might think. Doesn't it reveal the extent to which Americans have been mesmerized by their postwar myths—and the extent to which America's friends in the West are influenced by them?

The year 1960 was a watershed not only for Japan but also for our idea of Japan. We can consider it today as the year America's "Japan" was formally launched. A few days after the AMPO treaty became law Premier Kishi was replaced by Hayato Ikeda, another leftover from the wartime bureaucracy, whose mission it was to take people's minds off the troublesome matters of democracy, sovereignty, and world politics. Ikeda promptly instituted a program every Japanese, alive at the time or not, recognizes as a postwar turning point. It was called the Income-Doubling Plan. It was devised to give as many Japanese as possible a material interest in arrangements as they were. It may look today like a bribe, and it was—partly. But it was more in the way of an offer the Japanese could not refuse.

The reverse course, the Yoshida deal, and the 1955 system had prepared the ground well for this moment. The Ikeda plan produced a kind of madness—the madness of material growth at any human or environmental cost, of a ruling party whose sole task was good relations with America, the madness of a mutant democracy in which elections function to deprive voters of their democratic rights. Thereafter, production and consumption were everything. Ikeda also invented the notion of consensus politics. His slogan was "Tolerance and Patience." Everything was to be done by common agreement after 1960. Of course, tolerance and patience changed nothing in Nagatacho; they meant only that the opposition took its place at the table on the understanding that power would never change hands. The Liberal Democrats could still pass any law they wanted, as the treaty vote had proven. Consensus was advanced as a traditional Japanese value but it was really nothing more than another word for the disguised power of the political brokers who controlled Nagatacho.

Ikeda's plan succeeded admirably, at least on its own terms: the average salary doubled in seven years, three short of the goal. So began the era of Japan Inc., the name America gave to the obsessed nation it had created. It was almost as if America had chosen Ikeda for office for he did much to produce the country America wanted Japan to be. "High exports through hard work," George Kennan's prescient phrase at the start of the reverse course, was fixed as the national ethos. All at once Japan became a mass society, a corporate society, and a management society (that is, one planned and controlled by a technocratic elite, such as a business). But it was no longer a society capable of managing the democratic process, or even of sensible decisions, for Hayato Ikeda put Japan to sleep as a civic society. So it was that the Diet assumed the lifeless gait and the taste for immense corruption that have been its hallmarks ever since.

Edwin Reischauer visited Japan shortly after the AMPO crisis. At an academic conference in Hakone, a resort district south of Tokyo, he and other scholars elevated the paradigm to the level of doctrine. Thereafter it was known as "modernization theory," which assumed as truth the ideas Reischauer and a few other Americans had been advancing for years: Japan was a place of contented conformity, and the Japanese had handily regained the democratic track after a few misguided nationalists, now banished, temporarily diverted them. Gradualism in all matters was the correct prescription. The only way forward, anywhere on the globe, was the Western way. For its naivete (or cynicism, perhaps) and all-around inaccuracy, the new orthodoxy astonished the Japanese scholars at Hakone. But a few months after Reischauer returned to Cambridge the new American president, John Kennedy, named him ambassador to Tokyo. Kennedy no doubt had the revolt against AMPO in view when he chose the professor from Harvard. And in appointing Reischauer he presided over the formal marriage of American scholarship to Cold War ideology.

In his later memoir, *My Life Between Japan and America*, Reischauer made short work of these matters. He could not comprehend the vehemence of Japanese attacks upon modernization theory, he wrote. The idea of modernization theory was a fabrication in the first place; there was never any such thing. The Japanese scholars, in any event, were all "Marxists"— Reischauer loved the term—whose "deeply entrenched Marxist concepts" led them to misunderstand their own country; Americans understood it better. As to the anti-AMPO movement, that was a misunderstanding, too. Resurrected war criminals like Kishi were no problem; the problem was the Japanese people who lived and labored in the dark:

> Many Japanese ... felt helpless and resentful in their dependence on the United States.... They feared that America's adventuristic foreign policy, as they perceived it, combined with American nuclear power would involve Japan in a new tragedy. They saw themselves as being at the mercy of American callousness and political folly. Although they believed that they had no choice but to remain economically dependent on trade with America, they wished to distance themselves politically as much as they could from United States foreign policy....
>
> It was necessary for the Japanese to realize that the United States was not an inherently aggressive, militaristic country, but that it had to maintain some military strength in the Western Pacific....

It would be Reischauer's task as ambassador to correct "all these distorted concepts," as he put it in his memoir. He never entertained the idea that the Japanese, even if they were wrong, had a right to their mistakes. Or that they well understood the circumstances under which they lived—and how they arrived at them—and that they simply did not wish to host America's Pacific forces or continue living as they had for all but a very few years after their defeat.

Reischauer served in Tokyo for six years. We now know he actively planned the subversion of at least one election, in Okinawa, and it is difficult to accept that as the extent of his illegal activity. Reischauer never fooled the Japanese about the Americans. From his day to ours they have held to a hard-nosed understanding of their bargain with America, the old Yoshida deal, which is one reason Tokyo appears to be so relentlessly obstinate today in matters such as trade. But the professor from Harvard was a resounding success in fooling Americans, and to a lesser extent their allies, about the Japanese. Among Americans this can be measured by their failure to understand Japan's official behavior toward them. More broadly, it is reflected in the ease with which we all dismiss ordinary Japanese as conformist robots, or "economic animals" with no interest and no pride in anything other than production and export.

THE JAPANESE WENT through a long period after the war with the pervasive feeling that they were ugly. People who lived through the defeat will sometimes still mention this in passing. One also finds vestiges of a time of profound self-rejection in ordinary expressions. *Nihonjin banare shiteiru*—you look different from a Japanese—was a common compliment among young women well into the 1980s. A poignant sense of inadequacy dates from Japan's first modern contacts with the West in the last century. But defeat in 1945 intensified it dramatically. The Japanese wanted somehow to disappear after the war. And the Americans invited them to do so, to efface themselves before the world, with the idea that they were not nationalists but internationalists.

"Thus, the Japanese, not long ago one of the most militaristic peoples of the world, have now become ardent champions of internationalism," Edwin Reischauer wrote after the war. "Some may doubt the sincerity of this sudden conversion, but it is not difficult to understand in a people entirely at the mercy of foreign military powers and completely dependent on trade with the outside world."

Reischauer's reasoning worked well for the Chrysanthemum Club. For example, it excused orthodox scholars from engaging the thorny question of wartime coercion on the part of Washington's new friends in Tokyo. But as a piece of logic it is a little preposterous. The Japanese were not a militaristic people, any more than any other ever was or will be. They suffered under a militarist regime over which they had no control. Neither does Reischauer's conclusion stand up to scrutiny. It is precisely those at the mercy of others whose sincerity must be questioned. Only those who willingly supported the dictatorship could be considered candidates for conversion. And many of them did not convert; in the reverse course Americans allowed them merely to bury their sentiments or reinterpret them.

By embracing internationalism the Japanese were supposed to have repudiated any claim they may have made to nationalism. It is true that the pacifism and neutrality popular after the war remain so today. But that is not the same as professing internationalism to the point of giving up one's national pride and identity, even for a people who wanted to disappear out of self-loathing. To be internationalist instead of nationalist—this is a false equation, commonly proposed. It has left the Japanese themselves confused and inarticulate as to their place in the world and the meaning of the awkward but often used term "Japaneseness." And so it escapes us that beneath its calm surface Japan still suffers the same restlessness and unease that was evident until the summer of 1960.

If we are to understand Japan today, and what Japan is likely to become, we must recognize that this restlessness has reemerged, as inevitably it would. To put it another way, the Japanese have come to realize that it is impossible to disappear from the face of the earth, or to make the bogus exchange of nationalism for internationalism. Or another way again, the Japanese are outgrowing their feelings of ugliness and inferiority in comparison with others. And these realizations have now led them to begin to redefine themselves.

Among the curiosities of modern Japan are the many slogans it has produced. They are like capsule philosophies, rich in meaning. *Fukoku kyohei*, wealthy nation, strong defense; *wakon yosai*, Japanese spirit, Western things; *bunmei kaika*, civilization and enlightenment. These were some of the phrases Japan used to describe itself when it began to modernize, and each one stood for an idea. During the war the dictatorship exhorted the populace with "Desirelessly on to victory," a telling admonition to suppress the self for the sake of the state. In the late 1980s Japan invented a slogan in a single word: *kokusaika*, internationalization. It was a complicated notion, never well explained, but it, too, gave an insight into the age.

It was difficult to tell what *kokusaika* meant when bureaucrats, scholars, and television commentators used the term. It was supposed to mean nothing less than the reinvention of the national ethos. Somehow Japan Inc. would be decommissioned: the Japanese would work less, export less, and consume more of other people's products. They would take a greater part in world affairs. But these were rather large projects. Japan Inc., after all, could not be discarded just because some Japanese decided they were finished with certain aspects of it. American dispensation would be required. In any case, there were too many definitions of *kokusaika* and too little agreement as to its true meaning. How would Japan internationalize? What would it mean to the rest of us?

Japan stammered for a simple reason. "Internationalization" was the wrong word. It was trying to articulate a revived nationalism it feared the world (especially its neighbors and the Americans) would not accept. Along with "internationalization" came other notions—less often discussed but more to the point: "soft nationalism," "resurgent cultural nationalism," "prudent revivalist nationalism." And along with these came Japan's arrival on the world's economic stage. In the mid-1980s the yen began a climb in value that put it among the world's strongest currencies. At home interest rates were dropped to record lows, quickly producing the "bubble economy," a five-year period of high but frothy, speculative growth. The Tokyo stock market tripled in value. Land prices doubled in a year—and then doubled again the next year. The bubble brought the Japanese into the world's real estate markets, resorts, and auction rooms. Investors bought Hollywood studios and trophy properties such as Rockefeller Center. Japan became the largest aid donor and number one source of credit. At economic summits in Toronto and elsewhere, the world began to bow in Tokyo's direction. Can anyone doubt that these events were a form of national self-assertion—that the Japanese were making themselves visible again?

In certain ways the late 1980s resembled a party, as many Westerners who lived in Tokyo during those years understood. And like other parties, it was an occasion for both remembering and forgetting. The Japanese remembered nothing less than themselves. At home and abroad, they grew more confident—as a nation and as individuals. They began to assert themselves politically for the first time since the anti-AMPO protests of 1960. But in the intoxication of the time they forgot about their larger circumstances. They forgot the immense influence America still exercised over Japan. They forgot that Japan had placed its faith in efficiency and technology, not democracy, and that reversing that decision was their greatest challenge. They forgot, too, that all the property deals in the world would not change the fact that Japan was a nation that had "power without purpose"—a phrase famous by the decade's end.

The bubble lost its air in 1990 when Japan tumbled into recession. But something more abrupt than an economic downturn brought the Japanese back to sobriety. On August 2, 1990, Iraqi forces invaded Kuwait. And when the United States began gathering international support for a military response to Saddam Hussein, the Persian Gulf War became a critical moment for Japan. What was Japan to do within its constitutional constraints, which exclude it from collective security actions? As much to the point, what did Japan want to do? As Tokyo dithered, Washington grew shrill. Japanese leaders looked like fools—at least from America's perspective. They sent no soldiers to the Persian Gulf—no troops, no supplies, no ships until it was too late. Japan eventually pledged thirteen billion dollars and got more criticism than thanks for it. Twenty-nine nations contributed to the Persian Gulf effort; Washington gave twenty-eight of them regular progress briefings during the assault and pride of place at the celebrations that came afterward.

There was a singular irony in this obvious snub—the irony of America's blindness to the history Americans themselves had made. No one seemed to remember the old Yoshida deal, or that Japan's place in the Western security alliance had been imposed upon it. It never seemed to occur to anyone in Washington that Tokyo's fumbled response was partly the consequence of a document Americans wrote for the Japanese and then made law. And it was a measure of Tokyo's long habit of deference that no Japanese official ever pointed these things out.

The memory of those months will be long in fading among the Japanese. The Persian Gulf crisis suddenly ended the party of the late 1980s, the dream that Japan would never have to face the tasks of dismantling the Yoshida deal, rethinking the notion of internationalism, and becoming—the phrase was soon universal—"a normal nation."

THE CHRYSANTHEMUM CLUB survives in America and still extends its influence throughout the West. It is now supported, vigorously and generously, by Japanese institutions. There is a Mitsubishi chair of law at Harvard and a Toyota chair of anthropology at the University of Michigan, among numerous other endowments like them. The Japanese spend many millions on such positions, which are almost invariably occupied by the *geisha* of the Chrysanthemum Club. *Geisha* still direct Japanese studies in many of the most esteemed universities, not just Harvard, and as the scholar Chalmers Johnson once pointed out, "You never have to tell a *geisha* what to do."

The Berlin Wall was a year in ruins when the Gulf War broke out. Saddam Hussein's invasion was a mere taste of the complex new world Japan, along with the rest of us, entered when the Cold War ended. Products of the Cold War, the Chrysanthemum Club and its "Japan" could never survive the end of it. Neither could the postwar political elite in Tokyo, janitors of America's Orientalist creation. The Tokyo political landscape has changed forever since the late 1980s. Yet our postwar images linger, partly as a matter of inertia. We will eventually have to examine all our old assumptions if we are not to drift dangerously far from reality. But inertia, especially when it is rooted in a fear of change, can be a considerable force.

At the brink of the Cold War's end the Chrysanthemum Club was openly challenged for the first time in many years. It was the challenge of journalists and scholars known as the revisionists. They were (and remain) a loose group; on many questions they are far from universal agreement. None among them especially likes the revisionist label (as members of the Chrysanthemum Club did not like theirs). But they are legitimately bound by a simple assumption: The paradigm is false; the West should reassess the way it looks at Japan.

It is time to recognize, the revisionists say, that Japan is different from America and other industrial nations. At least as it is presented, it is a model of nothing. It has assumed the trappings of democracy but does not function as one. Its institutions do not serve the purposes we think they do. The government is not merely a regulator—an arbiter, as in the West— it is an advocate. It plays an active role in the economy, with defined social and economic goals, as governments do in many Third World countries. Chalmers Johnson, best-known of the revisionists and a scholar who has devoted his career to China and Japan, coined a new term for the Japanese system. He called it a "capitalist developmental state"—a creature unknown until postwar Japan came along.

The revisionists detonated an explosion with another simple idea: If Japan is different it should be treated differently. As revisionism spread into newspapers and magazines, this assertion was immediately applied to matters of trade. Suddenly America could understand its chronic deficit with Japan for it could dispense with the fiction that, apart from a few specific problems, the Japanese were free-market capitalists, just like the rest of us. The problem was systemic. Japan was closed, by virtue of numerous visible and invisible mechanisms, because Japan's political and business leaders liked it that way. And it would not open until the West forced it open—a task left chiefly to the Americans.

Revisionism arrived like fresh air in a windowless room. It was an act of creative destruction in that it began the work of dismantling the postwar paradigm. It bore no ideological load, no Cold War imperative, so that it made the prospect of clear sight, even among Americans, at last realistic. Revisionism held much appeal for ordinary Japanese who stood to benefit greatly from an economic system stripped of some of its elaborate controls. Not surprisingly, the Japanese elite quickly labeled the revisionists "Japan bashers," a term whose sole purpose was to preclude open discussion of the institutions whose levers they pushed and pulled.

Revisionism has had a considerable impact in the United States. The old picture of Japan advanced by the Chrysanthemum Club is scarcely credible now. That it continues to be taught in universities—in America and elsewhere—is faintly ridiculous. It is a vestige. Washington and Tokyo still guard the wall between trade and security that they erected after the war. But this artificial distinction is now under threat—as it should be, for it is a vestige, too.

The revisionist version of Japan has also begun to sway ordinary Americans—though not always in so favorable a direction. In the early 1990s they suddenly decided they were confronted with another version of the "evil empire." This kind of talk did not go very far elsewhere in the West. But as the Soviet Union collapsed there was serious talk in America that Japan would replace it as public enemy number one. All that remained was how Americans could protect themselves from the conspiring country across the Pacific.

Such notions have a long history in America. And it is of interest to others because, for better or worse, America retains immense influence in shaping Western ideas of Japan. For more than a century it has swung like a pendulum in its views of the Japanese. A hundred years ago Americans wondered how long it would take before the primitive but innocent Japanese would become Christian and democratic. Then came the yellow peril, when the Japanese were cast as predatory militarists with a love of the sword deep in their souls. During the war they were simply "beasts"—Harry Truman's judgment. Then they became diffident workaholics. And here were the Americans again, hatching conspiracy theories. Suddenly, nothing happened by accident in Japan. Narita, Tokyo's international airport, was not big enough because Japan wanted to limit the influx of foreigners and the foreign travel of the Japanese. Japan did not enter a recession in the early 1990s: it was "blindsiding" the West, a sort of sneak attack, the better to achieve economic domination. This view has receded precisely because Japan has been in a recession, but it is likely to return as soon as America's trade problems do.

Revisionism is partly to blame for this sort of paranoia—if not its originators, then those who popularized the revisionist perspective. What went wrong? Why did revisionism not mark the beginning of a genuine understanding of the Japanese—and so the end of the stories spun around various "Japan"s?

The revisionists' faults had something to do with their timing. When they appeared Japan had just finished a quarter of a century of gray, monotonous stability during which nothing seemed to change. Of course, there is no such thing as a static society—it is a human impossibility. On this point the revisionists should have learned from that other eternally unchanging nation, the Soviet Union. Instead, at the very moment everything was to begin changing, they posited a nation incapable of movement.

Most of all, the revisionists' advocates displayed little understanding of history. They seemed unaware of the extent to which America was responsible for the "Japan" that was suddenly so threatening. Every important component of Japan's postwar economic machine was in place by the end of the occupation in 1952. M.I.T.I., the demonized Ministry of International Trade and Industry? Up and running precisely one day before the first allied soldiers arrived in Tokyo in 1945, and its bureaucrats have never looked back. Targeted industries—ships, steel, electronics, cars? The policy to concentrate resources in them began under the Americans in 1947. It was called "priority production" then; the only thing the Americans did not like was the name.

One of the terms that came up often in the late 1980s was *gaiatsu*, which translates as "outside pressure." There was nothing new about *gaiatsu*, but the term was current then because *gaiatsu* seemed the only way things got done in Japan. Outside pressure almost always meant pressure from the Americans. Washington would demand, say, an open market for beef or baseball bats. Tokyo would resist until the last moment; then it would present the case to the Japanese public as "inevitable"—so relieving itself of responsibility.

Gaiatsu is indeed how many things get done in Japan. But what kind of relationship does *gaiatsu* imply? Is it one that does credit to either side— or does it diminish both? More, does it represent a long-term solution to the problems Japan has in its relations with America and the rest of the world, or is it, at its core, Orientalist? *Gaiatsu* was much favored by many revisionists and still is, which brings us to their most basic mistake. Like the Chrysanthemum Club, many revisionists failed to acknowledge Japan's complexity and humanity. Instead, they took Japan to be the Japan of its institutions—the Japan of the center, the Liberal Democratic, corporate, consensual Japan America did so much to create. This is the Japan Kenzaburo Oe described—an "official" Japan made of *samurai* tradition and efficiency. And it is a mistake for any of us to accept it at face value.

Oe drew a fundamental distinction when he talked about the other Japan, the "blank where the Japanese live." By this he meant a Japan that is more authentic but less familiar to us in the West. It is a country of ordinary people with ordinary desires, people neither more nor less efficient than anyone else, neither more nor less individual, neither more nor less given to feudal arts and formality. Borrowing terms from Buddhist history and bending them, we call the familiar, official Japan the Japan of "the great tradition." Beneath it is the Japan of "the little tradition," the Japan we do not easily discern.

The difference between the two is very old. In one form or another it is no doubt universal. But nowhere has it been so influential for so long as in Japan. For all of its recorded history there has been antagonism between the great and the little, the refined "above" and the ordinary "below." The famous saying of the late feudal period was "Revere officials, despise the people." This crude notion survived into the Meiji era as a clear line drawn between *kan* and *min*, officials and commoners, and it is not absent, to put it mildly, in Japan today. There is one other point worth noting. The great tradition has always reflected what Japan has borrowed from abroad. It is an imposed import while the little tradition has always been by nature indigenous.

The conflict between the great and the little is rarely explained in our mainstream accounts of Japan. Yet it is the coiled spring of Japanese history. It is as evident today as at any time in the past, and it will inform the rest of this book. To grasp it, at least generally, is essential to improving our understanding of Japan and the Japanese.

Consider again the matter of protectionism. In the West we have always taken Tokyo's protectionist trade policies to reflect the nation's essential ethos—its xenophobic mentality, its dislike of the foreign. Assuming protectionism enjoys universal support, we view it as a problem of "the Japanese." It has never been so simple. Who and what do Japanese policies protect? Is it ordinary Japanese people or the Japanese system, the bureaucrats and ministries at the center of Japan. Had this been considered, America might have thought better of *gaiatsu*. *Gaiatsu* does nothing to alter the system, and the system is the problem—for the Japanese as well as for the rest of us.

Because the revisionists, or most of them, did not make the distinction between the great and the little, they did not see that America's problems with Japan were merely symptoms of more fundamental problems, many of which America either caused or prolonged. And they exhibited no confidence in the ability of the Japanese to alter their nation's course by themselves. Isn't this, in a new form, the same mistake Westerners have made since they first arrived in 1542—the essential mistake of all Orientalists—that is, the failure to allow the Japanese their own past, their own history?

LATE IN 1995, three American soldiers stationed in Okinawa, Japan's southernmost prefecture, molested a twelve-year-old girl outside of their base. Two admitted to abduction, the third to rape. (In the end a Japanese court sentenced all three to roughly seven years.) A gruesome crime in any circumstance, the incident set off a storm in America's relations with Japan that went far beyond the conduct of guests in another country. Three G.I.s on a night off managed to put the entire postwar security system back on the table between Tokyo and Washington.

In this the incident was reminiscent of the AMPO upheaval thirty-five years earlier. The question soon became the American military presence as a whole—the core of the Yoshida deal. What were so many Americans doing in Japan? More accustomed to foreigners and less influenced by Japanese tradition, Okinawans are more direct than Japanese of the main islands. This was an unfortunate accident of history for the Americans, for the protests of the Okinawans made it evident once again that change between Japan and America is, sooner or later, inevitable.

It is not easy to hide almost fifty thousand troops from public view for nearly half a century—especially when thirty thousand of them operate seventy separate military facilities, spread over a fifth of usable land, as is the case in Okinawa. For a long time Washington and Tokyo did a thorough job of hiding these soldiers from Americans and were pretty good at keeping them out of sight in Japan. This was one reason three-quarters of the American bases in Japan were concentrated in the country's most distant prefecture. And it is why the rape incident once again challenged America's simple idea of Japan and of how it has conducted itself there.

Fifty years ago the Western allies interrupted the Japanese. We defeated them, of course, and in a time we briefly provided for them they took their first tentative steps toward resolving the tragedy their modernization had come to. Then America decided to delay such resolution—a delay that has lasted five decades. A paradox presents itself: America now claims the closest relationship with Japan of any Western country, yet it is also the most unhealthy. If it is to make its relationship a healthy one, it must now do what it failed to do a half century ago—stand aside—and what the first Westerners in Japan failed to do five centuries ago—look at the Japanese only for what they are.

The first thing we must all discover about them, ironically, is that they are accustomed to hiding—from themselves as well as from others. Every Japanese wears a mask. And within their masks the Japanese have learned to live close to one another by living far apart. But beneath the placid, unchanging surface of Japan's oddly vacant, undecided present are countless conflicts, tensions, crosscurrents, and anxieties. They have always been there. They have merely become more apparent now, as if a lid were lifted, or a mask partially removed.

In *Masks*, the novelist Fumiko Enchi describes her antagonist as possessing an "indestructible face." One of the essential questions the Japanese have begun to ask themselves—one posed in this book—is whether their masks are indestructible too or whether it is time to live without them.

2

HIDDEN

HISTORY

Look closely and you will see what an enormous variety of
human types are represented in the huge crowd.

—SHIMEI FUTABATEI,
Drifting Clouds, 1889

IN KANAZAWA, a city on the Sea of Japan noted for its old samurai quarter, there is a family that traces its ancestors back four centuries. Their name is Meboso, and they have made sewing needles and fishhooks for nineteen generations.

The Meboso's are as proud of their uncommon name as they are of their craft, for the two cannot be separated. "Meboso" comes from *meboso-bari,* narrow-eyed needle. In the sixteenth century their skill was such that the local daimyo, the feudal lord, let them take a surname and carry swords. "An unusual honor," Tadayoshi Meboso said when he explained this to me. "Almost no one of our status could have a name or own a sword." Today the Meboso's sell fly-fishing gear, along with boxes of tailor's needles, from the same shop they have run since 1575. It is on Meboso-dori—Meboso Avenue.

It was hardly unusual for people under feudal rule to have only a given name and to be identified according to their village or some other obvious attribute. But where else among the advanced countries is this point of a family name still important, still dwelt upon in casual conversation?

The feudal past is near in Japan. Until late in the last century only daimyo and samurai, and an exceptional few like the Meboso's, had family names. Everyone else was nameless. Allowing everyone a surname was among the early reforms of the Meiji era, Japan's great period of modernization, which began in 1868. It is because names were so recently granted that many still correspond to villages or rural features. Kurokawa: Blackriver; Ishibashi: Stonebridge.

What is to be learned from the simple historical fact that the great-grandparents of many Japanese alive today had no names? Seeing Japan as a group society, we conclude that there was no notion of individuality among the Japanese until a few generations before our own. No individuality, and for the vast majority no history—just as the serfs of feudal Europe lived out lives as unrecorded as the lives of farm animals.

Such reasoning is logical enough. It is a commonplace that the Japanese are given to groups. No matter what version of Japan one subscribes to, it is likely to include the assumption that the individual's worth and power are secondary to the worth of the collective, whether it is a village, a base-ball team, or a corporation. History offers abundant evidence to support this idea. The fact that the Japanese were nameless until little more than a century ago is but one of numerous examples.

But this is a misreading. For the group is a kind of fiction in Japan. It is within the group that the Japanese put on their masks. To assume a mask is to assume a role—a public, designated role in the group. The masks of the Japanese are also masks of sameness. By wearing them, the Japanese signify to themselves that there are no differences among them, and that having no differences is part of what it means to be Japanese.

One of the first Westerners to live in Japan, a Jesuit called João Rodrigues, seems to have understood the Japanese mask uncannily well. Rodrigues arrived in 1576, around the time the Meboso's got their name, and remained more than thirty years. He was fluent in the language and eventually translated for the shogun. The Japanese have three hearts, Rodrigues surmised: "a false one in their mouths for all the world to see, another within their breasts only for their friends, and the third in the depths of their hearts, reserved for themselves alone and never manifested to anyone."

To wear a mask among others: Is there a better measure of how thoroughly the individual is effaced, of how well the Japanese personality learned to peek out through the reed screen of a purposely blank expression that hides the true face from public view? These habits of mind and physiology have been so completely internalized that Japanese even today have difficulty discussing their own ways of thinking or feeling. But a nation of effaced personalities is different from one in which individual personalities—somehow, miraculously—do not exist.

Neither individuality nor a sense of history is missing from the assumptions by which ordinary Japanese live. Nor were they absent in the past. These basic aspects of human life have simply been submerged. So there is a more accurate conclusion to draw from the nameless majority that lived and died in Japan until a century ago. Then as now, it was not individuality that was missing so much as public individuality, the open manifestation of the self, the self unmasked within the group. In the same way, the Japanese did not live without their own history—no more, at least, than anyone else in a feudal society. Their history was merely hidden by the society that preferred them to remain nameless.

There is a vast chasm between the simplicity arriving foreigners often find in Japan and the furtive, unrevealed complexity that lies within. In this space the Japanese still make their hidden history—the record of their endeavor to achieve public, unmasked individuality.

THE TERM FOR "group" is *nakama.* The first character, *naka,* means "inside," and the second, *ma,* refers to an enclosure in either space or time—a room, a field, an interval, a long duration. The importance not only of belonging but of being hidden within can be judged from the first lines of poetry Japan ever produced:

> Eight clouds arise.
> The eightfold fence of Izumo
> Makes an eightfold fence
> For the spouses to retire within.
> Oh! that eightfold fence.

These lines are about the whole of Japan. There were eight clouds and eight fences because in the old chronicles Japan consisted of eight islands. One still finds a suggestion of the much-treasured fence in Izumo, a coastal city in southwestern Japan where an ancient god is said to have descended from heaven. The Izumo shrine, Shinto's oldest, is still enclosed by a fence beyond which ordinary mortals may not pass. Outside of it there are several torii, the classic Shinto gates, which reveal perfectly the essential abstraction of the belonging ritual. No fence ever flanks a torii. It is freestanding but nonetheless alters the space around it. The outermost torii at Izumo is most of a mile from the shrine along a busy commercial street. Candy stores, trinket shops, and garages stretch out on either side, yet the gate marks the difference between outer and inner space, the profane and sacred.

The duality of outside and inside, the enclosed and the exposed, is the first thing to confront the arriving visitor. The standard term for oneself is "gaijin," outside person. It is one's first notice that life in Japan will consist of a series of acceptances and rejections. Nothing is excepted. What is sumo, the popular wrestling tradition held to extend back to 23 B.C., if not a ritual celebration of the distinction made between the included and excluded? The two wrestlers purify the circle where they stand by dusting it with salt. They square off, squat, and stare. There is almost nothing to see, for the match usually lasts no more than a minute or two, and often mere seconds. What matters is the consequence. The sumo contest produces not so much a winner and a loser as a change in status: The vanquished is the man pushed out of the circle.

In feudal Japan the matter of belonging came down to one's *ie,* or household. The *ie* was more than a family in that those not related by blood could be adopted into it. Villages were groups of *ie;* commercial enterprises were organized as *ie.* The *ie* remained important until 1945, a building block of imperial Japan. In the *ie* one learned to suppress the self. And all of Japan was an *ie,* the emperor being the head of the Japanese household. The prewar ideologues claimed that Japan was unique in the world because it was a "family-state."

Today the Japanese live in a universe of intersecting, constantly shifting circles—"households" made of families, schools, graduating classes, universities, sports clubs, sects, social cliques, nightclub regulars, companies. The list is infinite, the question of belonging continuous. Alone, two people from different sections of the same organization are outsiders to each other; joined by a third from another organization, they become insiders, and the third is the outsider. Such variations occur over and over in the course of daily life and are signified in commonplace objects: not just fences and gates, but walls, bridges, banks of desks, paper screens.

Japanese is rich in its descriptions of this essential distinction. There are words denoting what is outside and inside, public and private, the spoken and authentic versions of the truth. One pair of these terms will be useful. *Omote* and *ura* mean the explicit and the implicit, the outer and the inner, the front and the back, or, more broadly, the revealed and the hidden. In old Japanese they meant "face" and "mind." Today one speaks of *omote-dori* and *ura-dori*, main streets and back lanes; *omote-ji* is kimono cloth, *ura-ji* is kimono lining. *Futo no omote* is the front of an envelope; *ura-niwa* is a back garden. These terms have numerous dimensions and, like others, can be revealing. *Urameshii* means to feel bitter, *urayamu* to feel envious, and *urami* is a grudge. None of these is an acceptable thing to reveal in Japan, where the group's primary purpose is to preserve harmony and the appearance of sameness. So feelings of envy and bitterness are by definition *ura*, hidden.

Common to the various terms for inside and outside are the values of belonging versus exclusion, revelation versus concealment. What is public has always been the higher social value in Japan. And what is public is associated with order and the group, while what is private is individual and therefore secretive, selfish, and corrupting. One may belong to a group, and that group to a larger group, but the price of belonging is the subjugation of the individual to the group, the private to the public, the authentic to the represented.

João Rodrigues, the Jesuit who found three hearts in the Japanese, was smarter than we are in one respect. Our images of the Japanese encourage us to assume that there simply is no individuality among them—that in some other than human way they are content to live, like penguins or lemmings, with nothing to distinguish one from another. Rodrigues understood that the individual was only obscured. But the Jesuit was wrong in another way. There is nothing "false" about the faces the Japanese present to the world, not so far as they are concerned, and nothing about unshared thoughts and feelings that make them truer or more valuable. This is a mistake only a Westerner could make, for we, like Father Rodrigues, do not share Japan's notion of the group as the superior value.

It is also true that the Japanese reserve a special place for what is concealed. They are dedicated diarists for the simple reason that so much of life must be hidden. One of Japan's aesthetic traditions, famously displayed in a temple garden in Kyoto, is called *mie gakure*, the seen and unseen. In the garden, fifteen stones protrude from a sea of combed gravel. But from no vantage point are all of the stones visible; wherever you stand, one is always hidden. In a friend's office I once saw an ink drawing of two peasants pulling a harness. The harness trailed off at the edge of the picture; nothing else was depicted. When I mentioned the drawing my friend smiled. "Yes," he said. "Can you see the cart?"

Mie gakure, applied to people, also means "to appear and disappear," or "to hide oneself." And there is nothing the Japanese are more accustomed to hiding than themselves, their inner beings. True heart, called *kokoro,* and *ninjo,* human feelings, are rarely manifest but all the more precious for it. Emotions are unsullied and innocent, which is why, when the Japanese expose them, they appear childishly sentimental—as, for example, when they are drunk, or singing in a karaoke bar. Emotions are part of the "*ura* of the *ura,*" the inside of the inside, and it is because they are withheld that each Japanese lives with a certain sense of crisis in his relations with the outer world.

"What is concealed is the flower," wrote Ze-ami, the fourteenth-century Noh master. "What is not concealed cannot be the flower." The thought survives in many contexts and is not irrelevant in this one. It is cited by the psychiatrist Takeo Doi in his explorations of the Japanese personality. Doi was a deeply traditional man. He believed that to live amid elaborate concealments was a normal, healthy thing. And he saw no tension between the security of belonging, which is undeniable among the Japanese, and the individual desire to break free of the group—which, though traditionally unacknowledged, is also undeniable. "The ideal condition of the mind, the condition from which mental health derives," Doi wrote in 1985, "is one in which we can feel comfortable having secrets."

The confinements in which the Japanese live are enveloping and complete, affording only the dimmest view of a life without them. Something as simple as asking directions in Japan can often reveal the peculiar isolation the habit of concealment produces at the core of Japanese life. It is perfectly ordinary to find a person willing to oblige. But it is also common to be completely ignored, as if you had not spoken, as if you were not standing there—as if you were a ghost. This is not so much impolite behavior as it is a recognition that there is (in the Jesuit's terms) no heart between you: With neither formal relations nor friendship there is only strangeness, a kind of nonbeing. Even if the passerby pauses to help, you may discover he knows nothing of a street or building only a hundred yards away, for it is not part of the tiny universe in which he lives.

Foreigners who reside in Japan are part of the system by virtue of their exclusion. Rarely does the "outside person" enter the intricate, burdensome web of duties and obligations that covers all interaction among the Japanese and binds each to the group. According to custom a resident gaijin, like a Japanese, will be known as Fuji Film's Wilson or Smith of the *International Herald Tribune*. One is considered to be part of a group, as every Japanese is. But the foreigner soon recognizes that just as Japan is a nation of insiders, it is equally one of "others."

There never seem to be enough groups to create new "others," new outsiders. It is as if people will resort to any ruse to obscure the matter of public individuality. Pseudoscience is popular in this regard. A European executive once sat with his Japanese manager to meet job applicants. After the routine questions, the manager ended each interview with, "And what is your blood type?" All but one candidate replied matter-of-factly and without surprise. (The exception laughed and did not know.) Later the gaijin asked about the strange inquiry. It is best, the manager explained, not to mix blood types in the same work space. The idea has many adherents; newspapers sometimes assess new governments according to whether cabinet members are A, B, O, or some other blood type.

When I arrived in Tokyo and began to staff my newspaper's bureau, I found many young Japanese intrigued by the prospect of joining a gaijin company—an act that carried a whiff of individual risk and nonconformity, even of defiance. The Japanese have made a womb of their society. But if the temptation to exit it was strong, most found their fears still stronger. The womb of life is confining, but it is also secure, and so most Japanese remain, as it were, unborn. By the time I met Kay Itoi, who worked with me at the *Herald Tribune* for the duration of my tour in Japan, I understood that I was looking for someone with a certain courage and restlessness, even impatience.

It is in restlessness and impatience and the temptation of risk that we find clues to the individual's struggle with the enveloping web. This is nothing new; it is a long thread in the history of the Japanese, and to describe the Japanese today is to note only the new prominence this thread has taken in the weave. It is a kind of eternal tension—between freedom and belonging, community and autonomy—and it is part of what I call hidden history because it, too, is concealed—submerged but never nonexistent.

AFTER THE PACIFIC war an interesting debate took place among the Japanese. It concerned something called *shutai-sei*. The term literally means "subjecthood," but it is translated variously as "subjectivity," "selfhood," "authenticity," or "autonomy." It refers to the perceiving, judging, deciding individual. To achieve *shutai-sei* was to leave behind all the old conventions: the enveloping mutual duties, the acceptance of inclusion and exclusion, the suppression of individuality for the sake of the displayed consensus. *Shutai-sei* meant to establish an autonomous identity. The term also had strong connotations. It implied an energetic, assertive individuality—what I have called public individuality. The autonomous person was capable not only of making moral commitments but of acting openly upon them.

It is remarkable to realize how little the Japanese of the late 1940s knew of such matters. Japan had recently deployed millions of soldiers, ships, planes, and weapons across vast parts of the Pacific. But, midway in our century, the Japanese had no socially accepted notion of something as ordinary elsewhere, as taken-for-granted, as individuality. Except in their private hearts, as the old Jesuit would have put it, or in open opposition to accepted norms, they could cultivate no sense of self. Their thoughts and values were the thoughts and values imposed by the community. We ordinarily assume that group identity is something the Japanese cling to so as to keep foreigners out. But we must consider the opposite proposition: Was the group not also made to keep the Japanese people in—and to keep them from becoming individuals?

Those who debated the meaning of *shutai-sei* believed that cultivating the autonomous self was postwar Japan's fundamental task, more essential than any other. It was the failure of the Japanese to make subjective judgments, they said, that led them to acquiesce when the wartime dictatorship draped a blanket of ideology over them and pushed the nation into tragedy. The core of the postwar project, therefore, was psychological.

As the best-known exponent of autonomy put it, "An internal reform of the psychological structure of Japanese society must occur."

These words belong to a man named Masao Maruyama. Maruyama, who passed away in 1996 at the age of eighty-two, was without question the most influential thinker Japan has produced in our century. In the great debate over *shutai-sei* he led a camp called the "modernists," who posited two kinds of autonomy. One was individual: the self as a private, independent being. The other was social: the free individual who also understood his place within the larger whole. These two ideas of autonomy were advanced in opposition to the old notion of community, in which people had no identity and no free choices. The object of all this theorizing was nothing more nor less than democracy. The modernists called for the creation among the Japanese of "a new, democratic human type." Their views are easily boiled down: Democracy does not work without individual liberty, and individual liberty is impossible to sustain without a democratic context.

The debate over *shutai-sei* collapsed in the late 1940s. The new democratic human type never appeared, a casualty of the reverse course. Under the restored prewar elite the Japanese were unable to escape from the old, confining notions of community. That is why Japan took on the machinery of democracy after the war but has had no authentic democracy. In the Cold War climate many of those who urged the notion of autonomy upon the Japanese, including Maruyama, were dismissed as dangerous leftists. And here we arrive at one of the fundamental ironies in the way we look upon the modern Japanese. There was indeed an active left in Japan after the war—a left of many hues. But so what? Examining the postwar situation today, the notion of a Soviet-style Japan looks a bit ridiculous. Much of what we took to be the subversive left stood not for collectivism but an escape from collectivism, not the suppression of private endeavor but the embrace of it. They had argued for the very thing Westerners profess to believe in most profoundly: the primacy of the individual.

The *shutai-sei* episode has many echoes in the past. So we must ask, Why has the group had such a tenacious hold on the Japanese? Where in history did so deep-seated a notion of community come from?

The group in Japan is as ancient as its people. Rice cultivation required communities based on mutual dependence. Geography isolated the Japanese: one community from another by the islands' mountainous landscapes, and the islands from the Asian mainland by the rough waters of the Japan Sea. There is nothing peculiar about the community ethos that resulted. Ancient Japan was a primitive society that had much in common with any other. Japan took its first unusual turn in the seventh century, under a scholarly prince regent named Shotoku. It was then the Japanese began to build the group society that would endure until our time.

Under Shotoku Japan began to borrow wholesale from China much of what we now think of as Japanese. Along with Buddhism, urban design, a central bureaucracy, and much else, Shotoku imported the Confucian classics. Through these Japan learned the revered virtues—benevolence, filial piety, sincerity, and so on—and the five relationships that define the human stations: ruler and ruled, father and son, elder brother and younger, husband and wife, friend and friend. We might consider Shotoku Japan's first great Orientalist—the first to imagine a "Japan" other than what it was. He brought order and hierarchy to people who had been notably informal in such matters. The Japanese court was typical: It, too, had been rather informal. Then it assumed elaborate ranks, all of them quintessentially Confucian—Greater Benevolence and Lesser Benevolence, Greater and Lesser Propriety, and on through the Chinese sage's catalogue of righteousness.

The feudal period began at the end of the twelfth century, when provincial warriors, the earliest samurai, forced the emperor into obscurity and built a military dictatorship that lasted seven centuries under a succession of generals—the shoguns. We are familiar with many of the samurai's features: his discipline and austerity, his rigorously simple aesthetic, his adherence to an honor code similar in outline to the chivalry of medieval Europe. The code of the samurai was elaborately Confucian, with a complex system of mutual duties: a system of give-and-take interdependence meant to keep samurai—professional killers, martial arts cultists—from destroying one another. Over time the shogun told the samurai what to wear, how to settle a dispute, how to prepare meals, what kind of pottery to have around the house, how much to spend on a gift. Rules were everything. Rank and "house," signified in the precise colors, fabrics, and patterns of one's clothing, were also everything.

For the nameless majority the samurai were the stuff of heroic legend, the doers of high deeds. But they were not really individuals. When they internalized the code they built an edifice within. Each act, no matter how perilous or against the odds, was at once a mark of distinction and an affirmation of conformity to the code. It was a display of will—which was also cultivated according to the code. There is, for instance, the matter of loyalty. The great sage was clear about the virtues. Loyalty was not first among them—benevolence was. And loyalty meant allegiance according to one's conscience. But the samurai made loyalty paramount and made no allowance for the inner voice. In the Japanese conception, loyalty and filial piety together required obedience, even at the sacrifice of reason or conscience. It is no wonder that the Buddhism of the samurai was Zen, a native-hatched sect. Zen taught emptiness of mind: the suppression of self by an exertion of will so complete as to enable action without conscious thought.

The samurai can be viewed as the first Japanese whose individuality was essentially private. How else to describe people who found purity in the utmost detachment from everything they did that was visible to others? Satori, Zen enlightenment, was a matter of private salvation. Seppuku, ritual suicide, was an honorable way out of disgrace because it was an act of private individuality. In this we can wonder about the excessive care with which seppuku was carried out: the crosswise cut through the belly, then upward toward the navel—incisions that made death certain but damaged no vital organs. Was it a ritual revelation of the intact self within, or a final, public assertion that there was no self, that the self was obliterated so that honor could be posthumously restored?

It is not difficult to see in the samurai things we try to understand today: the concealment of personality, rigorous loyalty to the group—loyalty to a fault. But how were these habits of mind prolonged so far into our own time?

In 1542 three Portuguese sailors landed on an island off the coast of Kyushu. The lost mariners were the first Europeans to reach Japan. Francis Xavier, the Jesuit from Goa, arrived seven years later to plant the cross. Notably, there was little interest in how these first Westerners lived and thought, but much in the things they brought: clocks, musical instruments, medicines, maps. Muskets prompted Japan's first try at industrial copying: They were reproduced in great numbers.

As Christianity spread, successive shoguns feared it would unite the daimyo, or feudal lords, each with an army of his own, against them. The first ban on missionaries came in 1587. By 1639, a century after foreigners first stepped ashore, isolation edicts called *sakoku*, "closed country," were in effect: Gaijin were barred with the exception of a few Dutch merchants; "Dutch learning," open to a select few, became the sole source of outside knowledge. Anyone attempting to leave Japan would be put to death; no ship could be built to carry more than a thousand *koku*—which was a ban on oceangoing vessels.* *Sakoku* was the work of a family of shoguns named Tokugawa. The first of them, Ieyasu, took power in 1603 and moved the military government from Kyoto, the decadent imperial capital, to a swampy hamlet then called Edo and now Tokyo (Eastern Capital).

The Tokugawa ruled for two and a half centuries, until 1868. Theirs was the most extreme form of feudalism Japan had ever known. The Japanese lived like figurines in a bell jar—locked in hereditary status and the ancient, cyclical time of masters and cultivators. Progress was prohibited—the enemy of changelessness. The Tokugawa were the greatest Orientalists Japan has yet produced. Their notion of Japan was grotesque, utterly static. It became more imaginary as the Edo centuries wore on, so requiring ever greater bureaucratic will to enforce it.

Edo Japan was a society of distinctions—beneath which lay a profound conformity. Everyone was ranked according to caste: samurai, peasants, artisans, merchants. Each caste had its assigned role. Each was segregated by dress, means of transport, and countless other details. Only the samurai could bear swords—long ones in the countryside, short ones in town. Samurai were permitted no contact with peasants, the peasants none with townsmen. A townsman's kimono was to be this long. Peasants must rise at this hour, consume such and such a meal, avoid tea, plant bamboo this close to their huts, dig latrines that far away.

Japan as a caste society was nothing new. The last family of shoguns—there were fifteen Tokugawa rulers before the end—merely took the feudal rigidities to their limits. They were Confucian fundamentalists. The Tokugawa were obsessed with edicts, decrees, prohibitions, gruesome punishments—everything needed to maintain a climate of terror. Edo kept an immense network of enforcers—secret police, frontier guards, censors, undercover agents. Villages were organized into five-person groups: Each member was required to spy on the other four, each group on other groups. In spite of this (or because of it) there were roughly three thousand peasant uprisings during the Tokugawa centuries—one a month,

---

* A *koku* equaled slightly more than five bushels.

on average, though they gained in frequency as time went on. There were another three thousand "disturbances" that never went as far as the house trashings and riots scholars count as uprisings.

Feudalism in this strangely illuminated twilight is an essential piece of Japan's past—not only because it lasted so long or because we can trace back to it so much of what the Japanese are today, but because the history of Edo has been the battleground in modern Japan, or a large part of it. Edo Japan gives us a classic example of the power of leaving things out. And what is always left out is the conflict and tension that existed just below the surface—the history that was hidden.

Today we have a peculiar idea of the Edo era—a half-true distortion of this bizarre age. Our received image is of a dull but orderly time, well expressed in the standard term "the Tokugawa peace." In *Japan: Past and Present,* Edwin Reischauer gave a neat summary of the orthodoxy, as uncomplicated as one of the period's woodblock prints: "The prolonged, complete peace of the Tokugawa period brought to Japan years of unprecedented prosperity, and industrial production and trade grew rapidly." Based upon such imagery, we are invited to think of the Edo era as "early modern Japan"—never the derogatory "late feudalism." This is an exceptional irony, for from the Edo era onward it has been a mark of Japan's leaders that they have, in one way or another, sought to defer the true arrival of modern society in Japan.

Edo's advances cannot be denied. Rudimentary manufacturing began; restless merchants laid the groundwork for modern trade, and a lively popular culture—Kabuki, pulpy literature—took root in the pleasure quarters of Edo, Osaka, and Kyoto. But there was no peace in Edo Japan. There was a sort of federalist settlement between the shoguns and the daimyo, but otherwise the era was marked by merciless exploitation, purposeful deprivation, paranoic police controls, coercion, more or less constant official violence—and more or less constant popular resistance to all of these things. In its terror and totality, its nightmarish bureaucracy and manipulation of knowledge, Edo Japan is usefully compared with the later Soviet Union. In its violent dream of Oriental agrarianism it suggests the Cambodia of the Khmer Rouge.

The lasting gift of the Tokugawa was to deliver the Japanese to the doorstep of the industrial age with the feudal edifice crumbling all around but still intact within each of them. Today there are the corporate samurai—as obsessed with "house" and hierarchy as the old warriors. The Japanese still puzzle over the precise value of gifts to be given for precisely which favors received, precisely the proper clothing for each occasion, the precise seating in a room according to rank, inclusion, and exclusion.

Many Japanese entertain a kind of ersatz nostalgia for the Edo era—ersatz because it is cartoonish, sanitized. Among the old sayings one still hears in the countryside, for instance, is "Three houses in front, one on either side." It is a simple admonition not to act before surveying all those around you. And it is a neat description of how the complex system of duties and obligations works. Those who still dwell in the old villages often advance this phrase as a measure of community spirit and the endurance of village values. Perhaps it is that, partly. But the saying requires its full context. Properly understood, it also suggests something of the individual's wariness toward all others, a wariness the Japanese learned long ago to carry within.

There is a remarkable description of the Edo era—remarkable because it remains so oddly apt today. It was written by Yukichi Fukuzawa, an educator in the era that followed, and it appeared in one of his best-known works, *Outline of Civilization*. Fukuzawa appears today on the face of the ten-thousand-yen note, stern but wistful, wearing a somber kimono but with a Western haircut. One senses he looks forward in that pose. But in *Outline*, published in 1873, he looked back to a people atomized but unrealized, intensely private but intensely unfree. The passage is a concise description of a society in which individuality lives only in the secrets of each of its members:

> They all depended on the government and did not concern themselves with national affairs. Among a million people there were a million different minds. Each person shut himself up in his own house and ignored the outside world as if it were a foreign country. They failed to consult one another even about the best way to clean their wells, let alone ways to repair roads. If they chanced to come upon a dog's excrement, they went around it. They were so preoccupied with trying to avoid getting involved in anything that they had no time to discuss things together. This long-ingrained habit became a custom and produced the present sad state of affairs.

Respect for and dependence upon authority, unswerving loyalty, austerity, and a rigorous work ethic—all are marks late feudalism has left upon the Japanese. We are invited to conclude that Japan is by tradition and culture a vertical society and that Japanese ethics are situational—based not on principle but on the ever-shifting net of relationships in which the Japanese live. The best-known explanation of these matters is *The Chrysanthemum and the Sword*, a book published in 1946 by the anthropologist Ruth Benedict. Benedict distinguished Japan as a shame culture as opposed to a guilt culture: "True shame cultures rely on external sanctions for good behavior, not, as true guilt cultures do, on an internalized conviction of sin."

These observations cannot be dismissed. But they obscure as much as they explain. The Japanese are shamed when they transgress, for they have disgraced their household. But are there really people in the world who never feel the pangs of guilt, who have no conscience? Loyalty can be a fine thing, but Japan's notion of loyalty, loyalty that admits of no questions, led it into a world war, after all. Hard work, by the same token, has historically been a matter of desperate necessity. As to respect for authority, it is better understood as obsequiousness bred of fear.

A clear picture of the past leads to a fundamental point about the Japanese, an understanding that changes everything. Once we recognize the conflict beneath the surface, we understand that group identity had more to do with coercion and power than with tradition and culture. Then we must rethink our conclusions about the attributes of the Japanese we are encouraged to admire. Are they so enviable as to be emulated? More admirable, by any measure, is the long, buried struggle against feudal terror and tyranny—the same struggle we admire in our own history. There is nothing especially "Japanese" about what we call the Japanese character or personality, we must conclude. We can talk only about people subject to certain conditions and their response to those conditions.

It was the primitive habit of confinement and exclusion, fixed during the Edo centuries, that the Japanese tried to overcome within themselves when they considered such questions as autonomy in the late 1940s. That is why they found themselves, then as now, only half at home in the modern world. Alone among primitive societies, Japan is "advanced"; alone among advanced societies, Japan has remained primitive.

WE KNOW JAPAN today as a late developer. When, in the 1860s and 1870s, it sent emissaries abroad for the first time in two and a half centuries, the objects of Western industry—threshers, railroads, air compressors, iron bridges—left them shocked. So, it must be added, did everything they attributed to Western individualism: political debate, labor strife, each person running off in his own direction. The West, especially America, seemed to live in a state of barely controlled anarchy. Capitalism struck the Japanese as "warfare in peacetime," as an early diplomatic diarist put it. These first travelers across the Pacific were like experiments with time, people who were born into the modern world but who had seen nothing of it.

We also know Japan as an addicted borrower, first from China and, beginning in the late nineteenth century, from us. In this the Japanese were discriminating, choosing from each country only what they wanted. From France they learned of oil painting, from England of warships, from America of manufacturing. But they missed something essential about all that they borrowed. They did not understand that a piece of machinery— to say nothing of a school system or a set of laws—had a long past, that it was an expression of the society that produced it. Like the feudal Japanese who encountered the first Europeans, Japan's first modernizers were concerned only with *mono*—things, hardware.

But as much as Japan was a late developer, it was also an early one— indeed, the earliest. If, among advanced countries, Japan was near to last, among Third World countries it was first. The Japanese were the first non-Western people to absorb the things of the Western world. And Japan's modern leaders did no more than what many Third World leaders have done since: They adopted the technological ways of the West while preserving the social, spiritual, and psychological identity of the past. A century ago the Japanese called this *wakon yosai,* Japanese spirit, Western things. Today they would profess to believe in "Asian values"—as distinct from universal values.

Japan quickly followed the West's belief in humanity's alienation from nature and so set about subjugating the natural world. That was a prerequisite of industrialization. But it rejected the West's notion of the sovereign individual. Instead Japan tried to remain a communal society—hence the idea of a "family state"—in which the individual was dependent upon the authority of the group. To put it another way, Japan rejected the idea that people were the makers of their own history, autonomous agents of reason and judgment. Such a proposition was blocked at the border like a contaminated vegetable or an uncensored foreign newspaper. In short, Japan did not become modern so much as a consumer of the modern.

Is this to say that, as the West had an Enlightenment, so must the Japanese and the rest of humanity? That is the error of the Chrysanthemum Club and its "modernization theory": To be modern is to be Western, and everyone must sooner or later follow our path. But neither do we want to make the opposite mistake—to assert that the liberation of the individual was something peculiar to Western societies at a certain moment in history. The Japanese never had an Enlightenment, but that is hardly the point. No one familiar with the coercion and resistance of the feudal centuries—and of the modern era, for that matter—can conclude that the Japanese failed to evolve toward greater autonomy and individuality because they did not want to or were not ready to.

In July of 1853 Matthew Perry anchored four steamships off the coast south of Edo. The shogun and his immense, creaking bureaucracy had advance word and expected him. But local fishermen on the water that day tell us more about Japan's true sentiment. They thought Perry's "black ships" were some sort of floating volcano, and they scattered like birds at the sight of a sudden intruder.

Japan was about to get its first dose of *gaiatsu,* foreign pressure. Four years after Perry arrived, the shogunate—confused, decayed, desperate— signed treaties with the United States, Britain, Holland, Russia, and France that extended their jurisdiction onto Japanese soil and limited Edo's right to tax imports. In 1867 the last shogun abdicated, and Japan began its age of modernization. It never forgot the humiliation of the unequal treaties. They shaped Japan's goal to make itself the West's industrial and military equal and lent the endeavor an urgency that left no Japanese untouched.

It is easy to misunderstand the West's part in all this. Perry's ships were merely catalysts, arguably not even constructive catalysts. At the moment of their arrival all the principal agents of the great change to come were within. Japan may have been better off without Perry, for it might have felt less urgency in the task ahead, and it might have done things less expediently, so avoiding the tragic consequences that lay in the future.

The Meiji era, named for its emperor's reign, began with the restoration of imperial sovereignty. For seven centuries Japan had been ruled by shoguns, and before that by regents. They wielded power in the emperor's name, but by 1867 the throne was far from public view, its transcendent authority a myth. With the restoration the emperor suddenly exited the neurasthenic shadows and stepped back onto center stage. So at the core of all the advances there lay a return. The emperor was to become a modern monarch, but he was also a god-king of the sort not seen since ancient days.

The events leading up to the restoration were extremely bizarre. In 1866 the political scene was a tangle of forces backing either the shogun or the throne. The fires of antiforeign chauvinism, long fanned by the bureaucracy, were raging. Crop failures and the new foreign trade—imports of manufactured goods, exports of gold and silver—had wrecked the economy. Popular unrest was at a peak: more than a hundred rural uprisings, and urban riots at the rate of several a month. A thread of premonitory superstition ran through all of this. A comet that year was taken as a portent of some imminent but incalculable change.

Early in 1867 everything went strangely quiet. Popular unrest more or less ceased. But in the autumn Japan broke out in ecstatic revelry—a combination of rioting, religious hysteria, sake-powered partying, and spontaneous, orgiastic street dancing. Houses were hung with brightly colored rice cakes, straw, and flowers. Dancers—men and women, young and old—clogged the streets to clamoring bells, drums, gongs, chimes, and whistles. Drunken commoners tramped through the houses of the privileged without—unforgivably—removing their shoes. Popular lyrics celebrated food, sake, and sex. People gave clothing away to strangers and threw money in the streets. The frenzy swept from Edo to Hiroshima after thousands of amulets, paper charms with Shinto and Buddhist gods painted on them, began falling from the sky.

No historian has explained the rain of amulets. But they were not the only peculiar feature of this altogether odd interlude. Cross-dressing was widespread. Despite all the pent-up anger of late Edo, there was no violence. A British diplomat traveling in Osaka remarked on the absence of fear or animosity. Everywhere the revelers repeated the same incantatory chant: *Ee ja nai ka!* This elusive term has numerous inexact translations.

Its nearest literal meaning is "Isn't it good?" or "Why not? It's all right!" A scholar recently described it as falling somewhere among "Right on! Go for it," "What the hell," and "No more bullshit!"

Odd as it seems, given our image of the Japanese, *ee ja nai ka* was the sound of modern Japan's beginning. The delirious chanting lasted until the spring of 1868. And amid the cacophony of a sexually charged carnival, two samurai clans loyal to the emperor, the Satsuma and the Choshu, found a singular opportunity. During the interim from the autumn of 1867 to the spring of the new year they secured the shogun's resignation and wheeled the new emperor forward as the new ruler of a new Japan.

Ee ja nai ka! The subtext of every shout was an open declaration of liberation, a jack-in-the-box release of pent-up desire. This alone would give *ee ja nai ka* a place in Japan's hidden history, but there is more. What does it mean when people of no great sophistication take to cross-dressing, or to trampling across tatami in muddy shoes, or, in abject poverty, to throwing money away? We cannot be satisfied with the notion that a commoner celebrating sex and gluttony in late Edo Japan saw no farther than the next sake barrel and a free-spirited companion. *Ee ja nai ka* was a shout toward the heavens, a rejection of the reigning order. It was as if people had seen through the roof of the great house of Tokugawa to glimpse an immensity of alternatives in the open sky beyond. Above all, it was an act of public individuality.

Edo's last months were both expectant and subversive. By the end, *ee ja nai ka* took on an explicitly political meaning—it was another inchoate expression of rebellion, like the constant protests of the Edo era. The evident sexuality offers us a clue to understanding this moment as one of undirected individual assertion, desire without an available language. But the formlessness of this rebellion does not obscure its psychological complexity. Speculating, we can wonder whether the shouts of *ee ja nai ka* were the deformed flowers of a Japanese enlightenment ready to sprout but without the ground to grow. More certainly, they reveal that the individual's struggle against the enfolding web was part of modern Japan from the moment it came into existence.

The emperor restored in 1868 was a brisk, intelligent sixteen-year-old named Mutsuhito. Even before he moved in a dazzling procession from Kyoto to the renamed Tokyo, he issued a kind of constitutional preamble called the Charter Oath, an open pledge to his ancestors. Third of its five clauses was this one:

The common people, no less than the civil and military officials, shall all attain their aspirations, so that the people's minds
shall not be made weary.

No number of bearded commodores or imposed treaties can account for
such an astonishing proposition. To attain one's goals—even to aspire—
was a bracing, revolutionary idea. But the Charter Oath is easily explained.
It was issued amid the confusion and anticipation of the *ee ja nai ka* interlude. The oath was intended to calm the nervous, the doubtful, and the
impetuous. And to do so the emperor and those around him chose to
acknowledge the popular desire for change of the most fundamental kind.
In one sentence the young Mutsuhito announced the end of a long, trau-
matic bondage. All boundaries between the official and ordinary, the high
and low, were to be erased. A society of fixed status was to be transformed
into one of mobility and striving individuals. When Mutsuhito left Kyoto
for Tokyo, for three hundred miles commoners pressed their faces to the
earth along the roadside. Mutsuhito may have been a god-king, but let us
understand this spectacle properly: He was also the man who banished the
terrorizing shogunate from the life of every Japanese.

But the society the emperor promised never arrived. Meiji freed the
Japanese from the feudal castes. They could entertain their individual aspirations. But the modern era did not give them the individual liberty to
pursue their aspirations. Meiji turned out to be nothing more than a transition from feudal absolutism to absolutism in nineteenth-century form.
Japan remained a communal society—closed instead of open, particular
instead of universal, a society of individuals who could cultivate no individual values. The contradiction made modern Japan what it is today—a
place of immense but unrealizable dreams, relentless competition, and
near-universal frustration. No matter how contemporary we imagine the
Japanese to be, the society promised in the Charter Oath is the one they
still struggle to attain, whose betrayal they seek to redress.

A period of liberal exploration did ensue after the emperor moved into
the shogun's palace. For half a dozen years Japan lived in a state of happy
inconsistency. A hundred flowers bloomed. Restlessness replaced the long
sleep of Edo, just as it would replace the defeated dictatorship in 1945.
There was no fixed way forward. Intellectuals read Rousseau's *Social*

Contract and Mill's *On Liberty,* among many other Western works, as quickly as they could be translated. Then the Satsuma and Choshu leadership, known as the Sat-Cho, retreated into conservatism (just as it would in the late 1940s), so making itself an entrenched, undemocratic oligarchy—the worthy successor of the shogunate.

But what was the early idealism made of? And why did it fail? The best answer comes from the educator Yukichi Fukuzawa, he of the ten-thousand-yen note. Fukuzawa was among the foremost exponents of liberalism and later a strident critic of the Meiji oligarchs. In 1876 he collected several years' worth of pamphlets under the title *An Encouragement of Learning.* Rendered in plain Japanese, the book sold more than 3 million copies. In it Fukuzawa invented the very notion of individualism for the Japanese. His term was *dokuritsu,* spirit of independence. The new word, like the book, was beloved for its simplicity, but we should listen carefully to what Fukuzawa meant, for it is a key to the ethos of the era:

> When the people of a nation do not have the spirit of individual independence, the corresponding right of national independence cannot be realized.

> Persons without the spirit of personal independence will not have deep concern for their country.

> Japan must be filled with the spirit of independence if we are to defend her against foreign threats.

In these passages Fukuzawa defines the intellectual failing of Japan's first foray into liberalism: He took the cultivation of the autonomous individual to be a means, an expedient to a greater goal, instead of an end in itself, the greatest goal of all.

Fukuzawa is ranked today among modern Japan's great *philosophes.* Liberals still claim him for his opposition to the reaction that followed the early period of possibility. The Bank of Japan puts his picture on its bills because his image lends a liberal veneer to early modern history. In his time Fukuzawa had many conservative enemies, men more interested in the Confucian virtues than in the "spirit of independence." But what was this great intellectual clash really about? Only method. Fukuzawa's adversaries wanted a strong state able to resist foreigners and renegotiate the unequal treaties. To them, the road ahead lay not in any notion of individuality but in continued reverence for the hierarchical order. Fukuzawa shared their goal—he never lost sight of it. He differed only over the usefulness of the past.

Meiji Japan became a cauldron of discontent with the defeat even of Fukuzawa's flawed liberalism. Indeed, the new Japan was not much quieter than the Japan of the old shogunate. Crowds gathered as suddenly as summer storms. Popular protests, riots, and resistance movements were features of daily life. Decommissioned samurai, along with intellectuals, small-time factory owners, village landlords, and ambitious rustics of all varieties, formed a loose, nationwide group to demand popular rights—an idea so foreign it required an invented word, *kenri.* These were Japan's first politicians. They also introduced the notion of *minshu-shugi,* which meant "people-masterism"—that is, democracy.

By 1881 civil unrest forced the Sat-Cho to promise the Japanese a constitution and a national assembly. These arrived on schedule in 1889 and 1890, respectively. By then there were political parties and a cabinet—as well as a self-appointed peerage modeled (like the constitution) on imperial Germany's. The first elections were held. But having promised the institutions of modern government, the oligarchy then made sure they had no modern meaning. The constitution vested ultimate authority in the emperor—in whose name the oligarchy presided. The imperial Diet, as the legislature was called, was elected by slightly more than one percent of the population—and had only an advisory role anyway. The cabinet declared itself to be "transcendental"—that is, beyond politics and party interests. So was modern government imported and rejigged as if it were another new machine.

By century's end Japan was what it would remain until 1945—an ideological state, a nation whose people could understand themselves only as members of the larger community. At the core of Japanese ideology, of course, was worship of the emperor. The emperor was the head of the *kazoku kokka,* the "family state." The family state was unique in the world because it possessed an ineffable quality called *kokutai,* "national essence." Being a family state, having an emperor descended from the gods, and having such a singular thing as national essence made the Japanese a chosen people.

These ideas were transmitted in a thousand different ways. Instead of encouraging critical thought, the individual as a shaper of society, the ideologues encouraged conditioned reflexes—the individual as society's object. Ideology is what the Japanese got instead of autonomy and democracy.

Japan's ideological stew was a rich concoction. The Tokyo elite was hardly alone in inventing tradition. Bismarck's new Germany was doing the same thing. Both nations needed legitimacy, some device to make people feel "German" or "Japanese." Being ex-samurai themselves, Japan's leaders turned to their own past to create the new Japanese. Japan would be a nation of noble warriors, all serving the emperor with the old, peculiar notion of loyalty and all the old inflexibility. This feature of the modern era is often missed, but it is essential. While Japan was busy westernizing, it was also busily "samuraizing." The first prime minister, Hirobumi Ito, a former samurai who took up the sword at thirteen, when Perry's ships arrived, explained this point to his colleagues in the 1880s:

> The major task facing us today is inculcating within the entire populace the spirit of loyalty, devotion, and heroism that was formerly associated with the samurai class, and making these values their values. Thus we must teach the common people to work and study hard for the sake of their neighborhoods and villages, and never to waver in matters that would lead to the destruction of their families. Moreover, they must develop a peaceful and obedient character, show respect for the law, and demonstrate an understanding of our noble moral ideals and highly refined national sentiments.

A nation of samurai would be a very different thing from Japan as it had been, a place of conflict between great and little, the elevated and the common. There would be no democracy, but there would be no tension, either. Everyone, however humble his circumstances, would think of himself as part of the great tradition. The old samurai code would become "the beautiful customs." In 1907, five years before the Meiji era ended, a bureaucrat with the benign paternalism of a true imperial subject explained how the beautiful customs were supposed to work. At the time, the nation's new industries were a riot of unrest and violence:

The old, beautiful customs existing in Japan are concepts of mutual love and respect from employer to employee. This master-servant relationship is not an evil feudal remnant but a benefit gained from feudalism. Will not these beautiful customs, namely compassion from above for those below, and respect from below for those above, be greatly helpful in harmonizing labor-capital relations?

Looking back many decades later, the scholar Masao Maruyama likened ideology to "a many-layered though invisible net over the Japanese people." Another postwar thinker described it as "an enormous black box, into which the Japanese unknowingly walked." Why did this happen? Why were the Japanese so easily led into xenophobia, extreme patriotism—and war? If we understand this about the Japanese we will have understood a great deal about who they were then, who they are now, and who they will become.

The ideological period is a tragic aspect of Japan's past, but it is not incomprehensible. When Japan began to embrace the modern, ordinary Japanese had no notion of what it meant to be part of a modern nation. They knew of nations only what the new oligarchy told them with shrill persistence. And among the most important ways they learned—an essential institution in creating nationality—was military conscription. Neither did they know what it meant to be an individual: The most liberal among them tied the idea to the nation-state. Fukuzawa's mistake, the mistake that said, "To be a person means to be a Japanese person," was repeated many times. And it would be hard to exaggerate the attraction of being "Japanese," and of participating as a recognized part of a modern nation, to people who had been so recently only nameless serfs.

This could not, of course, resolve the problem of public individuality so evident at the restoration. What became of all those shouting individuals? Enveloping though the emperor system was, we deny the Japanese any social or psychological complexity if we assume that, one and all, they became avid followers of emperor ideology. Instead, a kind of con game began in the space between the Meiji ideal and the reality of modern life, a con game played by the concealed individual behind the public mask. Publicly one strove in the new Japan for the emperor and the nation; privately one strove for oneself.

Few Japanese of the Meiji era ever resolved the contradiction their incomplete modernization presented them. What it meant to be Japanese, to say nothing of individualism, was hopelessly fogged. The ideological fanatics were many, selfishness their constant complaint—no surprise, for the con game was extensively played. It is no wonder that Soseki Natsume, the great novelist of the early modern period (and a great writer of any age and nation), was so saddened by the spectacle. The confusion that reigns over the Japanese today has its roots in his time.

Soseki led a troubled life, suffering often to the brink of emotional collapse. In 1900 he traveled to England, where he struggled to learn all he could about Westerners and their literature. Then he made the discovery that was to rule his life: The most profound lesson the Japanese could learn was not to be like anyone else, but to be themselves—to live their own authentic individuality. Soseki spent his life as a writer trying to convey this simple truth. But it never stopped weighing upon him—it was his blessing and his curse—because so few understood it.

In 1914, two years after Meiji ended, two years into the era called Taisho, Soseki gave a lecture titled "My Individualism" to a group of Japanese students. He was almost certainly circumspect in his remarks, for individualism ranked high at that point as a danger to the ideological state. But his message—that one must reject the false coin of Meiji in all its guises—is clear enough today. "You make peace with yourself when the individuality with which you were born arrives where it belongs," he told his young audience at one point. And at another:

> I urge you to accomplish this, *not* for the nation's sake, nor even for the sake of your families, but because it is absolutely necessary for your own personal happiness.

And another:

> Individual liberty is indispensable for the development of [the] individuality that I spoke of earlier.

And finally:

> As I see it, individualism advocates respecting the existence of others at the same time that one respects one's own existence. . . . More simply stated, individualism is a philosophy that replaces cliquism with values based on personal judgment of right and wrong. An individualist is not forever running with the group, forming cliques that thrash around blindly in the interests of power and money. That is why there lurks beneath the surface of his philosophy a loneliness unknown to others. As soon as we deny our little groups, then I simply go my way and I let the other man go his, unhindered. Sometimes we cannot avoid becoming scattered. That is what is lonely.

Soseki understood loneliness as the mark not only of an authentic individual but of someone isolated by his insight. Few Japanese saw, as he put it, "the distinction between yourself and others." They did not accept that individuality lay finally in rejecting the group and discarding the masks of sameness.

SOSEKI'S JAPAN, and the Japan that followed, was an unsettled place. The Russian revolution and unrest at home inspired numerous challenges to the status quo I have described. In 1918 a group known as the Association of New Men called for "a rational reconstruction of contemporary Japan." In the 1920s there was a period of party government—a direct affront to the old oligarchy. At this time the Japanese also shifted their focus from institutions to psychology: It was in the twenties that they first began discussing *shutai-sei,* autonomy. But the period of "Taisho democracy," as it is called, was short-lived. There was little social or political framework to support all the new ideas—which were imported ideas, after all. And as intellectuals reacted against the foreignness of the things that inspired them, democrats became nationalists and socialists, national socialists.

It was no long leap to the 1930s, when the military took power in Japan and turned out the lights on such questions as democracy and autonomy. All that had to wait until the end of the coming war—the "total war" against the West.

IN DECEMBER OF 1945, an American correspondent named Mark Gayn wandered one day in the Shimbashi district, south of Tokyo Station and the Ginza. Then as now, Shimbashi was a hectic quarter given over to small-time businesses, though all that had survived the war was a bustling black market. Gayn later recorded the excursion in his book *Japan Diary.* "Conductors are having difficulty with men who smoke in street cars, despite 'No Smoking' signs. The men say, 'Do we have democracy, or don't we?'"

Nothing better captures the confusion that greeted the Americans. What was this thing from abroad called (by this time) *demokurashi?* Did it not strip away the past, fulfilling at last the restoration's unmet promise? The promise of the occupation could arrive only as another misunderstood import—precisely what it was. Democracy requires institutions that balance a diversity of interests. But Japan had no such institutions. The Meiji oligarchy gave Japan a constitution and a parliament, but neither was democratic. Japan's one try at democracy, in the 1920s, ended with a military takeover. For centuries diversity was simply suppressed—hidden behind masks.

Wasn't the postwar debate over *shutai-sei,* autonomy, which began at the time of Gayn's trolley ride, in some way similar to the shouts of *Ee ja nai ka!* as the shogunate collapsed? Behind the need to achieve individual autonomy and the cries of "Go for it!" was the same desire to be released from the past. Within a year of the surrender more than three hundred political parties appeared. Many of them stood for nothing more than a single person's swollen ambition. Like the men on the trolley, they assumed democracy meant everyone getting what he wanted. These one-man bands are looked upon variously as good or bad measures of the post-war mood. But surely there was something positive in their brief appearance. After all they had been through, the Japanese were eager to take part in public life, even if they had no understanding of a system that mediated between individual desire and the rest of society.

Americans tend to think that it was their example that got the Japanese interested in democracy and the civic self. Certainly their arrival in Japan had something to do with the rise of democratic expectations. But we must be careful, once again, not to misunderstand the role of gaijin. Just as Japan might have been better off without Commodore Perry's black ships, it might have been better off without the occupation—at least as it turned out. Americans opened the door again, as it were, in 1945. But with the reverse course they closed it. Democracy became a showpiece again, for we made it impossible for the Japanese to build a civil society. We gave Japan a new constitution full of liberal freedoms and civil rights, but then we brought back the prewar elite, proven masters at manipulating "the beautiful customs."

No account of the postwar years captures its essential conflict as thoughtfully as *The Journey*, a novel by Jiro Osaragi written at the end of the 1950s. Osaragi never uses the term, but his real subject was *shutai-sei*. His main characters struggle against all the old conventions. They fight to make their own decisions, to rely upon themselves, to follow their own ideas and passions. These are Japan's heroes, we are told by the aging professor through whom the novelist speaks. In one passage the professor quotes an ancient tea master: "I exhort you to do all those things in the world that are bad." As with the Greeks and their vases, there is in these words an appreciation of the flaws that signal authenticity in things of beauty or worth, for the professor continues:

> The real point is that if a fellow can't do anything bad in this world, he also can't do anything good. Human beings aren't meant to consist just of style or appearance. We shouldn't become like mosquito-larvae bred in lukewarm water under the sun. . . . No lukewarm methods! We don't want the sort of fellows who just have conventional civilized educations. We need people with chips and cracks, twisted in ways, but with uncommon characters.

Osaragi ends in ascending chords. People pressed together by well-worn social conventions diverge along separate paths, so embracing society's multiplicity. But *The Journey* is no bedtime story. Other characters, seduced by postwar materialism and superficial notions of American ideals, fail to connect freedom with responsibility and end up submerged in the very morass of self-centered getting and spending that Tokyo encouraged after the anti-AMPO protests of 1960.

Midway in the book a student who once dreamed of blazing scholarly trails by tracing the path of Alexander the Great worries that his ambitions are shrinking to idle fantasies:

> Apart from the process of growing up, the social uneasiness of the postwar period was responsible for this shrinking process. The age of individualism had come to Japan too late. It was an excellent thing, of course, that the dignity of human rights had finally come to be respected. But at exactly the same time Japan had entered the age in which it was considered essential . . . that people suppress their egos and submit themselves to a system of centralized organization.

Osaragi was not a prophet, only a prescient recorder. By the end of the 1950s Japan was becoming a mass society. The old elite had entrenched themselves once again, bringing with them the old notions of what it meant to be Japanese. Under them the era of Japan Inc. began.

The term *shutai-sei* is not much used anymore. In the 1960s it enjoyed a vogue in the student movement. Opposed to the renewed social hierarchies in which they lived, university demonstrators eventually took the issue to be themselves and the edifices erected in their minds: *uchi naru todai,* the Tokyo University within, *uchi naru onnaishiki,* the traditional woman within. Community groups proliferated during this time. They engaged questions ranging from the environment and nuclear power to textbook screening and local political autonomy—each one an indication of a widespread desire to break free of the old constraints. A woman active through this period once put it perfectly: "We wanted to live without always looking from one side to the other, a habit planted deep within all of us." That the question of the public self became explicitly political was no surprise. Public individuality was always a political issue. The community groups eventually disappeared, and the protests of the 1960s went the way of protest elsewhere—into radical adventure and obscurity. But the task before the Japanese has since changed not an iota: It remains to throw away the masks while tearing down the walls within.

The psychiatrist Robert Jay Lifton, who has studied the Japanese for many years, once interviewed a student who came of age in the 1960s. Like most of his generation, the student was profoundly confused about the Japan that confronted him and his true place in it. Before he was twenty-five Lifton's subject had been in succession an ultranationalist patriot, a westernized democrat, a martial arts devotee, an Amerophile exchange student, a Christian, a leftist radical, and a dissipated idler. To the student these were alternative selves, different ways of being, yet he seems to have entered fully into none of his serial lives. They were roles or—better, perhaps—different brands of modern life to be pulled from the shelf and sampled. In the end he drifted into a desk job at a large corporation.

Lifton exposed a prevalent condition—the propensity of the modern Japanese to dream. And like the dreams of the Meiji era, the dreams of the postwar Japanese were always dreams of escape. *Sararimen* dreamed of striking out on their own. They had a slangy contraction for this: *datsu-sara,* to escape being a *sarariman.* It was usually enough to imagine such a step, so the idea of *datsu-sara* was merely a popular fantasy. In the same way the Japanese were famously obsessed with their entries in the *Guinness Book of Records.* They sustained an elaborate subculture of dreamer-achievers: climbers, trekkers in Africa, arctic explorers, single-handed sailors. Among the best known was a man called Naomi Uemura, who soloed by sled to the North Pole, lived alone in Greenland, and rafted the Amazon by himself. Uemura died alone in the Canadian tundra, which only enhanced his mystique.

Such preoccupations expressed an abiding desire among the Japanese to release their individual selves. But as dreams, of course, they proved only what they were intended to refute. The Japanese were still individuals who could not live as individuals. Autonomy, as the scholar Masao Maruyama would have put it, was still private. People had no public individuality. In public they still wore masks: They assumed roles from which there was no escape. "Many millions of people throughout Japan were sealed up in many millions of separate boxes, or separated by many millions of walls." That was how the educator Yukichi Fukuzawa described Japan just before the restoration. It was also precisely the Japan Maruyama found after the war—and the Japan one found until a decade or so ago.

Even now the Japanese share a profound ambivalence as to the need to escape the web of belonging. But the conflict between freedom and community has heightened dramatically over the past decade. In this Maruyama was something of a prophet, for the best way to describe the

Japanese condition today is the way he described it fifty years ago: It requires that same "internal reform of the psychological structure of society" of which he wrote. That is to say, the line between the private and the public must be redrawn so that the individuality that has been for so long furtive can be manifest. As Maruyama understood, this is necessary not only for personal autonomy to take root, but for democracy. Having neither an experience of public individuality nor the mechanisms to express it, Japan is again launched upon a messy experiment. "The underbelly of this exquisite society is beginning to surface," Lifton remarked in the mid-1990s. "The Japanese are seething within." This is a true description. It remains for us only to recognize that Japan has seethed for a very long time.

If the disintegration of the enveloping web is a gradual process—as it is, exceedingly so—it is also unmistakable. One sees it in schools, neighborhoods, offices, in a proliferation of subcultures of all varieties. Less and less do people identify with their old, traditional groups. The corporate samurai—loyal, dedicated, the quinessential Japanese belonger—is already on the way to becoming a figure of the past. One sees evidence of this change especially in the political world. Behind all the apparent chaos—the constantly shifting alliances, the rise and collapse of parties, coalitions, and cabinets—occurs the essential process of building a system able to accommodate the historic emergence of the civic self, "the new democratic human type," as Maruyama's modernists put it after the war—the unmasked, public individual.

We have noted the practical circumstances surrounding this momentous change. Japan has become the West's equal in material terms; the Cold War has ended. But societies do not evolve—not in any fundamental way—because of economic successes or an altered international climate. Like Perry's black ships a century and a half ago, these are only catalysts at work on agents of change already assembled. Societies change because the people who comprise them want them to. And such is the truth with which the Japanese now grapple, at once daunting and emancipating: People change institutions; in the end it is not the other way around.

The Japanese are much given to distinctions between generations. Each seems to be a point of departure. Each seems to have some assigned task. In recent years it has become impossible to discuss Japan without discussing the ways it will change, but change is seen as the responsibility only of the young. Others may desire it but feel no obligation to effect it.

"Change? Can Japan change?" an aging local official in western Japan once said over lunch. "Our generation is haunted by the old. We must wait for the next for change." This is not so, surely. Change cannot be but the consequence of desire and effort accumulated over many generations and transmitted from each to the next.

A decade ago a new generation emerged in Japan: the *shinjinrui,* the "new human species." The term described Japanese who seemed to be a people apart. The new species knew nothing of postwar reconstruction or the turmoil of the 1950s and 1960s. They were the first Japanese to know only affluence. They spent rather than saved, they felt no obligations toward society, they did not care for corporate loyalty or lifetime employment. To their elders their lack of vigor and direction was a source of worry. They seemed to have no point of view, no identity, no political perspective—nothing to distinguish themselves except the blank stare of indifference toward Japan's postwar values. By decade's end the rest of Japan simply shrugged, and the new species became *passé.* They seemed to reflect something familiar on the Japanese scene: the conformity of sanctioned nonconformity. Corporations reduced the *shinjinrui* to a marketing conundrum. The man who gave the new human species their name, a writer named Tetsuya Chikushi, repudiated it, saying there was nothing new about them after all.

We must wait to see if this is so, for it is not so easy to dismiss the *shinjinrui.* Rather, we must separate what is ephemeral about them from the things that are of lasting importance. Without even meaning to, the new species announced the end of "the modern" in Japan, the modern as the Japanese had understood it for a century and a quarter. Viscerally, they seemed to recognize that the past was somehow over and that they represented a decisive break with it. Their parents had completed the modernization project. It was the new species who, detached from history, could finally see the great price the Japanese paid for material success. This was their paradox: They consumed with abandon, for that was life's only reward—but always, it seemed to me, with a certain bitter contempt for consumption.

Many of the new species are no doubt *sararimen* by now, having drifted into corporate life as indifferently as Lifton's fickle student. But that is not the point. When one spoke with them, the people of this generation almost invariably explained that their primary concern was to reclaim time. What did they mean by this? Certainly it was not a matter of the passing hours and days. It was the way modern life has been divided in Japan. To reclaim time meant to assert control over themselves as individuals, to redraw the line between public and private—to make private life acceptable, not furtive and secret, and to live publicly as authentic, autonomous individuals.

Understood this way, the new species was aptly named. Its members signaled, it seems to me, the start of a fundamental renegotiation of the terms of Japanese life. They repudiated nothing less than the community ethos that has so long bound the Japanese—and so proposed a new way of being an individual that had nothing to do with being Japanese. They made the refusal to wear the Japanese mask the act not of a mountain-climbing hero but of an ordinary person. And they began, in all this, the final chapter of Japan's hidden history. That is why there is scarcely an aspect of Japanese society that is not now in flux.

"It is not true that we refuse to make any effort," one of the new species once explained. "We are dedicated to finding something worth making an effort for." The notion invites a useful comparison with the Association of New Men, the group that pressed, during the 1920s, for a fundamental renovation of modern Japan. Unlike the New Men, the new species has had no apparent political agenda—and certainly it has no organization. But the new species resembles the New Men in its advocacy of alternative ways of thinking and living. The project of the New Men was to partake of a society still in formation. The *shinjinrui,* by contrast, have confronted an altogether fixed society. They have sought not the right to participate in Japan as it has constructed itself but to quit that Japan in favor of one that admits of autonomy and multiplicity.

LET US RETURN briefly to the matter of names. From this story of names, names printed on paper, we learn the point of transition the Japanese have reached—a peculiar place, but one from which there does not seem to be any turning back.

Meishi, business cards, are essential equipment in modern Japan. They tell you not only a person's name and affiliation but—most important—his rank within the hierarchy. Without some indication of status, two Japanese would have a difficult time because they would not know the proper behavior. Who stands above whom? How deep should the bow be? You can fill drawers with *meishi* in the course of a busy year in Japan. Even the most casual encounters require exchanges of cards; the code they supply is essential. Is the *meishi* not in some way analogous to the samurai's dress—the meticulously displayed colors and patterns by which he identified himself?

The most interesting *meishi* I ever received was from a *sarariman* at the Nikken Corporation. Nikken was a going concern in the early 1990s; perhaps it still is. It did a thriving business leasing office equipment and industrial machinery. It had three factories, 160 sales offices, and almost two thousand employees. There were subsidiaries in Chicago and Bangkok and a listing on the Tokyo Stock Exchange. Yearly revenue came to 60 billion yen, about $600 million.

The man from Nikken who handed me his *meishi* was thirtyish, a "new human species." One side of his card read TARO HONMARU, GENERAL MANAGER. On the other it read MY REAL NAME IS KEIICHI NAKAMURA. What did it mean that a young Japanese executive had two names?

The system started naturally enough. After hiring a nephew with the same surname, Nikken's president soon tired of the confusion. So he called his nephew Imafuku-san, after the younger man's hometown. The characters for "Imafuku" happen to translate as "now luck," a fortuitous stroke, for it yielded a lasting nickname. And so the system evolved. The president was called Kane (Turtle), for his tough demeanor. An executive from a mountain village named himself Kodama-san, *kodama* being the echo heard across peaks. There was a sports fan called Rikishi-san (because *rikishi* is another name for a sumo wrestler) and a Hitomi Sakura (Iris Cherry Blossom). The general manager who explained all this was Honmaru-san because he worked in the head office's planning section. *Honmaru* were the central towers in the castles of the feudal daimyo.

Honmaru-san, tall and boyish, was much taken with the curiosities: the confusion at business hotels, the computer directory where real and invented names were matched. He did not seem to have considered what such a system said about Japan and the Japanese, or what it meant that one's real name represented the private, authentic self, and the made-up name the public self, the mask. Then, in his polite, diffident manner, he began to explain. We sat across from each other at a Formica-topped table in a bare conference room.

"One reason we do this—perhaps it's very Japanese—is that a lot of *sararimen* get confused between their private and public selves. They want to separate the two clearly. While at work, you should have the dedication of the professional businessman—the so-called corporate warrior. After five, you should return to your real self and do what you want to do."

Honmaru paused to judge my reaction before drawing his conclusion. "The Japanese are like actors," he said finally. "Actors can't refuse a role. You can't refuse your part in Japan."

Actors cannot refuse roles, but ordinary people can.

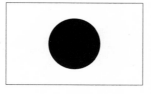

3

BECOMING
NIHONJIN

Education in Japan is not intended to create people
accomplished in the techniques of the arts and sciences,
but rather to manufacture the persons required by the State.

—ARINORI MORI,
Japan's first education minister, 1885

YOSUKE KOBAYASHI HAS a stocky build, an intent gaze, and the bristly
crew cut favored by aging nationalists. In conversation he brooks no hesitation, no pause for thought. Sitting around a kerosene stove with a half
dozen colleagues, he is their self-appointed spokesman. He smiles easily
but, son of a farmer, guards his self-possession and pride.

Yosuke Kobayashi is seven. He is in second grade at Sakai elementary
school, a two-story brick building down a narrow road in a village whose
name, Fujimi, celebrates its distant view of Mount Fuji.

Fujimi, a community of farmers and factory workers in Nagano
Prefecture, is below freezing in January. From the sloping streets in the
center of town, you can see well-packed ski trails across the valley below;
the winter Olympics will be played not far away in 1998. The lights of a
distant *ryokan,* a traditional inn, flicker even in the daytime. At Sakai

there is a crust of snow several inches deep, and the drive in is solid ice.

Yosuke Kobayashi's problem, one shared with six classmates on a windy Wednesday morning, is wet feet. All seven of them have retreated from the playground, shoes off, stockinged feet to the stove. They are reading quietly when I arrive.

"What do you do after school? Play on the farm with the animals?"

"I do homework or play with the family computer," says Yosuke Kobayashi, pleased to contradict.

"What about when you grow up? What then?"

"A *sensei!*" Kobayashi exclaims. "I want to be a teacher."

The others consider the question and finally get a word in edgewise. There are two aspiring bookstore owners, a novelist, and one who wants to take care of children. The two others, perhaps reticent in front of a gaijin, cannot really say.

"Nobody wants to be a *sarariman?*"

"I wanted to be a *sarariman* last month," Kobayashi puts in.

"What made you change your mind?"

"I always change my mind. I only wanted to be one for a little while."

Yosuke Kobayashi and his friends look upon life as an event of infinite choices. They all, it turns out, always change their minds. Even the shy ones grin uncontrollably as if in delight with this enviable privilege. Their clothes, of bright colors and carefree styles, convey the same exuberance: yellow ski parkas, red socks, green sweaters, woollen caps a near riot of hues.

"Who sent you in here?"

"We came in by ourselves," answers Yosuke Kobayashi.

"No one told you to?"

"We had wet feet. It's common sense."

"You just did it. No one told you."

"We told the teacher first."

I went to Sakai to meet Japanese schoolchildren. And Yosuke Kobayashi and his friends were Japanese, of course—born in Japan of Japanese parentage. But it was hard to find anything about them that was Japanese as we ordinarily use the term. They were in full command of that personal autonomy most Japanese find so elusive. They had no particular attitude toward authority. They were not especially concerned about being part of the group. And they wore no masks.

Not far from Sakai elementary, Minami middle school is an altogether more austere institution. Its front entrance is wide open to the cold: physical hardship as the instructor of the will. The hallways, unheated, with floors of worn wood, are spotless: They are mopped every afternoon by platoons of students, who mumble a greeting—*Konichiwa,* good day—with uniform, eyes-to-the-floor diffidence.

Students at Minami all wear the same dark tunics (fashioned after old Prussian military garb), the same blouses and jumpers, the same hairstyles, the same sneakers, socks of the same make and precisely the same height. Identical book bags hang from wooden pegs around the classrooms. Posters explain the proper methods of study: Use thick pencils, one advises; with a dotted-line diagram, another shows the exact distance (thirty centimeters) to be maintained between the eye and the page.

Later I receive a copy of Minami's regulations. Rule 1: "Be punctual and moderate." Rule 2 concerns clothing and appearance. The school badge and a name card are to be pinned to the left breast; shoes must be of the approved variety. "Boys' hair is not to cover the ears and brow. Girls' hair is not to cover the eyes. When binding hair, rubber bands are to be black, navy, or dark brown." Other rules have to do with motorbikes and pinball parlors (prohibited), part-time work (to be approved by the principal), and leaving the village (not without adult supervision).

In a social science class they are studying Suwa, the feudal name for the district; for a brief period in the eighth century the area was a separate nation called Suho. At the end there is a four-question quiz:

1. Please write something about the Suwa area.
2. Describe Suwa during the Nara and Heian eras.
3. What do you think of Suho-*koku?*
4. What would you like to study about ancient Suwa?

In an English class two old telephone sets sit on the teacher's desk. Pairs of seventh-graders take turns at them.

"Hello," one conversation begins.

"Hello."

(Long pause; nervous confusion.)

"Are you free?"

"Yes, I am."

(Another long pause.)

"Do you . . . do you like baseball?"

"Yes."

(Pause, then haste.)

"Good-bye."

"Good-bye."

It is surprising to see instruction in local history—it suggests a departure from the heavy weight of central control for which Japanese schools are known. And the quiz: It requires thought and imagination. The Japanese normally learn by rote, advancing simply by repeating what they are told.

The lurching uncertainty in the English class is closer to what I expected to find at Minami. True, this is their first year of language study—the first of a minimum of six. But the anguished pauses are otherwise explained: They reveal the confusion the Japanese typically feel in the face of the unplanned. The Japanese learn to perform only when the script is written. Put them in a situation requiring a flexible response—when the next thought, the next statement, the next act is up to them—and they come unhinged. How unlike young Kobayashi-san and his friends at Sakai, who think for themselves and manage their own small affairs.

The Japanese consider freedom the right only of the very young. Japan draws a circle around them, a container within which they are unexposed to either social or psychological limits. Inside the container they are the emperors and empresses of daily life. The Chinese, too, are famously indulgent of their children. But only in Japan would a parent say, "Our young are free because we know the rest of their lives will be burdensome."

One hears such sentiments often. But young children enjoy an attenuated freedom, after all, because it is given (and eventually taken away) by those above—parents, teachers, administrators. For all their independence of spirit, Yosuke Kobayashi and his friends were also getting their first lessons in dependence—the dependence upon authority that has been characteristic of the Japanese personality for many centuries.

It is as the young exit the container that freedom is gradually withdrawn and the submissive personality takes its lifelong form. Could there be a question more laden with unconscious irony than the first one posed in the conversation drill: "Are you free?" To become *nihonjin*, to become a Japanese, does not mean becoming an ordinary person. And it is the inverse of the comparable process in the West: Adulthood is measured not by the achievement of ever greater degrees of independence, but in the acceptance of the process by which choices are narrowed until there are none.

The principal in each of the schools I visited spoke earnestly of the ideals of liberal learning. "Truth is not just scientific facts," said Toshio Iijima, who ran Minami middle school. "It's also how to arrive at the truth by oneself in daily life. We want students to find problems in nature and solve them."

Teachers all over Japan announce similar beliefs. The problem with most such assertions is the old one in Japan, the distance between the ideal and the real. Most educators are at ease explaining their admirable thoughts about education, especially to gaijin, because of how they learned them: by rote. This often becomes clear as conversations go on.

"My duty is to make students grow into adults who can support the nation," Yu Hosono, an orderly but relaxed man in his fifties, told me at Sakai elementary. "My basic principle is 'Everyone can play any role.'"

That may not be a bad description of an educator's duty, depending on your perspective. But there is a danger in it, the danger Yukichi Fukuzawa ran into during the Meiji era: the contradiction between human development for its own sake and development for the sake of a strong country. After a century and a quarter of modern education Japan has yet to resolve this contradiction. It will do so: The Japanese are too restless, there is too much discontent in the schools, and the nation's economic imperatives are changing too drastically for there to be any other conclusion. But it will not be an easy resolution, or a quick one.

Today Japanese schools are a battlefield. This is not surprising; beneath the surface, most Japanese institutions are. At stake when teachers clash with bureaucrats, when students drop out, or when intellectuals take the Education Ministry to court over the content of national textbooks is nothing less than the kinds of people the Japanese are permitted to become.

Haven't Japanese schools produced the men and women who have built the world's second-largest economy? Yes—and the straight-line equation the question implies is precisely the problem. Look at education from the perspective of individual development, and the story of modern Japanese schooling immediately becomes one of truncated opportunity and stunted personal growth. Schools are merely preparation for the ceaseless assault on the individual that the Japanese must accept as part of the adult burden.

At Minami middle school, Iijima-sensei, thin, balding, and intent, had a more precise vision than Hosono of the system he worked within—and a more accurate one, at least for the moment. "Learning the truth is important," he said. "But learning to be Japanese is very important."

WESTERNERS DO NOT see the danger inherent in a system dedicated to building a population that can serve the nation. We associate education with liberal values—knowledge, rational inquiry, civility, civic-mindedness. We have our debates as to what ought to be taught and how; but we tend not to think of education as an empty vessel that can be filled with just about anything. Serving the nation may or may not be a fine idea. That judgment must always depend on the nation, and how it is to be served.

This is an extraordinary lapse, particularly for Americans. The occupation officials at G.H.Q. in late 1945 were horrified at what went on in Japanese schools. Emperor worship, Japanist ideology, state Shinto: Schools were building the old edifice within, as everyone saw. It was to dismantle the internal edifice that Americans were eager to teach the Japanese square dancing, billiards, and other ordinary pastimes. Less quaintly, the same zeal was reflected in the occupation's education reforms, which were among the most sweeping of its programs. Almost all of those reforms, however, were pushed aside after the reverse course. Then we began to kid ourselves. We still count the changes we made in Japanese schools among our great legacies. Of course, it has been convenient to maintain this fiction. It is a large part of our imaginary "Japan."

William Bennett, President Reagan's education secretary, issued a report in 1987 called *Japanese Education Today*. It was Bennett's indirect contribution to the heated argument among Americans about the collapse of their public schools. "Our educational ideals are better realized on a large scale in Japan than observers have tended to realize," he noted. Bennett admired the Japanese system; its excellence, so far as he was concerned, reflected America's postwar influences. "It is the American belief in the value of universal education that the Japanese have so successfully put into practice, and the American quandary over 'equality' and 'excellence' that the Japanese seem rather satisfactorily to have resolved."

That the Japanese learned the value of universal education from the occupation is among the hollowest of America's conceits. Official Japan has long found universal education desirable—for its use if not its value. But Bennett was merely repeating the orthodoxy. The same year he issued

Japanese Education Today, a Harvard lecturer named Merry White published *The Japanese Educational Challenge: A Commitment to Children,* a book that posed some excellent questions:

> In Japan the care of children is not regarded as just a domestic concern. Indeed the entire nation is mobilized behind children and their education. This national obsession may well be responsible for children Western parents and educators would be proud of, children whose lives and future prospects meet our standards of approval. In short, the Japanese national engagement in child development is something we should envy.
>
> What has fueled the drive to maximize the life chances of children? How does the intense commitment to children mirror the nation's conception of its past, present, and future?

Unfortunately, White's study neglects to answer her excellent questions. Instead her book veers off into explanations of educational "scarcity," pervasive feelings of insecurity in an agrarian society, and (quoting a teacher) "Japan's moral 'common sense.'"

Many statistics suggest the superiority of Japanese schools. Japanese pupils average seven hours of instruction a day and two hours of homework; Americans average five hours and twenty minutes in school and twenty-five minutes at homework. School-age Japanese read for twenty-five minutes daily—two and a half times what American children give to books. Japanese teachers are better prepared than their American counterparts. By any measure the Japanese student is more literate and more numerate than the American schoolchild.

But how and why do Japanese pupils become so notably disciplined—and to what purpose? What habits of mind do they acquire? What sacrifices are forced upon them? What are they like when they finish school—or (better put, perhaps) when school finishes with them? If we answer these questions, or the questions White poses, we might wonder whether the experiences and prospects of Japanese children would "meet our standards of approval."

With history in view it is irresponsible, to say the least, to assert that "the entire nation is mobilized behind children and their education," and that Americans ought to envy this "national engagement." National engagement in education dates to Meiji. From the 1930s onward it was a form of coercion, an essential tool in Japan's version of fascist totality. And the continuity between Japan's pre- and postwar education systems is nowhere considered even debatable.

VIOLENCE IN SCHOOLS—in America and to a lesser extent elsewhere in the West—is one reason we are encouraged to admire the Japanese system. But violence (rendered by both students and teachers) is common in Japan. It is only more institutional—better dressed. Every year the newspapers report incidents that seem to border on sadism: A seventeen-year-old's spleen is ruptured when a teacher kicks him in the stomach for reading a comic book; a thirteen-year-old suffocates when other students roll him in a gym mat and stuff him upside down into a closet. Teachers are reported to inflict more than a hundred skull fractures, sprains, broken bones, and the like each year. *Ijime,* student bullying, is a peculiarly Japanese problem. It is rampant in the school system: More than twenty-two thousand cases are reported annually.

These sort of things help to explain much about Japanese schools. There are troubling rashes of suicides among schoolchildren, for instance—a dozen in 1995. The dropout rate averages twenty students annually at every high school in the country; one student in six struggles with alcohol; truancy cases hover at just under 5 percent of all students because children in the tens of thousands simply refuse to subject themselves to Japan's educational regime. These numbers climbed dramatically during the 1980s and were at record highs in the mid-1990s.

We are rarely encouraged to think of truancy, violence, and drinking as endemic problems in Japanese schools. When these matters come up, they are placed somewhere in the statistical fringe—odd occurrences bound to happen in any large system. It would be wrong to suggest that Japanese schools are either dangerous or empty. They are not. But, once again, we cannot simply leave the statistics sitting there without explanation. Violence, the dropout rate, and other problems are symptoms of disorders that affect a vast number of students who never appear in the statistics.

The core problem is evident in the very term used for "education." *Kyoiku* is written in two characters, the first meaning "to impart" and the second "to develop." In the difference between the two lies the tragic failure of Japanese schools. Teaching methods, textbooks, and curricula, from ethics and history to morning exercise routines, are decided by the Education Ministry. All stress the dictation of knowledge to the neglect of the student's ability to manage knowledge—that is, the *kyo* at the expense of the *iku*. Pupils are taught not to think but to accumulate immense piles of disparate facts that can be repeated on command but cannot be connected. This is not an accident or a lapse. Rote learning is the child's next lesson in dependence. To think is an act of autonomy; to memorize the given is to rely upon authority.

Rote learning is measured by an intensely competitive examination system. Exams are a typical feature of Confucian meritocracies. They are administered not at the conclusion of a course of study but as entrance requirements. The Chinese used exams to select bureaucrats. The Japanese apply them to everybody, which leads to a peculiar kind of competition: It all takes place at once, and then it is over. This is why students spend much of their time in a state of intense preparation called "exam hell." One will either pass or fail, with no second chance to display improvement. Individual achievement is not the point; the point is merely to enter the school whose diploma accords the most privilege and social recognition— a very different thing.

Savage competition and force-fed information without the cultivation of critical thought go far to explain the character of Japanese graduates. The system's demands—years in exam hell, every other student an adversary— produce not exploring intellects but the narrow, machinelike people we assume the Japanese to be by nature. Wholly focused on achieving the highest possible place in the hierarchy, they are unable to form healthy ties with equals—horizontal relationships. They are indifferent to most public issues because they are unnaturally inward looking and (by official design) ignorant of large patches of their own history. Outside of a few conventional settings—karaoke bars are one—they display little sense of autonomy.

Those who stay the course become *shakai-jin,* social beings, people conditioned to live in society. What have they learned? What is considered important to live in Japan? To keep their individuality private. To persevere, to soldier on in the face of adversity. And to conform. These are essential habits for the successful *nihonjin.* They explain why bullying and physical punishment, while officially condemned, remain so ordinary. The

Education Ministry does little about them, except in the most extreme cases, because they are the best way to get the message across.

In Kobe I met a psychiatrist named Masao Miyamoto, who had been trained at Cornell Medical and practiced in America for a decade before returning to Japan. He had been working for the Health Ministry for seven years. Miyamoto's problem was simple: He was detribalized. His life was a kind of hell until he learned to cope with the relentless demands of sameness by resisting them, then ignoring them, and later writing about them. Miyamoto wore bright neckties. He went to dinner with his minister and some colleagues and ordered a different plate than the others. He did not work overtime and took all of his allotted vacation. The price was ostracism and *ijime,* bullying. And when he began publishing his observations about the difficulties he found in Japan after living abroad, he was invited to resign—not because his remarks were untrue but because he had betrayed his group to outsiders.

Bullying does not end at graduation. In one form or another it is part of every *nihonjin*'s existence from school days onward. Miyamoto called it "a sadistic impulse which seeks to bring straying sheep back into the fold." But how did his bureaucratic superior see things? "That's not bullying," Miyamoto was told. "We call it discipline. It's because of our loving feeling toward you that we want to acclimate you to the environment as quickly as possible. You simply don't understand our affection."

These two explanations of *ijime* do not contradict each other. Bullying is cruel and loving at the same time because at the root of both lies narcissism. To acquire a certain narcissism is a fundamental part of becoming *nihonjin:* One takes on the fear of difference and—the other side of the coin—the drive to see oneself reflected in all others. Doesn't turning little boys like Yosuke Kobayashi into "social beings" involve both bullying and love—both administered by society in heavy doses? The necessity of narcissism explains, in psychological terms, the suppression of public individuality. "You are allowed to have divergent thoughts," Miyamoto said of his work in the bureaucracy, "as long as they are not publicly expressed."

Among the most curious people to appear during the late 1980s were a group in their teens and twenties called *otaku. Otaku* is one of many terms for "you." In its ancient meaning it was used to address someone from another *ie* (extended household) and implied that one was unconcerned with the details of the other person's family and circumstances. To use it was to say, "We are from different houses. We have only this encounter in common." The word objectified the other while preserving the illusion of sameness. It prevented the discovery that there were differences between subject and object, "I" and "you."

Otaku today apply the term to those who share an obsession. They take their name from the old pronoun because they use it to mean, "I am not interested in you or your inner life. I share with you only our narrow interest." An *otaku*'s obsession is highly cultivated. It might be a deceased pop star, a cartoonist, rail schedules, or outer-space aliens. Computers are a favorite obsession. It does not matter as long as one knows the finest details of one's interest, preferably an obscure interest. I once ran into a group of *otaku* waiting at some subway stairs in the Roppongi bar district for a rock singer no one had heard of for years. Each one carried a rose. What were they expecting, I asked. They were sure he would emerge from the next train, at precisely 9:05, on his way to a party at such-and-such an address.

The *otaku* are an extreme group. But they cannot be ignored as marginal. Most university students display some attributes of the *otaku*, and many continue on with their obsessions as young professionals in their twenties. To be an *otaku* is merely the final word in private individuality. It is to reject anyone who would diminish the protected ego and to acknowledge an inability to achieve the intimacy of authentic human contact. The *otaku* draws a circle around himself—that fundamentally Japanese impulse— and withdraws within. He (almost all *otaku* are male) refuses knowledge of those who share his compulsion because the details of anyone's life would force the conclusion that even an *otaku* partner is an "other."

This is the purest imaginable display of the narcissism inherent in Japanese society. The *otaku* desires both an idealized union and an impregnable independence—the classic drives of the narcissist. He seems postmodern and marginal but is deeply traditional in his rejection of the unfamiliar. Students in the ancient schools of tea ceremony were like *otaku*. Every member had to be a mirror of every other member. The *otaku* represent rebellion as parodic conformity.

And how does the *otaku* spend his time? Like the typical Japanese student: accumulating disconnected (and therefore useless) facts. His fixation is a postmodern joke—the punch line being the meaninglessness of what passes for meaning in contemporary Japan. He is at once protesting what and how he has "learned," and performing an act of profound conformity and submission. Perseverance is an enviable virtue; one may even take conformity to be one. But it is another matter to envy these qualities once one understands how they are inculcated. The *otaku* show us that perseverance and conformity, both of which they possess, are like education: They can be good or bad.

The notion that Japanese graduates look out upon a bright, enviable future applies to a sliver of the 40 percent of students who attend university—the graduates of Tokyo University, say, or a handful of other institutions. But we ought to question whether even the privileged few are to be envied. Our efficient Japan, the "Japan" of Japan Inc., rests on a false picture. Graduates of Todai, as Tokyo University is familiarly known, are subject to the same dreary pressure to conform as everyone else once they begin moving through the system; if anything, such pressure is greater on them, for they are Japan's exemplars. Dr. Miyamoto's experience is typical of the Todai graduate's in all respects but one: Unable either to conform or resist, he spent his first year at the Health Ministry nursing gastritis and insomnia.

This sketch of the Japanese system can surprise only those who accept the conventional wisdom without questioning it, or who do not wish to see Japan as it is. Only in the West—from afar, where one sees the shiny surface of things but not the grim detail beneath—do people want to take credit for the Japanese system. In Japan the question is blame. How did our schools come to such a sorry state? they ask. No one any longer even pretends they work properly. But there the agreement ends, for solutions to the problem are widely varied.

Arinori Mori, Japan's first education minister, could not have foreseen the truants and the dropouts—to say nothing of the *otaku*. The record suggests he would have been horrified. But what is contested in schools, what lies behind these morbid symptoms, is the very notion contained in Mori's quotation at the beginning of this chapter. Education in modern Japan was to produce—"manufacture"—people more akin to machines than inquiring individuals. A century after his death, Japan has still not resolved the simple but fundamental problem of which serves the other, the individual or the state. Can anyone wonder that the descendant of Mori's system is among the most contentious in the industrial world?

ARINORI MORI HAD the way of the warrior in his blood. His education, as the son of a samurai, had much in common with a pupil's routine today: Up at six for sixteen hours of memorization and rote recitation—"without particular attention to meaning," his biographer tells us. Tears when his recall failed. Plenty of physical rigor—chores, the martial arts, occasional war games in the dark. He did not leave the fiefdom where his father served in the bureaucracy until he was eighteen.

For most of the next decade Mori was abroad: England, the Continent, America. And from these travels another Mori emerged. A photograph taken in 1872, four years after the restoration, shows a confident, exceptionally handsome man: a set gaze, flowing hair in the English-aesthete style, perfect bones, a well-trimmed beard. He wears a suit with wide lapels, a silk four-in-hand tied neatly at his neck. Mori was twenty-five and halfway through a three-year tour as Tokyo's first minister to Washington.

Was he a champion of "civilization," or a xenophobic samurai? Or perhaps the question is backwards: A craven imitator of the West, or an excellent steward of the great Japanese tradition?

Mori knew the West, arguably, more intimately than any other Meiji figure. Japan needed to absorb all it could, he preached—to evident excess. He advised young Japanese studying in the United States to improve the nation's gene pool by taking American wives; he wanted to scrap *nihongo* ("our meager language") so the Japanese would converse ever after in English. He was the first Japanese to marry in Western style and, giving his wife the rights then accorded in America, to set her free of Confucian ignominy. His favorite pastime was billiards, learned (along with much else) from Herbert Spencer, the English sociologist, at the Athenaeum Club in London. Hirobumi Ito, the first premier, called Mori "a Westerner born in Japan."

Then the other Mori reemerged. He divorced, then remarried in Japanese style. He became an ardent patriot. Mori's schools taught the *kokutai,* the national essence; the emperor's image hung in every one, his words on education recited frequently. Textbook censors were busy. There was no such thing as an individual who happened to be Japanese and who learned for the sake of learning—only *nihonjin,* who learned for the sake of Japan.

Mori's death was as contradictory as his life. In 1887 he went to the sacred shrines at Ise, south of Tokyo. The visit was in earnest, we may assume, but Mori botched the protocol. On entering he failed to remove his shoes; then he used his walking stick to part a sacred veil no mortal was to touch. So it was said: The details are lost. Two years later, on the day the emperor was to give Japan its new constitution, Mori was stabbed by a fanatic nationalist, a fallen samurai like himself, in revenge for the Ise incident. The newspapers made the assassin a martyr for ridding Japan of a sellout—a closet Christian, rumors in high places had it. The public did not know whether to pay respects at the grave of the honorable minister or of the fanatic nationalist, among the first of the modern breed, who killed him.

Early biographers sought to pin down the great switch in Mori's mind: His influences changed from America, a riot of individual enterprise during the Meiji years, to the new and nationalist Germany; he seemed to leave behind the liberalism of youth for the traditionalist within. But there was no such advance and retreat, no progress or regress. Mori seems to have held all his views at once—never bothering (or unable, perhaps) to reconcile the contradictions. Nationalist always, a statist at his ministry, Mori thought Japan should nonetheless be like the West he had traveled through: a place of open relationships, lively intellectual exchange, civic awareness—in short, a *public* Japan. Individual to the point of eccentricity in his personal habits (another source of suspicion among colleagues), Mori seems nevertheless not to have established the kind of sovereign self the novelist Soseki Natsume talked about.

Mori's life is a kind of biography of Meiji. If we cannot find a name for Mori we cannot attach one to his age. His confusion was everybody's. His "dual structure of the spirit"—the gentle phrase of a later historian—was precisely modern Japan's. But he never quite outgrew the long days and nights as a samurai-in-training, and so ended up inflicting a version of his own experience on the whole country. And the human tragedy of the modernization project—its immense missed opportunities—was nowhere more evident than in Mori's schools.

Upon his return from Washington in 1873, Mori began the Meiji Six Society, so named for its founding year by the imperial calendar: the sixth year of Meiji. Made up of liberal intellectuals and publisher of its own magazine, Meiji Six quickly became the center of the "civilization and enlightenment" movement. Yukichi Fukuzawa, champion of "the spirit of independence," was prominent among Meiji Six's members. He and Mori were friends. But they stood on either side of the Meiji era's great divide over education. And the chasm between them first emerged in the group.

In 1875 the new government issued the first in a line of libel laws and newspaper regulations intended to limit free speech and the spread of political discussion among ordinary Japanese. Sweeping but vaguely worded, they portended Japan's imminent change in direction. Reflecting on the Meiji Six Society, Mori advised his colleagues:

> It was not originally the intention at the founding of our society . . . that the discussion would relate to contemporary political matters. Thus let us be careful in the future to avoid becoming embroiled in such controversies.

Was this not akin to telling people to discuss their discovery of an ocean without reference to water? How could one discuss modern Japan's birth from feudalism without discussing politics? Fukuzawa was incensed; he saw no point in going any further. Meiji Six, for two years an influential voice in the new Japan, ceased publishing its monthly shortly after Mori's critique and dissolved entirely three months later.

What was the essential quarrel between Mori and Fukuzawa? Press censorship? If so, Fukuzawa would surely have argued for continued publication. The core issue was the ban on political discourse. Behind Mori's idea was the assumption that certain things were to be considered only in the restricted upper reaches of society. And behind that assumption lay another: that the motor of the new Japan, the source of its ideas and direction, was not the common majority but the educated elite. The implications were enormous. In our terminology modern Japan was to be top-down, not bottom-up. In the school system this idea produced a sharp distinction between learning (for the elite) and education (for the masses).

A neat summary of this principle was given in 1911, Meiji's next-to-last year, when, in a squabble known as the Northern and Southern Dynasties controversy, the legitimacy of the imperial line was thrown into question. How should this issue be described in textbooks without weakening the throne? Here is how a Todai scholar with an ideological bent reasoned:

When doing research and making judgments . . . there are of course two attitudes we can take. First, with regard to reality as reality, we must conduct our inquiries in a scientific manner, without sticking to questions of right or wrong, good or bad. In the other case we are obliged to pursue our researches and make our judgments from the standpoint of the national morality . . . in other words, what is good or bad for the state. It should go without saying that in the case of our national textbooks, the principle of selection is not to be found in the first of these attitudes.

Knowledge as power: In modern Japan it would be one thing to arrive at the truth, another to disseminate it.

Fukuzawa detested this sort of logic. Mori, as we have noted, was more ambivalent, but he had his own quarrels with the old Confucianists. He did not want schools to teach either ideology or Shinto as an official religion. In 1887, he tweaked conservatives in his resolution of a festering row over ethics instruction. After the Meiji Restoration the first ethics texts had been direct translations of American works. Confucianists gradually replaced these during the 1880s with their own tracts on moral education. Unhappy with the trend, Mori simply banned ethics texts of any kind. Already suspect for the Western tint in his thinking, Mori as an enemy of the true soul of Japan became an idée fixe among conservatives from this period onward.

But here we come to one of Mori's intellectual swamps. What did he want schools to teach? "It is a big mistake to think that the primary aims of education should reside in instruction in the three 'R's," he said the same year he banned the ethics texts. Mori wanted schools to produce "virtuous subjects." What would those be like? Mori asked this question himself and then answered it. "They will be imperial subjects who completely fulfill their duties, which means that when called upon to do so they will willingly give their lives to the state."

He may have equivocated about the conservatives, and they about him, but Mori handed them the schools they needed. Few decisions were left to local discretion in the system structured during the late 1880s. Curricula, textbooks, and standards became the business of the Mombusho, the Education Ministry. Tokyo functionaries inspected every school in Japan annually. Most private schools were shut down; to neutralize the rest Mori decreed that only pupils from state schools could sit for university exams. Then came the teachers, many of whom were liberals and populists who could not be entrusted with the task of molding the modern Japanese. The Rules of Behavior for Primary School Teachers banned instructors from political discussions. Intent on turning teachers into reliable conduits of *kokutai*, the national essence, Mori brought teacher training under Mombusho control. Candidates had to wear military tunics. When the bureaucracy was finished with them they were deployed around the country like soldiers.

Mori's system endured until 1945. High among his influences were France and Germany, the one for its central command, the other for a meritocratic system in the service of an emerging industrial economy. But what was put into the vessel Mori made was purely Japanese.

In 1890, a year after Mori's death, the emperor issued one of the two or three most important documents of the prewar era. It came amid great confusion. Mori's murder had shaken the government—not least because of popular confusion as to whether the assassin had been right or wrong. What kind of country had the oligarchy made? That was just the question addressed in the Imperial Rescript on Education. Like every other communiqué issued in the emperor's name, it was written not by the sovereign but by those around him who ruled in his name. It reads today like a harmless set of platitudes regarding the old Confucian virtues and "the fundamental character of Our Empire."

But the rescript's influence was immense, and extended far beyond Mori's schools. Rescripts were national codes, instructions to all Japanese. There is no paranoia in imagining behind the education rescript the roll of military drums. In it loyalty and filial piety were officially combined once more. To serve the emperor was to serve the state, and vice versa. This was the new edifice within: precisely what Fukuzawa, albeit with his faulty argument, had fought.

Mori's schools required no great change to accommodate the rescript. At the bottom there was universal education: Six years of compulsory schooling by Meiji's end, when enrollment reached just under 100 percent. Long before the years of military dictatorship—before, even, Meiji was over—education was legally defined not as a child's right or as a responsibility of parent to child, but as a parent's duty to the state. "The entire nation," one might have declared, "is mobilized behind children and their education."

At the top were the universities, places of learning as opposed to education. Only in the universities could ideas be explored in anything resembling an open atmosphere. Even there impartial scholarship was treated as a kind of radioactive experiment. There were seven imperial universities and a few private ones. (In 1868 Fukuzawa had the forethought to found one, Keio University, that is still put among Japan's best.) This handful was enough. Japan needed an elite, but a small, manageable one. Todai stood at the apex. In 1887 an imperial ordinance awarded Todai law graduates the exclusive right to advance directly into upper ranks of the bureaucracy—a privilege still apparent.

In shape the system resembled Meiji society: a pyramid with steep sides. Schools became what they are today: battlegrounds, all the more gruesome because the foot soldiers are so young. Mori's schools were the central venue of what scholars call successism, or the ideology of striving—that fierce competition created by the release of desire and ambition in a society that remained a hierarchy. While basic education was universal, no more than 15 percent of students went on from there. Schooling, no matter what it consisted of, no matter whose picture hung on the wall, became a mania among people finally offered a path, however narrow, upward.

EDUCATION MADNESS FIRST appeared in the 1890s. Successism produced too many aspiring students—too many commoners who saw that school was the only way up from the rice paddies. The primary schools were full, but they were not yet dependable; they did not turn out pupils of uniform qualifications. There were too few schools beyond the primary level anyway: The pyramid was too steep. Schools above the elementary level became addicted, as they are now, to entrance examinations.

Exam hell was bad enough at Meiji's end. A student's place in society, the course of his entire adult life, was decided by a test. But it got even worse after 1945. The occupation lit the fires of aspiration anew. Colleges and universities mushroomed: There are now roughly five hundred of them. But there could be five times that number and little will change so long as schools, and not a student's achievements, are rated according to a hierarchy strictly observed in both government and business. All that has changed is the number of aspirants looking toward the top—and the number of disappointed failures consigned to universities of indifferent quality.

Exam hell has produced numerous peculiarities. Japan is a society of *kyoiku mamas*—education mothers, obsessed with their children's success. There are many thousands of high school graduates, called *ronin* (after wandering samurai without masters), who failed the entrance exams and wait to retake them. As everyone in Japan knows, most matriculated students do little during their university years because their place in society is more or less fixed no matter what they accomplish. The companies they join will finish the task of turning them into *shakai-jin,* social beings. So their university years are not an education so much as a reward for surviving exam hell, a last fling at attenuated freedom.

Cram schools, called *juku,* are another oddity. They are a parallel system at least as important as the schools that award diplomas. Seventy percent of primary and middle school students attend *juku* or (in some cases) have private tutors; for high school students the figure is 80 percent. *Juku* are big business. Fees run to many thousands of dollars a year. Japan is lauded for the austerity of its educational budget: It is the lowest in the industrial world. But Tokyo depends heavily on the private side of education. In the average family, education consumes a quarter of income; more than half of what it spends on preuniversity education is taken up by *juku* fees and related expenses.

The *juku* once met a practical need. They resembled the temple schools of the Edo era, in which a scholar taught basic arithmetic and writing so that the children of commoners, as adults, could manage local affairs. After the war teachers minded the children of the millions of workers who drifted into the cities, where there were no villagers to share the burden and no grandparents in the household. But the *juku* have blown way off course. Not only are they part of the national obsession; in a way they drive it by feeding the anxieties of parents about the success of their children in national exams.

In Ikebukuro, a commercial district in northwestern Tokyo, there is a cram school called Shingakai, the Growing Bud Club. It occupies half a floor in a building called Sunshine 60 after the number of stories it has and because its height, unusual in Tokyo's low-rise sprawl, puts its upper floors far enough above the densest smog to allow them clear light. In Shingakai's large, bare rooms students prepare for the exam system by taking additional lessons—the work of any *juku.* In theory, at least, Shingakai graduates will have it over competitors in the race for places in the nation's most favored schools. But then there are many other *juku* like Shingakai—between fifty thousand and sixty thousand, most of them in the cities, where competition is fiercest.

Shingakai is special in one sense. It was the first *juku* for a new age group: one- and two-year-olds. No one I met there was quite sure when this ground was broken, but it appears to have been sometime in the early 1980s. This was a tragic but inevitable step—and a measure of how acutely competitive Japan had become beneath the harmony on the surface. During the 1980s *kyoiku mamas* began to talk of "education in the womb"—an expectant mother's recitation of numbers and words to give her fetuses a head start.

Shingakai's progress reflects the fraught path education has taken since the war. It did not start out as a *juku*. It was founded in 1956 by a man named Hideo Ohori, who studied psychology at university. It was like an old temple school, except that Ohori-sensei was a pied piper more than a Confucian scholar. He minded neighborhood children and got two or three hundred yen a day for each. Then Shingakai began to offer preparatory classes for exams to enter elementary schools: It became a *juku*. Now it has thirteen branches in and around Tokyo.

Tsutomu Matsuzawa, the general manager, looked more like an accomplished *sarariman* than a *sensei*. He was tall and thin with neat, oiled hair, a dark suit, and polished manners. He spent a good part of his day greeting well-to-do education mothers eager to enroll their children. But despite his practiced confidence, Matsuzawa grew hesitant when we began to talk about something called mock testing. Yes, Shingakai ran mock tests, he said, but it did not have the Spartan regime of other cram schools. "We emphasize adequate growth for each pupil. The education we give is through play."

Mock tests began in the mid-1960s, when private testing companies started to apply computer analysis to the tests they produced for schools. Mock tests were intended as practice for the real thing—the entrance exams. But with computers the mock tests were used to give each school a "deviation value" each year: The tests were graded once on a right-and-wrong basis, and again to locate each student's place in the school's average. The student's rating was then used to determine which school he could enter, in advance of the actual entrance exams.

Mock tests rank among the most powerful of the school system's addictions. The deviation measure is a kind of condemnation—of schools and students alike. It is frequently used to send students to schools they do not want to attend. Most educators believe this is one main reason 120,000 high school students drop out every year. Shingakai used the mock tests to determine where its five-year-old graduates could go to kindergarten.

Matsuzawa and I were joined by Shingakai's president, a more professorial fellow named Kigen Fujimoto. Fujimoto began his career at the other end of the system, training university graduates as they became "social beings" and actually learned things—simple, practical things. Fujimoto worked with graduates in training to represent their companies, and he was shocked by what he found among his charges.

"They were almost incapable even of a task as simple as a professional telephone call," he recalled. "I had to ask, 'What are we doing with our children?' One day I heard a lecture by Ohori-sensei, our founder. 'I feel that parents concern themselves too much with their kids. They interfere too much. Children should be left free. The job of a child is playing. It can't be right to manage the play of children. It isn't the accumulation of knowledge that is important but the accumulation of experience.' That was the basic content of the lecture. I was greatly moved."

I was moved, too. But when I asked Fujimoto why parents sent their children to Shingakai, he sighed wearily. "To put the conclusion first, because they want their children to enter the kindergarten or elementary school of their choice. So this is basically preparation for entrance exams."

Like white-coated clinicians, we filed into a room to watch a class in progress. On a gym mat, four teachers and ten toddlers engaged in "free play," as Fujimoto put it. There were blocks, balls, flags, plastic kitchen implements. A couple of education mothers stood nearby. Fujimoto said, "The important things are whether a child can work within a group and whether the child has enough confidence to work independently of the mother."

Fujimoto paused as the children lined up for a game. "What we do is make as many good memories as possible for the kids, and educate the parents. If they don't understand what education is, the child suffers."

Fujimoto was another idealist, another of the men and women who fill the school system and who understand what education ought to be. Parents understand, too—unfailingly. But understanding does not matter. Not all the free play their first *sensei* allows will keep the children on the gym mat—from affluent, ambitious families, the most privileged in Japan—from suffering.

I watched the children match red and blue balls with red and blue flags. They were well dressed, well behaved, and played by the rules. They were close enough to touch but seemed to exist at a great distance. At that moment they were more like experiments than children, the room not a room but some sort of scientific incubator.

It would have been easy to think of the children as the victims of those who stood around them—the teachers, the administrators, the education mothers—except that they were all victims. Teachers like to think their classes are a refuge from the system; parents, that they have chosen wisely for their children. But it is almost never like that in the Japanese system. Schools are merely rungs on a ladder. Shingakai was the first.

I visited a high school on a crisp, clear Tokyo morning. It was late February, end of term in Japan. I sat with four graduating seniors in a classroom that would never again be theirs. They had all been to cram school for many years. One had attended a cram school to get into a better cram school. She told me about her routine. "I would leave the house at eight, finish school at three, then go home. From six to nine I was at cram school. I got home again at ten, and worked until one in the morning." She wanted to go to a special high school, with a much higher deviation value than the one where we sat, but she had failed the entrance exam. "For a long time after I entered this school, I wanted to quit."

Her name was Ai Ogawara. After a time Ai and her friends began to argue among themselves. They reminded me that Japan has something in common with a Swiss watch, or one of those toy machines through which a ball tumbles, lifting a lever that activates an armature that sets off a rotary conveyor, and so on. Because Japan is so intricately made, to alter one part of the system means that you must alter them all. Otherwise, the machine will no longer function. Its gears and spindles and all the rest will no longer match.

"I don't like the system," Ai said. "It's just tests. Tests are one day. After that, you don't study at all."

"People think entering university is a form of torture necessary to be free," someone else said. "That's why I think the system is wrong. I don't want to waste my time."

"The system isn't wrong," the only boy of the group protested. "It's natural for people to want to get into good universities to get a good salary."

"Why say the education system is wrong?" Ai asked. "What's wrong is the social system."

"So we should change the social system," the boy said.

"But if we want to change the social system," Ai replied, "first we have to change the government."

IN 1960, JUST as Japan erupted into the anti-AMPO protests and Tokyo declared its high-growth economic policy, the Education Ministry gathered a committee of scholars and bureaucrats to consider the future of education. The report it produced (after five years of labor) had a somewhat sinister title, *The Image of the Desired Japanese*. It was written as an advisory to high school teachers and announced itself, in its preface, as "a map of virtues." In length *The Image of the Desired Japanese* was not much more than an essay, but it was an extraordinary document nonetheless— among the most revealing of the postwar period. It is a classic case of what the occupation's reverse course meant to ordinary Japanese. And it is a perfect example of why, as Ai Ogawara put it, improving Japanese education finally means improving the Japanese government.

The Japanese must be taught never to forget that they are Japanese before they are "world persons," the report began. They must respect the emperor and devote themselves to work, because "society exists for production." In the bargain they must recognize their reliance upon "the state, the society, and the household."

> Individual happiness and security greatly depend on the state.
> The way to contribute to humanity is usually opened through
> the state. To love the state truly is loyalty to the state. . . .

In theme and sentiment *Desired Japanese* was a return to the prewar era, a nostalgia piece. There is an implicit regret over the loss of nationalist spirit after the defeat. The nation must revive that "delicate affection" and "firm will" of which "the beautiful Japanese tradition" is made. "If we can make this delicate affection deeper and wider, we can be the tough, beautiful, magnanimous Japanese."

This sort of language was standard fare before 1945. Until the surrender, schools were (along with the military) the central channel for the diffusion of state ideology. The Education Ministry, packed with ultra-nationalists, was among Tokyo's shrillest bureaucracies. Teachers and other advocates of educational freedom had been trying to crawl out from under the ministry's control since the 1920s. Instead, instruction was reduced to nothing more than brainwashing.

In other circumstances—or if Japan had had a different modern history—it would be shocking to read invocations of "the beautiful Japanese tradition" that date to the mid-1960s. Shocking, not least, because the men who wrote *Desired Japanese* were managers of the system we are now encouraged to admire. But education turned out to be a tragic casualty of the reverse course. So *Desired Japanese* is not really much of a surprise at all. G.H.Q. was not even closed before the prewar nationalists reassumed control of the system, clawing back almost all of what they had lost to the early changes.

The occupation's reforms in education were sweeping and swift. Authority devolved to communities and schools. The Education Ministry, though far from cleaned out, was stripped of all but arm's-length oversight powers; even its right to certify textbooks was limited. The prewar system, which streamed roughly 15 percent of students beyond primary grades, was replaced with a single stream called "6-3-3-4," which opened the system from primary school through university to everyone. Education became not a parent's obligation to the state but a child's right. So declared the Fundamental Law on Education, written to replace the imperial rescript. The Fundamental Law was instantly sacrosanct among the Japanese. The Japan Teachers Union, which sprang up immediately after the surrender and became Japan's largest union, was a powerful voice in support of it.

But the reforms were doomed from the start. The Fundamental Law was passed in 1947, just as things began to change at G.H.Q. And the occupation appointed the Education Ministry to implement it. The prewar elite took to calling the early educational reforms "excesses of democratization," a common phrase as the 1940s turned into the 1950s. In 1951 the education minister, a survivor from the dictatorship named Teiyu Amano, drafted "An Outline for National Moral Practice" and remarked in it:

> Nowadays, as a result of too much emphasis on the "individual"
> and the "world at large," there has arisen a marked tendency to

weaken the ground of the state's existence. . . . The state is the womb of our existence, the ethical and cultural core of our collective lives and activities. Therefore, the very life of the nation depends on those activities which the individual willingly performs so as to contribute to the well-being of the state.

Amano's tract was tossed out of the Diet and popularly denigrated as "Amano's imperial rescript." But it set the tone well. The reverse course in education was completed in only a few years. The Japan Teachers Union was disemboweled. Legislation passed in 1954 declared the ministry the defender of educational freedom—so handing the nightstick to the convicted felon. When the ministry tried to reassert its authority over textbooks, riots nearly erupted in the Diet. But the ministry did regain control over local administration; most significant, it abolished school boards chosen by election and assumed the power to appoint them. Skipping the legislative process, the ministry revised curriculum guidelines and then made them legally binding, turning teachers who deviated into criminals.

This was enough to neutralize the Fundamental Law. The ministry's power was soon sufficient to control areas, such as textbooks, where it had failed legislatively. It was a neat trick, familiar enough in Japan: Maintain the *omote,* the front, while discarding the *ura* within. The Fundamental Law remained in place—as it still does, a shining badge of democratic education. But everything behind it had been altered.

The Image of the Desired Japanese was a declaration of victory in this postwar war: victory over the Fundamental Law, victory over liberal education. It was never submitted to the Diet: Its authors feared the reaction it would have provoked. But legislative approval was beside the point. *Desired Japanese* became the "guiding ideal," in its chief author's words, of the postwar school system. It called for nothing more or less than a reassertion of the *nihonjin,* the Japanese person, in his official version.

The oblique title raises an essential question. The desired Japanese: Desired by whom? To answer this is to understand much about the postwar system. *Desired Japanese* was not the work of brooding bureaucrats still nursing the sting of defeat—not entirely, anyway. Among its enthusiasts was Keidanren, the Federation of Economic Organizations, Japan's most powerful industrial group. *Desired Japanese* was intended chiefly to produce the kind of human being Japan required as it embarked upon its high-growth course. As Arinori Mori would have put it, it was intended to turn teachers back into manufacturers.

"WHILE THERE IS no one who cannot read or write due to nine years of compulsory education, the system is preventing the growth of free, individual personalities."

This appraisal of Japanese schools is notable only for who delivered it: Kunio Hatoyama, a career bureaucrat serving, in the summer of 1992, as education minister. Why, after more than a century of education wars, would the general in command of the castle take the position of the insurgents?

Education was a heated issue by the time Hatoyama spoke. No one (except foreigners, perhaps) could any longer pretend that discontent within the system—among teachers, students, and parents—was anything less than universal. Here are a few headlines from the first half of the 1990s:

STRESS PERSON, NOT TEST, EDUCATION MINISTER SAYS

INDIVIDUALIZING EDUCATION

ALL YOUNG JAPANESE ARE NOT THE SAME

MOCK EXAMS MOCK SYSTEM

TOO MUCH CENTRAL CONTROL

FOR LESS CONFORMITY IN EDUCATION

All but the first of these phrases introduced editorials in national newspapers. To read them in the organs that shape officially approved views would have been unthinkable for most of the postwar era. Yet the headlines alone reveal the key notions at stake in the eternal battles over education: diversity, liberalization, individuation, choice, creativity, initiative.

These were supposedly the new values of the education ministry. When Hatoyama spoke, and when the commentaries were written, Tokyo said it was preparing to make Japanese schools what people wanted them to be. Such a thing was to be no minor adjustment. Ministry bureaucrats called it "the third educational reform." The preceding two were those of the Meiji era and the postwar years.

But it is important to understand what officials mean, for it would be a mistake to accept their remarks at face value. It is more accurate to view the third education reform as another effort to shape a "desired Japanese." The only difference between the desired Japanese of the 1960s and the 1990s version lay in the kind of Japanese considered desirable.

Japan began to think differently of its future after the first abrupt rise in oil prices, in 1973. The high growth achieved over the previous two decades was unlikely to be repeated. The leading intellects in the business community, men such as Konosuke Matsushita, founder of the electronics giant that bears his name, envisioned a Japan less reliant upon the protective barriers to competition, erected from Meiji onward and tolerated by Washington during the years of reconstruction and Cold War tension. This elaborate complex would eventually have to come down. Japan would have to become genuinely competitive. In the 1980s a pair of neat phrases gained currency: Industry had been oriented toward *ju ko cho dai*, heavy, thick, long, and big. In the future it would be *kei haku tan sho*, light, thin, short, and small. Japan could no longer mass-produce or copy and modify products conceived and designed elsewhere. It would have to develop its own advanced technologies, and it would have to be quicker on its feet in the information and services industries.

Yasuhiro Nakasone, who became premier in 1982, well understood these imperatives. The economic preeminence he wanted for Japan meant more influence and responsibility in the world community. There would be more Japanese living and working abroad, and more gaijin in Japan. Above all, Japan needed a new kind of person in the era of high technology. A mass production economy required a few generals at the top and a vast army of foot soldiers to serve loyally in the war for raw economic power, simple girth. Preeminence would be another matter. Blue chip Japan would need imaginative graduates with a capacity for original thinking. It would need, in short, a new class of commissioned officers.

In 1984 Nakasone named an "extraordinary council on education." In its first report to the premier it wrote of "a state of desolation" in Japanese schools. Violence, truancy, exam anxiety, the mushrooming growth of *juku*—all were recognized as symptoms of a vast malfunction. What was Nakasone's answer? More moral education and more teacher training. Classes were to honor the *hinomaru* flag, the rising sun, and sing the *Kimigayo* anthem, although neither is constitutionally recognized. Textbook screening, the source of much dispute, would be "streamlined":

A book was either accepted or rejected, and the author had no recourse (and would not know the reasons behind the judgment anyway).

And here we come to one of the great contradictions of Japan in the late twentieth century. The school system would have to produce individuals, but not people who lost sight of their duties to the state, the beautiful traditions, the official idea of Japaneseness, and so on. But how can the nation social-engineer free-thinking, experimentally inclined individuals in the same way that it has turned out loyal samurai, soldiers and sailors, *sararimen,* and factory workers in the past? Nakasone displayed his own version of this contradiction: He was a dedicated privatizer in the fashion of the times, but he favored rigorous state control over schools.

Nakasone left office in 1987. Afterward one heard many answers to this conundrum: more diversity and choice; less emphasis on exams and more on a human environment. Overregulation, uniformity, and rote instruction would have to go. In a less competitive system time must be made for personality formation: sports, leisure activities. Local school boards must be revived. The reforms must be bottom-up, not top-down. Little of this has actually happened, though the third-reform idea is now in its third decade. None of it answers the central question anyway. The people who supplied these responses, senior bureaucrats at the education ministry, began to remind me of Arinori Mori and his muddled thinking. Their answers were merely the opening lines in a drama that will end in the next century. By its own admission, the ministry was feeling its way, trying one thing, then another—much as the first modern educators did.

An hour and a half by train west of Tokyo there is a new university, called Tsukuba. Tsukuba was intended to be a sort of Japanese M.I.T.—strong on original research and the sciences, home of high-technology breakthroughs, the sort of institution Japan needed to enter its next economic phase. Yet it has failed to earn the comparison, chiefly because of the caliber of students the system sends to Tsukuba's classrooms and laboratories. Tsukuba has no intellectual charge, no electricity—an absence as palpable when one strolls the campus as its ungiving architecture.

Tsukuba's president was named Leo Esaki. Esaki was a Nobel laureate in physics and a former research star at IBM. He had lived in America for twenty-five years. He peppered his writings with mentions of Socrates, Aquinas, Rousseau, John Dewey. In his energetic conversations, "independence" and "individuality" were his bywords. He was pleased with Japanese students, Esaki insisted when I went to see him. "But we want to produce peaks in the graph. In America you find people working at cash registers who can't even add. Yet America has more than a hundred and fifty Nobel laureates in science. Here the average person is very capable by comparison. But we have five science Nobels. That's thirty to one."

Esaki paused for a moment. I asked him what would happen to Japan if schools began to graduate classes of individuals. How would such people fit into the machine—the corporations, the bureaucracy, even the universities?

"Right now, about forty percent of high school students enter university. I don't think we can educate all of those people to be individual intellectuals. We're talking about a select group. You choose the most talented people. Selection is inevitable."

Esaki paused again. I asked if he were talking about creating a new elite, and he seemed pleased that I had used the word.

"That's basically it—an elite of about ten percent. Every society has an elite. There are leaders and followers. The Japanese system is already equipped to produce followers."

"But elites are not something you can plan," I suggested. "If you set out to create a new elite, can its members be very different from one another? They will all take the side of the power that selected them. What makes an elite acceptable is its diversity."

None of this seemed to matter to Esaki. He was known as the leading spokesman for the third reform in education. He offered me a glimpse of the schools of the future—or at least the future schools as those who ran them saw it. Yet he did not describe the future at all, but the past. In perfectly contemporary terms he spoke not of a new system, or even a reformed system, but the old imperial system, in which education and learning were two separate things and where there was no question of anything being bottom-up. In Esaki's universe, knowledge would again be power.

"It's relatively simple in the field of science," Esaki persisted. "We need a better way to select people. Then there's mass education. But I'm more interested in elite education—you know, scholarship."

IT IS IMPOSSIBLE to share the enthusiasms of Leo Esaki, or the gaijin admirers of Japanese schools, when reform means sustaining discriminatory and coercive practices invented by a nineteenth-century oligarchy, perfected by a dictatorship, and then, five decades ago, at least briefly outlawed.

But education is unlikely to arrive in Leo Esaki's idea of the future. It is no longer possible to control knowledge, for one thing. For another, there is too much energy at the bottom. The school system is like a jack-in-the-box, still unsprung. Much of this energy is negative—sullen and deformed. Yet on a journey through the system one also stumbles upon its rare treasures. There behind the facade of uniformity they suggest that, however long it takes, the Japanese will learn that they are individuals before they are Japanese, and that no method will ever be found to change this fact.

An hour from Tokyo by commuter train there is a school called Jiyu no Mori, the Freedom Forest School, so named for the dense pines surrounding it. I went there one late-winter afternoon, just as classes ended. It would be difficult to exaggerate the strangeness of the scene. When I opened the front door against the wind I was greeted by a cacophony of shouts, musical instruments, running footsteps, clanging lockers, slamming doors, and voices—singing voices, laughing voices, voices in many different conversations. As I talked with the principal, a flautist practiced solos in the next room. Yutaka Endoh, a thin, overworked man in a modest suit, seemed not to notice any of it.

"Our aim is to raise young people to be human beings, not just Japanese," Endoh began. "We're developing thought and intellect, emotional lives, and the will by which one directs the mind and body toward an ideal—a goal, a target. A student should have discovered himself by the time he graduates, and have an independent will to be free."

Endoh stopped to gauge my response before adding, "All this is natural if education regards humanity as important. But these are unusual goals in the Japanese social context."

Outside Endoh's window, something between rain and snow had begun to fall on the thick pine forest. It suggested a kind of tough winter idyll. An hour away were Tokyo and the examination halls through which Jiyu no Mori's students would have to pass if they were to continue on to university. For a moment it seemed an act of cruelty to prepare people for a world they would not find, and I explained this thought to Endoh.

"Let me give you a few figures," he replied. "We graduate two hundred and forty students from high school each year. Fifty or sixty go straight to university, twenty or thirty to junior colleges. Seventy take a year to prepare for entrance exams, and another seventy go to technical schools. Twenty find jobs right away."

"But how do they compete?"

"If you have a root you can grow branches. If you give students fundamental knowledge, they should have no difficulty preparing for exams—and with less effort than otherwise."

Endoh was in his sixties—of the generation too young to have gone to war but old enough to remember it. There are many Japanese his age like him: People who made the rest of their lives a kind of atonement for their failure to act against the dictatorship, the war, and the "black box" of ideology. After the defeat Endoh taught for twenty years in a progressive private school in Tokyo until he decided that, despite its intentions, the school (like so many others) could not resist turning students into devices made only to take exams.

Endoh started Jiyu no Mori in the early 1980s after raising 4 billion yen, about $40 million. Half of that was still debt, but it brought the school across the great barrier to alternative education: Without 4 billion yen of their own, private schools do not qualify for government subsidies. Now Jiyu no Mori had twelve hundred students, from junior high school through twelfth grade. "We're trying to give students wisdom," Endoh said after explaining the numbers, "the thing needed to assess the state of society and then to influence it."

Endoh's deputy, many years his junior, appeared at the door: It was late, and he wanted me to see the tenth-grade choir practicing for a recital to be held at the local town hall in two days' time.

The walk from Endoh's office to the gymnasium door, where the choir was assembled, was a passage through controlled chaos. A student greeted us by throwing a basketball into the deputy's arms. Another assailed him with a martial arts kick that came within inches of his face. Endoh's deputy smiled and tried not to lose the thread of our conversation. At the gym door he said good-bye and disappeared into a flock of students.

I began to wonder whether Jiyu no Mori was a kind of pointless overstatement—a purposeful anarchy created in reaction to the rigidities of the system, but nothing that would bear upon the future.

In the gymnasium the choir was between pieces and debating which to do next. The walls were smudged. Piles of loose books lay along the sides of the room. Bright colors were everywhere; no one wore a uniform.

Then, suddenly, they began to sing, a choir of about fifty behind an orchestra of maybe half that number. Without warning they swelled into parts of Mozart's *Requiem* and Vivaldi's *Gloria*. Then the *Agnus Dei*. I had to turn my face away. All the disorder had vanished. An extraordinary unison took its place, filling the room until the windows seemed about to burst against the rain and snow outside.

I waited to meet these students, the most exultant Japanese I have ever known.

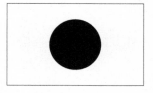

4

FENCES IN THE HEART

... one feels as though one's soul has found for itself a strange home.

— SOSEKI NATSUME
Kokoro, 1914

IN MY LAST year in Tokyo I moved from a gaijin flat to a central but unrestored quarter of the city. The local *fudo-san,* the rental agent, was called Shiino and shared the business with his father. The Shiino's operated from a room crammed with desks, chairs, filing cabinets, fax machines, telephones, portable heaters, and a tiny coffee table covered with a plastic doily, over which business was done. The room measured six tatami, a standard size, about the dimensions of a large Western bathroom. The front window was plastered with scribbled sheets advertising available apartments.

There was one for eighty-five thousand yen, about $700 at the time, on a lane in Minami Aoyama. It would be primitive, but it was less than I was prepared to spend, and I had a friend nearby.

"No," said Shiino the younger, a reedy, uncertain fellow in his forties. "You wouldn't like that one. What about—"

"But I like the sound of this place," I said.

"It's really quite dirty," Shiino replied. He frowned, shook his head, and drew on a cigarette.

"That can be fixed. Why don't we have a look anyway?"

"Sumisu-san, it's just not your kind of place. Very dark. Full of smells. It's not for you."

I was about to persist when Shiino the elder grew impatient. He was small and easygoing. In his seventies, he was of the generation that had fought the war. He wore an old suit of the same blanched gray as his stubbly crew cut. He lived in a tiny place upstairs; with a broom of bound twigs, he swept the street in front of the office just after dawn every morning.

"It's not for gaijin," the old man barked, half to me, half to his son. "The owner lives next door. He would never have a gaijin in that apartment." Then the old man smiled.

I finally found a drafty, weathered house—"They've had gaijin gentlemen before," the younger Shiino assured me on the way over—within the much-reduced estate of an old Tokyo family named Yamada. It was in a quiet cul-de-sac of a dozen dwellings. Hard by one another, these were miracles of folk engineering. I had no view of my neighbors, and they none of me, so long as we kept our paper screens and wooden doors closed. Open any one, and everything that had been private the previous minute was public.

An ugly canopy of corrugated plastic blocked sunlight into the kitchen, the only room that faced the street. It was like an old reed screen, hiding me from others and limiting my view to a few television antennae and a sliver of sky. One day I asked Mrs. Yamada if I could remove it.

"That's impossible," she replied without her usual grace.

I told her I did not mind the neighbors seeing through the window. "It's only the kitchen, after all."

"It's not the neighbors seeing in," she said. "It's you seeing out. It would upset all the other households."

My neighbors were the middle-class families of *sararimen*. Their curiosity subsided only after I went around at dusk one Saturday to introduce myself to each. (I was advised that I could skip the customary bowl of hot noodles newcomers are expected to offer.) I remained a novelty. But I was gradually accepted as part of the Yamada *ie*, and through the Yamadas as part of the village known by the address all the houses shared, Nishi-Azabu 2-chome.

It was a narrow lane where idiosyncrasies were tolerated, but only after the required process of establishing them. Someone played the harmonica in the evenings. Another house had a superb collection of jazz recordings. Someone returned from work on a bicycle with a loose fender and screeching brakes at precisely one-thirty each morning. A neighbor's dog barked all day Sunday (and for some reason only Sunday). All of this was fine. But I was not to hang laundry from my upstairs balcony: It dripped onto a neighbor's tin roof. And that, because it had never happened before, was a transgression.

In the autumn a man drove by before dusk in a tiny open truck with, improbably enough, an open fire in the back. Over it sweet potatoes roasted in the traditional way, amid hot rocks of luminous gray. Through a crackling microphone the man droned the old poetry of the village:

> Baked sweet potatoes,
> Baked on heated stones,
> Just baked, sweet and tasty,
> Can't I tempt you?
> Baked sweet potatoes . . .

Two blocks away were the boutiques of Moschino and Jean-Charles de Castelbajac, and beyond them a postmodern wonder done in raw concrete by the architect Tadao Ando. Just up the street was an elegant restaurant called Kihachi, run by a refined man partial to double-breasted suits and Issey Miyake shirts—a modern-day "high collar," in Meiji era parlance. He had gone to France and returned to combine his acquired knowledge with local custom in the kitchen.

At the Meiji Restoration Japan was a country of roughly 30 million people. Eighty percent of them were peasants eager to become the first people known as "Japanese." Edo's population at the moment it became Tokyo was less than a million. Then it began to grow: to more than 2 million at the end of the Meiji period, to almost 4 million by 1920, year of the first modern census. In August of 1945, half of the city's 7 million inhabitants were either dead or dispersed in the countryside. Then Tokyo began to grow once more: It reached 7 million again by 1952, and 10 million a decade later. In the 1960s an average of more than a hundred families a day left the old villages for Tokyo and the other cities along the Pacific coast. Today Tokyo is the world's largest metropolitan area; 40 million people live and work within twenty miles of the center.

Modernization made Tokyo a city of dislocated souls. With the restoration in 1868, the new "Eastern Capital" became the powerful center Japan never previously had, a magnet whose field was all of the islands. Even the emperor was an immigrant. In Tokyo, samurai formality combined with the novelty of Western things to create something odd for the common Japanese: distance, unfamiliarity, urban anxiety. And at bottom the detachment of the new city dwellers was a detachment from themselves, for they had turned themselves into "others."

From the plain surrounding Tokyo, called Kanto, southwestward to another plain surrounding Osaka and Kyoto, called Kansai, is a slim corridor known as *omote nihon,* the front of Japan. And after a century and a quarter of furious modernization, it is still what we mean when we talk about Japan and the Japanese. It is the showplace of the postwar "miracle." Two-thirds of the Japanese population live in this space, which accounts for 14 percent of the islands. Three-quarters of the nation's industrial output comes from there, which makes the strip of land at the front edge of the country roughly half again the size of Germany in economic terms. It is home to almost all the nation's banks, insurance houses, financial markets, corporate headquarters, publishers, universities, media, and manufacturing plants. Those few large enterprises with head offices elsewhere (Matsuda, which makes Mazda cars; Komatsu, the builder of construction equipment) keep considerable presences in Tokyo to be near the bureaucratic center of power.

There are other cities like Tokyo. A great many Parisians arrive in Paris from distant departments only to make their names or fortunes before returning to towns they never really left behind, or to their *maisons secondaires* someplace else. Paris, like Tokyo, is an overgrown village. But the comparison stops there. The French never became strangers to themselves when they went to Paris. Many generations of Japanese who went to Tokyo did.

The modern era gave the Japanese capital, like other cities along the Pacific coast, two distinct faces, or—better put—a revealed face and hidden interior. Tokyo became a city full of references to other places: to the West (French restaurants, dance halls, Victorian brick facades) and to the village (rustic wooden houses, backyard rice paddies). One went to Tokyo to participate in the new Japan—to work for a large, new enterprise. Cutting his topknot and donning a frock coat, the new urban dweller became a "high collar." But he also retreated from the modern city, the Tokyo meant to be seen, to the Tokyo within. Today Tokyo is a city of noisy restaurants and skyscrapers full of bars, broad thoroughfares, office buildings, ministries, and stylish shops. But a few steps from any major intersection the avenues still give way to a warren of barely passable lanes, where in the evenings men walk about in pyjamas and slippers. A friend who lived a block from Roppongi crossing, among the world's busiest and most neoned junctions, used to awaken every morning to the crowing of several roosters.

"'Even in the town you will find the countryside,'" noted Kurt Singer in *Mirror, Sword and Jewel: The Geometry of Japanese Life.* Singer's brief book, written in 1946, remains among the most insightful a gaijin has ever written on Japan, and one can easily see what he meant. But the old Japanese saying he quoted to describe the city is no longer as true as it must have been then. Today Tokyoites are no longer strangers to themselves, no longer at odds with what they used to be. The past of most Tokyoites is now in Tokyo: a simple demographic fact. And so the city no longer defines itself by either the Japanese past or the West it used to imitate. Tokyo is becoming simply Tokyo—neither a display case nor a city nostalgic for the village. And in the same way the modern Japanese are beginning to accept that they are the Japanese as they really are—crowded together in apartment buildings and offices, rather different from one another after all, with none of the sameness of villagers and no mud on their shoes.

In the 1980s a writer named Hikari Agata published a story titled "A Family Party." It is about a mother and her children whose neighborhood has been redeveloped. An eighteen-story hotel stands on the family plot. Urban rootlessness beckons. "This neighborhood had always given the impression of being disorderly," the narrator says,

> and yet, I was always relieved whenever I returned to it from the jungle of high-rise buildings. It had been a neighborhood where browns and grays melted nicely together, and the natural colors were gentle on my skin.

Tokyoites will sometimes still reveal this lingering attachment to their *ura-dori,* their backstreets. The uncomfortable old houses, the more weatherworn the better, have given refuge as much as physical shelter. At the same time, the wrecking ball provides one of the great urban dramas of the modern era. It is common to see entire neighborhoods transformed within weeks. In place of village houses come houses in a thousand contemporary styles. In place of wood in tones of brown and gray come raw concrete and charcoal-shaded granite, the postmodern materials much favored by Japanese architects.

When I lived in Tokyo the change provided some small, tactile sense of the unnerving speed of Japan's modernization. I could go away for a week and return to find a house down the block demolished, gone, and something entirely different already half built in its place. The scene repeated itself again and again—an urban renewal that also extended to the way the Japanese live and work in their cities.

"WE LIVE UNFREE lives, shoulder unnatural burdens, and suffer under an irrational system," a Tokyo shipyard worker wrote in a union magazine in 1922. "Where is our value as humans? Racing to the factory on icy mornings, rushing home under the stars, we have no chance to enjoy life. We live an inhuman existence."

It is remarkable how early and often the theme of humanity denied appears in the accounts of the modern Japanese. Unnatural burdens, an irrational system: It is as if Japan's first modern generations understood immediately that something strangely irregular, even aberrant, lay at the core of their transformation into "the Japanese." The primal experience of the modern, shared by millions of migrants to the cities, was one of departure. Had they somehow lost themselves and their humanity when they left the village behind to become the samurai of the future?

In *Kokoro,* his 1914 novel, Soseki Natsume gives us a poignant picture of the early, aspiring *sarariman* through a character he calls simply K. K has left his village for Tokyo, where he throws himself into his pursuit of "the true way," though he knows not what the true way is. He cultivates an unbending will. Seeking "concentration of mind," he drives himself to the brink of exhaustion. He devotes himself to "modern concepts" yet is equally given to honoring heroic figures of the past, self-flagellating samurai who disdained all comforts and embraced all hardships for the sake of the *do,* the way, of virtue and masculine reverence.

Soseki was prophetic, for we recognize this man: In our own time he would aspire to a standard blue suit and a standard white shirt and a middling position at Toyota or Toshiba—section manager, assistant department manager, or some other precisely defined rank. Because the line between the public and private is drawn in so peculiar a place, we see in him also the odd intersection of economics and psychology that is unique, perhaps, to modern Japan. Soseki's character sacrifices everything to make himself a firm, resolute Japanese according to a tradition he finds elusive even as it consumes him. But in his endeavor he becomes, in the narrator's word, inhuman. "Set up fences in your hearts against wandering or extravagant thoughts," a samurai house law advised many centuries ago. That is to say, fences against ordinary thoughts. So we recognize this about the modern Japanese warrior, too. There is something inhuman in the ideal to which he is supposed to dedicate himself.

I once went to an office building in Tokyo to meet a man named Terutaka Kawabata, who was descended from a family of samurai. Kawabata was thin and graying, a business executive somewhere in his late fifties, but he had a kinetic vitality that made him seem much younger. Kawabata was dressed in the pyjamalike trousers and abbreviated kimono of the warrior. We were in a large basement room with a wooden floor, like a ballet studio. There we watched his Wednesday evening class in *yaido*, an early form of kendo, "way of the sword."

As we talked and drank green tea, a half dozen middle-aged men dressed in identical costumes practiced the fixed movements of which *yaido* is made. Each one traced meticulous replications of the old choreography. It was as if they called upon memories embedded in their arms and legs. Each face— lips tightened, eyes half-closed—was a blank. But for the crack of swords together, or the occasional thump of a bare foot on the wooden floor, the room was dead silent. "The object is to move in a perfect and beautiful way," Kawabata whispered. "You must learn it. You can't innovate."

Kawabata was not a hobbyist. His lessons were meant for life outside the windowless room where we sat. "I use the same tactics in business and with friends as I use in *yaido*. I'm always ready to react. The Japanese like to protect themselves from changes in life. But it's important to learn the techniques." He continued in this vein until his students finished. They were from companies whose names I recognized easily. It was odd to see chemical salesmen, shipping executives, and securities traders paired off to duel with wooden swords. But here was Soseki's K, eighty years on and gainfully employed, the corporate warrior who was supposed to approach his paperwork or his sales quota with precisely the determination of the samurai who once roamed Japan with the purest of motives, the clearest of minds, and concentration willed from within.

Except that Kawabata's students did not possess these qualities. There was about them a certain timidity, an absence of clarity and purpose all the more evident for finding itself in the same room with Kawabata's vitality and focus. In a word, Kawabata's charges were altogether ordinary. And what did these men really want to learn from their *yaido* master? Ancient gestures across the air, or how to be alive, to feel passion for the task—to be good Japanese according to rules that required them, like K and like Kawabata, to squeeze the ordinariness out of themselves?

At the foot of Mount Fuji there is a place called the Management Training Institute. It looks like a boot camp—more or less what it is. There are drill fields, flagpoles, a few radio towers, and two long, low barracks that form an *L*. The Management Training Institute is for fallen warriors, whose companies are unhappy with their marketing results, or their production schedules, or simply their attitudes. They are up at six and quit at nine-thirty in the evening. There are night marches of twenty-five miles, and shorter, faster ones of fifteen or so. Trainees call the institute "hell camp" and their tours there "walking the floor of hell."

Yasuo Motohashi, the president, was a deliberate man with silver hair. He was interesting in his views of *sararimen.* "In a single word, the training is to make people discover their spirit—the spirit to work hard. It is difficult for the *sarariman* to do things with sincerity and passion. We go quite deep into our trainees. And this is the larger point: We find that people are not in touch with themselves. They act only because they are obliged to act. We want our trainees to realize how dull their lives have been, how empty of true feeling."

Living in Japan, one sees *sararimen* every day in Tokyo, Osaka, Kobe, and other industrial cities along the Pacific coast. And you find everywhere the same struggle to cross the yawning chasm between the ideal and the real—the same detachment from the great national task of economic production, the same groping for some source of motivation. Isn't such detachment endemic in the industrial world? It is, but only in Japan, where the public and private have been so closely woven, has the idea persisted that the properly conditioned psyche is essential not only to national economic success but to existence in "the front of Japan." One is still supposed to strive out of the same inner conviction that drove the samurai. But there are few *sararimen* with the zest and passion of a swordsman such as Terutaka Kawabata. So the absence of proper motivation comes to be looked upon as a national pathology.

One despairs of explaining this to foreigners who take the *sarariman* ideal to be the authentic thing. The unstoppable corporate warrior is a central ornament in our imaginary "Japan." It is a pernicious image in that it makes the Japanese, to use Soseki's word, inhuman—and therefore fearsome. The reality is rather different, as the shipyard worker understood, and as ordinary productivity comparisons between Japanese and, say, American workers invariably reveal. There is nothing heroic in the *sarariman*'s unending slog. When the psychiatrist Masao Miyamoto remarked upon the inefficiency he found in the Health Ministry, the director general replied with an excellent description of the system as it really is: "It is the accumulation of inefficiency that leads to efficiency."

The government publishes a remarkable book purporting to explain the corporate warrior to foreigners—remarkable because it is utterly devoid of the standard mystique. It suggests that there is indeed something inhuman about the *sarariman,* though this has nothing to do with omnipotence born of will. The cover of *"Salaryman" in Japan* pictures a middle-aged man with sundry things floating around him: a newspaper, a computer, a barking boss, a *bento* lunch box, a subway strap. These are the components of the man at the center, it suggests, as if he were a manufactured assemblage. *"Salaryman" in Japan* explains each tiny aspect of the *sarariman*'s life. Young *sararimen* carry this type of briefcase; the middle ranks, this type; and those over fifty, this type. Middle-ranking *sararimen* must cope with unreasonable superiors, selfish subordinates, large mortgages, and cheating wives. Here are the *sarariman*'s six variations on the smile; here is the order by which *sararimen* of various ranks assemble themselves when riding in a car. These points are advanced as if they were laws, which, in a way, they are. The certainty of the text—this is how the Japanese are, and there are no deviations—is an essential subtext, testimony to the stringent conformity to which the *sarariman* submits.

The average *sarariman* approaching retirement becomes a "window sitter"—someone rendered useless, whose desk is given to a younger manager and who daydreams away the final years of his working life. In retirement he will be known by another cruel nickname: "industrial waste." The little book describes its *sararimen* at this stage with exceptional candor:

Salarymen in their 50s turn to *haiku, bonsai,* or other traditional arts. Many have begun to sense their own human limi-
tations and use these pursuits to fill the emptiness they feel
with regard to everyday life.

My first encounter with a *sarariman* outside of an office occurred late on
a rainy evening when I almost ran over one. Through a spring downpour,
I spotted a blue-suited body lying in the street not far from one of the train
stations serving suburban commuters. I stopped to look down upon him:
He was of early middle age, his face prematurely lined. He was drunk and
drenched, but alive. When he opened his eyes to discover a gaijin peering
down at him, he sucked in his breath and tried to compose himself, as if
we were engaged in a routine business encounter.

One cannot draw too many conclusions from such an incident.
Drunken *sararimen* chasing late trains are an ordinary sight in Japanese
cities. But that is precisely the point. We must consider closely the truism
that after-hours drinking with clients and colleagues is an established part
of the *sarariman* routine—a requirement of the job. For to witness the
habits of the *sarariman* at close range is to recognize the vast gulf between
the image of the *sarariman*—an uplifting study in discipline and dedication—and the often degraded reality.

For a long time the corporate-warrior ideal was a deception not only of
foreigners, we who look in from the outside, but a deception of the Japanese
themselves. There were many generations of aspiring K's. For a century and
a quarter after the oligarchs decided to make Japan a nation of samurai, the
Japanese struggled with the finer points, endeavoring to conform to the
image of the Japanese. Salvaging the corporate warrior was a thriving industry during my years in Japan. The institute at Mount Fuji was reputed to be
the toughest of hell camps, but there were numerous other companies whose
business it was to cultivate the inner selves of *sararimen*. Is it possible to
induce an inner spirit in another—to plant it, or inspire it, or even create it?
Or does the effort itself assume its object to be a commodity—"human
material," as the institute at the foot of Mount Fuji called its trainees?

In Soseki's novel, K never becomes a modern samurai. Try as he will he
is unable to deny his humanity—his emotions, frailties, hesitations, and so
on. In the end he recognizes that his real weakness lies in his impulse to

take refuge from the complexity of ordinary human relationships in the idealized, unattainable past of the unbending warrior. Afraid to face life as an individual, the warrior's code no longer any help, K commits suicide.

Doesn't the *sarariman* industry suggest precisely the same point: that the company samurai is essentially an imaginary image—and a rather destructive one at that? When the oligarchs turned the way of the warrior into social convention it atrophied; as all such ideals do, it became mere form. Today the Japanese call the first decades after the war the "golden age" of the *sarariman*. But this is mere myth. There was never a golden age for Japanese employees—only a brief period of acquiescence. The institute at the base of Mount Fuji was founded in 1967—when the golden age was supposed to have been at its height. It was then, in the late 1960s, that the long deception of the modern Japanese began to reveal itself for what it was.

THE SAMURAI WITH a briefcase is an old figure. In 1616, early in the Tokugawa peace, a warrior near Kyoto took the radical step of putting away his blades. "No more shall we have to live by the sword," he told his household. "Great profits can be made honorably. I shall brew *sake* and soy sauce, and we shall prosper." This may sound like dissonant advertising copy, but Sokubei Mitsui turned out to be a clever man. With those words he founded what is now the world's oldest industrial corporation (which still bears the family name).

After the restoration, when the Meiji oligarchy withdrew their rice stipends and sent samurai into the new society to fend for themselves, the old soldiers rushed into the era's rising new enterprises. They soon staffed the offices of favored firms and became skilled workers at the shipyards, munitions plants, and machinery factories designated (in today's terms) strategic industries. They made little distinction between office workers and those on the shop floor: They were all still warriors together.

The decommissioned samurai were just the kind of employees a nation in a hurry needed. They believed in loyalty and they had some notion of national purpose. And it was natural that they brought the samurai code with them. The early *sararimen* were the first modern Japanese rewarded with ranks and regular wage increases. Companies became their *ie,* their households, so translating into the modern world the sense of belonging they had drawn from being part of a daimyo's army. But there were not enough samurai to go around. Industries were burgeoning. Who would work in them? Commoners had little sense of the old virtues as the samurai understood them—to say nothing of national purpose. So the story of the corporate foot soldier has mostly to do with how Japan remedied this problem by encouraging commoners to take up "the beautiful customs" found in the samurai code.

When the modern system finally took shape, during the 1920s, loyalty did not come naturally from the past. Japanese enterprises bought it—a wise transaction from their point of view. The promise of lifetime employment produced managers and wage earners prepared to devote their lives to prestigious companies. These companies sought not talent but a certain character—moldable clay. It did not matter what one learned at school, apart from elementary skills and some fundamental discipline. An employee was instructed not only in practical talents but also in the corporate equivalent of moral education—company values, the true character of a Sumitomo employee, and so on. Lessons absorbed, the new company men were *shakai-jin,* social beings—that is, recognized members of society.

To commoners in from the countryside—hayseeds who had never worn a suit or sat in a chair—the modern company was something like their household and something like the old village. From their companies flowed their new sense of social place. Neither office managers nor factory hands identified with their skills, or even their careers—only with their companies. And it is when companies are understood as households or villages that corporate dormitories, company-arranged marriages, and all the other practices that blur the public and the private in urban Japan are comprehensible. That is why, even today, any earnest *sarariman* introduces himself by putting the company name, like the family name, first. "I'm from Sankei Steamship. Watanabe." "I'm Nissan's Fujimoto."

Corporate values took the place of the civic values modern Japan never developed. One could not switch companies any more than one could switch households or families, for example. To do so was to display such lack of virtue that it was impossible to be hired by any other large enterprise. One could leave a company only in favor of an existence outside the system; some did, but it was always to enter a less certain way of life, a life beyond the circle of the chosen.

The circle of the chosen was small. In prewar Japan the large enterprises propelling the country forward employed less than a third of the labor force. In its rush to match the West, Japan built a few modern industries—textiles, mining, steel, shipbuilding—and left the rest of the economy more or less to its own devices. Japan became two things at once. It claimed, with justification, to be a rising industrial power; five years into our century it proved the point by defeating the Russians at sea. At the same time, Japan remained an underdeveloped nation. The latter condition remains surprisingly large and well hidden today, though it is right before our eyes. What we consider typical Japanese companies—with company songs and uniforms, robots, and spotless dining halls—account for less than 1 percent of all businesses. The rest, those with less than $1 million in capital and fewer than three hundred employees, ship half of all Japanese manufactures and account for 80 percent of retail sales in Japan.

Behind the names familiar to any consumer—Sony, Toyota, NEC—are their captive subcontractors, where employment is uncertain and conditions unattractive. A company such as Honda controls many thousands of suppliers. This is called the satellite manufacturing system. It was invented during the 1930s to maximize munitions production, and since Japan now exports it, it will be more or less familiar to any British or American employee of a Japanese subsidiary. Beneath the subcontractors are front-parlor factories—households where parts are assembled, stamped, or cut and packed off up the production ladder. Enter one and you find a single piece of equipment squeezed into a tatami-matted living room. Husband, wife, daughter, and neighbors will take regular shifts on the family machine. Living room factories doing piecework number in the hundreds of thousands.

As they did a century ago, most Japanese still work in the small factories down the narrow back lanes of the cities, or at the end of dirt tracks in the countryside. Small enterprises employ as few as one or two workers and as many as three hundred. But there are many thousands of them. They were on the periphery of the modernization project, but they were the backbone of the economy. Today, small subcontractors employ about two-thirds of the manufacturing workforce.

Few Japanese—roughly one of five employees—enjoy the benefits of the genuine corporate warrior. In blue chip Japan, wages and salaries are as much as 45 percent above those paid by smaller companies. But the economy is an immense field of aspiration, as it has been since 1868. Small and medium-sized companies struggle to follow the practices of blue chip corporations as best they can. And the *sarariman,* like the samurai, is idealized and emulated by the great mass of ordinary people, who can only dream of becoming one.

What was the object of this dream? The answer seems obvious. There were the pay and the perquisites, of course, and the security. Still, why would someone wish to emulate those who strive to make themselves "inhuman"? In the beginning, in the years of K, it must have been simply to belong, for the early *sarariman* was the modern Japanese—Western in method, native in spirit. After the war it was more or less the same: The *sarariman* carried the nation forward in its newly defined purpose. So the dream was understandable in these respects, a dream of identity: Who does not want to make good in whatever way society defines it? But can a dream survive as the harsh reality reveals itself? Does one want to make good when making good might mean, quite literally, working oneself to death?

EARLY ONE MORNING in July of 1990, a forty-seven-year-old section chief at Mitsui & Company stepped into the shower in a Nagoya hotel room. Fluent in Russian, Jun Ishii was to lead a tour of Russian clients through a plant that made machine tools.

Ishii never finished his shower. Midway through he collapsed and died of heart failure. He had made ten trips to Russia over the previous year—he had, in fact, just completed one—and he had taken countless groups of Russians around Japan. Mitsui soon paid Ishii's family 30 million yen, about a quarter of a million dollars, in compensation. Two years later, a Tokyo court ordered the government to pay Ishii's widow 2 million yen yearly for the rest of her life. It ruled that Ishii was a victim of *karoshi,* death from overwork.

Jun Ishii's fate was not unusual. The year he died an organization assisting the families of *karoshi* victims estimated that ten thousand employees per year die from the stress of overwork. Other claims had been recognized as legitimate before Ishii's death, but those cases involved manual laborers at small companies. With Jun Ishii, Japan officially admitted for the first time that a corporate warrior could die of dedication.

Karoshi victims often haunt their families. Spouses recall prefiguring signs they failed to read: chronic fatigue, peculiar silences, insomnia, headaches, unfocused eyes. Sometimes those who die leave behind suggestions that they knew what was happening to them but, in typical Japanese fashion, kept it to themselves. The living are usually left with the feeling that the company and the country have betrayed them, which is why many families of victims enter lengthy legal battles to win recognition of what actually caused a *sarariman*'s death.

In 1988 a group of lawyers, professors, and physicians founded the National Defense Council for Victims of Karoshi. The council set up hot lines around the country and offered consultations to grieving families. By its own account, the group was overwhelmed. There were 135 calls the first day; after two years, the council had almost two thousand cases on its books.

The council also published a book, *Karoshi: When the Corporate Warrior Dies*. It included this diary entry, by a forty-three-year-old man named Toshitsugu Yagi:

> Let's think about slavery, then and now.
>
> In the past, slaves were loaded onto slave ships and carried off to the new world. But in some way, aren't our daily commuter trains packed to overflowing even more inhumane?
>
> And can't it be said that today's armies of corporate workers are in fact slaves in almost every sense of the word?
>
> They are bought for money.
>
> Their worth is measured in working hours.
>
> They are powerless to defy their superiors.
>
> They have little to say in the way their wages are decided.
>
> And these corporate slaves of today don't even share the simplest of pleasures that those forced laborers of ages past enjoyed; the right to sit down at their dinner table with their families.

These observations belong to someone who has discovered something that contradicts what he has long believed about the meaning of his life and the justness of his difficulties. The important point in the diary entry is what is missing. There is nothing there about the sort of dedication we attach to the *sarariman* and much to suggest that the modern corporation in Japan has never been the sort of benevolent community it was supposed to be. Yagi sounded like the plaintive shipyard worker who wrote of his inhuman circumstances in 1922. Like the shipyard worker, Yagi described relations based on the very unmodern notion of above-and-below, in which the one below is powerless.

Of course, people die of overwork in places other than Japan, often of the same maladies. But we must be clear about the Japanese work ethic so praised in the West. It has deep, unenviable roots in the feudal era. Edo bureaucrats were quite conscious in their effort to make the common majority a population of driven producers. Their motto was, "Don't let them live, but don't let them die." They kept commoners desperate while advancing a peculiar idea of moral duty. Virtue was measured in crop surpluses; filial piety meant paying one's rice tributes. Samuraization only reinforced the established compulsions. That is why Japanese employers have preferred the beautiful customs to the rule of law. And it is why the case of Jun Ishii, the Mitsui executive, had within it an echo that sounded far back in history.

While keeping his diary, Toshitsugu Yagi worked for a Tokyo advertising agency that specialized in real estate ads. His death, in 1987, of a myocardial infarction, occurred shortly after he wrote the above passage and was the indirect result of a property frenzy that began with the economic bubble in 1985 and lasted the rest of the decade. In the two years before his death, Yagi was required to absorb a flood of new business, manage a new financial subsidiary, and compensate for company cost cutting by extending his overtime. Living almost two hours from Tokyo, Yagi rarely got home before midnight.

The case bears the usual marks of Japanese management practices. Pressure to reduce costs is more or less constant, and overtime, especially in a strong economic cycle, is more or less mandatory. Because such practices are essential to Japan's ability to compete internationally, they are termed "social dumping"—that is, the use of exploitative employment standards to keep prices below those of competitors. I once visited a maker of construction equipment where each employee worked thirty hours a month in overtime—360 hours a year. In effect, each six workers did the work of a seventh. Put another way, the plant's forty-three hundred employees did the work of just over five thousand, were overtime eliminated.

Mitsue Yagi, the ad executive's widow, was denied compensation in her claim of *karoshi* after a two-year battle with the Labor Ministry. The ministry cannot be faulted for failing to acknowledge the *karoshi* syndrome. It does. But it recognizes overwork only if the victim was on the job for twenty-four hours immediately before death or sixteen hours daily for the preceding seven days. By 1996 fewer than a hundred claims had been officially recognized of the many thousands that were probably legitimate since the term was invented, in 1978, by Tetsunojo Uehata, a physician who helped start the council for victims' families. The Mitsui case was important, but no second case involving a *sarariman* has been recognized since.

When Dr. Uehata invented the term, he defined *karoshi* as

> a condition in which psychologically unsound work processes are allowed to continue in a way that disrupts the worker's normal work and life rhythms . . . and finally result in a fatal breakdown.

The council applied this definition to the fifty thousand employees between thirty and fifty-nine who die annually from strokes or other heart ailments. The conclusion it reached—that 20 percent of this group are *karoshi* victims—is usually considered a conservative estimate.

Karoshi is a perfect example of the unusual integration of the Japanese system. High land prices force employees to accept long, crowded commutes, cramped housing, heavy mortgage burdens, and poor leisure facilities—all of which encourage overwork. In such an unpromising environment, parents seeking maximum advantage for their children push them into cram schools and long hours of homework. Keeping children in the right schools forces fathers to accept *tanshin funin,* one-body transfer, the practice of leaving families behind when a *sarariman* is moved to another city. There are no reliable statistics regarding *tanshin funin,* but executives living solitary lives away from home are commonly thought to number at least half a million, and they are prime candidates for death by *karoshi.*

Toshiro Ueyanagi, a lawyer at the defense council, discussed these things one winter afternoon at the council's offices, down a narrow street in Tokyo. In the 1970s *karoshi* was concentrated in a few categories, he said—journalists, night-shift workers, taxi drivers. It grew after the oil shocks, when companies began talking about "stripped-down management." And in the 1990s, he said, "the problem is everywhere." New technology helped *karoshi* spread by allowing drastic cuts in the labor force. Nissan Motors, to take one example, eliminated 15 percent of its labor force between 1985 and 1988. But automakers are not to be singled out. Despite their prominence in Japan, they are typical companies. So are the lives of their employees. Here is how the wife of a Toyota employee described her family routine to the defense council:

> Night shift is extremely trying, living in two small rooms (four and a half and six tatami mats) and a kitchen and caring for a one-year-old and a three-year-old. After my husband goes to sleep the children can't shout or play, let alone cry. So we spend most of the time outdoors, taking diapers and snacks to the park. Rain presents a real problem. At times like this we visit neighbors or friends whose husbands work the opposite shift. We cope by helping one another out in this way. From about the third day of the night shift, fatigue makes my husband uncharacteristically ill tempered. At the company he works under the same conditions he would working days, even though he has not been able to sleep properly for a week. There have been times when I have found myself unthinkingly bringing my hands together in silent prayer as I watched my exhausted husband set out for work.

In 1992 the government declared that it would reduce the hours the average employee works annually to 1,800 by the year 1997. At the time of the announcement, officially measured hours were 2,200. This figure compared with 1,900 hours in the United States and 1,650 in Germany. The plan was part of a broader idea to make Japan a leader in *raifu-sutairu*, lifestyle—a favorite government theme at the time. But most experts greeted the plan with skepticism. The government, after all, had been talking about a five-day workweek and reduced working hours since the mid-1970s. One problem, if not the principal one, was the difficulty of controlling overtime no matter what companies did to reduce the hours of a regular work shift.

Overtime is an essential feature of Japan's social dumping. It comes in several varieties. Apart from paid overtime, there is the overtime expected of *sararimen* who work at home, and there is the overtime worked because employees are not expected to take their allotted vacations. Corporations have brought court cases against employees who refuse to work overtime. Most important, though, is unrecorded overtime, known as "service overtime," in which employees work without pay as a token of loyalty. Even a government survey calculated that, with overtime included, actual hours worked at the start of the 1990s came to 2,400 yearly for the average employee, and 2,600 for the average male. Other studies showed that year in, year out, service overtime brought the hours of many *sararimen* well above the 3,000 mark.

Toshiro Ueyanagi, the lawyer for victims' families, was pessimistic about changing such practices, because they were so deeply entrenched. "I'm skeptical about changes in the political system or the core economic system, and that's where change first has to take place. There's a reluctance to see the reality of the lives of ordinary people because there's reluctance to change the way ordinary people live."

Ueyanagi gave me the telephone number of the Ogawa family, who lived in a three-room apartment at the end of a long train ride into the western outskirts of Tokyo. Takamasu Ogawa, a balding, heavyset man of fifty-nine, was not strictly a *karoshi* victim. He had survived the stroke he had suffered six years before I met him, but only to witness the frustration and anguish his family went through afterward.

Ogawa had worked for a small firm that traded in electrical products—tapes, tubes, treated paper, chemicals. Some of these items weighed a hundred pounds when packaged in bulk, and Ogawa serviced clients with them in an area that required two hundred miles of driving daily. According to his time cards, Ogawa routinely worked twelve hours a day, excluding commuting time of almost three hours. He had every other Saturday off, but keeping his account books took up his free weekends.

Several days before he collapsed at the office, his wife, Yoshika, noticed signs of stress that she understood only afterward. He had complained of headaches; he dozed frequently and breathed heavily in his sleep. In the evenings just before March 28, 1987, he would crawl from dinner to his futon, skipping his customary hour of television. That day, while discussing a troublesome client with his supervisor, Ogawa felt an intense pain rush to his head. Then he collapsed. The coma lasted three weeks.

It was hard to look at Ogawa directly. He sat in a wheelchair at the kitchen table, the right side of his face and the left side of his body paralyzed. He had round, thick features and a gray crew cut. A photograph taken a few years earlier showed a fit, athletic man: He had grown heavy only since his stroke. Now he recounted his breakdown in clotted phrases. His golf clubs, in a large leather bag, stood in the kitchen corner.

After a time he paused, and Yoshika started to speak.

"After the stroke we called the company president about using disability insurance toward the hospital costs," she began. "At first he said, 'I understand.' On our next visit he said, 'We can't do it.' Then the company said he should resign without any guarantees. Finally he came home from the hospital, a year and a month later."

Impatient with details, Ogawa caught my eye. "My eldest son got married two days ago," he said. His face broke into something between a laugh and a cry, and I was unsure which.

Yoshika resumed talking. Her trail eventually led to the victims' defense council. It helped her apply to the local ward office, the metropolitan labor office, and the Labor Ministry, the last arguing that Ogawa had had too many Saturdays off to qualify for disability benefits. None of these applications had received a final ruling. At that moment, Yoshika was trying to obtain copies of Ogawa's company files, which both the government and the company were withholding.

Ogawa interrupted again. "It's taking too long," he barked. "We have lives to lead."

Then Ogawa's face broke up again. For a moment he looked like a large, helpless infant. This time I was certain it was the closest he could come to crying.

THE IDEA OF what it meant to be modern took a fundamental turn after 1945. Until the imperial state was defeated, making Japan modern was a means to an end. Japan needed industry so that it could resist foreigners. Modernization, it could be said, was a way to preserve identity, culture, and "tradition." After the war this notion was turned upside down. Modernization became the goal, and "tradition" the means. There is another way to put it: At the odd intersection of economics and psychology one finds ideology—imperial ideology before the war, the ideology of growth afterward. The postwar ideology's detractors called it "GNPism," denoting the new obsession with gross national product. The critics were many, and GNPism may indeed seem a grim prospect. But for many more it was liberating when put against what had come before. GNPism gave the defeated Japanese something to strive for other than the discredited imperial state. And soon enough the ideology of growth led to the myth of the *sarariman*'s golden age.

The myth of the golden age was not solely about striving at the workplace. The Japanese also became consumers for the first time. The Americans, who developed their own consumption mania after the war, were an important influence. The Japanese were awed by the easy manners of the occupation G.I.'s and the flood of postwar Hollywood films full of sprawling houses and unimaginable appliances: That was the way one lived the modern, independent life. With the Income-Doubling Plan, begun after the AMPO episode in 1960, the national idée fixe switched from reconstruction to high growth, and consumption was more or less as patriotic as making one's quota at the company.

But consumption has always been a complicated business for the Japanese. It had a peculiar past when the Japanese first turned themselves into consumers, and it has had unexpected consequences in our time.

For many centuries austerity was more than a habit—it was a virtue, an aesthetic value, and finally a legal dictum. The Tokugawa shogun put strict limits on consumption, especially of the conspicuous kind. Merchants indulged themselves with relish in the pleasure quarters of the main cities, sumptuary laws or no. But they were feudal Japan's shame, the lowest of the castes. In the modern era there was a consumption craze during the 1920s, the high point of prewar westernization. It was during the twenties that an urban middle class first appeared. But there was something a bit unseemly about consuming then, too. It was too individualistic; it was private—which was to say selfish. It suggested that one had thoughts of one's own that had nothing to do with the emperor and the good of the state.

After the war to consume was to declare one's autonomy, but it was a self-deceiving declaration. Consumption was less about the "selfhood" intellectuals were debating than the Japanese propensity to dream. There was the relatively early phenomenon of the *burenda*, the electric blender. The rage for blenders in the early 1950s must have been extraordinary, for Japanese alive then still remember it vividly. And here is the curious thing about it: The foods one could process in a blender were nowhere to be found in the markets. Most blenders went straight onto the top shelf, hidden icons honoring the dream of another life. It was the same with cars. Widespread car ownership became possible only in the late 1950s. But a driving license was a mark of status much earlier, and the *pepa doraiba*, the paper driver, was a familiar fellow in urban neighborhoods.

Things accelerated in the mid-1950s, along with the economy. The fashion for blenders eventually turned into the *denka bumu,* the electric boom, the compulsive acquisition of household appliances of all varieties: vacuum cleaners, refrigerators, and so on. A decade later came *maikara* (my color, that is, my TV set), and *maikura* (my cooler, air conditioner), and so on. An insightful advertising copywriter coined the term *maihomu,* my home. *Maihomu* was more than an ad slogan: The borrowed possessive captured the new tilt toward private gratification. The newspapers marked 1966 as the first year of *maika,* my car.

Maika reveals something of what lay beneath the consumption phenomenon. No modern invention is better equipped to plow roughshod over the old Confucian constraints. In any city or town one can cruise through crowded streets with a kind of anonymous, private aggression. One shuts out the world and its burdens and obligations simply by rolling up the windows. Certainly this helps explain the persistent popularity of cars in a nation that barely has enough road to accommodate the number purchased. It also explains why people ordinarily so observant of the inbred politesse are atrociously combative behind the wheel. A few years after the national dailies declared the year of *maika,* the car became known as *hashiru kyoki,* the runaway weapon.

In the consumption *bumu* lies another of the ironies of postwar life in Japan. In the end it did nothing for the *sarariman's* sense of independence. It was merely a retreat into privacy, which is a different thing. Dreaming and consuming, the one encouraging the other, are an expensive combination. It was the *sarariman,* of course, who paid the bills for the urban household's acquisitions. And far from keeping the corporation out of the home, the new consumption was the corporation's way of reentering it. The line between public and private life was not redrawn but further obliterated. During the car craze of the 1960s and 1970s it was not unusual for the crowded urban household to turn the front parlor into garage space for *maika*—a perfect expression of what really happened to the *sarariman* during his golden age.

There is an unbroken line between the relentless *mai's* of the 1960s and the binge consumption of the 1980s. Products developed toward the end of the last decade—computerized toilet bowls, toothpaste flecked with gold— suggested a consumption culture run amok. The mass-consumption dream reached such an extreme that the urban Japanese ran out of room to put things in their cramped houses and apartments. Waste disposal became a national preoccupation. When I arrived in Japan the volume of refuse had begun to overtake the capacity of artificial landfills in Tokyo Bay—city dumps named, with no intended irony, the Dream Islands.

But in a certain way consumption had again taken on the subversive edge it had in the deep past. It is true that Japanese consumers fueled the bubble of the late 1980s, and that the bubble dramatically increased Japan's imports—so easing a trade issue that had reached a critical stage. But the consumption of the time was like the indulgences of the feudal townsmen: The shogun disapproved of the rich merchants of Edo and Osaka because consumption made apparent the matter of difference. And that is just what the indulgences of the 1980s did.

Famously, 90 percent of postwar Japanese long believed they were part of the middle class—an impossibility, but an article of faith nonetheless. It is nearer the truth to say that, as in many primitive societies, difference was suppressed to contain envy. The control of envy has a long tradition in Japan; everyone knows it lurks just beneath the surface of sameness. Consumption in the 1950s and 1960s was all about sameness: Everyone had a *burenda,* everyone a television. The 1980s were different. Not everyone had a mink-trimmed Mercedes; not everyone bought floral bouquets wrapped in sheets of uncut dollar bills. The consumption of the eighties, based not on hard work but on stock and land speculation, created a new and conspicuous class of *narikin,* as the Japanese call the nouveaux riches—*niyu ritchi* in the parlance of the decade.

And as the mask of sameness dropped, the self-denying corporate soldier, modern Japan's ultimate conformist, began to seem an anachronism, even a bit of a dupe.

TO UNDERSTAND THIS we must return briefly to the early 1970s, when Japan took several serious blows—*shokku,* it called them. The yen was revalued against the American dollar after two decades at a favorable rate. Then the system of floating exchange rates began. Then came the first oil shock. The *shokku* wreaked economic havoc. Japan Inc.'s bureaucratic engineers did not handle them well. Growth slowed and inflation soared. Tokyo had to choke off the consumption spree to combat spiraling prices. Companies retrenched, and unemployment reappeared for the first time since the economic confusion of the late 1940s. This was the period, incidentally, when *karoshi,* death from overwork, also made its first appearance.

Japan quickly recovered from the *shokku*. By mid-decade the economy was back on track, and many years of growth lay ahead. Japan Inc. was fighting trim—a little leaner and meaner, we would say. But Japan never really came back from the *shokku*, which is why they are worth recalling. The Japanese began to separate economics from psychology for the first time. Eternal economic growth was discredited as an overarching value. Even before the *shokku* many Japanese had begun questioning the human and ecological costs of GNPism; afterward, a purely material response to life no longer seemed adequate. At the moment the economy entered its mature phase—which is what the *shokku* were all about—the old collective effort gave way to renewed ruminations as to the place of the individual. That is why one needs both economists and psychologists to understand this singular moment. "After the oil shocks," one of the latter once told me, "we lost our belief in unending progress. We lost our transcendent guide."

It was precisely such a Japan—unguided, without beliefs—that began to look once more at what it meant to be modern. And it could only be a matter of time—a decade, to be precise—before the Japanese began to look with a certain distance at the way they had chosen. Did they really need the way of the warrior to be good, modern Japanese? Did they need the corporation as it had presented itself to them—the corporation as village, as household?

In the spring of 1993 a politician named Ichiro Ozawa, a rising star in conservative circles, published an influential book about the future of Japan. Among the many striking observations in *Blueprint for a New Japan* were these about the *sarariman* ideal:

> Individuals have to be liberated from their companies. It is only when each individual becomes able to act autonomously that we will see the birth of a richly diverse and dynamic society.
>
> The way we are employed is in no way a traditional Japanese construct. It is something that developed during the period of rapid growth . . . Japan is no longer catching up. We now rank alongside the United States as an economic power. The social framework tied to rapid growth is no longer appropriate.

No member of the political elite, least of all someone of Ozawa's prominence and authority, had ever thought to demolish the myth of the corporate samurai. Ozawa did so in a few direct sentences for a simple reason. Japan could no longer afford "the beautiful customs." With the economy in transition, neither were they any longer useful. Employment figures offer a clear explanation. Japan reckons its jobless rate at roughly three percent. Factor in the window sitters and so on—the "efficiency of accumulated inefficiency"—and the rate triples, according to some experts, who believe it will have to go higher still before Japan regains its economic health. "Japan's most pressing need is a change in the consciousness of our people," Ozawa wrote—pressing because lifetime employment, seniority raises, and all the rest of the samurai code in its modern form had become a hindrance rather than an advantage.

But what did Ozawa really mean? Who would direct these momentous changes? Change has almost always taken place in Japan from above rather than below, autocratically rather than democratically. And that is the most pressing change of all. Ozawa wrote as an official of the central government—as a man "above," a man of the "great tradition." What about the ordinary Japanese—the "little tradition"? Ozawa was right about the need for a change in consciousness. But what would it consist of? Many people—many *sararimen* and their spouses and children, the generation of the "new human species"—were way ahead of Ozawa on this point. It would be impossible to change the system as Ozawa proposed without changing the dependence upon authority Japan's leaders have long cultivated. That, again, is the most pressing need of all. The outstanding question is whether men such as Ozawa, and the corporations employing Japan's army of *sararimen,* will accept such a change. For there were many signs of it by the time Ozawa attacked the mythical corporate warrior.

In 1991 a *sarariman* named Akio Koiso published another unusual book, called *Record of a Fuji Bank Man.* Not much had ever been written about the *sarariman* and the way the individual worker actually related to his company. Koiso broke the colossal silence of the corporate warrior. And then a slew of other *sararimen* gave firsthand accounts of the auto industry, the press, the transportation industry, the mammoth life insurance companies—the institutions of Japan Inc. These were not stories of harmony and unified purpose. They were tales of what Koiso called "coercive labor," full of intimidating managers, corrupt union officials, executive suicides, *karoshi* incidents, "service overtime" scams, vindictive personnel departments, and employees banished to various Siberias for being too independent of mind.

Akio Koiso was not an easy man to find. Whenever I called his office I was turned away: He was in a meeting, he was traveling, he had not come in that day. I finally reached Koiso at home. Yes, he said, the bank was no longer letting him take telephone calls. We eventually met in the lobby of a Tokyo hotel. Koiso turned out to be a modest man in his fifties. He wore his hair in a low part, combing most of it over a balding pate. When he offered his *meishi*, it read simply, "Akio Koiso, Fuji Bank Employee." No rank, no section—no clue to his place on the pyramid.

Koiso began working at Fuji, a large commercial bank, at the beginning of the Income-Doubling Plan, in 1960. His career coincided with what he called "massification"—torrid competition between banks for the savings accounts that provided industry with the cheap, stable capital that paid for the "miracle." Massification has produced workloads that increase with each technological advance. In his book Koiso recalled a "maximization of efficiency" plan from his early days at the bank:

> Branches were assessed according to targets set by headquarters and by comparisons with other branches. This assessment included expansion of clients, fixed-term accounts, savings accounts, direct payroll deposits, and so on. People in charge of favored clients had to visit twenty or more daily. Twenty-five percent of the marketing staff was to be eliminated in three years, along with 10 percent of total personnel. Reducing expenses meant rationing ballpoint pens, removing lights, and "spontaneous rejection" of overtime pay. . . . Twenty-five years after its introduction, this system is still in place. . . .

From the beginning Koiso had concerned himself with the way Fuji treated its employees, and he soon rose to the top of the union local. It was not a good career move. Koiso's fate was sealed when he insisted on reporting all his overtime and, later, when he opposed the bank for ignoring even the government's lax labor standards. Not surprising, he was transferred five times, usually from one desolate rural branch to another. Unable to dump Akio Koiso, whose hard work often won him the support of branch managers, Fuji Bank tried to bury him.

Koiso was a product of the AMPO era: He had expected Japan to change at that critical moment and had lived with disappointment ever since. But he saw the system passing, partly because banks and corporations had new, global ambitions. In *Record of a Fuji Bank Man* Koiso wrote, "This kind of contradiction—depending on internationally unacceptable working conditions to become an international company—cannot go on forever."

As we sipped coffee Koiso expanded on this point. "When you enter a firm, substantially what takes place is a *giri-on* relationship, the old type of relationship in which obligations are created and then must be observed. By giving *on* to employees—benefit, kindness—management creates *giri*, duty. It weakens the employees' sense of autonomy. That is how Japan works. But you can't impose these kinds of practices overseas."

Koiso was eager to pursue the theme. "Another thing carried into the workplace after the war was military style. We call the branch manager *oyagi,* an informal form of 'father.' This is true in most big companies. It came from the army, where you would call the platoon leader *oyagi.* An order from the *oyagi* was an absolute order. The practice began after the Russo-Japanese War. It fostered 'familyism,' the idea that you should think of the army as your family."

I wondered what would replace the system beginning to fade. Koiso did not know. "I don't think it'll be like France or Germany or the United States. It'll be Japanese. I've got no concrete image in mind. Younger people are good at putting things into practice. But the example of Meiji tells us something. Lower-ranking samurai learned from the West, but they didn't pass on what they learned—they modified it. This will happen again to change the system into something socially, morally, and internationally acceptable."

When Koiso got up he turned toward me and, as if to leave behind some reassuring message, said simply, "The power of the past is weakening." This was a shrewd view of things. Turmoil among Japanese wage earners and managers is now an evident feature of the economy, as it is in America and elsewhere. Then, it was just beginning. Companies laid off senior managers—proven corporate warriors. They reneged on their *naitei,* job guarantees extended to university seniors, an institution as sacred as lifetime employment. People found it difficult to give up the security of the old system. But I had no doubt Koiso was right: The past was fading.

During my last year in Japan I used to meet with researchers at the Recruit Company. Most foreigners familiar with Recruit know it as the company behind a late-1980s political scandal. But Recruit was central to the Japanese employment system. It helped corporations connect with graduates entering the job market—hence its name. Recruit had grown rich in the 1980s because companies were ever more mystified about the people they were trying to attract. It was an important nexus in the system. The researchers I met were young, stylish executives in a group called the Work Design Institute. Their job was to advise corporate clients how best to appeal to young, stylish executives-to-be. The institute was started in 1989. It published a great deal of research and statistical matter. Periodically it produced a glossy magazine on a single theme: how Europeans spend their leisure time, for instance. It is fair to say that those at the institute had the task of simply explaining themselves and their generation to those who did not understand them.

It was remarkable to find, among the ten or twelve people who attended these sessions, unqualified derision for the system their parents had accepted—the system that had produced the affluence they enjoyed. But as a shared sentiment this was a given, something not even discussed. When I first arrived, I asked one of the leaders what he did. He beat his chest and said in English, "I am Mister Company, a business soldier." Everyone laughed. People no longer even used that phrase, I supposed. "Only ironically," said one of his colleagues, a woman in her late twenties.

The irony masked mystification. I sensed as the meetings went on that it was hard for these people to find enough distance to know even themselves, to say nothing of their parents and what they had lived for. These people worked hard, too, but that was not the issue. Among much else, the group was struggling with the idea that people could live in a variety of ways. Such a thing had not occurred to the Japanese since the early postwar years.

"Why is there the phenomenon of *karoshi?*" someone asked in one session. "There is no answer to this."

I suggested, "People overwork because they have no mechanism within themselves that allows them to say no."

"Then why are young people not the same way?"

The group slipped into a discussion in rapid Japanese. A younger member of the institute turned to me and explained. "At this moment we are asking, 'What is a corporation?' and 'Why did men think in a way that produced something like *karoshi?*'" The conversation was part of a long study they were finishing. It would go to the core of the matter: the relationship between the *sarariman* and the company.

"There was the corporation, and the *sarariman* belonged to it," the group leader said. "But people don't feel the same loyalty anymore. So companies have to come up with a new method of management. The issue is how to make fundamental change in the way companies relate to their employees. Most companies share the same problem. They simply don't know how to treat people."

There was something peculiar about the group. Amid all the rumination, its members were skeptics. Older people like Akio Koiso, who had lived through the system for so long, were more optimistic about change than those younger, from whom change was supposed to spring. Perhaps they did not trust themselves as they watched friends graduate and step quickly onto the treadmill. Like many generations before them, they evinced that common Japanese mix of emotions, desire without hope. But within a year of the meetings at Recruit such companies as Honda, Toyota, and Nomura, the sort of blue chip corporations emulated by all others, were trying new salary systems, promotions based on merit, and short-term contracts that left people free to change jobs—left them loyal to themselves.

I ONCE TRAVELED to the shores of Biwako, Japan's largest lake, northeast of Kyoto, where forty young men and women were in training. They had just joined the Toray Corporation, a leading maker of synthetic fibers. I arrived on a warm day in April, not long after university graduations. A gray-haired man in a light blue suit—trousers and a waist-length Eisenhower jacket—stood on a raised platform in front of a microphone. An oval above his breast pocket gave his name as Muneishi.

A veteran *sarariman*, Muneishi-san was part drill sergeant and part camp counselor. He divided the room into four teams, each of which appointed a salesman, a receptionist, a junior *sarariman*, and a *kacho*, a section chief. The exercise was simple: The salesman arrives, greets the receptionist, asks to see the *kacho*, is shown into the *sarariman*'s office. The *sarariman* then fetches the *kacho*: end of exercise. There was much bowing, exchanging of *meishi*, talk of the weather, business chat, and so on. Each skit lasted a few minutes. Sometimes the actors spoke so diffidently that you could hardly hear them. When they finished, Muneishi-san gave his scores.

"Team A, your manner was quite good. But you left out the discussion of price and deadline. These are important in business. Minus one point."

The score went up on a blackboard. The people at Team A's table fidgeted in their seats.

"Team B, your salesman didn't offer his *meishi*. Minus one. Then your junior clerk didn't present his *meishi* at the right time. Minus one."

Someone on another team didn't say, "Thank you very much," when a *meishi* was presented. Minus a point. Someone else put a proffered *meishi* in his pocket. Minus three: The *meishi* must remain on the table between two people for the duration of a meeting. Someone else left his briefcase half opened during his encounter with the junior *sarariman*. Minus one.

A hand shot up.

"I learned that you don't give a *meishi* to the receptionist. Is this true?"

"Hmmm." Muneishi-san wrestled half aloud with the conundrum: It is true, but if you don't give your *meishi* to the receptionist, how does she know whom to announce? "In my opinion," he concluded at last, "it's best if you give your *meishi* to the receptionist, too, but only on the first visit. But let me check on that."

Afterward, I pulled aside a man named Yasuhiko Takibayashi. He had been a salesman for his team and had incurred a minus or two—demerits he evidently took to heart. "It was difficult to grasp the timing—to say what I wanted to say while listening to my counterpart. The polite form was hard, too."

"What was difficult about the polite form?"

"I'm not used to 'respect language.' And to complete a sentence clearly was also hard."

He was fresh from Hokkaido University and had grown up on the cool, pastoral island in the north. He had the reticence one would expect of a farmer's son transported, like millions before him, to the city. Takibayashi wanted to work in the marketing section. But why Toray? "O.B.'s at university—I mean 'old boys'—who went to manufacturing companies. One who went to Toray came back and left a good impression." What was the impression? "I learned that in Toray your opinion is valued, and you can do what you want."

Over the two days I spent at Toray's training camp they played with clay—each recruit fashioned a traditional flute—and they played with words: Half of each team was shown a map to a factory and, using only description, had to tell the other half how to get there. They made telephone calls to departments within the company. They wrote business letters and scheduled appointments. To prepare for each task they studied thick manuals that resembled the text-and-pictures format of *"Salaryman" in Japan*. Could I see one? No, they were for "inside people."

They were becoming *shakai-jin,* social beings. Making a flute taught them something about creativity and about working alone. They learned how to communicate with strangers. In the enacted scenes they began to grasp the rules of business conduct, which were as simple and rigid and precise as any of the decrees Tokugawa bureaucrats had issued to the samurai or the peasants centuries earlier.

When I arrived, a group of Toray executives greeted me. They had all seen many freshmen begin their paths through the company. There was not much new under the sun, it seemed to them. But one manager, a portly, severe man who wore metal-framed glasses, did not especially approve. He said, "My very personal opinion is that the younger generation still has some thinking to do about whether they want to stay long-term with a company or quit. There's still some doubt about it. They're undecided and uncommitted."

I met a young woman named Yukiko Hayashi. She was not a migrant, but a born-and-bred Tokyoite. Hayashi had graduated in sociology from Waseda, a prestigious private university in the capital. She was small and alert and casually dressed. Something of the undergraduate's slouch lingered about her. It was easy to imagine her carrying a backpack full of books. "For me, a woman, the priorities are different," Hayashi said. "I put more emphasis on the atmosphere inside a company. I'm less interested in a company's name than in a company where I can work freely."

She was not unlike Takibayashi. But I wondered whether she considered herself different from her parents' generation. "A little," Hayashi said. "People want to work, but they want to enjoy their own time. It's not either-or, though. You work to live, and not the other way around—it's getting that way. I hope the company will accept that."

Maybe Hayashi had left behind disappointed friends when she packed off for her weeks near Biwako. Maybe she left behind a piece of herself, also disappointed. But there was nothing final about her commitment to Toray— the severe *sarariman* was right about that—except her judgment of the future. It contained something more than the familiar pessimism and desire.

"Will young people change companies," I asked, "or will companies change young people?"

"It goes in both directions. This company, like most of the others, sticks to the old ways. Before I came I thought, I want to change these attitudes. But it's hard to change that quickly. On the other hand, we have to change."

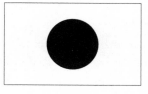

5

HAPPINESS IN A HIDDEN CORNER

Our ancestors cut off the brightness on the land from above
and created a world of shadows, and far in the depths of it
they placed woman, marking her the palest of beings.

—JUNICHIRO TANIZAKI,
In Praise of Shadows, 1933

WHEN MICHIKO FUKUSHIMA smiled, which was often, her eyes narrowed until they nearly closed, and her crow's-feet grew. Fukushima was small, energetic, and sixty-two when I met her, in the early 1990s. In conversation she combined curiosity with bemused detachment, a distance she would rather not cross. She had offices in a residential quarter of Tokyo: two rooms crammed with folding chairs, bookshelves, stacks of film reels. There was an oversized table with folding legs, the sort of thing that belonged in a school auditorium.

Fukushima was a rarity in late-century Japan—an independent woman who had made her own way in life. She was as aware as anyone else that few women younger than she, the generation then emerging, would accept the standards she had set for herself long earlier. She was like a mountaineer, pleased with her conquest but lonely for it, too. There did not seem to be anyone scaling the peak behind her.

Fukushima's life spanned many of modern Japan's different phases. She was born on a farm outside Tokyo in the 1930s, one of six children in an *ie,* an extended household. Like the other girls and women—her mother, grandmother, sisters—she was considered her father's property. They ran the house, but they obeyed in all matters outside of it—including marriage, of course. Among Fukushima's earliest memories were the relentless complaints of visiting aunts about their husbands and in-laws.

"I was six when I decided I would never marry into such a situation," Fukushima said in one of our conversations. "I'd have to study, then build a career. But my father and mother never agreed about higher education. They saw no need: That was only for my brothers. They thought if I were educated no one would marry me."

Fukushima stopped for a moment, lost in memory. "So I never explained my desire," she continued. "I always obeyed. But inside, the desire to escape grew and grew."

The war saved Fukushima from the fate of her mother and her unhappy aunts. The occupation abolished the *ie,* and by the mid-1950s, when women's education was universally accepted, she was working her way through Tokyo University. One day she saw a film called *Ashes and Diamonds,* by the Polish director Andrzej Wajda. It told the story of a young resistance fighter who, after the war, found his identity as a brave partisan worthless and had nothing with which to replace it. The predicament resonated with a young woman raised on the prewar diet of patriotism. And the film became the inspiration for much that followed in Fukushima's life.

The year she saw the film, Fukushima married an engineering student a year ahead of her, with whom she had a son. Somewhat unusually for the time, it was not an arranged marriage with a go-between, awkward meetings, and family-to-family negotiations. Fukushima chose her own husband. He had promised to respect her independence but turned out to be, as Fukushima put it, "very Japanese." She went to work at a small production company, but the toll at home soon mounted. The domestic issue, perhaps not so oddly, came down to a desk.

"It sounds funny, but I very much wanted my own desk," Fukushima said with a quiet laugh. "My husband would point to the one he had and say, 'Use this one. It's ours.' But I wanted my own. I wanted my own world."

Fukushima entered her own world at thirty-one: She divorced in 1962—another rarity at the time—and was more or less disowned by both her husband's family and her own. While the neighbors whispered, she made herself a scriptwriter and director of documentary films. It was a rough business, made of frequent moves, heavy equipment, male crews, shared rooms in cheap hotels. It was a world in which a woman had to prove her worth against the inconveniences she caused. But it was also one of the few in which, once a place was achieved, no distinction was made between men and women.

Fukushima paid heavily for her independence. She was allowed no contact with her child again until her husband died, of cancer, sometime in the late 1980s—she was not sure when. Her son was thirty-five when they met again; she had not seen him for three decades.

Fukushima never precisely regretted her choices. But neither did she ever seem far from the edge of sorrow when the course of her life came up, which it did almost as often as she smiled. "I felt nothing, I believed in nothing," Fukushima once told me about the end of her marriage. "I just wanted to leave." On another occasion she said: "I've been through a lot, but I always did what I wanted." And on another: "I'm happy with how life turned out. I don't have too many regrets—I can say that now, anyway, at a certain age. I chose my way. It's my responsibility, my choice."

To depart from the norm in a society as intricately knitted as Japan is always dramatic: That is the simplest explanation of Fukushima's experience. And that is how it has been for modern Japanese women. They have not built much together. Only alone have they found paths of their own. To step outside the crowded circle of conformity is still to accept a harsh and lonely unknown.

It is easy to imagine Fukushima as an exemplary feminist in a Western country. But in Japan her life reflects a larger problem; it cannot be confined to the question of feminism alone. Japan, in its obsessions with above and below and inside and outside, has been notably cruel to its women. Japanese men have made victims of them for many centuries. But feminism has never proven an adequate response. Women have often been complicit in their victimization—often and deliberately. And it is more obvious in Japan than anywhere else that as women suffer, so do men—that in every act of subjugation, both subjugator and subjugated are victims.

The larger problem between Japanese men and women, the problem that lies at the bottom of Michiko Fukushima's brittle, radical choices, is the pervasive lovelessness one finds in modern Japan—that is to say, the profound absence of sympathy between the sexes. Nothing seemed more evident, when I met Fukushima, than her courage and isolation, and the pride with which she stood outside the confining circles of Japanese life. But choosing to live as an independent person—to take responsibility for herself, as she put it—did not bring with it some new emotional blight. In her own words, her life was empty even in marriage: "I felt nothing, I believed in nothing." In the end Fukushima's courage lay in her simple, unabashed honesty about herself and her society.

The absence of intimacy, inherent in the very fiber of society, is resolved neither in marriage nor in the giving up of marriage. It is part of the inheritance of history, for it is the past that has made Japan a place where a certain subversiveness attaches to the very idea of intimacy. To resolve the problem—to discover love and intimacy and then to make them public—is to effect an escape from the formal relationships constructed in the modern front of Japan, *omote nihon*.

In a novella called *Star Time*, published in 1980, a young girl on a city street tries not to step on the cracks in the sidewalk, which is made to stand for the social grid into which everyone in modern Japan is expected to fit. "The child was walking unnaturally, avoiding the cracks in the pavement," *Star Time* begins. Adults pass her, indifferent to her contortions. Then:

> As she attempted to keep off the cracks that didn't match her natural stride, with every step the child's body recognized the lack of love in a world absolutely indifferent to her—a lack of love she couldn't accept, nor adapt to, in any way. What she was actually doing now was probing the source of all those hurts that for some reason had steadily become part of her life, day by day, since the very first time her needs—for a hug, for a suck of the breast—had gone unmet.

The longing for intimacy ranks among the central themes of modern Japanese culture. It is not that the Japanese are somehow incapable of loving. Countless novels, films, and dramas describe a society that renders men and women powerless to manifest their desires for love and intimacy because the expression of love is, among many other things, a supreme act of individual self-assertion.

WHEN I MET Michiko Fukushima, women in Japan seemed to have many more choices than she had had. They seemed to face many fewer risks. These were the apparent consequences of the late 1980s. In 1986 the Diet passed an equal-opportunity law. The bubble economy made more room for women in white-collar jobs. Women became a force in national politics. It was easy to think the situation of Japanese women, like that of women elsewhere, was beginning to change.

But the 1980s were a cruel trick, as the deflated bubble proved. Women were the first to be laid off in the recession that followed. Then companies resisted hiring them altogether. In Nagatacho, the political district, women seemed to get lost, their voices drowned out. The equal-opportunity law made no difference, as anyone who read it should have understood from the beginning: It was never equipped with penalties; it was a guideline. In 1995, 60 percent of women graduates looking for work failed to find any. To be independent still carried the high price Michiko Fukushima had paid.

The most famous of the missions Japan sent abroad after the Meiji Restoration included five girls, aged six to fourteen, whose task it was to learn the habits of upper-crust Westerners. When they returned they exposed Japanese women to new social customs for the first time in many centuries. The intention, however, was less salutary. The dispatch of a few females to take instruction in the West was merely another feature of the campaign to display Japan as a civilized nation worthy of equal treaties with the Western powers.

It is useful to view the 1980s with this bit of history in mind. Japan suddenly showed the world an economy, a bureaucracy, and a political system open to women because these things were part of what it meant to be international. They went along with affluence and global influence. But substance was never at issue. The apparent encouragements that greeted women in the 1980s were the same as they were a century earlier: They were matters of face.

Feminism has a long history in Japan. In November of 1911, near the end of the Meiji era, Ibsen's *A Doll's House* was staged in Tokyo for the first time. For more than a decade afterward women argued as to whether Nora was right to defy her husband and leave home. Today women count those not always friendly discussions and the ferment that attended them as the beginning of Japanese feminism. They marked the first time women discussed their own ideas about their assigned place in society. Nora struck a chord because the place of women inside or outside the home was the core of the feminist question in Japan. The issue is the same today: Where do Japanese women belong? But the problem then is also the problem now: There has never been anything to hang new answers upon, no change in society to support the choices of independent women—women like Michiko Fukushima.

Questions of independence and equality are complicated in Japan by the role women have played in the past. They have been defined—carefully, purposefully, and by men—as social inferiors, second-class citizens. But they were not without power or purpose. A comparison is sometimes made with Kabuki drama. Only men can appear in women's roles. Women, because they are women, are not qualified to depict even themselves. Instead they are like the *kuroko,* literally "black people," those dressed in black who prompt Kabuki actors and change the scenery. They are there on stage, but the conceit is that they are unseen.

The Meiji ideologues, intent upon their family-state, gave the place of women in the home an explicit political value. As in Michiko Fukushima's *ie,* the place of women was inside, the place of men outside. There was a contradiction, still unresolved: Women were an important part of the workforce. Despite this classic chasm between the ideal and the real, the official status of women was a matter of ideology. To change it was to change the way Japan worked—never a small project. The status of women has greatly changed—at least officially—since the defeat of the imperial state. But the old attitudes about women are still evident; Fukushima's life after the war is evidence enough of that.

The feminist movement renewed itself in the 1970s, as it did elsewhere. Women began to connect sexual inequality with larger concerns: the psychological structures they learned as children, the autonomy of individual women. They engaged the question of *uchi naru onnaishiki,* the traditional woman within. The feminist movement eventually collapsed—a victim, its members say now, of relentless sensationalism in the media. The charge is entirely fair. But the better explanation of feminism's eclipse was that it struck too close to the architecture of authority and—closely related—faced women with too difficult a task. Feminism came to be "rights-and-careers" feminism, as a 1970s activist once put it—an imported feminism that did not really address the specific problems of Japanese women. Rights-and-careers feminism then became the feminism of the 1980s and 1990s.

There is a saying in Japanese, *Dansei joi, josei yui*—Men superior, women dominant—that, while not new, has been current since the 1980s. It is still invoked by conservative feminists who believe women should not give up the place in society they already have. Women could be satisfied with small equalities within the larger inequality, or they could face the more imposing problem of "the traditional woman within." At bottom, "Men superior, women dominant" is an empty temptation. What does it offer beyond ersatz freedom in exchange for the continued submergence of identity, the continued effacement of female individuality? It is a bribe, but it is a bribe many women have accepted.

In this the years since the late 1980s have been cruel a second time. When the easy choices afforded during the bubble evaporated, younger women had to face their unwillingness to make the harder choices. They seemed to retreat from the present. They did not particularly want the responsibility that women such as Michiko Fukushima stood for. They did not understand the generation of feminists before them. They seemed to resent such people, as if they, the younger women of the 1980s and 1990s, had emerged too quickly from the shadows of the past and were distressed by the idea that they could live with fewer boundaries.

At about the same time I met Michiko Fukushima I met a much younger woman named Nobuko. She was twenty-five. Well schooled, she had begun her career a few years earlier at the Bank of Japan, the central bank—an auspicious start for any graduate. Then she began to drift: two years at Morgan Stanley's Tokyo office, a year with an importer of Czech glass. When I met her she was working in the research department of a large American brokerage. She had begun this odyssey in search of an independent life of her own. But by her own account she did not fit into the world that seemed to beckon. Nobuko represented the new, international Japan, yet a palpable disquiet pervaded her life, the anxiety of a traveler without maps.

Nobuko was bored by the men of her generation. She was unmarried at a crucial age, and Japan is not kind in this respect. Women in their twenties are traditionally called "Christmas cake"—much in demand until they reach twenty-five, unwanted afterward. The age at which the cake is considered stale has crept higher—it now approaches twenty-nine or thirty—and women's eligibility is generally less rigidly defined. By the 1990s nearly a third of women aged twenty-five to twenty-nine were still single—a vast increase. But women like Nobuko still felt keen pressure—from family, friends, and from themselves.

"Yes, people are marrying at an older age," Nobuko said when I broached the subject. "But the younger generation, watching ours, might conclude it's better to get married younger. Without knowing the background, they might say it's a waste of time working in a man's society, since society doesn't change."

Nobuko always gave the impression that the choices she was making embarrassed her, as if she knew there were better choices but could not make them. Her life as a woman never seemed something she was proud of, something she stood by the way Michiko Fukushima stood by hers—with frankness, independence, and responsibility.

"We get too much information. We have too many choices, and we don't know how to evaluate them," Nobuko once told me. "It's like walking into an antique shop. There are valuable things and there are fakes. If you don't know anything about antiques, you can't tell the difference. It's the same in our lives. What is valuable? What is fake?"

Before I left Japan I heard through a mutual friend that Nobuko had abruptly decided to marry—a young *sarariman,* entirely conventional but, within the usual limits, entirely promising. He sounded like the sort of man Michiko Fukushima had described her husband to be.

WOMEN WERE POWERFUL in ancient Japan. This is evident even in the creation myths, which cast the sun goddess, Amaterasu, as Japan's cosmic protector. Amaterasu (Heaven-Shining Deity) was a radiant child, while her first brother, Susa-no-o, was an unhappy storm god. From the mists of their breath they gave birth to the deities the imperial family claims as its ancestors. But Susa-no-o (His Swift Impetuous Male Augustness) behaved badly toward his sister—ruining her rice fields and befouling her palace. His problem was familiar: Like all Japanese men since, he missed his mother. In the end Susa-no-o was banished to the nether regions, and Amaterasu's light was again unobstructed.

There is much to suggest that the creation myths were the legends of a matriarchal society. The conflicts they depict may have reflected the triumphs of clans led by women over others led by men. Women were considered closer than men to the magical and the divine. Some of the women whose names survive in the myths were shamans as well as chieftains. And they ruled over a Japan very different from the Japan of later ages. The first hard historical account of the Japanese was written by Chinese travelers in the third century. "In their meetings and in their deportment, there is no distinction between father and son or between men and women," it said. Men and women were at home in the natural world—delighted, thankful, unafraid. Shinto, the animist folk religion, saw gods everywhere—in the sun, the moon, the rice crop, the river water. Fertility cults abounded. And neither love nor intimacy were hidden. Sexual and marital customs suggest an Edenlike innocence among the ancients.

In the eighth century scholars compiled what is arguably Japan's greatest collection of poetry, the *Manyoshu*, the *Anthology of Ten Thousand Leaves*. Its forty-five hundred entries were written by poets of varied backgrounds: the accomplished and the merely noble, the lowborn and the anonymous. We can assume from the content of this entry that the poet was a peasant girl:

> You'd better go after dawn.
> Now the grasses under the cherries and hemp are wet with dew.
> I don't care if my mother notices.

This poem suggests a practice known as *yobai,* night crawling, a term for young suitors. An eligible village girl slept in an accessible part of the house when she wanted to encourage a farm boy to enter for the night. He conveyed his desire to marry by remaining until morning. These lines, still as fresh as the dew they describe, can thus be read as its author's desire for a lifelong commitment.

It is for such poems that *Ten Thousand Leaves* is treasured today. It is considered a record of the authentic sentiments of the Japanese heart and soul—native notions of love and human bonds before the overlay of Confucian morality and the stratification of classes and genders. But even as the anthology was compiled the ancient innocence was already disappearing under the blanket of Chinese influence. Women flourished briefly during the Heian period (794–1192), when they produced *The Pillow Book, The Tale of Genji,* and other literary classics in reaction to the weight of imported orthodoxy. Then came the great tradition of the shoguns and the samurai, whose culture submerged the ancient ways almost entirely.

In the warrior's household women conformed to the most rigid of inner-outer distinctions. A wife was confined to the *oku* of the samurai house, the innermost rooms, and so was called *oku-san,* inside person. Wifely involvement in *omote-muki,* public matters, was out of the question. The psychiatrist Masao Miyamoto relates an interesting word in this regard. *Anshin* means "security," the feeling of relief or assurance. Its first characters picture a woman within a house.

Love had no place in *samurai* culture—at least, no public place. Intimacy was associated with secrecy, even with weakness. And marriage was a link between households, like an early corporate merger. This was also the way marriages were made in medieval Europe. But love was different between East and West, as legends and literature suggest. In general, the courtly love invented by medieval knights contrasted sharply with the earthier Japanese view: The Japanese considered love only in its carnal aspects, with no notion of it as a transcendent emotion. But there was idealized love in Japan, surely, and there was carnal love in Europe. The real difference was that love was publicly expressed in the West but became private in Japan.

The most popular play of the great playwright of the feudal era, Monzaemon Chikamatsu, is called *The Love Suicides at Amijima.* Jihei, a paper merchant, and Koharu, a courtesan, are in love. But Jihei cannot reconcile love with loyalty toward his wife. He is a pathetic character for much of the play because he is too weak minded to find a way out of his dilemma. He becomes a hero when he enters into a suicide pact with Koharu. Life is duty; only in death does one find the freedom of unobstructed love.

In 1672 a scholar of the Chinese classics named Ekken Kaibara published one of the better-known books of the Edo era. *Onna Daigaku* (*Greater Learning for Women*) resembled all the other Edo codes intended for the various classes. As farmers were told what to eat and where to dig the latrine, women were informed of the ideal behavior of their sex: "Take no naps," "never write to young men," "don't go to places where many people gather," and so on. But the lasting renown of *Onna Daigaku* stands partly on this unbashful assessment:

Women have five defects—disobedience, anger, slander, jeal-
ousy, and ignorance. These infest seven to eight women of
every ten, and it is these that account for the inferiority of
women to men. Reflect on yourself and improve your faults.
Ignorance is the worst defect of all, and the parent of the other
four. Women are negative. Negative is night and dark. . . .

So did Japan create its "world of shadows," as Junichiro Tanizaki put it, with
women in its inaccessible reaches. One must marvel today at what gender
memories of women's preternatural potency urged men toward such thoroughgoing persecution. Surely to cut women off from brightness reflected
an irrational, primordial fear. Why else deprive them so purposefully of the
sun, that primal source of power with which the ancients identified them?

Onna Daigaku was not intended for many people—its saving grace,
perhaps. For the whole of the feudal era the peasant majority and most
other commoners, excluded from the great tradition, were left to their own
devices in matters of family and marriage. Many vestiges of the old matri-
archy survived in the countryside, sometimes into our own century. Long
after the wives of samurai were shut indoors, one would have found a
culture of considerable equality among the rustics. Nobody became
anyone else's property. A new husband might be absorbed into his bride's
household—just the reverse of the high-culture practice. Village life was
always difficult, but for all the hardships, peasant women led freer lives
than those in the upper strata.

This leads us to a peculiar irony of the modern era. Women were
among the greatest losers after the Meiji Restoration. Modernization
brought samuraization, and samuraization meant less freedom, not more.

Meiji did not begin this way. After the restoration Yukichi Fukuzawa,
who seemed to have something to say about almost everything, wrote *Shin
Onna Daigaku* (*New Greater Learning for Women*), a crisp refutation of
Ekken Kaibara's work. But the notion of an equal position for women
soon went the way of liberal education, democratic discourse, and the
other ideas of "civilization and enlightenment." In 1887 the Education
Ministry came out with its own answer to Kaibara's classic—*Meiji Greater
Learning for Women,* a tract much closer to the original than Fukuzawa's.

The Meiji constitution and the civil code institutionalized women's place. Along with students, teachers, soldiers, police, and others, women were banned from politics. They could own property but could have no say in running it. They could enter into legal agreements, but not without their husbands' consent. And they did not share their husbands' right to divorce for the plain reason that they were legally defined as their spouses' property. These laws prevailed until 1945.

Among Meiji's great concoctions was the "traditional Japanese woman." All women were "inside people" after 1868. The traditional woman was to be educated—so her children would be good imperial subjects. She was to be frugal—so her savings could finance industry. Above all, she was to manage the household, where her word was *tsuru no hitokoe,* the call of the crane—meaning, in old Japanese imagery, the final word. These arrangements were essential in the family-state, for the household was the building block of ideological Japan. The Education Ministry described the traditional woman as "Good Wife, Wise Mother," a phrase as familiar now as a century ago. The good and wise woman was essentially a civil servant. In *Meiji Greater Learning for Women,* the education bureaucrats put this point succinctly: "The home is a public place where private feelings should be forgotten."

To control the front door—to regain the distinction between the public and the private—has been among the central issues for women from Meiji until our own day.

In one obvious way the Meiji social architecture never actually applied. Industrialization was the enemy of the idealized woman. Women of the common classes had always worked—in shops and on farms, in primitive industries, as geisha in the urban pleasure quarters. After the restoration women became essential. In textiles, Japan's first great foreign exchange earner, the workforce was never less than 80 percent female. Early in our century Japan became the world leader in cotton textiles, a position it kept until its military endeavors of the late 1930s. So women gave Japan its first "number one." And industry's dependence on their nimble hands has been a tradition ever since—never more evident than in the age of chip assembly and consumer electronics.

The contradiction between the ideal and the reality made it all the more important to build "the traditional woman within," as the feminists of the 1970s called her. And we cannot lightly dismiss the attraction the concocted ideal held. Women had a recognized role, even if it was officially confined to the home. To have a sanctioned place in society, to be included in the idea of being Japanese, to participate in the construction of modern Japan—these were strong temptations for women as well as men. It is the same temptation evident today in women's confusion, and in phrases such as "men superior, women dominant."

In the debates after *A Doll's House* premiered in Tokyo there were many points of view. Early socialists cast the question of women in the larger context of capital and ownership. Conservatives considered "Good Wife, Wise Mother" to be just about right. Others argued for motherhood and state subsidies: the childbearer as government worker. A poet named Akiko Yosano argued for independence and equality of the sort Western feminists would easily recognize.

Akiko Yosano remains a hero of Japanese women. The League of Japanese Women Voters still sings one of Yosano's suffrage songs. But why? Why is she an icon?

Yosano ran away from home and married for love. She wrote daring poetry—personal, sensual, individualist. She had ten children by a temperamental writer jealous of her success. In her life and writing Yosano posed vital questions: What role should the state have in deciding how women lived? Could love, sexuality, marriage, and family be placed beyond the reach of political power? But these questions did not make Yosano a hero. Her heroism was the consequence of the way she lived, in a category of her own. She was like one of the record breakers that fascinated the Japanese after the war: the round-the-world sailor or the champion ice climber, someone to look up to but not to emulate or to follow.

And what of the women who favored the "good and wise" role during Yosano's time and after? Having no critique of imperial ideology and the nationalist regime, they ended up supplying spouses and sons for the war in the 1930s and 1940s and then cheering from the sidelines, because for the first time in history the imperial state had given them a *role*. The word leads us back to our earlier comparison with Kabuki. Women were finally able to play the women's parts, and this they called progress, even if the parts were grotesque.

Nora created a muddle among the Japanese, as imports often have. She became the model for the new woman, the urbanized female struggling out of the shadows and, sometimes at least, out the front door. Then came the new woman's daughter, who appeared during the 1920s as the *modan gaaru,* the modern girl. The modern girl had style and (in the popularly accepted version, at least) no politics. But she lived beyond the shaded interior, so presenting an implicit social challenge. She worked. Instead of marrying, the *modan gaaru* drank gin and nightclubbed in the Ginza; she wore flapper dresses and consumed with apparent abandon.

Japan did not know what to do with the *moga*, as she became known. So it made her a joke, deflecting the question of her psychological freedom. In comic strips and sensational newspaper stories the *moga* was reduced to a promiscuous, empty-headed slave to imported fashions. Tanizaki wrote a novel called *A Fool's Love* in the mid-1920s with a flighty *moga* named Naomi as its antagonist. By the standards of the day, Naomi acts like a man. The narrator is obsessed with her open sexuality. At the novel's end, he is reduced to supporting Naomi while she sleeps late, peruses *Vogue,* and conducts her varied affairs in a grand Western bed.

The *moga* had her activist side—or her activist sisters. By the close of the 1920s women had built a national movement to win the political franchise. In 1930 the Diet's lower house passed a bill giving it to them. But the next year the imperial army attacked the Chinese in Manchuria, beginning what the Japanese call the Fifteen-Year War. The feminist movement disappeared, and women went to work in munitions factories or prodded spouses and sons to distinguish themselves for the emperor. Universal suffrage was not to be for another fifteen years, when the occupation decreed it.

IN THE FIRST elections after the surrender, in April of 1946, two women out of three voted—all of them for the first time. They sent thirty-nine women to the Diet, giving women almost 10 percent of lower-house seats. But it was a proportion never again matched.

We have seen this pattern elsewhere—among labor unions, in the school system: a burst of energy, then a reversal. Postwar Japan soon sent women home for another round of "Good Wife, Wise Mother." They became the housewives of corporate samurai, then mass consumers and education mothers. The first three decades after the war are the only time in modern Japanese history that the number of women in the workforce declined.

But women were never true "inside people" again. They were active in local politics and community affairs. They vigorously opposed the reverse course in education—delaying, at least, the worst of it. When the rush into high growth put Japan among the earth's most polluted nations, women were essential to the nationwide movement that forced the first environmental laws onto the books.

In 1954 a group of Tokyo housewives formed a writing circle—a typical activity at the time. One member, a woman in her forties named Yasuko Awata, eventually published an essay called "The Awakening of Housewives and Their Small Happiness." It described the conflict women felt between the part they took in public affairs and their officially designated role—their small happiness, their "happiness in a hidden corner," as Awata also called it. It offers an acute insight into the novelty of selfhood after the war, especially among women. And it reveals the tension they still feel today between freedom and security, autonomy and belonging:

> Sometimes our public involvement gets us into trouble and we feel we would be better off without it. . . . On the other hand, if we immerse ourselves in our small happiness, we are disturbed by the feeling that we are not fulfilling our duties. . . . Until five years ago we were all . . . isolated individuals. But through our five years' work in various groups, we came to get at least a wider perspective from which to reexamine what our small happiness consists of.

The daughters of this generation became the feminists of the 1970s. And if Mrs. Awata had one among them, surely she understood the attack launched against "the traditional woman within," for she had begun in her gentle essay to question that very being. But four decades have passed since then, and despite the efforts of Mrs. Awata's feminist offspring, there has been no progress. In the 1990s women still wrestle with the temptations of happiness in a small corner.

The late 1980s were supposed to be the great watershed for women. In a 1990 general election voters sent almost fifty women to the Diet—6 percent of seats. The leader of women into the Nagatacho political elite was Takako Doi, who headed the Social Democrats. "The mountain has moved," Doi famously exclaimed. This was an adroit reference to an old but shiny shard of feminist history, a poem Akiko Yosano wrote in 1911, the year *A Doll's House* was staged. It is her best-known piece:

The day the mountains move has come.
I speak, but no one believes me.
For a time the mountains have been asleep,
But long ago they all danced with fire.
It doesn't matter if you believe this,
My friends, as long as you believe:
All the sleeping women
Are now awake and moving.

Many Japanese knew the verse and the inspiring story of Yosano's life. In eight lines she at once invoked the ancient vitality of Japanese women, the long, silent suffering that followed, and the animating optimism that has come and gone over and over from her time to ours. Takako Doi tapped into all of these. The woman most emblematic of a rising generation of female politicians declared that a long-held aspiration had just been fulfilled.

A few things survive from the years that followed. Women saw new issues onto the national agenda: legally mandated maternity leave; equitable tax treatment; compensation for "comfort women"—mostly Koreans and Chinese indentured as prostitutes for imperial troops during the Pacific war. Few such questions had even been discussed before the 1990 elections. And there has been progress in some of them, though not all.

But Doi was either reckless or deliberately misleading—or both. There was no poetry in women's predicament at that moment, only possibility. Doi merely invited women to do what the Japanese have often done when change seems imminent: to let dreams alone satisfy them, to be content with empty symbols, the appearance of change without the reality.

Women have not changed Nagatacho so much as they have been changed by it. Apart from their votes on certain issues, they have been unable to coalesce into an effective political force. Those who entered the Diet tended to be swallowed whole: some too privileged to understand discrimination, others unwilling to confront the elite who control the legislature. Nor did new Diet women want to risk disfavor in their districts by appearing too radical. Everyone in Japan knows the phrase *Onna no teki wa onna*—women's enemies are women—and it cannot be dismissed as the crudity of complacent mysogynists. It is the legacy of the "traditional Japanese woman," the ideal constructed after the restoration.

"I don't particularly want to think of myself as a woman. I like to think I'm an individual. And I don't like to raise 'women's issues.' I'm not especially interested in them." Wakako Hironaka, serving in the Diet's upper house, was fifty-nine when she made those assertions. Well bred, well dressed, and well traveled, she once told me that as a young woman she was like the young Betty Friedan: "an upper-crust woman without fulfillment." She was conversant with Ibsen's women—Hedda Gabler, Nora. She had lived in America off and on for two decades, beginning with a stay on a New Hampshire farm after university graduation, in 1958.

"While living in America I looked at Japan for the first time," Hironaka once said. Then she made a comparison: "Some Western women felt like Ibsen's heroines. But I couldn't imagine my mother feeling that way. In Japan, although the position of husband and wife was very structured, she controlled the family, and there were many important things to do around the house and in the community.

"Then I thought of American women. At the farm in New Hampshire, the husband was the authority. But the wife was just as powerful. Everyone had a role. I thought, Same situation. When a woman has a role, she's confident. That was the situation in Japan a century ago. My mother was like that. There were many strong women during Meiji, women we could count on, in spite of the feudal system."

Hironaka was silent for a moment. Then she said, a bit sullenly, "The change came after the war."

"What happened then?"

"Women lost their inner strength."

"They 'lost their inner strength'? What caused that?"

"The constraints of society make women strong. They give women dignity, as opposed to a *Doll's House* situation, when Nora left her family. In other words, I'm not the kind of person who pushes for rights."

I MET WAKAKO Hironaka in an interesting way. She was lecturing at a school for women who wanted to enter politics. The school, the first of its kind in Japan, or perhaps anywhere, was started by an opposition party, the New Japan Party, after the 1990 elections. Hironaka made an odd instructor. Product of a privileged family, she was given to the samurai formalism of the great tradition. Few in her audience shared such a background. She preached a version of "Men superior, women dominant." But this, the samuraization of women, was the very reason they needed a school to learn how to enter politics.

What were ordinary women really doing at the moment Hironaka addressed them? At some point in the mid-1970s women reversed the postwar pattern and returned to work in large numbers. By 1990 two of every three worked: 25 million women, 40 percent of the labor force. But look closely at a few more numbers. A quarter of women employed in 1990 worked part-time. Eight part-timers of ten were women. The number of women employed part-time roughly doubled in the decade and a half after 1975, during which Japan turned itself into a powerful manufacturer. Part-time workers enjoy poor benefits, if any. In a nation where women's wages are roughly half of men's, women working part-time earn three-quarters of a full-time woman's wage rate—slightly more than a third of a man's wage. It is no surprise to discover that the demand for part-time female labor has been more or less limitless. By 1990 there were three openings for every applicant; the recession that followed diminished demand but otherwise changed nothing. Part-time women are like *kuroko* on the Kabuki stage of industry: essential but unacknowledged.

Why did this situation come to be? How did Japan manage to turn women into a new version of the Meiji textile workers?

"A country's tax regime is an expression of how it really views things," Wakako Hironaka once told me. Assuming that to be so, it is worth considering a system that allows women a tax exemption if they earn less than a million yen yearly, about $10,000, and penalizes households in which the wife brings home more than that. The incentive is evident: Women are encouraged to assume part-time work but discouraged from developing careers. It is a pin-money mentality. Women call the tax statutes "the million yen wall."

Wakako Hironaka spoke of the tax system with approval. It encouraged women to go to work, she said. Yes, only part-time, she allowed, but it treated women as individuals, not just as family members—and that, she said, was the important thing. The tax system is the perfect example of how women are a gear in an intricate machine. To alter it is to change the way industry works and to begin the task of dismantling the "traditional Japanese woman" as a social pillar. The tax issue, still sitting in the Diet, will eventually be resolved. But it is hard to see what women such as Wakako Hironaka will have to do with resolving it.

Japan remembers the 1990 elections and the years afterward as "the madonna boom." The national newspapers invented the term to trivialize the election results, as they had the *modan gaaru* of the 1920s and the feminists of a half century later. The "madonna" who got more attention than any other was named Mariko Mitsui. And it was precisely because what she said and stood for was not easily dismissed that she was made into a walking symbol of the boom in political madonnas. After the 1990 elections the big dailies took to calling her *gonso madonna,* the original madonna.

"We need a new strategy, new priorities, new thinking, new ways of putting issues on the agenda," Mitsui once told me. "There are no effective laws now, no public policies. We're not accustomed to raising new issues. But if you don't raise an issue, it's not an issue."

What happens to women who say such things, who are intelligent enough, or honest enough about themselves and Japan, to see the yawning chasm between the ideal and the real, and to see that little can be accomplished within the idea of "Men superior, women dominant"?

Mitsui was forty-four: slight, eternally tired, but always vibrant. In her clear, striking features one saw the old sun shine. She was as much a woman of the countryside as Wakako Hironaka was of the city. A grocer's daughter from the poor north, she did not know inequality until she went to Tokyo after university to look for work. Like Hironaka, Mitsui had lived in America, but Mitsui's America was not Hironaka's. Mitsui had spent her time on barricades and marches; she had lobbied for abortion rights, equal employment, the environment. Speaking of those years, Mitsui described an awakening. American women amazed her with their commitment, she said once. I think she meant their assertiveness, their rejection of passivity. And it was among Americans that Mitsui looked back at Japan and made her first political plans.

When she ran for a seat in the Tokyo Metropolitan Assembly, she set herself apart from the somber flock of candidates with garish red clothes and a concern for feminist questions. She spoke to her constituents— women to whom "Men superior, women dominant" meant only unshared housework and the million-yen wall—in blunt Japanese free of the gender-laden syntax of everyday speech. Elected in 1987, she forced the assembly to drop an old, demeaning term for women from official documents. She refused the green tea served by old women during assembly sessions. These were gestures. While making them Mitsui fought for reform of communal property laws, protection against domestic abuse, and a national alliance of women lawmakers. After a time she aspired to the Diet.

Mitsui's most celebrated act was her break with the Social Democrats, in 1993, when she abruptly charged several colleagues with sexual harassment. The political world was stunned; her supporters felt betrayed. This was the party of Takako Doi. It was Mitsui's only access to the sort of money she needed to find her way into national politics. "There is no allowance for free discussion or debate among the Social Democrats," she explained to her supporters one evening. "Democratic politics cannot issue from such an inflexible organization. If we expect innovative policies from the Social Democrats, we are dreaming." I recall thinking that Mitsui met both her political future and her future as a Japanese woman that evening. At that moment she entered the aloneness that seemed to have been waiting for her all along. She became another Akiko Yosano, the early feminist poet, or another Michiko Fukushima, the filmmaker who left her family behind.

Mitsui's bid for the Diet, as an independent with no political machine behind her, went nowhere. She could be faulted for her theatrics. And she imported too many of her ideas—a familiar mistake. In her books—she had written several—she held up Americans for their legislation, Norwegians for equalities already achieved. She interviewed Madeleine Kunin, then the governor of Vermont, and Gro Harlem Brundtland, the prime minister of Norway. I imagined Mitsui in these encounters, bent forward in the posture of the student before the teacher. She offered Japanese women gaijin as models, as they were models for her. This was not enough. But she followed her ideas to their logical end. She had endeavored to explore a broken world and then began the work of fixing it. She made herself a person she could respect. These were worthy things.

IN 1992 THE emperor's eldest son, Crown Prince Naruhito, married a commoner named Masako Owada. Owada was a twenty-nine-year-old bureaucrat at the Foreign Ministry, a linguist who had attended Harvard. The newspapers and networks had a field day with Owada-san, as she was known to all Japanese. Their stories and broadcasts about her shoes, handbags, and scarves bordered on fetishism. They turned her wedding into a kind of morality play about women in Japan.

Masako Owada was something new in the imperial family: a modern woman with overseas exposure, a diplomatic career, and an intellect she did not feel compelled to disguise. One could applaud these things. But the media, which never stray far from official opinion, were bent on reassuring Japan that roles were not being abandoned, lines were not being crossed. Television clips about Owada's overseas education, her several languages, or her foreign friends usually ended with something like, "But she can also cook!" or, "She's a good homemaker, too!" A few weeks after the royal engagement was announced a headline appeared: CROWN PRINCE WON OWADA'S HEART AFTER PROMISING TO PROTECT HER. This was published on page one, above the fold, in the *Asahi Shimbun*. Protect her from whom? As everyone understood, from the Imperial Household Agency, keeper of the royal family. As everyone also knew, the agency, with its fetishistic insistence on the old formalities, had years earlier driven Naruhito's mother, the reigning empress, to a nervous breakdown.

By all accounts Owada had resisted the prince's proposal until the pressures to accept—from the royal family, her own, and the Foreign Ministry—left her little choice. After that her public story took shape. It began with notions of "imperial diplomacy" and a mere shift in jobs, for Owada was somehow to maintain her professional role. The story ended a few months later with explanations of why her hats and makeup would require approval from the Imperial Household Agency, how long her skirts would have to be, and how many steps behind her husband she would walk.

The intended lesson was simple and familiar: Institutions still changed people in Japan, as they always had, and it would never be the reverse. Even Owada's appearance reflected this—an important point in a culture that stresses form as much as substance. Her wardrobe went from efficient professional to dowdy matron; her once-animated face seemed fixed with a complex, troubled smile, like those on the ancient Noh masks now preserved in museums as national treasures.

Women, especially those of Owada's generation, attached great symbolic importance to the royal wedding. This was a mistake from the beginning, surely: What royal union is ever likely to signal fundamental change in the lives of men and women together? Far before his time, Soseki Natsume had offered a superb image of the loveless individual in modern Japan; it is, again, the observation of *Kokoro*'s narrator concerning K: "It was as though his heart was encrusted with a layer of black lacquer, so thick that no warm blood could ever penetrate through it." Soseki described the samuraization of feeling and intimacy. And that is what the royal wedding was made to stand for: the formality of the past brought into the present, the superiority of reverence over individual love.

Women had begun careers by the 1990s. Three percent of lawyers were women, and 3 percent of chemical engineers; one civil engineer in two hundred was a woman. At the time Owada-san married her prince, women held slightly less than 3 percent of management slots. (These proportions represented considerable improvements.) But all the imagery associated with the time—the self-conscious executive fashion, the ubiquitous profiles of high-flying career women, the go-it-alone "lifestyle" magazines—was eventually recognized as so much *omote*—surface, front, presentation. The *ura,* the invisible back, proved rather grimmer. How serious about advancing women was a society in which day care was almost unheard of, in which nursery schools opened too late for the children of working women and closed too early? Lifetime employment and advancement by seniority—hallmarks of corporate life—are simply not practices geared to women. Neither are obligatory drinking sessions after work or the long commutes caused by high land prices. To alter the position of women meant, as it always had, altering too many other aspects of the system.

I once put this to Kay Itoi, my colleague during my years at the *Herald Tribune.* It turned out to be a propitious moment for such a conversation. She had just rented a new apartment and was unable to sign the lease until her father guaranteed it. Kay was bitter. "An older brother would've been O.K., but never an older sister." Then she said, "It's all proven to be so superficial for women who began in the nineteen eighties. We have no models, no one to pass laws that protect us." I told Kay about Michiko Fukushima. She said, "Someone like that looks stupid to younger women. They'd say, 'She's given up too much—and for what?' They can't relate to anything she's done. They don't understand hard work or sacrifice for the sake of achievement. It's too difficult to live as a single woman in Japan. We live in a society made for dependents."

And a society of dependents is not a society in which love and intimacy flourish. A dependent person is neither loving nor lovable, after all.

In 1993 I met a woman who made a thriving business out of the emotional problems of the urban Japanese. This became possible, I was convinced, only at this time, when such problems were more acute than ever and when the Japanese seemed finally prepared to face them. Satsuki

Ohiwa was a sign of her times. She was not a psychiatrist, though she functioned somewhat like one. "What we do is present human love to our customers," Ohiwa explained soon after I entered her office. But who were her customers? "Our customers are people who want to enjoy life and are full of the feelings of human love."

Neither did Ohiwa run the kind of business one might assume from this exchange. Japan Effectiveness Headquarters, Japan Success President: The names of her enterprises, despite their oddly combined foreign words, suggested something purposeful. So did Ohiwa, a trim, intense woman with short, briskly brushed hair and oversized eyeglasses. She was direct and determined, and pleased that she had mastered in herself the inbred reticence of the Japanese in public. She said, "In the eighties people began to say, 'Human beings are important. Individuals are important.' But Japan still thought about material wealth alone. People had no idea how to live any other way—how to communicate their feelings, their individuality. We decided to provide actual services, not just an idea."

Ohiwa started by training *sararimen,* after realizing that many of them had not the vaguest idea of how to interact with others. They had been through the rigors of the school system and the corporate advancement rituals; most had married and begun families. Yet they remained unformed as personalities. She taught the same things offered by the management institute at the foot of Mount Fuji: courtesy, voice modulation, and so on. After a time this sort of fix did not seem enough. So she burrowed further into the problem.

"The instruction we provide cannot be grasped without an understanding of human beings," she said. "So we try to explain the machinery of the body—the essence of human desires and how they are manifest, the essence of human emotion and how it changes. Basics. Then we teach people how to express themselves. Now, totally free self-expression can be simple selfishness. So before we teach people how to express themselves we teach the basics of humanity—how to coexist with others, even the joy of making others happy."

Ohiwa prospered in her peculiar trade—making humans of the dehumanized. And from her contact with *sararimen* she discovered another need. We can call this end of the business "rent-a-family." Confronted with the emptiness and disorientation of the urban Japanese, their half-hidden but pervasive sadness, she began a subsidiary that provided professional actors ("entertainers," she called them) to clients who missed having certain family members—real or merely desired—around the house. The most common case was to provide a young couple and child to an elderly man and wife. The second-most-popular request was the reverse: young couples who wanted their children to have grandparents. Third: singles who wanted families. "A man will ask for a wife and child so he can go on a picnic."

Ohiwa had a waiting list of a hundred clients. Each would pay 120,000 yen, not quite $1,200, for an initial visit (of five hours), and then less for two or three visits per month. As a business, she said, it did not pay. "We hope people won't always need this service. But we do it because it's something people do need now."

"Why?"

"Japan is that kind of society. Human love is basic to any society, but it is forgotten here."

"Why do people see this now?"

Ohiwa went back to her initial point. "Japan has been a country where adults express their love with material gifts. We in our thirties and forties were children who received love in the form of things. We did the same to our children once we became parents. What happened in the nineteen eighties? Among other things, people realized material goods alone don't make them happy. They have begun to see what they've forgotten—or what they never had. They don't know what to do about it yet. They're not sure. But renting a family is one of the things they've done."

It is odd by any measure to hire out people to assuage one's loneliness. But it is not difficult to understand the impulse behind such an enterprise—not when we consider Ohiwa's point about the human cost of the drive for economic success after the war. In 1963 the Harvard scholar Ezra Vogel published a book called *Japan's New Middle Class*. It is an account of the postwar *sarariman* culture based on a year spent living in a Tokyo suburb. Although written with evident approval, it describes urban families suffering some degree of dysfunction. It describes husbands and wives who are strangers to each other. It describes not just a division of labor between men and women, but a division of consciousness:

> The salary man is essentially free when he returns home; home is a place to relax. . . . However, the wife generally knows little and cares less about her husband's daily activities at the office.

The husband's assignments in the company generally are limited, and the problems in which the husband is interested at work have little meaning to the wife. Even if a curious young wife expresses an interest in her husband's work, he has difficulty explaining his work in a way that she can understand. . . . Because she is so completely separated from the husband's daily world and he knows so little about her community activities, the area of mutual interest tends to be the children and the relatives.

To dwell upon damaged families and the extremes of lovelessness is to portray a nation of suffering people—to provide a picture that may be discounted as an extreme in itself. This is not my intention. But we cannot be surprised at the prevalence of lovelessness, sweeping as such an observation may seem, in a society that long turned human ties, even those behind the front door of the home, into matters of form—political relationships. The great book of imperial ideology, *Kokutai no Hongi*, was widely read by ordinary Japanese, essentially as an instruction manual for living, until 1945. Its authors were careful to devalue the private relationship between husband and wife, lest love disrupt the ideological project. Love, along with individuality, was cast as another unwanted Western notion, harmful to social harmony. The family was not to rest "on such a thing as individual or correlative love." It was to rest upon "reverence and affection." And it was not so different after the war.

We commonly describe Japan as a society that serves the corporation and not the individual—"rich Japan, poor Japanese," a long-accepted cliché. What do we mean? The material burdens imposed upon the Japanese—the sacrifices and deprivations of daily life, the intense pressures to conform, all of which are also well known and often noted—must be understood to have consequences other than those that are apparent. The material burdens are pervasive. We should assume the spiritual burdens are equally so. Otherwise we have satisfied ourselves with another image of an imagined "Japan."

THERE IS AN interesting comparison to be made between women in Japan today and the women who wrote the classics that reflected the flowering of culture at the Heian court. Women were freer than men when Shikibu Murasaki wrote the *Tale of Genji*. They experimented with hiragana, the new system of Japanese script, which had a liberating ef-fect. Men were still in thrall to Chinese tradition. They committed the borrowed canon to memory and then copied it in dry treatises and vapid verse, using Chinese that was half a millennium old. Only if they wanted to write of something immediate or sensual did they use hiragana, and then they posed as women. Women were innovators, men prisoners of the orthodoxy.

There is a parallel today. Women travel abroad more than men. They experiment in their careers more frequently. They are more curious and seem psychologically freer than men—more agile in their lives, more flexible, imaginative, and adventurous. This was immediately apparent when I arrived in Tokyo, and the explanation is simple: Women are not required to participate directly in economic life, the core of the modern orthodoxy. The average length of service among continuously employed women is slightly more than seven years. Like women of the Heian aristocracy, they are not bound to social prescriptions as strictly as men and are more receptive to shifts in the social and cultural wind.

The comparison is usefully extended. The women of the Heian aristocracy were not truly independent or autonomous. Their freedom was attenuated, even artificial. For all but a few women it is again the same today. After a brief hesitation, most choose, instead of autonomy, a pleasantly furnished version of the far depths, as Junichiro Tanizaki put it, the interior of Japanese life. As Kay Itoi explained, they do not understand those among them such as Michiko Fukushima. Such women are mysteries.

Japanese women have come to complain in ever shriller tones about the emotional inadequacies of men. They cast men as feelingless dolts, bores with no human sympathies. This is why young women marry later, or set out not to marry at all, or why they hesitate, like Nobuko, before passing through the door to the life summed up in the phrase *Dansei joi, josei yui*, Men superior, women dominant. It is in these complaints and hesitations, or in the few years of false freedom, that we find a suggestion of the future.

What do women mean when they ridicule men as dullards, people who can never remove their masks? What is the core of their critique? Not simply men, surely, but the subjection of men to the social orthodoxy—which is different. Women cannot progress in Japanese society, they seem now to say, until men progress, and neither can progress until the notions of "small happiness" and "dominant" but unequal women are discarded. It is likely that women will lead Japan to an answer to this essential conundrum. If they do it will be because they learned what Michiko Fukushima, or Mariko Mitsui, or the feminists of the 1970s, have had to teach: that there is no changing others before one changes oneself. And it is by such a realization that women can shape their own feminism, a Japanese feminism, for the first time.

6

CONCRETE

AND DEMOCRACY

Japan can't get along without borrowing from the West. But it
poses as a first-class power. And it's straining to join the ranks of
the first-class powers. That's why, in every direction, it puts up
the facade of a first-class power and cheats on what's behind.

— SOSEKI NATSUME,
And Then, 1909

A STORIED OLD road called the Tokaido runs southwest from Tokyo. It
was built by the Tokugawa shogun to connect Edo to Osaka (the
commercial hub) and Kyoto (the imperial seat). The Tokaido was the
backbone of late feudal Japan, like Rome's Appian Way. It carried the
daimyo from their fiefdoms to Edo for required periods of residence in
the capital. It was celebrated in the prints of Hiroshige, and in a
Chauceresque satire called *Shank's Mare.* A photograph taken just before
the restoration shows a broad dirt path lined with high pines. Two samurai, with topknots and swords, stand in the center. Here and there
commoners carry baskets on poles across their shoulders, or rest along
the roadside. Though indistinguishable now in the tangle of highways
emanating from the capital, the Tokaido still follows its original course.

The northern end, running straight into the Ginza district, is Tokyo's best-known shopping street.

The Tokaido is modern Japan's landward boundary. It is roughly between the Tokaido and the Pacific that the Japanese built *omote nihon,* the front of Japan. All the rest became *ura nihon,* the back of Japan. The restoration did not create this internal divide. Meiji was more in the way of a geographic revolution. For the many centuries Japan learned from China, the Pacific coast was the back of Japan, and the countryside along the Japan Sea the front. When Japan turned to the West in the last century, back became front and vice versa. On one side of the Tokaido the Japanese made themselves modern, while on the other they were supposed to stand still.

The term *ura nihon* is considered slightly impolite today. N.H.K., the state broadcasting network, banned the expression from the air some years ago. It once meant the poor villages along the Sea of Japan, isolated from civilization, battered by Siberian snows. But when *ura nihon* is used today it implies more than a geographic area. The better translation is "hidden Japan"—the Japan of bamboo groves, rice terraces, and one-lane tracks, of fireflies, the smell of straw, and raw rice wine. *Ura nihon* is village Japan— all that the modern Japanese sought to escape. There is another term whose evolution makes the point perfectly: *inaka.* A rural official once told me its characters came from ideograms that signified a rice terrace with a building next to it. In the dictionary I use it is "one's home, one's native place." A farmer I met said it meant "not Tokyo." It is generally taken today to mean "the countryside," but if you ask any ordinary city dweller he is as likely to tell you the *inaka* is "the sticks" or "the boondocks," with all the condescension these terms imply.

It is possible to live in Japan many years without venturing much beyond the Tokaido. Japan encourages such an existence because it has been so centralized for so long and because *omote nihon* still wants to persuade you that modern, technocratic Japan is Japan. Traveling with Tokyo friends, I often discovered on the way to Kyushu or Hokkaido or most places in between that they had never been there. They would know Honolulu or New York but not Sapporo or Kanazawa or even Niigata, which is a couple of hours by bullet train from the capital. But you cannot accept the inertia the city encourages and understand even the city itself, for when Japan became modern it made the city and the countryside mirrors of each other.

For many generations *ura nihon* really was "not Tokyo"—all that Tokyo was not, a good definition. For the millions of new urban dwellers streaming in from the countryside the old villages became anchors, places where, they imagined, everything remained as they had left it. The village had to stand still for the simple reason that the city was in constant motion. To recall the village, even as one rejected it, was a defense against urban disorder, strange neighbors, and the sensation of living in a world made of borrowed things and ideas. How is it that people said to be so ungiven to change are so faithful, even frantic, in following the latest trends and products and fashions? The question could have been asked at any point over many decades and would have yielded the same answer: because the immutable village was ever present in the urban imagination. The traditional farmhouse has next to it a *kura,* a building of thick walls with one or two tiny windows cut into them. It is where the farming family stores valuables and heirlooms. This was *ura nihon,* the land outside the Tokaido: It was the *kura* of modern Japan, where the old customs were supposed to be uncorrupted and where *ninjo,* human feelings, the sentiments buried beneath the formality of modern life, were unobstructed by fences in the heart.

The Tokaido, then, has been more than a geographic boundary, or a divide between two economies. It is a kind of emotional border, too, a physical representation of something otherwise unseen. For between modern and unmodern Japan lies not just an ancient road but the tension of a divided national character. The Japanese have always thought of the front of Japan, the westernized and samuraized part, as a world without feeling: rational, scientific, calculating, capitalist, masculine. And in *ura nihon* they sought the communal, the nurturing, the intuitive, the sentimental, and the feminine—what they considered a truer, natural version of themselves.

The most famous journey in modern Japanese writing starts at Ueno Station in northeast Tokyo and ends in *ura nihon.* "The train came out of the long tunnel into the snow country," Yasunari Kawabata began his best-known novel. Every Japanese understands this simple sentence. *Snow Country* records a passage between two worlds. Its protagonist is a modern Japanese completely detached from his life in Tokyo—a dance critic who has never attended a ballet. At a hot spring in the cold, remote mountains a geisha opens the door upon a life of natural ease and intimacy. In these two characters lies the discord between what the Japanese made of themselves and what they had been. Written over a long period in the 1930s and 1940s,

Snow Country derives its power from the impenetrable barrier it depicts: the inaccessibility of the past—a past that Kawabata mourned on behalf of many modern Japanese.

Japan will no doubt always entertain a certain sentimentality about its countryside, just as Americans treasure the town meetings they will never attend and the English love the brick-and-flint cottages they are never likely to live in. But the great divide between city and country is disappearing—for better or worse. It is not simply because the urban centers are sprawling outward, though they are, but because the Japanese have accepted the truth of Kawabata's book: There is no going back, only forward from where they have come to. So the front and back of Japan have begun to resemble parts of a single country, just as the Japanese have stopped looking across the Tokaido to discover who they are.

In *A Wild Sheep Chase*, the 1982 novel by Haruki Murakami, there is another train ride out from Tokyo, remarkable (when put next to Kawabata's famous account) for its utter lack of sentiment. During his journey the narrator scarcely bothers to look out the window. Instead he puzzles over an obscure history of the village he is heading toward. The book he found of desultory interest. "But if the truth be known, Junitaki today was a dreadfully dull town," he observes. "The townfolk, when they came home from work, watched an average of four hours of television before going to bed each night."

THE TOWN OF Kakeya lies in a valley amid the desolate hills of Shimane Prefecture, in southwestern Honshu. Though hardly a hive of activity, it is nonetheless one of Shimane's healthiest towns. Kakeya is where the family of Noboru Takeshita, prime minister in the late 1980s, has brewed sake since 1866. Takeshita was kind to his hometown during his long years as a Tokyo politician—kind to a fault. For some miles before you arrive all the hillsides are neatly concreted. So is every riverbank and irrigation ditch. In the village off the main route, signs worthy of an expressway indicate narrow lanes; a bridge leading out to a few farms scattered along the valley floor could handle rush-hour traffic in Tokyo. Takeshita's kindness has made Kakeya a little ridiculous. But there is no poverty. Every house has a television antenna, every driveway a late-model car, and the shops along the abbreviated commercial streets are full of the latest gadgets from the other side of the Tokaido.

A town such as Kakeya would have looked very different at various moments in the past. In the Edo era it would have grown rice, of course. But its peasants would also have made a few things—paper, perhaps, or textiles or ceramics or ironware—and traded them with neighboring villages where other things were made. Kakeya would have had its own identity, even a certain autonomy, in a district that was, apart from the intrusions of Edo bureaucrats and the rice tributes due the local daimyo, more or less self-contained. There might have been a few products made in the emerging commercial centers, but only a few.

Kakeya would have changed after the restoration. It became part of the new Japan, and the new Japan made all its decisions in Tokyo. There would have been no question of autonomy, or a regional trading system, or any sort of distinct identity. Products from large new enterprises elsewhere, along with imports from the West, would have flooded the local market. The simple industries that could not compete would have disappeared. Locals who made marketable products would be integrated into the new national economy with cash infusions from distant investors. They would have made the same things, but those things would have been sold off someplace far distant, and profits would no longer have stayed in Kakeya.

Tokyo was quick to make peasants landowners after 1868. It was also quick to tax them—and not on the yearly yield, as the daimyo had taxed, but on land values, good crop or bad. Feudalism was gone, but the cash economy and the Meiji land reform led only to a new kind of desperation. Many farmers sold land a piece at a time and sent their daughters off to work in factories. Mortgage debt and foreclosures created wealthy, usurious landlords and poor tenants. Kakeya would have been crowded with struggling farmers and landless idlers—idle because dispossessions occurred more rapidly than the economy produced new jobs. Amid all the modernization, the Kakeya peasant was still where he always had been: a foot in the past, at the bottom of the pile.

That is how Tokyo "cheated on what's behind." The new economic arrangements did little for the villages. And the Meiji land settlement turned out to be one of prewar Japan's most tragic mistakes—leading it, in no small way, to war. Rural poverty kept the home market small, making markets overseas a growing necessity. By 1930 70 percent of farmers were sharecroppers who could no longer buy much of anything but who dreamed always of land. It was in those straitened circumstances that despairing tillers, the less thoughtful captains of industry, and sentimental militarists found sympathy for one another, and a common enthusiasm for an expanded empire.

Things changed again after the defeat in 1945. Land reform was among the occupation's most effective policies, immune even to the reverse course. Absentee landlords were banished and tenants were propertied again. The drain of people from farm to city swelled to a river after the war, as we have noted. But Tokyo made rural life manageable, even comfortable, with price supports, import protection against foreign farm products, subsidies, and vast public-works budgets. This was a great reversal. In effect, the countryside began to live off the capital after centuries during which it was the other way around.

But Tokyo cheated again after the war, for one thing did not change. Kakeya and the rest of village Japan did not become part of the modern economy, the postwar miracle. The countryside remained, so to say, in the cyclical time of the peasant. Even today Kakeya is a dependent, a ward of the state. That is why there are still two industries in Kakeya besides the Takeshita family's brewery: rice farming and construction subsidized by the central government. One is much older than the other, but both reflect established traditions.

Noboru Takeshita was mired in many scandals when I visited Kakeya, each more revealing of Tokyo's political malaise than the one before. The rest of Japan had had enough of him—he was long out of office—but he was still the patron of Kakeya. Along the streets and in the shops he seemed to be accepted as some cross between a political boss, a daimyo, and a peasant who did not forget his *ninjo* when he went off to the modern city. Local people did not believe in the scandals—or so they said. Takeshita had come to Kakeya for a few hours the night before I arrived. He gave a speech in the local hall, and people believed him when he told them the newspapers and networks had made up the scandals. Takeshita was a man worthy of trust and respect, the local folk told me again and again. But they would not give their names, and when I asked what else he had said the previous evening people told me curtly to read it in the newspapers—the newspapers that had created the scandals.

The town hall was of recent vintage. I had no appointment with the mayor, but he received me in his large, simple office as soon as I said I wanted to talk about Takeshita. Yoshio Ochiai was sixty-seven, roughly

Takeshita's age. He had tufty eyebrows and a deeply lined face. "It would be disrespectful to say I was a friend," the mayor told me with boyish humility, "but when I was twenty we were in a youth club together." This fact stood for itself so far as the mayor was concerned, a kind of validation. The mayor told me that the construction ministry and other Tokyo agencies gave Kakeya at least 200 million yen a year, almost half the town's budget. That seemed to stand for itself, too, and upon delivering this news, Yoshio Ochiai smiled.

Mayor Ochiai's smile was the wry smile the countryside often offers the other side of Japan. People in Kakeya accepted the handouts from Tokyo because they needed them. But no one seemed especially grateful for all the money, for the simple reason that they would rather not need it. No one, perhaps not even the mayor, precisely liked the man who sent Kakeya so much concrete. They would never acknowledge disliking him, and I doubted they did, at least not actively. But the praise was faint. People preferred to talk about the family sake, which no one especially liked, as if it could be made to stand for the man. At the brewery, a place of old vats and wooden paddles behind mud-and-plaster walls, no one would talk about Takeshita, so I asked about the sake. There was a long moment of hesitation. Finally, a young man in an apron and a cloth cap said, "I can't tell you it's bad, because I'm not supposed to. But"—he paused again—"we're a small brewery."

Two hundred million yen, about $2 million, is a handsome subsidy for a town of forty-three hundred people. The local school is modern and well kept, as are the streetlights, the police station, and everything else Tokyo paid for before the town ran out of projects and the spending turned to bridges with steel I beams and heavy guardrails. Kakeya is special, the hometown of a man long noted for his ability to raise and disperse political funds. But there are towns with less money and the same problems all over rural Japan, where funds from Tokyo are accepted with subtle, unstated resentment. Even Kakeya's money has not given it the ability to make a life for itself. Kakeya, like much of *ura nihon,* is a well-dressed welfare case.

The countryside has never recovered from the breathtaking wave of urbanization that began after the war. Fifteen percent fewer people live in Shimane now than in 1949—an extraordinary decline when one considers that Japan's population grew by three-quarters during this period. Shimane is among the poorest prefectures, but it is otherwise unexceptional. In one way or another, most of Japan outside the Tokaido beltway engages in a day-to-day, year-to-year struggle against social and economic erosion.

One of Noboru Takeshita's most famous policies was called *furusato,* old hometown—a term with a clear echo in the past. *Furusato* was an agrarian ideal invoked during the later Meiji decades. The hometown was always a reliable place to withdraw from foreign habits and industrialization and all that went with them—from the "other" that modern Japan was making of itself. Early in our century, when *furusato* was the sentimental rage among anti-Western ideologues, a Tokyo professor advocated an arresting response to the modern city's rise: The Japanese should boycott the cities by refusing to send them any more people. Then the cities would disappear, and Japan would go on being Japan.

Takeshita's plan, intended to revive rural Japan, was only slightly less dreamlike. He gave every town and village in the country—thirty-three hundred in all—a gift from the national treasury of roughly $1 million. The towns were to use it to make themselves more attractive to people from the cities. But what did they do? One village took residents on helicopter rides. Another bought gold. Another sent housewives on European vacations. Another spent half its windfall on a study to determine how to spend the other half. Though in the end Takeshita was simply trying to buy votes in the bluntest way possible, it was interesting to see where a prime minister in the late twentieth century located the soft spots in the popular consciousness. More interesting still was the extent to which he no longer understood either the urban imagination or the people living in the old hometowns.

TO GO BEYOND the Tokaido for the first time gives the sensation of entering another country. The scattered cities are jammed with the same cheap construction, cars, shops, neon signs, and game parlors that you find along the Pacific coast. And the occasional towns along the main roads are smaller versions of the same thing. Concrete electricity poles, with tangles of wires between them, clog the view from any street, just as they do in Tokyo or Osaka or Nagoya. But it is different, nonetheless, because the back of Japan was, so to say, colonized by the front. While Tokyo excluded the countryside from the new, ambitious Japan, it did manage to turn the other side of the Tokaido into an internal periphery. Nothing that is modern is precisely indigenous to *ura nihon.* It wears the architecture and artifacts of modern Japan the way India or Singapore assumed the red mailboxes and neoclassical buildings of imperial Britain—awkwardly, uncomfortably, incongruously.

Much of *ura nihon* is still untouched, verdant, and uncrowded. There are villages so detached from the frenzy of Tokyo or Osaka as to confirm the impression that they are removed in time as well as in space. In Yamagata Prefecture, far to the north of Shimane, there are three mountains held to be sacred by Buddhists and Shintoists. From one you can look south onto vast plains of rice terraces, each neatly bordered with summer grasses, and begin to understand something of the impulse to keep the countryside from changing. It is like looking into another century. And who among us is untempted by the dream of keeping the clock of technological progress from running, or turning it back?

But when you see modern Japan pay for unmodern Japan so that it will remain as it is, you recognize the cruelty of such an act, because it turns the countryside into a museum and its people into exhibits intended to give others the illusion that they can still claim to be what they once were.

There are forgotten villages in rural Japan, where the fuel pumps are abandoned and the streets deserted even at noon. There are others so remote in the mountains that people move into the valleys for the long months of snow, returning home only for the growing season. These are just as important, to the urban imagination, as the villages in snow country rich enough in subsidies to heat their streets in the winter. Few villages are as well off as Kakeya, but many are favored by hometown politicians doing well in Tokyo. Only slowly does it emerge that the *inaka* is a patient suffering a progressive disease. Subsidies keep the patient alive: Shimane gets back almost four times what it sends Tokyo in taxes. But subsidies do not keep the rail stations open, or houses occupied, or young people in the village.

In the mountains of Kyushu there is a village called Oguni, surrounded by dense cedar forests. Oguni must have been used to the old days, when the countryside was crowded with dispossessed farmers and the unemployed: For a long time the town was pleased to see people take jobs in the cities. After the war the young people who went away were called "golden eggs" because they sent part of their wages home every month. This went on until 1960 or so, when there were sixteen thousand people in Oguni. Then the tide turned. When I went there three decades later the population was down to ten thousand and no one spoke of golden eggs anymore. The money orders families received from their young were like the remittances wired home by expatriate Pakistanis or Filipinos working in the Middle East. Oguni had 150 high-school graduates in 1990, and thirteen hundred companies came to recruit them. Half the graduating class left as soon as school ended, and most of the rest drifted away within a few months. Oguni now dreams of keeping its young, or getting them to return—a phenomenon called "U-turn." There are U-turn cases here and there around rural Japan, but not many—and almost none in Oguni. Its median age was fifty when I last visited. It had shut its rail station six years earlier, and the town planner was struggling to save the bus service that had replaced it.

Villages invent many schemes to stay alive. These often reflect the submerged desire to regain some sense of the old identity and autonomy. In Oguni people showed me a locally developed architecture—domes made of interlocking beams—that they hoped would revive demand for cedar. A new dairy produced cheddar and Gouda cheeses ambitiously labeled in English and French. Elsewhere in the countryside there are vineyards and wineries, indoor orange groves, exotic mushroom farms. There are many examples of desperate extremes. A village in Yamagata, most of its women gone to the cities, recruited Filipinas to marry some of its two hundred brideless farmers. Another, in Toyama Prefecture, planted thousands of camellias and launched an annual flower festival, hoping to make itself famous; then it held a national songwriting contest; then a lottery with plots of land as prizes. During the bubble a well-known actor spent $15 million on a project—failed—to buy a Scottish castle, haul it across Siberia stone by stone, and reassemble it to improve the attractions of his hometown in Hokkaido.

In Inokuchi, the village that planted the flowers and held the lottery, timber-and-plaster houses with ceramic roofs announced a prosperous community. It was spring when I arrived, so the rice paddies were flooded up to front doors and the edges of driveways. But Inokuchi offered the familiar tale of the *inaka*. Its population was down by a third from its peak, in 1951. The village school, made of concrete slabs in need of mending, was built for three or four hundred students and had 150. It looked like something one would expect to find in Eastern Europe. Hard winters had left the asphalt playground buckled and cracked.

Along the road a sunburned old farmer sprayed his paddy with pesticides from a tank strapped to his back, and I waited by his tractor until he finished. He was named Yoshio Kobayashi, and he seemed not the slightest surprised to find a gaijin at the edge of his field. He had a small but sturdy frame; a lifetime in the paddies had left him slightly stooped, as it had many of his generation. His wife worked quietly nearby, weeding the rows in a kerchief, a straw hat, and tall rubber boots.

Kobayashi had a familiar story, too. His children had jobs in the cities, one distant, one a couple of hours away. Only his eldest son, who taught school nearby, remained to help him. In the spring and autumn, Kobayashi relied on the rest of the village to help plant and harvest—an ancient practice in the village. He had one hectare, about two and a half acres, and there was no way he could earn a living on it. He would need ten to twenty hectares to make a go of it, he told me. Why had he carried on, then? Kobayashi was a little taken aback at such a question. "This is where I was born. Where you know you love—isn't that true for you, too?" Not necessarily, I replied. "Well," the old man said, "this is my village, my home, my land. It came from my parents, so I have to protect it."

Almost no one lives by farming alone anymore—less than 1 percent of households. Most farmers depend on other income—from factory work, casual labor, remittances. Kobayashi-san was a rare man, the ideal citizen of the *inaka:* a man who lived a hugely impractical life but who lived it according to *ninjo* and the old values and customs. If Kobayashi had not existed, I was tempted to conclude, the politicians in Tokyo, along with a scholar or two and the lost city dwellers of his generation, would have invented him. Except, of course, that they had invented him: They subsidized the price his rice brought, his pesticides and tractor—and his village.

I found only one factory in Inokuchi, down a dirt lane, near a well-tended Shinto shrine. It was a small cinder-block plant that made road signs. For a long time one or two little factories were typical of the village economies, but *ura nihon* is changing in this respect—again, the way colonies changed over many years. Along the main roads the landscape often presents rice terraces bordered by a large plant and a parking lot, then more terraces, then another plant. In Akita Prefecture, in the north, manufacturing overtook farming as the main economic activity in the mid-1980s. Within a few years industrial output was five times greater than what the rice and fruit growers produced. The new jobs are welcomed, of course, but the arrival of industry does not tell a story of positive change. Most of the factories that dotted the Akita landscape assembled consumer-electronics products, things Japan was then making in Malaysia and Indonesia. This was the case all over the countryside, because when it comes to modern industry the countryside competes for Japanese investments with Southeast Asia, South Korea, Taiwan, and China.

In effect, *ura nihon* is an N.I.E., to use the economists' term, a new industrial economy—that is, a Third World country struggling to acquire capital and technology. And considered as a Third World country, rural Japan is an expensive place for a Tokyo company to invest. More often than not it loses the competition with the other N.I.E.'s, because its currency, the yen, is really the currency of the rich nation on the other side of the Tokaido. Once in Tokyo I met the president of a firm that made small electric motors, the devices that power car windows and kitchen appliances. He had just invested in a new factory in Thailand. There were company apartment blocks and a company plane that ferried managers back and forth to Japan. Studying a map with him, I asked why he had spent so much overseas and not in the prefectures. He said, "There are only two differences between Thailand and the *inaka*. Thailand is cheaper and in Thailand you need a passport."

The company president reminded me of my first trip beyond the Tokaido. I flew to Izumo, a small city on the Sea of Japan coast, to meet the new mayor. Tetsundo Iwakuni was an unusual man, a hometown boy who had done well in the wider world and then went home again: a high-profile U-turn case. He had taken a degree from Tokyo University and gone into merchant banking. After three decades in Tokyo, New York, London, and Paris, Iwakuni went back to Izumo for what he intended to be a brief visit. He soon decided to quit his job and stay. He ran for mayor and got elected. And he was among a handful of officials I met who understood rural Japan for what it was, perhaps because he had seen enough elsewhere to recognize it.

"What I found after three decades abroad is that my own town is not part of an advanced country," Iwakuni told me in Izumo's modest town hall. "My town is typical of what you find in the underdeveloped world."

FEW PEOPLE ON either side of the Tokaido like admitting the truth of Mayor Iwakuni's observation. But it is evident in large ways and small, and as true in people's heads (where colonization begins and ends) as in the villages and along the roads. To the traveler, Japan outside the Tokaido can be like Africa or Latin America, where the footprints of empire fade slowly. To go from Nairobi to Lagos, or from Rio to Guayaquil, it was long thought the better alternative to fly through London or Miami, respectively, because links across the continents were either tortuous or simply did not exist. It is still the same in the *inaka,* and the same in the way ordinary people understand themselves, as it is along the route. The prefectures, most of which draw their boundaries according to the *han,* the old domains of the daimyo, are like spokes on a wheel: Their ties are to Tokyo, not to one another.

Modern Japan inherited an ancient separateness. Together the *han* harbored an abiding resentment toward the shogun and the military bureaucracy in Edo. But each *han* was distinct. The corrugated terrain did not encourage extensive trade and other contacts. Instead there were jealousies and isolation. There are many villages in rural Japan that got roads to the outside world only in the 1920s. In Toyama Prefecture there is a district of high cliffs and dramatic drops called Toga, which meant "punishment" in old Japanese, for the shogun sent his convicts there knowing escape was impossible. The place is still speckled with thatched-roof farmhouses and barns that seem to stand in another era, or in an ink drawing. Only when the snow melts are they accessible.

In the summer of 1876 a painter who had just taken up oils in the Western style went to Hokkaido, northernmost of the main islands, and produced a landscape with several notable features. It depicts a virgin forest of tall trees with huge, gnarled trunks. A dirt track is cut through the center. Halfway along it a group of mounted soldiers lingers. Further toward the vanishing point is a finely drawn telegraph pole. The painting is of the place where imperial troops defeated Hokkaido's last resistance to the restoration. It was a celebration of the new central government's power and reach. The painter, when he returned to Tokyo and finished the canvas, presented it to the war minister.

It is easy to understand the powerful impulse to centralize after 1868. "Abolish the *han,* establish the prefectures" was Tokyo's slogan almost immediately after the emperor was restored. That was accomplished quickly—in 1871. And with the transformation of *han* to prefectures the fragile balance of power between daimyo and shogun shifted decisively toward the center, a shift Tokyo has refused ever since to mitigate. Meiji's leaders were keen to erase *han* identity in favor of the new national consciousness: They were nation building, as we would put it today. But as we know well in our own time, trying to eradicate local identity causes people to dwell upon their differences only more intensely, and often produces not one nation but many.

In the early days of the modernization the attitudes of village dwellers were treated with much derision. In the countryside people made up tales about the noise of the railroad at night. They thought iron beds were human roasting grills and that telegraph poles had something to do with Christian witchcraft. It would be easy to mistake all this for xenophobia. But xenophobia is easily misunderstood. Villagers did not necessarily want to cut their topknots, sit on chairs, and wear felt hats just because the center—the metropole, the colonizer—decided that this was how Japan would enter the modern age. In the countryside modernization brought unwelcome departures. It meant forsaking the little tradition for the great and becoming a modern samurai. It also meant *nu-o,* joining the West; joining the West meant *datsu-a,* quitting Asia. And to resist quitting Asia in favor of one's own inclinations, one's natural evolution, was less a matter of xenophobia than it was ordinary common sense.

Japan has a long and famous tradition of xenophobia. But Japanese nationalism and the attendant chauvinism were inventions of the city, not the village—the great tradition, not the little—because it was in the city that Japan confused itself as to what it meant to be Japanese. Today one is often told to expect little more than silence and discourtesy in the countryside, xenophobia at its purest, and sooner or later village Japan will not disappoint. But that can be said of any countryside, and it is certainly no more true in rural Japan (and perhaps less true) than anywhere else. Xenophobia is still more evident in the large cities of the Pacific coast than in any backcountry village. And in rural Japan one must still distinguish between a dislike of the foreign and a dislike of what Tokyo imposes upon its periphery.

It is 120 years since the Meiji painter celebrated Tokyo's early campaign to obliterate local identity. We can still recognize its success in the sameness of the Japanese countryside today. Homogenization was slow in coming. Only in the postwar era did the uniformity and ugliness first evident between the Tokaido and the Pacific overtake the whole of the islands: the mishmash architecture, the billboards and neon, the acres of used car lots, the forests of concrete poles. These mark the same extension of political and economic power suggested in the Meiji painting, power that has turned *ura nihon* against the very affluence modernization has produced. All over Japan there are the same franchises, the same department stores, the same movies in the national theater chains. They provoke the same resentment that "civilization and enlightenment" once did. The high growth of the 1960s and 1970s made the phrase *taiyokano nakano toitsu,* monotony within diversity, familiar around the country. One can still hear it today. It is part of what makes the resident of *ura nihon* smile his wry smile.

MODERN JAPAN HAS always been obsessed with speed. We can attribute to a fundamental sense of urgency many of the mistakes it has made over the past century, including its decision to erase local identity rather than incorporate it. The frenetic pace set by modern Japanese leaders, to make the matter clear, has never had anything to do with culture, tradition, or innate character traits. It began with the desire to catch up, which reflected anxiety, felt inferiority, and fear. Then came Tokyo's abiding concerns in our century—empire, wartime production, and after the defeat, reconstruction and high growth. These only reinforced the urgency at the modern era's core from the beginning.

So Tokyo "cheated." It was as if it had deliberately set out to create two Japans, a visible front and an obscure back. A good geographic spread of productive assets—a goal one might expect of a modernization project as self-consciously planned as Japan's—was never much considered. Neither did time alter the situation, except to make it worse. The economy did not immediately lapse into imbalance. The first modern industries spread through the islands like magnets, drawn along by pools of labor and raw materials. But by the last years of Meiji, and substantially in the 1920s, when heavy industry came on a large scale, the front was decisively front and the back left behind. The magnetic field had reversed, and labor sought out factories. Economic concentration was evident near ports and markets. In the 1930s Japan built four big industrial zones. Though the economy is changing, they are still its core. The only one not along the Pacific coast—in northern Kyushu—would be another stop on the Tokaido were the old road extended.

After the war, when the drift to the Pacific coast cities reached epic proportions, conditions in the countryside were grave enough to interest the United Nations. In the mid-1960s a team of U.N. advisers toured the country, much as they did the new nations of Africa and Southeast Asia. They advised Tokyo to build highways, bridges, and rail lines that would make the islands into a single country. "After the execution of all these interconnections," they wrote, "the picture of Japan would look different." The idea of "a new Japan," or "a new regionalism," has been a running political theme ever since because it resonates well with voters: among city dwellers because their impossibly cramped lives are less tolerable with each passing year, and among villagers because modern Japan has neglected them.

Extreme centralization is not unique to Japan. It is common in the developing world—in Malaysia and Indonesia, Brazil and Mexico. France is another apt comparison. It, too, suffers from population drift, industrial concentration, and underpopulated villages. But France, as an advanced country, does not cause the problems that Japan does. France's economy, its relations with others, and the lives of its people are not distorted because of the way it modernized industry. Japan is different. It has trouble importing substantially more of what the rest of the world produces because it cannot consume more: In the cities there is not the room and in the country there is not the income. Nor, for the same reasons, can it export significantly less of its own output. These problems are rarely discussed outside Japan; but the rest of the world, whether it understands the causes, knows the consequences well. "Overcentralization isn't Japan's number one problem. The international trade friction we generate is," Mayor Iwakuni once told me. "But unless we solve the internal imbalances, we can't solve the external ones."

One of the notable books on this subject was published in 1972 by Kakuei Tanaka, the great kingmaker of postwar politics, just before he became prime minister. *Building a New Japan* proposed a sweeping remake of the islands, a "grand design" as befitted the most powerful of all modern politicians. Tanaka came easily to the sentiments that then appealed to ordinary voters—men and women made dizzy by the pace of growth and change after the war. He was a coarse son of the Niigata soil who never forgot his *ninjo,* his heartfelt, countrified sentiment. He once sang earthy Japanese folk songs at a meeting of the International Monetary Fund. In *Building a New Japan* he wrote:

> Rapid urbanization has bred increasing numbers of people who
> have never known the joys of rural life, chasing rabbits in the

mountains, fishing for yellow carp in streams, whose only home is a tiny apartment in some huge city. With such a situation, how can we pass on to future generations the qualities and traditions of the Japanese people?

Tanaka was ambitious. He had been a contractor before the war and as premier proposed no less than "remodeling the Japanese archipelago," as if it were a two-up, two-down house in a crowded suburb. He promised to decentralize the whole of Japan, to "rebuild the home of the Japanese people, which has been lost and destroyed." But for all its nostalgia, *Building a New Japan* was not shy of policy proposals. Tanaka would revise land-use regulations, relocate industries, and build links that had never before existed: the roads, rails, tunnels, and communications networks that had been talked about for years. The kingmaker took an unbalanced economy as an opportunity. He wanted to bring as much of the poor Japan as he could within the high-growth Japan defined by the Tokaido.

Building a New Japan, though the kingmaker's underlings wrote the book for him, displays the clarity of vision characteristic of a great leader, which Tanaka could have been. What makes it extraordinary reading a quarter century later is our familiarity with the near-absolute cynicism that Tanaka and his followers in politics and industry brought to the tasks laid out so frankly in the book he addressed to ordinary people. The evidence of this cynicism is literally everywhere in Japan, for Tanaka is to be credited as the architect, if not the originator, of what the Japanese call "the construction state."

The construction state lies at the core of the postwar system. It helps to account for Tokyo's deranged pursuit of economic growth at any cost. It is what we mean when we describe Japanese democracy as "money politics." And it is why we sometimes picture Japan as a machine with no one at the levers, a machine out of all control. There are people at the levers, of course: the politicians, the bureaucrats, and the industrialists, the triumvirate that has managed Japan (apart from the war years) since the 1920s. But since Tanaka's time the machine has grown bigger than its operators. It is a Frankenstein.

The workings of the construction state are very opaque. It is hard even for Japanese to see through all the layers of the onion. But in outline the system is simple: It begins in Tokyo, which spends heavily on public works projects. Each year it awards construction contracts worth hundreds of billions of dollars after only the faintest pretense of competitive bidding. These projects help keep voters happy, or at least fed, even though the costs must be highly inflated, for part of each award supports the political system. A percentage is immediately taken off the top. Later in the cycle the construction companies make large donations to political campaigns. And finally they hire politicians retiring from the system—or at least the end of the system involving elections.

Given that all of the money involved belongs to Japanese taxpayers, the construction state is without question the largest instance of official corruption in the advanced world. The scholar Gavin McCormack offers these figures to put the system into perspective: In 1993 Tokyo spent $320 billion on public works construction—not quite half of the entire national budget. Based on population, that is two and a half times what the United States spends on public projects. When we factor in the size of the two nations, Japan's expenditures are thirty-two times America's. Not surprisingly, the construction state has saddled the Japanese with an immense public debt: $78 billion by the end of 1994, more than a quarter of the nation's annual output. To put that in perspective: The European Union now limits members to a debt ratio of 3 percent.

Tanaka did not invent the construction state—he only mastered it. He took the 1955 system, which made one-party rule the norm in Japanese politics, to its logical extreme. The national public works budget rose by a third during his first year as prime minister. By the time Tanaka was through Japan had invented a term for his way of doing things: *kozo oshoku,* structural corruption, corruption so immense and entrenched that it did not so much impede the system or even disgrace it; structural corruption became the system. It is what the Japanese got instead of a working democracy.

We remember Tanaka today as the kingmaker who presided over the Lockheed influence-peddling scandal of the mid-1970s. But for Japanese villagers of his generation the Lockheed payoffs are a footnote. Among them Tanaka is universally revered. He gave Niigata, his home prefecture, an expressway to Tokyo and a high-speed rail line that cuts through the surrounding rice paddies like a Roman aqueduct through the Italian countryside. The city of Niigata on the Sea of Japan remains a showcase for Tanaka's grand design: It is rich, busy, pulsing with ambition and industry. It is the envy of many other prefectures. But elsewhere Tanaka's plans are revealed for what they actually were: a bottomless barrel of pork. Throughout Japan today there are countless highways to nowhere special, useless bridges, unneeded sea breaks, ruthless land-reclamation projects, half-built resort schemes, and deserted "technopolis" centers intended (it is said) to make rustics familiar with high-technology devices. These projects have done little for the decentralization of Japan but everything for Japanese contractors.

Tanaka has had numerous political heirs. Best known among them are Yasuhiro Nakasone, prime minister for most of the 1980s, and Noboru Takeshita, the sake brewer from Kakeya, who succeeded Nakasone. We generally credit Japan's long line of postwar leaders, along with the bureaucrats who stand beside them, as the dull but efficient directors of Japan's rise as an affluent nation. The affluence cannot be denied, but neither can the near destruction of much of Japan as a human and natural environment. The front of Japan, between the Tokaido and the Pacific, is not only grotesquely overbuilt: It is also badly built, as the earthquake in Kobe in 1995 revealed. The back of Japan is partly dumping ground for the cities (toxic waste sites proliferate) and partly a playground made of ill-conceived golf courses and resorts. Japan is often accused of disbursing foreign aid to the benefit of its own companies. Tokyo treats the N.I.E. beyond the Tokaido in the same fashion. Projects awarded to corporations in Tokyo or Osaka are among the principal funnels through which Tokyo sends subsidies to the countryside.

One of Tanaka's great themes was environmental conservation, an ironic subject in his day and ours, given the ecological price of Japan's success. There is now one river left in Japan without a dam on it, and it is the object of heated contention between builders and environmentalists. Mountains have been leveled to make way for golf courses. Diseases have been named after Japanese towns: Minamata disease, a mercury poisoning; Yokkaiichi disease, a lung ailment caused by chemical emissions.

The construction state rolls on, as if on automatic pilot, which is why foreign builders have had so little success in winning Japanese contracts. There is a disturbing truth at the core of it: The frenzy of building has had little to do with what the Japanese need to improve their lives, or how they want to live. The building has continued, needed or not, to keep the postwar machine in motion. That is why Tokyo has not brought *ura nihon* into the modern economy so much as imposed the modern economy on *ura nihon,* and why the culverts and hillsides in Kakeya, Noboru Takeshita's hometown, are covered with concrete.

THE JAPANESE HAVE always harbored a secret regret about the way they have made themselves modern. And it has been the countryside that has preserved this silent reproach, with its smile and its silent gaze toward the cities beyond the Tokaido. A regret of the modern, even a certain self-revulsion, seems the very point of such ideas as *furusato,* old hometown: the countryside as refuge, as conscience, as a dream in which what the Japanese once were is retrieved and somehow reenacted.

The Japanese offer an unspoken critique of the West, too—not a xenophobic rebuke so much as a regret of the habits and things Japan has taken from the West: its excessive corporatism and materialism, the animosity toward nature that displaced the ancient intimacy. That is why Japan can devastate rain forests and hunt whales while presenting itself to us as a guardian of our lost symbiosis with the natural world. We cannot look at the mess modernization has made of Japan without seeing ourselves reflected in it. Japan has merely taken the sovereignty Westerners claim over the planet furthest toward its fearsome far point.

"Having come this far we cannot turn back," Junichiro Tanizaki once observed. It was 1933, six decades after Japan entered the modern world and six decades ago:

> However, there can be no harm in considering how unlucky we
> have been, what losses we have suffered, in comparison to the
> Westerner. . . . We have met superior civilization and have had
> to surrender to it, and we have had to leave a road we have
> followed for thousands of years. . . . If we had been left alone
> we might not be much further now in a material way than we
> were five hundred years ago. . . . But we would have gone only
> in a direction that suited us. We would have gone ahead very
> slowly, and yet it is not impossible that we would have discov-
> ered our own substitute for the trolley, the radio, the airplane
> of today. They would have been no borrowed gadgets, they
> would have been the tools of our own culture, suited to us.

The Japanese fool themselves somewhat about nature. Their oneness with the physical world was buried long before Westerners came along. The decisive break with nature came with the importation of Chinese culture, as the scholar Saburo Ienaga has pointed out. After that nature and man were distinct. Nature became a refuge from the sufferings and corruption of human society. The scholar's hut became a religious and literary ideal. But the *yamazato,* the mountain retreat, brought sufferings of its own to a highly socialized people: the suffering of loneliness. By the fifteenth century, retreats in the wild gave way to visits to a symbolic nature. And the teahouse—along with gardening, flower arranging, and so on— became the arts that still define high culture. Nature savored is nature tamed; nature tamed is nature as a cultivated artifice, a contrivance.

Was Tanizaki right, nonetheless? Can the Japanese not still turn back? This is among the most important questions they face as our century ends. Of course, the Japanese can never regain their ancient unity with the physical universe, though a desire to recapture the past is often evident. There is no such thing as pristine nature for any of us. But there is no reason (not in principle, at least) they cannot reconsider the Western impulse to conquer nature—to go back part of the way and explore alternatives not taken as a way of going forward. And because the Japanese put on Western habits like a suit of clothes, it is arguable that they are better placed than anyone to shed assumptions and practices that are no longer sustainable.

It is hard to find anyone in the countryside who does not think economic renewal is a fine idea. Everyone wants it. But *ura nihon* is unusual in the advanced world as a place ordinary people can still ask, "What kind of renewal?" By their exclusion they have a chance to step back to consider a notion of progress that is fuller than anything *omote nihon* has ever imagined. In the 1960s, as the era of high growth began, Tokyo designated a number of "new industrial cities," and those not chosen felt left out. When I began traveling beyond the Tokaido twenty-five years later, the excluded were counting their blessings. Looking toward the Pacific coast, they see only ecological damage, frantic consumerism, urban density, suburban sprawl, lost identity, and everywhere an emptiness of spirit. People inside the Tokaido also understand the price, of course. But there the meal has already been consumed. Those who did not partake, precisely because they were given no seat at the table, have a chance to suggest another way into the future.

What is the missing ingredient? Why does an alternative idea of progress sound like an altruistic fantasy—another of the indulgent dreams the Japanese are fond of? The thing left out, demolished at the restoration, is autonomy. It is the same quality stifled in the individual Japanese. Just as he is conditioned to accept direction only from above (while simultaneously resisting it in private), so it is in the forty-seven prefectures. The Americans understood this after the war. The occupation ranked local autonomy high among its reforms. But the devolution of power got lost, like so much else, in the reverse course. The result is evident today all over Japan: large local administrations whose only authority lies in sweeping the cemeteries and executing the central government's orders. After many years of contention prefectures have discretion over only a third or so of their own budgets. A prefectural governor cannot move a bus stop without Tokyo's authorization.

But centralized power, like the individual's desire for autonomy, has never been a settled question. There were the peasant rebellions of the feudal era and, closer to our time, the groundswell of resistance in towns and villages to GNPism and the social, economic, and environmental problems it created. There is a long tradition of those below exerting themselves against those above. In the 1980s and 1990s it has influenced a new generation of political leaders on the far side of the Tokaido. Mayor Iwakuni in Izumo has been one. The best known of them has been Morihiro Hosokawa.

Hosokawa is an appealing man, with polished manners and an aristocratic background. He was descended from daimyo who ruled Kumamoto, a *han* on the island of Kyushu, during the Edo era. Over a twelve-year period in Tokyo Hosokawa held numerous posts in government and the Liberal Democratic Party only to discover, as he put it, that the capital was too wrapped up in the "little politics" of fund-raising and corruption to have any time for "big politics"—that is, the substantial questions facing the Japanese. In 1983 Hosokawa quit his Diet seat and was elected governor of Kumamoto Prefecture. He returned to begin "a revolt from the periphery," as he once put it. And he devised an audacious slogan for his campaign: "Abolish the prefectures, reestablish the *han*." It reflected not nostalgia but a desire to reverse "a growing sense of betrayal at the hands of the bureaucratic state." Hosokawa was eager to revive the autonomy of the *han,* not the *han* themselves.

Hosokawa eventually saw the beginning of his revolt. In a certain way, he and others in his camp resembled the samurai from distant parts who led the restoration against the crumbling shogunate—a bit of history that helped account for the public's fascination with them. Like the last samurai, at least until they betrayed the early promises, they stood for an alternative idea of power. Hosokawa and the others often spoke about a completely new model—a "United States of Japan." Izumo developed clean industries and became (according to national magazine surveys) Japan's most livable city. Kyushu turned itself into Silicon Island: It grew to supply 40 percent of Japan's computer chips (a tenth of the world's). Hosokawa set environmental standards that became a national model. "Creating another Tokyo or another Osaka is not my idea of success," he once told me. "Tall buildings are not a barometer of healthy development."

In the early 1990s Hosokawa sent Tokyo a set of policy recommendations intended to shift authority from the capital to prefectures and localities. They represented seven years of thinking. Prime ministers had read twenty-one such proposals since the early 1950s, Hosokawa told me after sending it off. His, like all the others, was rejected. At that moment he decided to return to national politics. Soon afterward he resigned from the Liberal Democratic Party and formed Nihon Shinto, the New Japan Party.* In July of 1993 Hosokawa was elected prime minister.

Hosokawa was famous the world over for ending thirty-eight years of Liberal Democratic rule. His government, a coalition of seven small, bickering parties, lasted less than a year. It is fair to ask what it accomplished, apart from breaking the Liberal Democrats' grip. There was not enough time to crack the central issue of Tokyo's power. So the balance of power between the front of Japan and its back remains unredressed. To claim a measure of regional autonomy and identity—which is to say, to build a democracy—remains a long-term project. But Hosokawa's election stood, nonetheless, as a brief assertion of the periphery's interests at the center of the Japanese system.

During Hosokawa's campaign for the premiership we met at the Tokyo headquarters of Nihon Shinto, then his new political party. A large poster faced the front door: BEFORE JAPAN DIES, it read on top. And at the bottom: *Change Politics. Then History Will Change.* Hosokawa came out of

---

* Literally the Japan New Party, as it was commonly known in the newspapers.

his office to greet me and we stood in front of the poster for a minute. I told him about Kakeya and a few other places I had visited since I had last seen him. Then I asked if he thought the same way, given that he was back in the capital, about the front and back of Japan and whether they could find a healthier path into the future.

Hosokawa's reply was startling. It was the reason the Japanese elected him, and it described the task they are now looking for someone else to assume. "We're at the edge of something," he said. "In a way, I've come back to Tokyo to destroy it."

PART 11

AMONG OTHERS

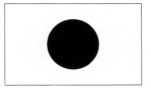

7

THE SPIRIT THAT RUNS
THROUGH HISTORY

The past does not only draw us back to the past. There are
certain memories of the past that have strong steel springs and,
when we who live in the present touch them, they are suddenly
stretched taut and then they propel us into the future.

—YUKIO MISHIMA
The Temple of the Golden Pavilion, 1956

THE JAPANESE MEASURE time by two calendars. The *gengo* system is
based on imperial reigns, which are named as they begin. The last year of
Hirohito's life was Showa 63; then came Heisei 1, the start of the era of his
son Akihito. A newspaper, a parking citation, or the bill for a bowl of *soba*
is always dated by the *gengo* system. The other calendar, the Gregorian, is
used on things more likely to be seen by foreigners—annual reports, press
releases, certain types of government business. It is as if linear time were in
some official way qualified as inauthentic—a formality, a fiction—and in
Japan time and history must remain cyclical. So are the Japanese kept
attuned to eras and the passage of generations. The end of each imperial
reign is like the harvest: Everything, even the calendar, begins again.

Many older Japanese think in the *gengo* system as a matter of course.

When did you first run for office, Watanabe-sensei? *That was in Showa 42.* Suzuki-san, when did you begin painting? *Showa 21.* Then one joins Watanabe or Suzuki in the awkward business of counting on one's fingers: *Showa 42 would be, let's see . . . 1967.* Showa 21 is easier. Twenty years on from the start of Hirohito's reign lands you in 1945 (a good counting aid), so it was 1946. Younger Japanese do not have the *gengo* habit. If older people pause to reckon because they are not quite accustomed to the Roman calendar, the younger ones have the same trouble because they rarely use the old system. You are unlikely ever to hear someone say, "I graduated from Todai in Heisei 3" (which was 1992).

The *gengo* system is not old. It was started in 1869 as part of the new imperial "tradition." Today it lingers uselessly on, too small a matter to be more than occasionally irksome, for one simple reason: Those who govern Japan prefer to keep it. It is one more reminder to the Japanese that they must regard themselves as different from others, a nation apart and all the same under their shared timekeeper, the emperor. The measuring of years by reigns tells us why the past intrudes so forcibly into the present in Japan: because it is officially put there. It also tells us where the past is at its most assertive: in people's minds.

It is common to observe that the Japanese move with remarkable ease among the objects of our age. Nothing new seems to surprise them. Nothing lasts—a notion some Japanese eagerly attribute to the Buddhist idea of impermanence, or to ancient traditions. It is easy enough to support this view. Wherever one looks in a Japanese city, something is always coming down and something else going up in its place. Near my neighborhood a row of wooden houses was replaced by an art museum, which was razed a few years later and made into a parking lot, upon which a string of retail shops and a fast-food outlet were eventually built. The average life of a dwelling in Tokyo is eighteen years. At Ise, south of the capital, the great Shinto shrine has been torn down and rebuilt every two decades since the year 690. The important thing is not the building but the building method, carried within: From one generation of craftsmen to the next, the way Ise is reerected never changes.

"Come to see my traditional Japanese teahouse," Kisho Kurokawa, a philosopher-architect of powerful and eclectic intellect, proposed in his office one day. Nothing better stands for samurai culture in all its fixed ritual and formality. Thinking I had an invitation to some sort of warrior's retreat in the countryside, I accepted with delight and asked where his teahouse was. "In Akasaka," Kurokawa replied, referring to one of Tokyo's most congested quarters, "on the eleventh floor of my apartment building." Then he smiled, satisfied that he had taught me something about the Japanese.

After the Berlin Wall fell it became popular to compare Japan with Italy. Both were frozen in time during the Cold War; both saw their political institutions corrupted as a consequence of it. This was a useful parallel: Both countries had to shake themselves awake again. But the differences seemed to outweigh the similarities. The past is never in doubt for Italians. It is in the stones and libraries, the naves of churches and the marble fountains. The past is everywhere, perfectly visible. There is no question of its place in contemporary life, or its validity.

The contrast with Japan and its fragile, invisible past could scarcely appear more stark. The Japanese enjoy nothing of the Italians' confidence. What they have of the past exists primarily as an idea. And how do the Japanese express this idea? What is supposed to distinguish them from the rest of us, the notion held in reverence for as long as Japan has existed in recorded history, is the Japanese spirit. Ancient as the idea is in Japan's case, we can define "spirit" by its meaning among nineteenth-century nationalists in Europe, for that is where the Meiji modernists looked when they sought to redefine themselves in modern terms: It is the "native genius," as the Europeans would have put it. It is *Kultur,* blood and soil, race and rank. These are what the Japanese have long been encouraged to depend upon to know themselves as Japanese.

In the late 1960s, a couple of years before Yukio Mishima took his own life, a correspondent went to his seaside home south of Tokyo to interview him for French television. The reporter later recounted his surprise at seeing the house where the novelist lived. Mishima was by then a passionate nationalist, yet his residence was gaudily Western. There were French doors and wrought iron balconies; a statue of Orpheus adorned the garden. "How do you explain the fact that the whole of your house contains nothing specifically Japanese?" the correspondent asked.

"Here," Mishima replied, "only what you cannot see is Japanese."

There is something to be said for all this—but not overmuch. We do not want to cast the Japanese as unworldly exotics unfazed when a fire or an earthquake destroys their houses and belongings. Impermanence is a practical matter as much as it is anything else. The rebuilding ritual at

Ise is surely rooted in traditionally available building materials. Wood and straw rot: nothing especially spiritual there. In the modern cities impermanence has less to do with Buddhism or the native spirit than with cheap construction and the politics of the construction state. Spirit must be understood for what it is: a creation, no more peculiar to the Japanese than a given way of counting the days.

Mishima well understood the prison the Japanese made of their past and the idea of spirit that resides there. He devoted his later life (and his death by seppuku) to the Japanese spirit. From it he drew his identity. Yet he had seen, earlier in life, that the never-changing thing passed down through the centuries was his captor. And it is that captor the Japanese have begun to destroy—that lid they have begun to lift.

MUCH IS TO be learned about the Japanese spirit from the way the idea began. The old phrase for it is *Yamato damashii.* Yamato was the ancient name for Japan, or one of them. It was literally a reference to the Japanese mountains, where heaven and earth were divided. But Yamato really meant the Japan founded by Jimmu, the mythical first emperor born of the gods. So Yamato signified the Japan of imperial culture, which is why the term is still invoked by nationalists. But the notion of a Japanese spirit did not spring up along with Yamato. It came some centuries later, after Japan had borrowed vast amounts of its culture—first from China by way of Korea, and then from China itself.

In one of the ancient myths the gods chopped off part of the Korean peninsula and attached it to the Japanese islands—a probable reference to a wave of mainland migrants. There is no separating Japan from the mainland when it comes to what it took from Korea and China. Japan had a culture—the culture of simple cultivators rooted in community. There was no rigorous moral code (as the first Chinese travelers discovered), no hierarchy, no distinction between man and nature. The language was extremely simple. The Japanese liked to drink and dance, and they ate with their hands from plates made of bamboo. This was the original Japan, the Japan before Yamato. Its name, the first name Japan ever had, was Land of Abundant Rice, and there was much to admire in it. But it did not stand up well when put against the mainland, whose culture was decidedly material by comparison. Korea gave Japan iron tools and weapons (in addition to waves of immigrants). In the fourth century a Korean scribe brought the Chinese writing system. Next to the Koreans and Chinese the Japanese seemed recessive, feminine. Theirs was not a culture that would ever project itself, as the mainland projected itself upon the islands.

Shotoku, the prince regent who reigned in the sixth century, was the greatest of all borrowers, at least until the Meiji era. He redrew Japan on the Chinese model. He is famous in history for giving Japan its first constitution. He reinvented the emperor, changing him from a first among equals into *tenno*—heavenly sovereign, the supreme, highest being. And Shotoku gave Japan yet another name: Nippon, Land of the Rising Sun—rising, of course, when viewed from the mainland.

All the borrowing from China is not difficult to understand. Innovation came slowly to isolated islanders content to cultivate. But to borrow so fully from another culture is at some point to posit the insufficiency of one's own. And to borrow from China had fateful consequences for the Japanese. Sinicization imposed the culture of patriarchs—Confucian hierarchy, sexual inequality, male lineage—upon a culture probably rooted in matrilineal clans. Japan has never resolved the tensions caused by its first great borrowing—to say nothing of its second, more than a millennium later. It is, in a certain way, part of the coiled spring that drives Japanese history. For the Japanese have wrestled ever since Shotoku with the question of who, precisely, they are.

This brings us to Shotoku's most durable gift, arguably the most unfortunate. It was not an import at all, but the native-hatched Japanese spirit. Swamped in *chinoiserie,* the people who reckoned their very position on the planet by way of the mainland could only wonder where lay their own center. So they looked within, contriving to find the essence of Japaneseness in their perseverance, their bravery, their loyalty, and their nobility of soul. No one else possessed these qualities as did those of old Yamato, the Japan before "Nippon" came along. Spirit made the Japanese unique. A few centuries after Shotoku's reforms they coined a notion that, with adjustments, came down to the modern era. *Kara-jie, Yamato damashii:* There were "Chinese things," but there was a "Japanese spirit," eternal and unchanged, everywhere. The Japanese have ever since taken a lively interest in copying the material culture of others while resolutely rejecting their principles.

The first to display the greatness of the native spirit was Yamato Takeru, a mythical figure held to have been born of a first-century emperor. When he first appears in the ancient writings, his father asks him to reproach his twin brother for not showing up at meals—a mark of disloyalty to the throne. Yamato Takeru goes off to perform his duty and returns, but there is still no sign of the twin at table. "And how did you instruct him?" the emperor asks. Yamato Takeru's reply is straight to the point. He waited in an outhouse until his brother came one morning. "I seized him, smashed him to pieces, tore off his limbs, wrapped them in a straw mat, and threw them away."

Yamato Takeru was at once a man of unbending principle and no principle at all. He slayed all manner of malefactors in his quest, which was to pacify the land whose name he shared. In Kyushu he cross-dressed as a beautiful girl to gain a dinner invitation from a rebellious chieftain, then murdered him while they ate. In Izumo he befriended another troublesome chief and suggested a swim. Yamato Takeru got out first and pretended to admire the chief's sword. Then Yamato Takeru sliced the defenseless chief to death when he emerged from the water. Whatever could be said of Yamato Takeru's methods, his devotion to the land of the gods lay beyond question.

Yamato Takeru's exploits are recorded in the first books Japan ever produced. The *Records of Ancient Matters* and *Chronicles of Japan* are eighth-century compilations of the creation myths and the early legends of Yamato. It is an irony that these could be set down only after Japan adopted the Chinese writing system. While pretending to be native in thought and sentiment, they are shot through with Confucian influences. But that, in miniature, was Shotoku's legacy: to give Japan the means to know itself only by way of others.

Japanese history is made of layers. None quite covered the one before, but each went in a new direction. In these early layers we find the first suggestion of Japan's long and unfortunate neurosis in its relations with the outside world: borrowing balanced by a defensive brand of nativism, the seesaw of admiration and xenophobia.

Much has come of "the spirit that runs through history," as the prewar nationalists called it in the 1930s. With it Japan has altered everything it has ever imported, from Buddhism to baseball, making each its own. Little else has derived from the Japanese spirit that does not contain some measure of tragedy: the tragedy of felt inferiority dressed up as its opposite, of overripe feudalism and its attendant deprivations, of Japan's psychological violence toward its own people and its reckless aggression toward others.

As I have already suggested, among the distinguishing characteristics of our time is the slow death of this spirit among those supposedly in possession of it (but who have been, of course, possessed by it). But we must follow this imprisoning thing through the modern era before we can watch it go.

THE PURVEYORS OF the Japanese spirit across the centuries were the samurai. It is true that their ideal drew heavily from the Chinese treasure chest. But only to a point. The samurai were also fierce nativists nostalgic for old Yamato. The greatest of feats was to display in action their Japanese spirit. In the end they transcended everything they took from the Chinese—that is, they Japanized it. Their Confucianism became the inordinately complex web of duties and obligations known as *giri* and *on*. Their Buddhism was Zen.

In the mid-1600s a Confucian scholar named Soko Yamaga codified the rules of the samurai for the first time. He called it Bushido, "the way of the warrior." This was a curious moment in history. In Yamaga's time the Tokugawa had ended the wars that once consumed the warrior class. Many of the idled samurai administered the provinces and entered the vast Edo bureaucracy. The grander townsmen took up bits of the samurai conventions, if in vulgar form. Customs once followed by warriors were assuming a secular purpose. So the samurai's idea of Japaneseness as resident in his spirit was spreading. Writing down the old house rules was a step toward the samuraization of Japan from top to bottom.

One of Sogo Yamaga's disciples was a samurai who featured as the leader in *The Tale of the Forty-Seven Ronin,* the best-known legend in Japanese literature. It is an account of events that occurred in 1701–2, midway in the Edo centuries. *Forty-Seven Ronin* illustrates the extremes to which the notion of spirit led the Japanese. What happens to practices that survive their purpose? Later generations fix them—and in fixing them make them fetishes. Consider the plot of *Forty-Seven Ronin*.

A daimyo draws his sword against an official of the shogun who has insulted him, and he is ordered to commit seppuku. His samurai thus become wandering, masterless warriors. Out of loyalty to their deceased master, they determine to kill the Edo official. They make great sacrifices to accomplish the deed. They accept the deaths of parents, wives, and children. They finally trap the official—in a shed at his palace—and the fatal blade is buried. They are heroes for their loyalty to their daimyo. Then they, too, must die by seppuku in the name of the highest loyalty of all— loyalty to the shogun.

Samurai intellectuals debated this incident until the restoration, a century and a half later. Philosophic treatises turned the right and wrong of it this way and that. *Forty-Seven Ronin* was immensely popular among commoners. The tale, as famous as *The Three Musketeers* in the West, remains a national legend. Yet it is a narrative of tragic senselessness. It suggests a society dedicated to the complete eradication of individual judgment in the name of spirit. The extent of such a society's malevolence could be limited only by the instruments of violence available to it.

One of the interesting things about the spirit is the way the Japanese use it to obscure their emotions and character. *Forty-Seven Ronin* is a good example. The warriors sacrifice family to the honor of a dead lord's name: not a very sympathetic position, but let us accept the premise. Then, having done the right thing by their own consciences, they willingly accept the ultimate punishment for it. There is an obsessive self-denial in this sort of irrational rigidity. Seppuku is another example. In 1869, a year after the restoration, the new government debated whether to outlaw the practice— as in many other matters, because it might offend Westerners. Here is how the defenders of ritual suicide spoke of it in the new imperial council:

> *Seppuku* has its origin in the vital energy of this divine country and is the shrine of *Yamato damashii.*

And:

> It is an ornament of our country and is one reason of its superiority over the countries beyond the seas.

And, most telling:

> Why should this custom be prohibited in imitation of the effeminacy of foreign nations?

The "effeminacy" of others? This was hardly the issue, of course: The issue was Japan's "effeminacy," that long-buried ease and recessiveness associated with the Japanese before Yamato came along. Consider the classic image of the samurai as he comes down to us: four-square stance, drawn sword, and (most of all) the tough, squinting eyes and the downturned mouth—the grimacing visage without which a samurai simply would not be a samurai. One sees this today in things like film and advertising: "Gekkeikan, sake of the samurai!" was a popular tag line during my years in Tokyo. And there he was, in his awe-inspiring masculine glory, knocking back his Gekkeikan. There is something in the samurai as we know him that is frightening, pathetic, and laughable all at once, because in the end it is an act, pure theater, a cover for aspects of the Japanese character—a givingness, a femininity, if you like—that are admirable rather than shameful, and still apparent, for all the effort to bury them.

It may seem bold, or uselessly general, to assert that an entire nation suffers a collective neurosis because of the way it has advanced through history, with layers of the past obscuring what it had been at the beginning. Yet it has been an inescapable question ever since the restoration, when all Japanese were made into samurai. In Meiji's penultimate decade, Lafcadio Hearn published an essay entitled "The Japanese Smile." Hearn, the noted Western interpreter of early modern Japan, wanted to explain why the Japanese smiled when they returned from funerals, when they were beaten by gaijin masters, when they were banished from service in a European house. Behind these smiles lay neither the levity nor the insincerity most gaijin presumed, Hearn wrote, but the same profound confusion that had haunted them a millennium earlier. Hearn saw the hollowness at the core of Japan's rush to modernize and described with astonishing prescience the nostalgia that was eventually to envelop the samuraized Japanese, a nostalgia they feel now, a century later, for what they have lost:

> Yet to that past which her younger generation now affect to despise Japan will certainly one day look back. . . . She will learn to regret the forgotten capacity for simple pleasures, the lost sense of the pure joy of life, the old loving divine intimacy with nature, the marvelous dead art which reflected it. She will remember how much more luminous and beautiful the world then seemed. . . . She will mourn for many things. . . . She will

wonder at many things; but she will regret. Perhaps she will wonder most of all at the faces of the ancient gods, because their smile was once the likeness of her own.

THE IDEOLOGUES WHO launched modern Japan were resourceful in their use of the Japanese spirit. Meiji was a hothouse of desire and ambition, as we have noted, but the new state was efficient in getting the new Japanese to link their lot to the old idea of Yamato.

Meiji's invocation of spirit had a full measure of rustic sentimentality. To glorify the villager with mud between his toes kept people in their places; it deflected some of their ambitions and dreams while they were turned into modern samurai. The Meiji ideologues reinvented a figure to stand for this aspect of the spirit, a legendary farmer named Kinjiro Ninomiya. Kinjiro-san was the ultimate hayseed—focused on his lot, devoted to his work, thankful to all above, ever willing to stretch a yen. In American terms he was a kind of Johnny Appleseed. The ideologues more or less canonized Kinjiro. When American soldiers arrived in 1945 they found many villages with statues of Kinjiro carrying firewood on his back and reading a book at the same time. (The real Kinjiro was an Edo-era peasant who rather miraculously rose to a position of some prominence as a land manager for the daimyo.)

Spirit, as the Meiji era went on, became explicitly anti-Western. Advocates of democratic and civil rights wound up singing lyrics denouncing the unequal treaties. Just as the Japanese once surrounded themselves with Chinese things, Meiji brought floods of European and American imports. So "Chinese things, Japanese spirit" became "Japanese spirit, Western things," *wakon yosai*—an idea any ordinary Japanese would have little trouble supporting.

What other borders are so clearly marked as those geography gives Japan? Yet Japan revealed to itself, in the last century as in the sixth, that at important moments in its evolution it seemed to have no borders at all. Surely one of the striking aspects of Meiji was its precise duplication of Shotoku's pattern: an imagined new Japan, a great borrowing, then an insistence upon a unique spirit whose fierceness reflected only a self-induced sense of inadequacy. In the last analysis, to invoke spirit again was to supply the borders that seemed to be missing.

The spirit invoked by the Meiji elite came wrapped in the notion of *kokutai*. It was with the *kokutai* flickering through their minds that the Japanese, in the half century beginning in 1894, defeated the Chinese, beat the Russians at sea, conquered Korea, and took on the West in World War II. In an earlier chapter I defined *kokutai* as "national essence," a standard translation. No historian has ever really defined *kokutai*, but then, neither did any of those who gave the word prominence. From the time the idea was concocted (as it was) late in the Edo era, the essential question was whether it was necessary to consider it unique. The educator Yukichi Fukuzawa thought of *kokutai* as nothing more elusive than "nationality." But to others it meant "national polity," or even—as if Tokyo borrowed from Rome—"mystical body of Japan." It was something like "a sense of nation"—a thing less important to understand than to feel. Not even the emperor's advisers were certain about it. The *kokutai* was immutable; no, it changed with the times. Everyone had a *kokutai*, the British, the French, the Americans; no, only the Japanese possessed it. The last and most earnest effort to clear this up was that volume of biblical solemnity and clotted usage called *Kokutai no Hongi*, published in 1937 as the principal ideological tract of the wartime period. Its *kokutai* was unique and eternal after all, "and shines resplendent throughout our history."

In his autobiography, the film director Akira Kurosawa gave a startling account of the day Japan admitted defeat. He was required to report to his studio (where he had been making propaganda films for the dictatorship) to hear Hirohito's surrender speech. As he walked through Tokyo it seemed to him that everyone he saw was prepared to die to honor the emperor, the *kokutai,* the noble Japanese spirit. "The atmosphere was tense, panicked. There were even shopkeepers who had taken their Japanese swords from their sheaths and sat staring at the bare blades." The young Kurosawa listened to Hirohito over the radio, one of 70 million Japanese who heard his voice for the first time. Then he left:

> When I walked the same route back home, the scene was entirely different. The people in the shopping street were bustling about with cheerful faces as if preparing for a festival the next day.

There are many similar stories about the afternoon of August 15, 1945. Some people recall empty streets and the sound of weeping from behind closed doors. But always they speak of sorrow mixed unmistakably with relief. How could the Japanese change so swiftly? Kurosawa offered his own answer: "In wartime we were all like deaf-mutes." A French correspondent, among the only Westerners present, put it this way: "Something huge had just cracked." The great cause had failed. Japan had counted on spirit to overcome the material superiority of the enemy. Now the Japanese were face-to-face with an inferiority that could not be denied. But consider Kurosawa's account once again: In a single passage he reveals not only how enveloping the idea of spirit was, but also how shallow. And so it has been since the surrender.

The notion of *kokutai* died with the imperial army in 1945—but only officially. The Americans made certain to kill it as swiftly as possible. MacArthur banned *Kokutai no Hongi,* the wartime text, a few months after he arrived in Tokyo. But something so essential to the way Japan was ruled cannot be uprooted and thrown into the dustbin of the past as if it were military ordnance, or a codebook. *Kokutai,* as an ideological assumption, was a little like a lump under a blanket. A year after G.H.Q. censored *Kokutai no Hongi* the Japanese cabinet declared "the national essence" to be intact. So, like the *gengo* calendar, *kokutai* has lingered on. It is implicit in such notions as the corporate warrior—or in the idea of "Japanese democracy," the Chrysanthemum Club's term for the preposterous political system the elite evolved after the war. One cannot claim a dysfunctional system works simply by renaming it, of course. But the concept of a Japanese version of democracy is widely accepted, even by the Japanese. And implicit in it is the belief that the Japanese are somehow able to infuse their unique way even into humanity's most enduring ideals.

When the psychiatrist Robert Lifton interviewed young Japanese in the late 1950s and early 1960s, he found that matters of spirit and national essence were thoroughly discredited. The very word *kokutai* was absent from the postwar idiom; Lifton reported that his subjects "dismiss it as the propaganda of militarists, and even find it laughable." But like the smile Lafcadio Hearn wrote about, the laugh Lifton heard was the laugh that conceals. The postwar Japanese did not identify with such things as *kokutai,* certainly, but neither had they found anything to replace it. They were lost, in a vacuum of belief. What Lifton discerned behind the laughs was the eternal tension felt by every Japanese,

> the polarizing tendencies that still haunt Japanese thought—
> the urge to recover *kokutai* and make things just as they were,
> and the opposite urge to break away entirely from every
> remnant of *kokutai* and make all things new.

The most interesting thing about *kokutai* and the samuraization of Japan is not that their traces reveal themselves even in our time. It is that the process of samuraization was at bottom a failure. The Japanese were samuraized, relentlessly, over a period of seventy-five years. But the task was never complete. As Lifton discovered, the imposition of the Japanese spirit only prolonged the most enduring of all divides among the Japanese, and within each one: between how the Japanese really are and how they are supposed to be, between an understanding of oneself as primarily Japanese and as primarily human. This divide is as old as *Yamato damashii* itself. It is also the divide between the great and little traditions. Japan has advanced its official, imperial version of itself and its culture—a narrative filled with princes, warriors, and unifying heroes, all exemplars of loyalty and the other great virtues—ever since the national spirit made its first appearance. But the little tradition, too, runs resplendent through history.

Consider briefly another Edo-era legend. It concerns a village headman named Sogoro, who lived near Narita, north of the capital, in the early 1600s. The daimyo raised the rice tribute so high that Sogoro's village faced starvation. When appeals to the local official failed, Sogoro took the dangerous step of leaving the village to confront the daimyo himself at his alternative residence in Edo. He was rebuffed again. It remained only to approach the shogun—a move certain to end in execution, for in the order of things Sogoro's right of appeal began and ended with those directly above him. The narrative continues:

> His heart contained only the thought that by sacrificing his
> own life, he would take upon himself the entire responsibility
> for the peasants' sufferings and save the masses from their hard-
> ships. How firmly resolved was he to act, and how incompara-
> ble was his courage!

Sogoro prevailed after planting his petition in the shogun's rubbish bin. It was discovered and taken to the shogun, who ordered the excessive tributes withdrawn. Then Sogoro was crucified with his wife and four sons because he had "treated public authority lightly."

The Sogoro legend comes from the little tradition: the periphery, not the center. You will never find it on the reading list of any Japanese grammar school. *The Tale of the Forty-Seven Ronin*, by contrast, comes from the great samurai tradition and is taught to every young pupil in Japan. And how are they different? What do we find in the little tradition? No evidence of grimacing warriors and their Japanese spirit. The core sentiment in Sogoro's story is nothing more or less exotic or Japanese than the survival against all odds of the ordinary, universal human spirit.

Sogoro's tale has been retold countless times. Though it bears no seal of approval it has tumbled through the centuries all the way to our own. Sogoro became a Shinto deity. Later, with the rise of popular culture in the cities, he was depicted in woodblock prints and Kabuki drama. His modern fate is revealing. A local shrine still honors him. In the late 1960s, when Tokyo appropriated land in Narita for a new international airport, farmers and their student supporters began a protest that continues even today. It is one of the longest-running disputes in postwar politics, a classic confrontation between the little and the great. Narita, guarded as heavily as a dictator's palace, is the first and last thing most visitors to Japan see. And so, while most travelers do not realize it, the conflict between the great tradition and the little is also what greets and dispatches them. They pass right through it.

The Narita farmers set out with a keen sense of history. From the beginning they chose Sogoro as a kind of patron saint.

NOSTALGIA FOR THE past is hardly peculiar to the Japanese. But it is hard to think of any others who can look back to find themselves so self-consciously re-created through history: in the "Japan" of Yamato, of Shotoku, of the samurai and the Edo-era castes, then the "Japan" of the modern era. Each one is like a coat of paint over the one before. So does history leave the Japanese oddly homeless, adrift in the twentieth century. They chip through the eras for the Japan that was not someone's vision, someone's dream.

Nostalgia persists—a characteristic emotion—but it grows fainter as the years go on. For a time the Japanese made themselves experts in it, scientists.

But there are various kinds of nostalgia for the simple reason that there are various "Japans" to pine for. There is the false but popular nostalgia for the "Tokugawa peace." The ultranationalist fringe remains nostalgic for the spirit of old Yamato. There is an aesthetic nostalgia for the samurai arts—Kisho Kurokawa's delight in his teahouse. Most of all there is a nostalgia for the very first Japan, the simple Japan that existed before Yamato covered it over.

In the late 1970s a group of Japanese built a primitive longboat to sail from northern Luzon, in the Philippines, to the southern tip of Kyushu. In the manner of Thor Heyerdahl's *Kon-Tiki,* the trip was supposed to demonstrate what certain scholars call the southern origin theory: that the ancestors of the Japanese, or some of them, migrated from Southeast Asia or the Pacific islands. The longboat made the journey, but no Japanese seemed any the less confused afterward. Today the hull sits outside a marine museum on Tokyo Bay, rotting lumber exposed to the elements. I was taken there once by Japan's preeminent yachtsman.

"What did it prove to take a boat to the Philippines and sail it back to Japan?" I asked him.

He shook his head derisively. "Absolutely nothing."

The sailing project was an example of what was called *nihonjinron.* It meant "discussions of the Japanese" or "theory of the Japanese." *Nihonjinron* asked again the age-old question: It asked who the Japanese are.

Nihonjinron was immensely popular. From the 1960s well into the 1980s its proponents chattered through many late-night television shows and wrote many best-selling books. A typical *nihonjinron* production was a 1985 volume called *The Japanese Brain,* which began:

> My findings seem to provide an explanation of the unique and universal aspects of Japanese culture. Why do Japanese people behave in their characteristic manner? How has the Japanese culture developed its distinctive features? I believe the key to these questions lies in the Japanese language. That is, "the Japanese are Japanese because they speak Japanese." My investigations have suggested that the Japanese language shapes the Japanese brain function pattern, which in turn serves as a basis for the formation of the Japanese culture.

Tadanobu Tsunoda, doctor of otology and audiology, claimed scholarly detachment. He professed surprise when his book drew international attention. Clearly he was less coy in his basic assumption, which also turned out to be his conclusion: The Japanese are unique. That was the starting and ending point of every *nihonjinron* expert.

The theory of the Japanese was never much more than quackery, a parody of scientific inquiry. And the yachtsman was right: No trip across the East China Sea would ever establish anything about the Japanese. Neither would brain scans or any other exercise in *nihonjinron*. Trade negotiators used variants in talks with irate Americans: Japanese snow is different from snow elsewhere, they argued (so Japan must ban foreign-made skis); Japanese intestines are longer than those of Westerners (and cannot digest imported meat). Such assertions only made matters worse, of course. Among foreigners the theory of the Japanese was considered a bad joke, innately xenophobic—which was true so far as it went.

But xenophobia was not all there was to it. What was *nihonjinron* all about? What does it tell us about the Japanese? The theory of the Japanese was a phenomenon of its time. It is impossible to imagine any spirited samurai or wartime nationalist indulging in such a question. For them the equation was simple: "Our unique spirit means we are not Chinese." After a millennium of that, "We are not Western" was the necessary assertion. Physiology, geography, or anthropology never had anything to do with the Japanese being Japanese.

The Japanese are unique: That is actually true. The theorists failed to reason through the next step in the logic: The Japanese are not uniquely unique—that is, they are no more unique than anyone else. The theory of the Japanese suggested only what it sought to refute: that the sense of uniqueness and belonging once supplied by the Japanese spirit was dying—along with the old notion of the spirit itself.

Nihonjinron is now a faded discipline, if that is the word for it. It died, I believe, because the idea of Japanese uniqueness is no longer sustainable. The Japanese spirit was finally exhausted in the 1980s, or—better put—it was no longer of any use. *Nihonjinron* was briefly popular because for the first time the Japanese could not define themselves simply by saying who they were not. They are challenged to explain—to themselves as well as others—who they actually are. In *nihonjinron* the Japanese cast their eyes backward once again. But it was junk science, cheap nostalgia. The

Japanese are still in search of a spirit—not the old one, the *Yamato damashii,* but the spirit of a modern nation, which they have never had. So the Japanese still want to rediscover their past. The difference is they no longer want to live in it.

JAPAN NEVER LIKED the idea of the "postwar era," tied by definition to the war itself. Starting in the 1950s it declared the end of it whenever a chance presented itself. In 1956, the newspapers named a spurt of economic growth the Jimmu boom, after the mythical first emperor, and Tokyo proclaimed the postwar era closed. In 1964 came the Tokyo Olympic Games. The same year Japan joined the O.E.C.D., the club of advanced nations. Two years later the World Bank classified Japan as an advanced country. These were all supposed to be the turning point. This search for the post-postwar era reflected a profound longing: The Japanese wanted to break from the past. But nothing really took. Nineteen fifty-seven was much the same as 1955; 1965 the same as 1963: hard work, economic advances, a national purpose redefined in material terms. The postwar sense of drift and loss lingered like a stain that could not be erased.

Japan has finally entered its post-postwar era. It is not because the Japanese have achieved economic parity with the West, or because the Cold War ended, or because the Liberal Democrats have been challenged, or because Hirohito died. What truly marks the beginning of a new phase for the Japanese is less easily measured. The events of our time, each in its own way, have helped the Japanese free themselves of the burden of felt inferiority—and of the past: not just the immediate past, the past of the war and the cult of emperor worship, but the long, imprisoning past of the Japanese spirit, too.

As it happens, to be free of the past is no more unique to the Japanese than their nostalgia for it. At millennium's end it is our universal condition, everybody's blessing and curse. We all proceed forward without maps and charts. But how much more momentous is this break for the Japanese, for whom the past has been not merely a guide but the rule of life, what they kept intact instead of stone buildings and statuary?

Sensing their break with all that has come before, the Japanese were for a time much tempted by the vague but fashionable thought that they were the world's premier postmoderns. *They have completed history, arrived at the modern era's far shore, and so stand at "history's end." Humming with the subdued regularity of a sewing machine, Japan is devoid of either conflict or ideology. Meaning has evaporated. Reality is replaced by its "virtual" represen-tation.* Such were the ideas, highly popular, expressed as the 1980s turned into the 1990s. But this is only another imaginary "Japan." Nothing could be less the case, nothing matches so fatuous a reading of Japan, past or present. It is the Orientalist, Chrysanthemum Club "Japan" brought two steps forward and dressed in postmodern black, another "project" for consumption in our age.

The Japanese began the modern era reading Rousseau, John Stuart Mill, and others in the long line of thinkers launched by the Enlightenment. Then they put aside the books and ideas. They built a modern economy but (as we have considered from many perspectives) not a modern society. After the war they made themselves citizens instead of subjects, but they did not make a civil society in which to participate. They possess democracy's machinery but no democracy. Whatever one thinks of postmodernism, the Japanese simply do not qualify. Strip away the high technology and the fantastic dreams of the future, and you find that their perspective is often not postmodern but pre-.

Where are the Japanese now, and where are they heading? These are logi-cal questions, but we should be careful how we answer them. *They stand at the brink of their own belated Enlightenment. They are about to become, at long last, more like us.* These have long been common assumptions in the West. And as the Japanese set about remaking themselves and their society, these assumptions may be right. Or the Japanese may go in an entirely different direction—an interesting possibility, given that the West itself has now begun to question whether the Enlightenment has run its course, or if there was something wrong with such a course in the first place.

But to cast the matter in these terms is to miss the point entirely. The endeavor is not to be like us—to keep on borrowing. The endeavor is to understand where they have been and go on from there—precisely with-out, for the first time, borrowing from anybody. It is to accept all of their own past—as past. One cannot claw back the parts of the past that were a mistake. Neither can one go on dreaming fantastic futures. The Japanese are not just simple rice farmers with easy manners. They are also the people who borrowed from China, who lived in strict castes, who borrowed from the West and then made war on it.

And with all this in view it is perhaps not too paradoxical to conclude that the Japanese will embrace the future simply by becoming more like themselves, comfortable for the first time in their own skins.

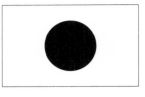

8

THE SACRED "NOTHING"

I am determined not to tell your name,
and you shall never say I am to blame.

—ANONYMOUS,
from the *Manyoshu* (*Anthology of Ten Thousand Leaves*),
book XI, compiled circa 750

EMPRESS MICHIKO, née Michiko Shoda, the daughter of a mill owner, was eleven when Japan surrendered, in 1945. Yet she remembered the war with unusual clarity later on. In 1985, twenty-six years the crown prince's wife, Michiko wrote of her time as a refugee from Osaka in a tanka, a five-line poem of thirty-one syllables, called "Thunder":

I recall those days
Of early childhood
When, in the countryside,
I would count the moments between
The flash of lightning and the thunderclap.

When Michiko married Crown Prince Akihito in 1959 she was the first commoner to enter the imperial household. But in her poetry she followed a noble custom at least as old as the eighth-century *Manyoshu*. The tradition provides a voluminous supply of egregious verse—weightless balloons, leaden clunkers, and everything in between. "Thunder" counts among the exceptions. It captures both the uncertainty and whimsy of childhood. It evokes that first youthful awareness of forces beyond understanding. "Thunder" is about specks of time that are out of time. It records the epiphanies of emptiness.

Michiko was five years away from becoming empress when she wrote "Thunder." But she had hovered long enough in the antechambers of Fukiage Palace, the imperial seat, to suggest the essential nature of what postwar Japan calls, a little antiseptically, the imperial institution. With an intuition displayed by no other Japanese royal in living memory, Michiko caught something of its peculiar emptiness, its invisibility, its claim to timelessness and the embodiment of spirit.

Fukiage sits amid verdant grounds in the middle of Tokyo, urban real estate so immense and central as to define the city's daily pulse and rush. Yet it can be seen—bits of it, never the whole—only from a few vantage points on the upper floors of skyscrapers along nearby boulevards. For all its "thereness," the palace is not there at all: It is only suggested. In *Empire of Signs*, Roland Barthes, the semiologist and philosopher, described this as Tokyo's "precious paradox." "It does possess a center," Barthes wrote of the Japanese capital,

> but this center is empty. . . . Daily, in their rapid, energetic, bullet-like trajectories, the taxis avoid this circle, whose low crest, the visible form of invisibility, hides the sacred "nothing." One of the two most powerful cities of modernity is thereby built around an opaque ring of walls, streams, roofs, and trees whose own center is no more than an evaporated notion, subsisting here, not in order to irradiate power, but to give the entire urban movement the support of its central emptiness, forcing the traffic to make a perpetual detour. In this manner, we are told, the system of the imaginary is spread circularly, by detours and returns the length of an empty subject.

The paradox Barthes found in modern Tokyo, the empty center around which everything spins, has existed since the ninth century, when a family called Fujiwara established a hereditary regency that lasted until the first shogun took power, in 1185, and the feudal era began. Throughout the centuries, the emperor gave legitimacy to civilian and military dictatorships while remaining in ever more frivolous seclusion. The Tokugawa especially liked this imperial evanescence, the better to check any emperor with temporal designs. It was against this background that the Emperor Meiji, a decisive figure of pronounced appetites, put away the pancake makeup and exited the shadows. But the elite who created modern Japan under him were still fond of the old mysteries: The invisible man above the clouds was their greatest organizing tool when they set about creating the family-state after the restoration.

Postwar rightists are practiced travelers along the detours and returns of myth and ideology surrounding the Chrysanthemum Throne. One of them, the composer Toshiro Mayuzumi, explained to me as Hirohito lay dying in the autumn of 1988, "The emperor has no power but is the source of all power." This was the age-old formulation, commonly employed after 1945 to excuse Hirohito from responsibility in the Pacific war. It, too, reveals something of the emptiness Barthes described, and the silence Michiko captured in her tanka.

Even now, with Hirohito dead and Michiko's husband installed (by an entirely mythical count) as the 125th emperor (124th successor to Jimmu, whose ancestors dwelt in the heavens) the peculiar emptiness of the emperor and the system sustaining him remains like a Zen koan, a one-hand-clapping riddle. An emperor sits at the center of Japan, but there is neither a throne within Fukiage Palace nor an empire beyond it. It is as if the palace and the man within are hollow vessels into which anything can be placed and so given meaning. Except that Hirohito was not so powerless, after all, and for a time there was an empire.

So we ask: What will the emperor mean in our time? Who will Akihito be, and what the palace's place? It is interesting to pose these questions, not because the emperor is still so important in Japan—I do not think he is. It is likely that he has reoccupied the place of minor importance, even obscurity, that his ancestors held before 1868. But the answers suggest something of Japan's transition nonetheless—from looking obsessively back to looking forward, from the ancient spirit to the spirit of a modern nation, the ordinary human spirit.

Akihito must ask himself these questions, too. It is easy, at least, to imagine that he does. He is the first emperor to begin his reign as a human, not a god. According to the postwar constitution, he is merely "a symbol of the unity of the Japanese people." To one degree or another, all of Akihito's ancestors fostered that dependence so central to the constructed Japanese personality. What will become of Akihito if he does not fulfill that role? And what will become of Japan and the Japanese?

HIROHITO DIED AT 6:33 A.M. on January 7, 1989. There was something oddly official about the way he passed away—something that suggested the final phase of his fatal illness was secretly controlled, or paced. Afterward, the theory of a choreographed death was widely discussed— the idea that the Kunaicho, the Imperial Household Agency, had planned everything, even the monarch's moment of departure. To picture an expiring eighty-seven-year-old as no more than a body through which fluids were passed until the decided day and time argues for a cold-blooded view of the imperial chamberlains. But many held this view, and it cannot be discounted.

Hirohito had been frail for some years by the autumn of 1988. He had undergone surgery, and his public appearances were even rarer and briefer than usual. There were rumors during the summer that he was losing his battle with pancreatic cancer—a disease everyone knew he suffered, but about which nothing was ever said. On a Saturday in September came the Kunaicho's terse announcement: The emperor had vomited blood and was in critical condition. Not in his worst moments had the cultish agency told the Japanese anything so graphic, so bluntly revealing. X Day—the official but widely understood code for the date of death—was coming.

To recall that autumn, it was as if a soft rain fell steadily for several months. It could not have been so; but that season survives in memory as a chain of days when umbrellas made an unbroken patchwork outside the palace gates. Daily crowds began to appear immediately after the official announcement. Well-wishers signed scrolls on rows of tables beneath long canvas canopies. Some wept as they paused to peer within the gates, some bowed, some talked, and some looked blankly ahead. The scene reminded me of a 1930s news photograph taken during a similarly dour season. Men in dark overcoats stand three-deep and bow toward Nijubashi, the ornate stone bridge leading into the palace grounds. It was as if nothing had changed over half a century of war and history.

From the *Herald Tribune* bureau at the north side of the palace, I watched the columns of people on their way to pay respects. Sometimes I went with them to the graveled field near the east gate. I met a retired unionist named Kamezaburo Takeuchi, who had come an hour and a half from Yokohama after the television reports about the vomiting. "I've been a man of the left all my life, but politics doesn't matter at a time like this," he said. "The emperor is the head of the Japanese family." On another cold, drizzly morning I encountered a twenty-five-year-old *sarariman* named Hiromichi Hashizumi. He said, "I've never believed the emperor was god as my father and grandfather did. But now that he's struggling for his life, I realize that he's kept our nation together."

One heard these things over and over. Much had happened since 1868, but—outside the palace, at least—one could still imagine the emperor as the instrument of authority that the restoration leaders intended to create when they moved him from shabby obscurity in Kyoto and declared him both a god and a modern monarch.

But the sentiments of those lingering at the gates were not matched elsewhere. A period of *jishuku,* self-restraint, was observed, but *jishuku* was a curious thing. Harvest festivals and office parties were canceled, weddings postponed. The season's sumo champion had no victory parade. Words like "new" and "congratulations" and "birth" were removed from packaging and advertisements. Then *jishuku* became complicated. It was disrupting the economy, merchants complained. A communist mayor signed a get-well scroll and his constituents forced him to apologize. Rock concerts were called off, but promoters and stars had to obscure so unfashionable a reason. The Mitsukoshi department store, long in the service of the imperial family, was reported to have withdrawn red fish paste, a celebratory food, from its shelves. No, the manager protested, supplies had merely run out. Along with the sadness came a certain resentment. In the end, *jishuku* was sustained by that most profound of anxieties, the anxiety of not conforming.

The Kunaicho is a jealous and obsessively secretive guardian of the imperial family. It is essentially the administrator of palace affairs—partly a protocol master, partly a pedant of history, and partly a severe baby-sitter. It shepherded the crowds near Nijubashi with decorum and solemn authority.

But elsewhere it seemed utterly at sea as to how to manage Hirohito's easily foreseen death. Until he died it issued daily statistics on his condition—pulse, temperature, volumes of blood lost and transfused—in a singular combination of reverence and vulgarity. These became, as when a word is repeated over and over, a nonsensical litany. A bowel movement was heralded on page one of the national dailies, as were ingestions of arrowroot and the emperor's success in sucking on tiny ice cubes.

Hirohito's funeral, held more than a month after his death, took place outdoors at a park named for the Emperor Meiji. Strains of ancient, discordant music haunted it. Elaborate and obscure, the ritual was incomprehensible—so reminding foreign guests that they were there partly to be excluded. Yet the present intruded, for the emperor's keepers had to observe constitutional distinctions between religion and state. Midway through, the funeral abruptly stopped. Then curtains were drawn to block a Shinto ritual from view, leaving hundreds of dignitaries staring at a blank barrier in a driving, freezing rain.

Crews from N.H.K., the national broadcasting network, set up cameras on either side of the central proscenium. On television later, the news showed a long shot as each foreign leader approached the bier; only if the dignitary bowed before it—a very few refrained—did the picture cut to a close-up and linger upon the gesture. The picture returned to the long shot as each guest walked back to his seat, and an N.H.K. commentary began. "Here we see the president of the Federative Republic of Brazil, Mr. José Sarney," a typical voice-over said. "While he is in Tokyo, President Sarney will be attempting to renegotiate part of his country's debt to Japan, which totals more than sixteen billion dollars." And then on to the next gaijin mourner.

The imperial transition was a lesson in the old enthusiasm for imagery and the surface of things. It was also the product of the new Japan, a Japan not sure if it was newly rich but still traditional, or simply rich. No one knew how to handle an event that had not occurred for sixty-two years. Officials studied photographs and films and old newspaper accounts, but there were few left in authority who could remember the death of Hirohito's father, the Emperor Taisho, and how the tradition was observed or embroidered then.

Akihito did not become emperor for two years following his father's death. In the interim, all the confusion Japan felt about itself came to the fore, all manner of monsters were bred. A private school in Shimane Prefecture boasted that it had revived the prewar practice of reciting the Imperial Rescript on Education. Ultrarightists called for a new restoration, in which the emperor's divinity, renounced by Hirohito after the war, would be reasserted. Ultraleft sects dormant for years, forgotten in absurdly fortified suburban hovels, blinked in the daylight and threatened to shell the imperial palace.

Everyone met at the vanishing point, for these were all contributions to a long-delayed national conversation. At times Japan seemed to have forgotten what year it was, but that was because so much in need of saying, about the emperor and the past, had been left so long unsaid. From Hirohito's death to Akihito's accession was a long season of uncertainty between the end of one era and the beginning of another, like the moment between the lightning and the thunder.

IN THE FINAL days of 1926, his father having died on Christmas day, Hirohito began his reign, the era of Showa, Enlightened Peace. Early in the new year the *New York Times Magazine* published an article by a correspondent in Tokyo named Adachi Kinnosuke. In hindsight we can only marvel at its ironies:

> A young emperor who has broken more than one rigid tradition observed by his 123 predecessors comes to the throne in Japan when public opinion for the first time has found its voice and universal suffrage is a fact. This combination foretells interesting events across the Pacific.
>
> The Nippon which the new Emperor . . . sees as he ascends the throne is a far different country from that seen by his father. . . . The latter came to power when his country was still under the thumb of a few old men known the world over as the Elder Statesmen. . . . Today the Elder Statesmen are passing into history. . . . For the first time in centuries the military oligarchy is in the thickening shadows, and one of its leaders, General Baron Tanaka, has forsaken a military career for a political career. The country has already passed through the first stage of industrialism. . . .
>
> To reign over this new country comes at the age of 25 a young Prince who has had two great experiences such as no

Son of Heaven upon the throne of Yamato had ever known in the twenty-five century history of the dynasty. One of them was contact with the world outside of Japan, and the other was with love. . . .

It has been the fate of each Japanese monarch since Meiji to begin again as a modernizer. The Emperor Meiji set in motion the great roll forward. Taisho, his son, who was progessively deranged his entire adult life, was so far gone by 1921 that Hirohito assumed the imperial duties as prince regent. But Taisho's reign, from 1912 to 1926, was nonetheless notable for its liberalism and its enthusiasm for the currents of European modernism. The interlude of "Taisho democracy" was brief, but the phrase evokes nostalgia and a certain wonder today, even among Japanese too young to have known it.

Hirohito had his frontiers, too, as the *Times* correspondent noted: love and travel. Hirohito was the first crown prince to leave Japan, when he toured Europe in 1921; his reception at Buckingham Palace was the stuff of legend. His marriage, three years later, was "the first love match known to the annals of the imperial house," as Kinnosuke reported. Against official objections, Hirohito had helped choose Princess Nagako himself: He hid behind a screen to watch a tea ceremony his mother arranged for several candidates.

So Hirohito, like his father and grandfather in their day, was much the progressive monarch in January of 1927. True, he had cast his eye upon China even while still crown prince; the weapons buildup that would soon change the world had begun during his regency. But the mood outside Fukiage Palace, if not within, was still Taisho liberal.

Hirohito's ventures among women and gaijin paled next to his son's. Akihito was tutored by a foreigner just after the war, a Philadelphia Quaker who, more than anyone else, made him an internationalist. His later travels ranged from Wyoming to Peru, Iran, Spain, and Afghanistan. More legendary was his introduction to Michiko Shoda on a tennis court in Karuizawa, a summer resort favored by foreign missionaries. Before their marriage (and for a long time afterward), the couple faced disapproval from the Kunaicho at least as strenuous as what Hirohito had confronted. But that only improved the story for ordinary Japanese.

Karuizawa became something of a shrine among young, romantically inclined "office ladies," and tennis a favored pastime.

That Akihito emerged as another imperial modernist is scarcely surprising. And at first glance it is remarkable how little the boundaries moved over the course of six decades. Love and travel, encounters with the self and the other, were still the frontiers of symbolic change. As Akihito prepared to replace his father, Japan was again trying to push its elder statesmen into history, and popular opinion was again heard in politics. But the elder statesmen of the late 1980s were direct descendants of the earlier generation; and while the public may have found its voice, in the 1980s as in the 1920s, it was not yet clear who was listening to it.

Japan's modern monarchs embody the nature of change in Japan, even if they are not its agents. There seems to be progress and yet no progress from era to era, like the observable shifts and the observable sameness in Japanese cities. It is the emperor himself who suggests most clearly that most enigmatic of realities, a nation always on the crest of great change, ever in the act of becoming—a thrilling and depressing prospect all at once. But Akihito would be different, a break in the chain. Hirohito was the last emperor to be considered a god. This alone said something essential about Akihito's time: It would be a departure, and there would be no turning back from it.

When Hirohito died he assumed the name of his era—becoming, by the recently established custom, Emperor Showa. Soon afterward, Akihito's handlers announced the new era's name. It would be Heisei, Achieving Peace. It was not one of the Kunaicho's most successful contrivances. People found the calligraphy an awkward pair of characters, just as in English there is something tentative and ill fitting about the phrase, the world's only officially sanctioned dangling participle. Commentators explained that Heisei signaled an enduring commitment to the postwar constitution, in which Japan officially renounced its right to wage war. But that peace was already achieved, surely. If there was a peace still to come it was with the past, a peace among the Japanese themselves as well as with their neighbors. Something new had to be placed inside the sacred nothing, and this meant another paradox, for it was something about which, for the first time, there could be nothing sacred.

Akihito spent many years elaborating his imperial imagery. He used a colloquial version of the language, in contrast to his father, and spoke often to ordinary Japanese, especially the young. He wore stylish suits and

threw out baseballs at opening games in the spring. These were signals—
subtle to foreigners, perhaps, but read by the Japanese as easily as billboards. A certain tension between Akihito and his Kunaicho minders was
sometimes suggested. He let his second son marry while his eldest,
Naruhito, the future crown prince, remained a bachelor: To the tradition-
alists this was a grave transgression. But in conversations, officials who
favored Akihito's tilt smiled upon these matters. They especially welcomed
the comparisons frequently made between Akihito and Prince Charles.

Akihito versified industriously as crown prince. In 1986 he and
Michiko published *Light*, a collection of their tanka. Here is one from a
three-poem series called "In Ethiopia" (1961):

> Seeing the acacia trees
> With nests of birds
> Hanging from their branches.
> I deeply feel
> I am in Africa.

And from 1985, "The Return of Prince Naruhito from Oxford University":

> Having spent
> Two years at a university
> In a foreign country,
> My son has now
> Come home again.

They may sit like potatoes on the page, but the lyrics served a purpose, as
much imperial verse no doubt did in its time. No one before had ever
evoked East African gum trees and English classrooms. But no emperor
was ever charged with making a worldly human of himself. To alter the
imperial imagery is enough to change the imperial system: That was the
conceit, at least. It was one way at one of the Chrysanthemum Throne's
essential problems, the problem of survival in a changing Japan. But to
alter the imagery is not enough to change the past, and the truth about the
past was another of the throne's problems.

THREE NOTED PHOTOGRAPHS describe the progress of Hirohito's reign. From the 1930s, there is Hirohito in high black boots and a Prussian-style tunic astride his famous white charger. In September of 1945, a month after the surrender, Hirohito wears a morning suit as he stands beside General MacArthur, who is tieless in khaki, hands thrust into his back pockets. Sometime later, probably in the late 1940s or 1950s, Hirohito sits before a microscope. Over a cheap *sarariman*'s suit he wears a white laboratory gown: He is pursuing his interest in marine biology.

Perhaps the Kunaicho should add the image of a chameleon to the three ancient symbols of the throne—the mirror, the sword, and the jewel. As a quick-change artist, Hirohito was a master who gave up the stage only when he died. Akihito has a far less dramatic script to follow, and so has managed the part with more subtlety. But the exercise is the same. Like the lizard that lives long without sustenance, the emperor changes color according to his environment.

The most famous speech Hirohito ever made, with the exception of his surrender broadcast, dates to January 1, 1946. The idea for it came not from the palace, but from G.H.Q. Neither did Hirohito write it—the Americans did. Hirohito was merely one of eight editors who worked on the document between its initial draft and its final form.

The speech was a muddle, as words uttered reluctantly often are. It began with a lengthy reference to the Emperor Meiji, the very wellspring of modern Japanese nationalism, and continued on to assure the nation that it would henceforth enjoy the democracy his grandfather had promised when he issued the Charter Oath. Well toward the conclusion the emperor remarked, as if in passing:

> The ties between Us and Our people have always stood on mutual trust and affection. They do not depend on mere legends and myths. They are not predicated on the false concept that the Emperor is divine and that the Japanese people are superior to other races and fated to rule the world.

Hirohito acknowledged his mortality with all the grudging dignity he could muster. Behind the scenes, though, his horse-trading with the occupation over this statement had been intense and decidedly down-to-earth.

MacArthur and the Tokyo lobby in Washington had decided even before the surrender to spare the emperor the fate of those to be tried for war crimes. History would record—though by no means to universal satisfaction—that the erstwhile Son of Heaven had been powerless against those who prosecuted the war in his name. The renunciation speech was part of this postsurrender deal. Most immediately, Hirohito saw it as a useful concession in negotiations over war criminals and in his furious (but finally failed) effort to save the constitution he inherited from his grandfather.

The speech marked the beginning of Hirohito's new life. He had traded in his plumed Prussian cap for the negotiator's chimney pot, and that day he put on the crumpled fedora of the postwar *sarariman.* He traveled a great distance downward from his place beyond the clouds, for the American plan was to make him mundane. Hirohito was the reverse course made flesh. In July of 1946 Washington formally informed MacArthur that preserving the imperial system was occupation policy. "The supreme commander is therefore ordered to assist secretly in popularizing and humanizing the emperor," an official directive read. "This will not be known to the Japanese people."

An impressive effort followed. The remade Hirohito came to resemble an innocent bumbler, a little like a Buster Keaton character. He pottered in his garden, fussed with his microscope, and spluttered when greeting his former subjects—people previously not allowed even to look at him. He was photographed reading *Stars and Stripes,* the American military daily, and traveled by ordinary train to every prefecture save Okinawa. He had grown up speaking an antique tongue; his surrender broadcast had required a translation into everyday speech. But he learned to address his countrymen in the modern vernacular. Soon enough Hirohito was known as Mr. Ah So Desuka, Mr. You Don't Say, for that was usually his remark when conversing with the ordinary mortals into whose midst he had entered.

The emperor's reinvention was easy in one respect—or seemed so. Few official records of his activities survived the two-week interval between the surrender and the conquering army's arrival in Tokyo. The war makers destroyed almost everything. After the defeat, MacArthur censored *Stars and Stripes* to eliminate any reference to Hirohito's role during the war.

This allowed a rewrite of history worthy of Stalin (who did not disapprove of it as much as others among the allies), but the occupation, as we have seen, was nothing if not ambitious in the matter of remaking Japan.

One might forgive America its ambitious deception, except for the havoc and heartache it caused the Japanese for the next half century. By excusing the emperor the occupation launched in a single stroke the culture of irresponsibility from which Japan has ever since suffered. History was made deniable. Ordinary Japanese would have to fight over and over against the false representations of their own leaders. With the victors' dispensation, the entire project of recasting the country began with a charade. The ethos of irresponsibility seeped in everywhere—politics, education, diplomacy, and so on. Show was enough, substance beside the point.

What did Hirohito think of all this? We do not have to look far for an answer, for he had more to say on the day he denied his divinity. He also presented the Japanese with a New Year's tanka, a tradition begun by Meiji in 1869. It was a surprising departure from the speech on which he and MacArthur had separately labored:

> Courageous the pine
> That does not change its color
> Under winter snow.
> Truly the men of Japan
> Should be a forest of pines.

Here was a thirty-one-syllable commentary on how the Japanese should react to all that was to occur under their occupiers: Bear it, Hirohito advised, but keep the spirit intact. His final two lines neatly presaged the postwar corporate warrior—each a part of the whole, each indistinguishable from any other. It was an imperial rescript, in miniature and in metaphor.

Four decades later this salutation seemed a bitter gift from father to son. With it Hirohito revealed his postwar intention: He would stop time— political and historic time—and delay the evolution of Japan and the Japanese. The Americans cannot be left out in this respect: They made the imperial institution part of the stopped time of the Cold War. Forty-three years afterward it was an odd coincidence that Hirohito passed away and the Cold War ended more or less simultaneously. The throne was still the center of controversy. And amid this controversy stood the old forest of pines that had never changed color, the tennoists, as devotees of the emperor (*tenno*) were called.

Tennoists were numerous before the war, a fixture on the political and ideological scene. Professors made careers out of hairsplitting contributions to *tennosei ideorogii,* the ideology of the imperial system. Theories of the state and theological interpretations could bring down ministers, weigh on military strategy, send people to prison. The best known of many controversies erupted in the mid-1930s. Its focus was whether the emperor was an organ of government (as the Meiji constitution stipulated) or a divine being who reigned beyond the temporal state (as nationalist ideology stressed). The "organ theory" spat was a political ploy to influence military strategy. It went through the upper reaches of power like a virus, eventually producing an indirect challenge to Hirohito's authority. In the course of resolving it he prevailed in his fateful judgment that Japan should avoid the Soviet Union and strike south into China and Southeast Asia when it made war.

Among the best known of the postwar tennoists was a man named Hideaki Kase. Kase had been an adviser to two prime ministers and was a blunt, provocative proponent of the emperor in his purest prewar form. I saw him on the eve of Akihito's accession. His office was in an ugly modern building, cramped and cluttered, but the floors were of polished wood and tatami, and the windows were covered in delicately framed rice-paper shoji. "I'm sorry to say that Akihito is going in the wrong direction," Kase began. What followed is worth quoting at some length:

> He's trying to project the image of a Western monarch, we can assume after the British model, which is totally mistaken. Royal houses in the West are basically families of entertainers. You could say that Elizabeth is the pope of the Church of England, but she doesn't perform any of the rites herself. She isn't an intermediary between heaven and earth, as the Roman pope is. In the East, holy people are not to be seen in public. This year, last year, Akihito has shaken hands with young people; he allowed his second son to marry while the crown prince is still a bachelor. This is grossly wrong. We expect members of the imperial family to be guardians of the Japanese

tradition. That's their role. I'd like to see Akihito go back to Kyoto and live in seclusion. Instead he's trying to be a modern monarch, competing with TV stars.

Kase was entirely correct: The image of a Western monarch was precisely what Akihito was after. In the era of Achieving Peace there would be no place for Talmudic bickering over the emperor's place, no hocus-pocus about divine ancestors. The throne's most devoted followers no longer fit into the entourage. The time of the true believers was over. But Akihito shared one important thing with the lingering tennoists. Like them, he wanted to cleanse the imperial institution of the smear his father had placed upon it. Like them, he wanted to avoid the questions his father left behind: questions of imperial guilt and responsibility. Like them, he thought manipulating the imagery would be enough.

AKIHITO'S ACCESSION RITES were many: There were forty in the year before he assumed the throne, in November of 1990. They cost the government $95 million. Not quite a fifth of that sum went toward a rite called the Daijosai, an overnighter in which Akihito entered into mystical union with no less a figure than Amaterasu, the ancient sun goddess. These occasions were duly reported in the national newspapers, but other than that no one seemed to take much notice. Postwar Japan, the Japan of production, political apathy, alienated youth, and consumer spending, had resumed its rhythm, flowing over the accession rites as ineluctably as a tide.

Modeled after harvest rituals, the Daijosai is said by some scholars to date to 350 B.C. or slightly later. It requires sacred paddies for the cultivation of rice that the new emperor offers to the gods. The exercise evolved over many centuries, but only after the restoration was it given much importance. Fertility was always the theme, but for a long time the gods and goddesses changed from one Daijosai to another. Amaterasu entered the picture only when the imperial system was established, in the sixth and seventh centuries.

The emperor's behavior during the Daijosai is a secret undiscussed even among tennoists. This much is known: The emperor enters a primitive hut in the evening and lies on a sacred bed. The bed rests on a seat once occupied by the deceased emperor. At least one female from the court is present during the night. It is then that the emperor assumes the spirit of Amaterasu—that is, he is deified. The secret ceremony ends the following morning. Then the emperor offers the gods rice, gruel, and sake, all from the sacred crop.

Does the emperor have intercourse with the female? Some scholars have said so. The sexual overtones are curious, in any event: a relic of the uninhibited society of the ancient cultivators, but a slight embarrassment in the fastidious atmosphere of modern, samuraized Japan. The female is there to renew the new emperor's soul. But does he also assume the soul of his predecessor, thereby confirming the lineage? In the mid-1970s this notion led one scholar to postulate the existence of a single "imperial soul" that passes on and on, from one monarch to the next. Some say the body of the dead emperor was placed on the sacred seat. In the old days, then, was the continuous soul conveyed when the new emperor bit into the corpse of the old? That has been postulated, too.

The interpretations of this rite are nearly as various as the Japanese gods. No one knows precisely what the ceremony means. No one was certain that Akihito's Daijosai was historically accurate. The past is everything and nothing in Japan. The Daijosai is the essential example of the modern state's manipulation of the past to create the power and authority rendered by tradition. Fertility rites are universal. The Inca emperor, who was oddly Confucian in certain respects, used to plant the year's first quinoa, "the mother grain," with a spade of solid gold. But it is only in Japan that the head of state continues to lead such ceremonies. The first recorded Daijosai took place in the year 691. For a time later it fell into disuse, but the Tokugawa revived it in the late seventeenth century. The moment of deification appears to be an occurrence no older than the restoration, a concoction of creative tennoists during the Meiji and Taisho years.

In 1990 this piece of the muddled past, like the Shinto rites during Hirohito's funeral, was constitutionally off-limits so far as the use of official funds. But then, the Kunaicho was run by fiercely nostalgic remnants of the prewar nobility, and it had a fairly free hand in organizing the accession. Disputes erupted. It was not simply the money to be lavished on the Daijosai, the $17 million required to build Akihito's primitive hut, which turned out to be a complex of thirty thatched-roof buildings on the imperial grounds. It was the spectacle of postwar Japan still living in the autumn of 1945, grudgingly giving up of the prewar order only what it was forced to give up.

Two weeks before the ceremony, a Socialist member of the Diet submitted five questions to the house speaker. In one he quoted a prewar textbook that described the Daijosai as "a divine event at which the emperor is unified with the Oogimi"—the greatest of Shinto gods—"and it is made clear that Japan is a divine nation." Would it be possible, the Diet member asked, "to deny such an old definition explicitly, and if so, what changes would be made in this year's Daijosai?"

Many days passed with no official response. When one came, two days before the ceremony, it was cast in the indirect language characteristic of Kunaicho utterances. There was nothing about altering the rite: "It is noticed that there was the description you pointed out, but it is believed this was due to the special circumstances of the time." On television that evening, the news announcer included a one-sentence brief on the matter just before the weather report: "A government spokesman stated officially today that Emperor Akihito would not be transformed into a god during the upcoming Daijosai ceremony."

The accession itself had plenty of Confucian distance designed into it. Heads of state and other guests were separated from the platform on which Akihito and Michiko sat by more than two hundred feet, and they were four feet below it. Onstage, the royal couple's seats were raised an additional three feet closer to the clouds (reduced from an elevation of almost twenty feet when Hirohito acceded). The ceremony lasted but half an hour; only those who craned their necks saw much of it. The Kunaicho must have been pleased: By manipulating space it had more or less forced foreigners into the position of the worshipful.

After the accession, I went to see a man named Seizaburo Sato. Sato was a tennoist. Sober in appearance, balding, a bit mean faced, he did not suffer foreigners lightly, especially Americans. But he effervesced when I told him I had come to talk about the accession. "It was simple, aesthetic, serene, and quiet," he said crisply. "It was neither gorgeous nor rhythmical. There was no music. Everything was just as expected—no more, no less."

I told Sato that I had watched the ceremony. It was indeed serene, but partly because Akihito appeared rather uninvolved. During many of the various rites he looked as if he wanted to fold back the sleeves of his voluminous kimono to look at his watch. The young Hirohito considered his divine status ridiculous, but he expressed that only in private, and he certainly made use of the power it gave him. So I suggested to Sato that, for the first time, Japan may have an emperor who was openly detached from his own status.

"Is it really necessary for a public figure to believe in the essence of the ceremony he performs?" Sato asked abruptly. "To follow the ritual is enough. The issue you raise is not something that's on my mind. My answer is, 'I don't know. It doesn't matter.'"

"Is that really so, Sato-sensei? It doesn't matter?"

"Japan is a nation-state. Every nation-state needs its fictions to unite people. You Americans have your fictions—the constitution, democracy, 'the American dream,' 'the American way of life.' The emperor is also a kind of fiction."

This was a startling admission for a man of Sato's reputation. It suggested that the pines were finally changing hue—that Akihito was to be cleansed of the musty odor of his father's boots and tunics. The Kunaicho had never acknowledged that the emperor was anything less than a god. The tennoists argued for half a century that the New Year's speech on the subject was coerced (which it was, more or less). Now the emperor was reduced to a fiction, or a colorful exotic, like a tourist attraction—or even an entertainer.

"That's quite different from what was held true during the last imperial transition," I remarked. "What else has changed?"

"One remarkable thing is that when Taisho passed away and Showa was enthroned, no foreign dignitaries came—only diplomats stationed in Tokyo. This time more than a hundred and seventy foreign dignitaries came. But this is natural. Japan is a powerful nation."

In one of Akihito's rituals at the accession rite he kicked a small globe at his feet three times, signifying his supremacy over the universe. Who knew how old this rite was? It reeked of prewar ambition. Still, the Kunaicho kept it in, and it made for an apt moment, especially because most of those 170 gaijin who sat below the emperor probably missed it. Unseen, the gesture became a precise expression of how little any of those present seemed to understand of what their attendance meant to Japan.

There were awkward moments during the transition period. Commotions erupted in countries with more accurate memories than the Americans': Australia refused to send an official to Hirohito's funeral, and

New Zealand sent a minor one after heated public debate. The headlines in London when Hirohito died began with HIROHITO TAKES HIS GUILT TO THE GRAVE (in the *Daily Telegraph*) and went on from there. LET THE BASTARD ROT IN HELL, a tabloid shrieked.

That was only one side of things. Japan got what it wanted from the imperial transition, at least in matters of form. At century's end it gained the throne's acceptance in the outside world. Tokyo had long earlier developed the habit of purchasing what it could not provide for itself. In the same way the new Japan could turn affluence and technological acumen into power. When Hirohito died, you could almost rank a country's hard-currency reserves by the solemnity of its response. India and Cuba, among others, declared national days of mourning.

POPULAR INDIFFERENCE TOWARD the palace was much noticed during the transition. Evidence of it appeared everywhere. An American scholar took me to the Roppongi bar district during Hirohito's illness. "You see," he said with satisfaction, "all full, like any other night." An English stockbroker reminded me that the market had gained 15 percent between the day Hirohito vomited and his death. An Italian correspondent dropped by my office. "Look!" he said, cupping his hands together and shaking them at me. "I've checked all the airlines and the resorts within a few hours' flying distance. What did I find? The weekend of the enthronement—all booked solid for the past three months."

Busy bars and crowded airports made official Japan pretend. It pretended that the whole nation would have been at the palace gates, if only it could have been. But to pretend in this way made the distance between the palace and ordinary Japanese seem only the wider and emptier. When Hirohito acceded, six hundred thousand people lined the streets of Tokyo, Kyoto, and Nagoya. The official estimate in 1990, delivered with the customary precision, was 116,877. There was no television in the old days, officials rushed to explain. There was less traffic then. And there was no official effort this time to mobilize people (which did not seem strictly true).

During the accession rites I went buttonholing again near Fukiage Palace. Thirty-seven thousand policemen were ranged around the city. On the day of the Daijosai I met a *sarariman* in an exercise suit who kept glancing away, or down at his running shoes. "I haven't been much interested in this kind of thing," he said. Was all the ceremony unnecessary? He didn't think there was much choice, he replied. "We should have it because we're Japanese. But it's expensive—and it's our taxes that are being spent. I have my doubts."

I spoke to a middle-aged woman who owned a shop in the Ginza. She said, "The enthronement is an important thing for all Japanese, but they should have divided the ceremonies more clearly into religious and national events. The religious events should have been more discreet. And the security is too heavy. That part is ridiculous. I can't stand it."

There was a tough-looking man in a leather athletic jacket who had come from Hokkaido to watch a rugby match. I asked whether he liked Akihito. He seemed to search for something to say. "I honestly can't say yes or no," he finally replied. Did he think the emperor system was a good one? "I'm sure we need it. It's a good national system. But I don't want to talk about the war now, or the emperor's responsibility. I'm not sure we were happy that the United States controlled us after the war. But I'm not sure either whether it would have been better if we had won the war."

I met two high school girls in navy-blue uniforms. One said, "No we haven't spent much time watching the ceremonies." Was that because they weren't interested? "We hardly talk about it at school—the emperor, the enthronement, and all that," the other girl said. "The emperor changed from Showa to Akihito, but it hasn't changed anything else so far."

It was hard to interpret these encounters. That many Japanese were uninterested in Akihito's solemn doings was evident enough. But the mournful crowds at the palace and the indifferent rush of traffic along the encircling boulevards could also be read as mirror images. The two displays of sentiment, side by side in apparent contradiction, suggested in combination the very essence of the imperial ideal since Meiji: The fullest acceptance lay in a form of disregard. The emperor, after all, was supposed to be at his most powerful in the psyches of his subjects. "People should-n't take an excessive interest in the emperor," the tennoist Hideaki Kase once told me. "He should be like an uncle, existing in our subconscious."

There is a kind of childish dependence implicit in such an idea. An infant develops a passive reliance in an exclusive emotional bond with his mother. It is when the child most desires to be securely enveloped that he counts most on the protective boundaries created by this intimate connection. This is universal. Peculiar to the Japanese is the social acceptance of this desire within the range of legitimate adult emotions. It is incautious to generalize on such a point. But the adult search for passive dependence is a traceable element in a society so thoroughly given to hierarchical relations, where adulthood is made so burdensome, and where emotional warmth and vulnerability are so closely identified with the private, the shielded, and the hidden.

There is no translation for the term that defines this feeling: *amae,* or, in its infinitive form, *amaeru.* The psychiatrist Takeo Doi established *amae* in *The Anatomy of Dependence,* his 1971 book, as fundamental to the psychological makeup of the Japanese. An adult seeks throughout life to reproduce that closed field of emotion that in infancy allows him limitless self-indulgence, Doi asserted. To presume upon, to rebel, to act with indifference: These were the adult expressions of *amae.* Doi insisted that to *amaeru* was common to all human beings, even if the act was not always named. But the Japanese

> idealized amae and considered a world dominated by amae as a truly human world; and the emperor system might be seen as an institutionalization of this idea. . . .
>
> It was not until the emperor himself denied the myths and became the "symbol" of the Japanese people that it became possible to bring into the light the *amae* lurking in the heart of each individual Japanese.
>
> The present age has seen the collapse of the emperor system as an ideology. . . . This does not mean, however, that everything in the nature of a system has disappeared. . . .

Doi made an important point. The psychology of dependence has not disappeared. One cannot talk about autonomy without raising the question of dependence. So one must view displays of indifference cautiously. And dependence was indeed fostered through the emperor. But there is a problem with Doi's analysis. There is no place in it for politics and history. To leave these things out is to posit some peculiar trait about the Japanese, something in the culture or the tradition or the soul. And that is to assert that the psychology of dependence cannot change. In the end, this is another Orientalist version of the Japanese.

I went to see Doi, a slight man then seventy, during the imperial transition. I told him that a prominent conservative thinker had called the emperor a kind of fiction. At this Doi pounced. "He deliberately used the word 'fiction'—that's my interpretation. He didn't want to give the impression that he really believes in the system. People are embarrassed when you, a foreigner, ask what they feel about the emperor. The general understanding is that we shouldn't make too much of a fuss about it."

Doi complained about news commentators, who referred often to the "symbolic emperor." They used a term that meant "something light," he explained, "something that has no weight, not the real thing." He said, "It's as if they were trying to protect themselves, as if they're saying, 'It's a puppet emperor, not a real one.' They feel it's not fashionable to say anything positive about the emperor. They want to minimize the value of the system and the tradition."

The image of a weightless man, tethered only by the gravity of his many-layered kimono, reminded me of something a professor had told me a few days earlier. Some of his students had compared Akihito's accession to a festival young girls celebrate each spring. In it they display dolls modeled on the emperor and empress during the feudal era.

"That's it, exactly!" Doi exclaimed. "People see them as dolls."

Doi would say nothing about his own feelings. He parried my questions impishly while fingering a well-worn paperback of *Roget's Thesaurus* in his lap. He seemed intent on sparring his way through the conversation, as if he wished it (and I with it) would go away. When I got up to leave, I asked bluntly, "Are you embarrassed, too, Doctor Doi?" For a moment he said nothing.

"I could tell you I'm indifferent, as many people seem to be," he replied. "But that would be too"—he searched for a word and laughed when he found one—"that would be too fictive."

Doi had considered radical political groups and how they, too, displayed the pervasive drive for *amae*. From the feudal era onward, he wrote in *The Anatomy of Dependence,* "the spirit of resistance to the authority of the time invariably used the imperial family as its starting point."

This was not strictly true. The spirit of resistance in Japan can hardly be reduced to a psychological habit, however pervasive. One cannot discount the thousands of peasant uprisings during the late feudal period—or any modern political group—simply by citing *amae*. Yes, many peasant leaders turned to the emperor to intervene against a harsh daimyo. Commoners turned to him as the Tokugawa shogunate collapsed. But this did not make them tennoists. The emperor stood for a political force at that moment. Doi seemed to give a name to a discernible phenomenon. Time and again in Japan (and elsewhere in East Asia, for that matter) one finds opposition groups more concerned with striking heroic poses than with building a reasoned position that could win acceptance and eventually prevail; power was the furthest thing from their minds. But how much did this have to do with *amae* and how much with the more complicated question of political immaturity?

There was a radical group called Chukakuha, the Central Core Faction, that was still active in the late 1980s. It claimed responsibility for dozens of minor acts of sabotage during the transition, including several primitive shells launched into the palace grounds. I went to see a man who went by the name Yoshihisa Fujiwara, a Central Core leader, in a shabby section of northern Tokyo, where the group had an old building barricaded with sandbags and steel doors. So far as I could make out, Chukakuha occupied a small plot in the farther reaches of the Trotskyist tundra. Among other things, it asserted that under Akihito Japan would again turn militarist and that the new emperor would lead another invasion of neighboring nations.

What, if anything, did Doi's notion of *amae* have to do with this somewhat deranged sect. How universally did it apply? Fujiwara spoke at immense length, if not very coherently. As he did I searched his face, behind the furrows, the fatigue, and the expression of deep concern. I imagined him as someone who had spent his adult life grafting a defensible political position—Japan would be a better place without an emperor—onto a set of emotional drives that had long ago become a cage in which he lived. I was never certain I found what I was looking for. Fujiwara, with the help of four hardbound volumes that contained the history of the Central Core's political adventures, droned on after each question—convolutedly, dementedly—until I stopped him by asking another one.

He said one thing of interest midway through our encounter. "If we didn't fight against the emperor, everyone would've been disappointed," he declared after an hour. "Because of our activities, the enthronement didn't go as expected. It was disturbed, not smooth. That's the important thing. We've succeeded completely."

NOT LONG BEFORE Hirohito was buried in February of 1989, WGBH in Boston, a station of the Public Broadcasting Service, scheduled a documentary called *Hirohito: Behind the Myth.* Produced by the British Broadcasting Corporation, the film was based on a book by Edward Behr, an Anglo-French correspondent who had a long record of service with Reuters, *Time, Life, Newsweek,* and other news organizations. The book and the film used diaries, memoirs, and other documents to assert that Mr. You Don't Say, the shuffling amateur who loved his microscope, his gardens, and his family, was in fact a generalissimo intimately involved in planning and prosecuting the Pacific war.

Behind the Myth was aired without incident in Britain. In America an unholy row erupted among scholars and writers even before the film was broadcast. "Ridiculous!" one author shrieked. Such learned critiques followed a campaign begun by Edwin Reischauer, by then retired from both scholarship and diplomacy. Ed Behr's work required nothing less than censorship, Reischauer asserted. "It's nonsense," he told the *New York Times.* "It's entirely wrong as to what the position of the emperor was and what his powers were. No emperor of Japan had any real power for many hundreds of years. It's bad taste and so incorrect that it shouldn't be shown."

It is an irony that such an argument was advanced in the nation where speech is freest. But then, it is in America that scholars such as Reischauer have made themselves so fully and eagerly available to Washington in the second half of our century. *Hirohito: Behind the Myth* was broadcast on schedule. The Reischauer rupture soon faded. But it occasioned one of our most public displays of the Chrysanthemum Club at work. And it was as shameful as anything else Reischauer and his colleagues in education and government did to rehabilitate the man in whose name so many suffered.

Behind the Myth, in film and print, was not flawless. Critics expended considerable energy dilating upon errors in fact and interpretation. But the nitpicks, of which there were not unduly many, were not the point. Washington and Tokyo had spent forty-five years deflecting any notion that Hirohito bore responsibility for Japan's wartime conduct. No contradicting account had ever met with less than sniper fire and creeping barrages of criticism that relented only when a work's reputation was judged wholly discredited.

Once, during a visit home from Tokyo, I found a book called simply *Hirohito* in a New York City shop. *Hirohito* was published in 1988 as part of a series of a 157 volumes called World Leaders Past & Present. It began with an introductory essay, "On Leadership," by the historian Arthur M.

Schlesinger, Jr. A slim book with many pictures, it was written "especially for young adults."

Hirohito contained a neat summary of the mainstream history of the emperor. In his introduction Schlesinger is eloquent on the power of individual leaders, "leaders in action—the leaders described in this series." We must read this faux pas with irony, for it is the essence of official history that the man described inside was possessed of a passive, troubled soul full of reticence and reluctance. The wartime Hirohito feels isolated and alone as he withdraws into the shaded rooms of Fukiage Palace. He orders nothing but acquiesces in all. He is forever kicking the dirt as he goes along, "persuaded by his advisers." Here is the Hirohito fit for consumption by American students:

> He was more at ease collecting marine specimens than with affairs of state.

> Hirohito was kept uninformed about the details of the "China Incident," as the Japanese referred to their war with that nation . . . and it appears he never knew of the Nanjing massacre.

> Hirohito played a minor role during the war. For the most part he remained in the palace.

The postwar play given to the emperor's interest in biology is perverse in view of its curious genesis. Hirohito had proven a motivated naturalist—and no amateur—even as crown prince. He was adamant as to the military uses of science, urging former tutors to develop the fungi and viruses needed to wage biological warfare. Thus were deadly bacteria bombs tested in China during the mainland campaign. By then Hirohito had approved the creation of the infamous Unit 731, a germ-warfare brigade distinguished as the only section of the army ever authorized by imperial decree.

As to the palace, Hirohito did spend much time there—because he ordered his Grand Imperial Headquarters built within it. This was Hirohito's war room. He first occupied it just before the Rape of Nanjing began. Twenty thousand women were raped in Nanjing and something over two hundred thousand people massacred. Hirohito quickly rewarded the officers who oversaw this terror (and whose commanding general was an uncle by marriage). Eyewitness accounts of Nanjing were published almost immediately; voices of disgust were raised worldwide (and in Japan). Yet somehow the man in the palace comes to us knowing nothing about it.

Just before Hirohito's bitterly cold funeral, the *Mainichi Shimbun* published the story of a man named Aristides George Lazarus. Long retired in a New York suburb, Lazarus was moved by the moment to unburden himself to correspondents in the newspaper's bureau in Rockefeller Center. He figured in none of the big histories, official or revisionist. But Lazarus, a Marine Corps officer and an attorney, had been assigned to the legal defense team at the Tokyo war-crimes trials, which took place from 1946 to 1948. As the trials began, Lazarus recalled, a Truman administration official asked him to make a private approach to General Hideki Tojo, Hirohito's famed wartime premier, in his cell at Sugamo prison in Tokyo. The mission was to explain that Tojo was to be found guilty at his trial so that Hirohito could be spared and Japan rebuilt under him. Lazarus did his duty but never forgot his objectionable orders. As we know, Tojo was hanged, having accepted his final assignment in the service of the *tenno*.

Historians had long posited pressure on Tojo. Lazarus supplied a first-hand confirmation of it and an account of how it had been applied. But like so much of the evidence relating to Hirohito's wartime years, the small shard of history Lazarus offered passed virtually without notice.

This was an old habit. Among the few important documents on Hirohito published before his death was the *Sugiyama Memoranda,* a memoir written by Hirohito's army chief of staff, Hajime Sugiyama. Nicknamed "the Bathroom Door" after his inexpressive features, Sugiyama was a noted waffler whose life ended in suicide in 1945. However much he dissembled, Sugiyama privately recorded numerous conversations with the emperor while he waged the war. Most significant, he asserted that Hirohito not only was aware of plans to attack Pearl Harbor but had, in January of 1941, ordered a secret feasibility study of the idea. This was a shattering revelation—history-altering in import. Yet when the *Memoranda* was published in 1971 it went unremarked—on both sides of the Pacific.

The Japanese are copious diarists, the private journal a function of their acutely private individuality. For politicians, palace officials, and other public figures the personal record also offers potential protection amid the intrigue rampant in high circles. Most of the accounts of Hirohito that survived the postsurrender purge of documents were based on diaries, though these were often falsified or heavily edited. There was not much to go on. Historians chicken-scratched, and the official version of things, supported by the lapses of the media, survived sporadic challenges more or less intact.

Hirohito's death changed that. Akihito did not accede before six diaries were published describing Hirohito's life and concerns, sometimes his words, and his role in the affairs of his reign. These came from a prime minister, a chief cabinet secretary, a chief military aide, and three imperial chamberlains. They were only the most notable of post-Hirohito productions, for with his passing some essential stone in the wall came loose. Scholars, fading veterans, schoolmasters, war widows, daughters of the dead—here and there around the country such people launched research projects, gathered memoirs, and recorded testimony. Overnight, the trickle became a torrent.

The most important of these documents was cast in Hirohito's own words. Hidenari Terasaki had been a diplomat in Washington at the outbreak of war and by all appearances a liberal much in sympathy with the West. (He also seems to have been an accomplished spy, which renders appearances suspect.) After the war Terasaki was assigned to assist Hirohito in his dealings with MacArthur. It was then he produced what is known as the *Monologue,* an account of discussions Hirohito had with Terasaki and four other officials assigned to the palace.

The *Monologue* is a remarkable document. Concerned in early 1946 as to whether he would be named a war criminal, Hirohito gathered his aides to rehearse his replies to a military prosecutor. The format was question-and-answer. In five sessions over three weeks, the emperor covered the whole of his first two decades on the throne. Terasaki wrote a shortened version of these sessions and left it to his daughter when he died, in 1951. Thirty-nine years later she published it—first in a monthly magazine and then in a book that included Terasaki's personal diary.

Hirohito intended to cast himself as a constitutional monarch—that is, a titular head of state with limited power over government and the army. But Terasaki's *Monologue* reads rather differently. Here is Hirohito the god-king and warrior asserting his control over the military. Here is the consummate insider, a petty and mean-spirited man intimately engaged in wartime political intrigue. In his introduction to the *Monologue,* Terasaki never took up the matter of Hirohito's guilt and responsibility: He merely let the emperor speak for himself.

Hirohito was a restorationist in his own right, bent on reversing the decline of imperial power and the rise of party rule under his debilitated father. In the *Monologue* he identified the very moment he took up this task. In mid-1929, less than a year on the throne, Hirohito banished his first premier. This marked the fateful turn from "Taisho democracy" to a government that involved an active emperor (and soon enough the military). From this point onward Hirohito pursued his dream of empire with growing dedication, playing political chess at home while keeping up with coded cable traffic and the minutiae of military logistics abroad.

One fatal flaw in the official reinvention of the emperor was its remoteness from reality. It was simply too ambitious an undertaking, despite the paucity of documents. Official historians may never explain why, if Hirohito was so demonstrably the powerless bystander, MacArthur, Reischauer, and the rest of the Tokyo lobby had to make so much covert effort on his behalf. But official history became less compelling after 1990; it looked atrophied and hollow. The *Monologue* and other newly available documents made possible a lasting picture of the man and his era—a true picture that can no longer be assailed.

A MONTH BEFORE Hirohito died, Hitoshi Motoshima, the mayor of Nagasaki, suggested in the city assembly that the question of imperial guilt should no longer be so fraught for the Japanese. A lifelong Catholic, Motoshima had a little of the outsider about him, though he was, at sixty-seven, a longtime Liberal Democrat, too. "Forty-three years have passed since the end of the war," Motoshima replied to an assemblyman's query,

> and I think we have been able to reflect sufficiently on the nature of that war. From reading various materials abroad as well as the writings of Japanese historians, and from my actual experiences in military service . . . I think that the emperor does bear responsibility for the war. However, by the will of the great majority of the Japanese people as well as the Allied powers, he was released from having to take responsibility and

became the symbol of the new constitution. My interpretation
is that we must adhere to that position.

Motoshima delivered these remarks with such modesty as to suggest they
were a foregone conclusion. For many Japanese this was so. But
Motoshima had turned the unspoken truth outward. The mainstream
media flocked to his hilly port city, wondering what could have prompted
such an utterance. Dozens of right-wing sects arrived to jam the streets,
demanding an apology, a retraction, a "divine retribution." The last arrived
a year later, though in earthly form: A right-wing extremist nearly took
Motoshima's life with a bullet that passed through the aging mayor's lungs.

The Motoshima shooting was treated as a sign that Japan was still a
dangerous place—that a resurgent right still lurked just below the surface.
What actually occurred revealed something else. Motoshima became an
overnight hero after his assembly speech. More than seven thousand letters
arrived in support of his view; within a few months almost four hundred
thousand signatures were gathered in support of his right to voice his view.
The shooting that followed was better understood as a nostalgia piece, an
aberration that proved a new rule.

Motoshima later published the letters. They read as a testament to how
far the Japanese had traveled since the days of coerced emperor worship.
And they revealed another fatal flaw in Hirohito's remaking. It was a mark
of the Tokyo lobby's contempt for ordinary Japanese that its members
assumed they could repackage a commander in chief and sell him to his
former subjects as a frail man of peace. This was hubris. Too many people
knew wartime Japan and Hirohito as they were, and the letters of a few of
them made a kind of retribution, too.

Another of the documents published before Hirohito's death were the
diaries of Koichi Kido, keeper of the privy seal during the war, an aristocratic friend of the emperor since childhood and his most trusted adviser.
Parts of Kido's diaries were made available at intervals from 1945 onward.
In 1987 another section was published. It included a secret memorandum
to Hirohito in which Kido urged his old patron to abdicate. This was in
late 1951. "If you do not do this," Kido noted,

then the end result will be that the imperial family alone will not have taken responsibility and an unclear mood will remain, which, I fear, might leave an eternal scar.

Kido was prescient. The unclear mood lasted the rest of Hirohito's life. It lingers today in the persistent refusal of Japanese leaders to acknowledge the past. It remains to be seen whether the scar upon the throne will prove eternal. That will be determined only when official Japan decides to acknowledge the truth to the world.

Akihito made three journeys abroad within three years of his accession—each a carefully calibrated display. In Southeast Asia and China, where no emperor had ever been, he edged closer to a direct apology for wartime aggression than his father ever had. On a later trip, to the United States, the imperial couple returned to the imagery Akihito favored as crown prince: casual attire, easy conversations, a dinner with Joe DiMaggio. The message, which was also beamed homeward, was clear: This was a new era and a new Japan, a Japan whose emperor others accepted.

But the apology the rest of Asia had so long awaited never came. And no dinner with a baseball star could compensate for Tokyo's later decision to cancel abruptly the imperial couple's planned visit to Pearl Harbor in 1991, the fiftieth anniversary of the attack. So the lesson of these journeys was clear, too: No amount of imagery and design can take the place of a true assessment of history.

THE HABIT OF thinking in imperial eras fades slowly. Like the *gengo* calendar, it is a declaration of Japaneseness because it acknowledges the emperor as the being around which Japaneseness revolves. The most sophisticated of Japanese look to the change of reigns as a reference point. A few months after Hirohito's burial, Hanae Mori gave a dinner party to mark her thirty-fifth year in fashion. Elegant and worldly, the designer had just arrived from her headquarters in Paris and seemed, as she often did, more French than Japanese. But her words were startling. "Showa has ended," she announced to her guests. "It's time to reassess myself."

When MacArthur argued for protecting the emperor he warned of "a tremendous convulsion among the Japanese people" if he were indicted as a war criminal. "Destroy him and the nation will disintegrate," he advised Washington. These points can be questioned. There may have been no convulsion. Or perhaps the Japanese would have welcomed just such a convulsion. But it is certain that Washington's decision helped to delay for at least forty-five years the birth of any greater sense of pluralism, or an expanded notion of Japaneseness. It is in these ways that Hirohito's death was a great relief to the Japanese, a relief not unlike that induced by the surrender. Diversity of thought and an openness in matters of national identity are foreign to Japan only because they were so long forbidden. Unless I mistook her, Madame Mori was not so much saddened by Hirohito's death as she was renewed.

To overcome the unhealthy effects of the emperor system can no longer mean removing it. That moment passed long ago. It requires altering the emperor's place among the Japanese. Hirohito's assignment in the postwar constitution, to be a symbol, was a severe limitation of the *tenno*'s role. Yet the Kunaicho and the governing elite manipulated it nonetheless to keep the nation encircled and others excluded. For the rest of his life Hirohito was Japan's ultimate import barrier.

What would Akihito put in the empty vessel, now that the sacred nothing was transformed into the nothing sacred? Though his father and grandfather and great-grandfather all began as modernists, they all failed, more or less conspicuously, to deliver on the early promise. The new emperor faced the same opportunity and the same risk. It was conceivable, during the imperial transition, that he would let the Japanese lift the old encirclement—let them unbuild some of what his ancestors built. That, at least, was his promise. He seemed intent on making a bourgeois monarchy out of the world's oldest divinity cult. But his success in that ambition will depend on how he responds as the Japanese rewrite their history to correct it. The many references to Britain during Akihito's accession were interesting: It is an island nation, like Japan; like Japan it is not overfond of foreigners. And it has a monarchy bearing many eternal scars, the scars of empire. But it has survived them.

ON A SATURDAY in December of 1990, I took a bullet train to Kyoto. I was only a few hours behind Akihito and Michiko, who were to spend that weekend at the Kyoto-gosho, the old palace. The previous day a bomb, courtesy of the Central Core Faction, had taken a large chunk out of an embankment along the track the imperial cars were to travel. But the emperor and empress arrived without incident. In Kyoto, home of Akihito's long line of obscure, powerless ancestors, they were to perform the last of their rites. When they were finished, the imperial transition would be complete.

The following morning, a crisp autumn Sunday, Kyoto television was taken up with local talk shows and coverage of the first Japanese to enter space, a broadcast reporter whose network paid the Russians $12 million for a seat on a research mission. At noon I taxied to the palace and found myself alone except for the security police guarding the entrances. At the Palace-Side Hotel, on the western edge of the grounds, I asked at the desk where the emperor would arrive. No one knew. At lunch I asked two students at the next table. They shrugged. One went away, and when he returned he said, "The road opposite."

"The East Road?"

He went away again. "No, the South Road," he said when he came back.

A little after two, the police began to string thick nylon cord between the lampposts along the South Road. Over the next hour the crowd grew until it was two or three deep—there were maybe a thousand people in all. The police tended us like shepherds so that we were spread evenly along the curb. Then the traffic stopped. At 3:25, twenty-five minutes behind the official schedule, a black Japanese-made limousine carrying the royal couple passed by at a courtly pace. The crowd sighed audibly, and there were a few scattered shouts of *Banzai!* I saw the dove gray glove of Michiko's left hand as she waved languidly from within. Then the limousine disappeared through the palace gates.

It was over in less than a minute. The police relaxed and began conversing. They left open the high gates of weathered wood, wheeling low steel barriers painted black-and-yellow in front of them. Within a few minutes the crowd dispersed and the order imposed over the previous couple of hours erased itself. People milled. Dusk was near. The symbolic emperor was at home in the house of his ancestors.

9

THE UNFINISHED
DREAM

We are up to our necks in Western culture. But we have
planted a little seed. And just as a seed takes root and grows,
we are beginning to re-create ourselves.

—KENZABURO OE
in conversation, 1993

YOSHIRO KATO LIVES in a half-deserted district of Brooklyn. Surrounded
by his paintings, Kato and his wife, Kazuko, inhabit a third-floor loft opposite a row of abandoned docks and the skyline of lower Manhattan. He is a
reedy man with a tightly drawn face and graying hair that hangs to his
shoulders. At the crown of his head he has a bald spot as round as a monk's
tonsure. By conventional standards, Kato also has a profane imagination.

In Japan during the 1960s Kato led a group known for its "ceremonies," as he calls them—"happenings," in the American parlance of
the time. The group wore blue *sarariman* suits and eyeless, expressionless
masks, like the faces on Greek statues. In one ceremony they knelt on a
futon at the entrance to a busy subway station and took off their clothes
while passing around an automatic masturbation machine (a Kato invention). In another they wrapped a naked woman in clear plastic and

carried her on their shoulders through the cars on the Yamanote line, the train that circles Tokyo.

What were Kato's ceremonies about? Fantasy and desire, obviously, and women—themes still evident in Kato's work. When he explained what he did during the 1960s, Kato said the ceremonies had to do with Japan's abject imitation of America after the war. Industrialization and mass consumption were making Japan "unlivable, like a spaceship." Japan had lost the ancient tradition that did not separate people from nature. If civilization were a train, Kato said, he wanted to get off it. "By taking off my clothes I took off what was Western. I made myself a representative of nature. When I created art I used my body to create nature itself."

The paintings stacked against the walls in Kato's loft were startling, an orgy of color and surreal imagery. They showed women sitting, standing, sleeping, sometimes naked, sometimes in kimono, sometimes in the street, sometimes in modern kitchens and other times in traditional rooms. Each figure wore a grotesque artificial penis painted in steel gray. In other paintings there was a figure resembling Kato, with the bald spot atop his head painted to resemble the female sex organ. Perversely, naively, humorously—I could not tell which—Kato made his canvases a uniform size so they could be installed as *fusuma,* the sliding doors in old Japanese houses.

Thirty years separated the canvases from the ceremonies, but not much had changed. Kato still entertained what seemed to be an extreme resentment. By other means, he still protested the path Japan had chosen and lamented the loss of the Japan that existed before Meiji and before the samurai, the Japan that was once, as he put it, "a country of women, in which women and men were free." Along with the old idea of humans in nature, Kato said, that, too, is gone now, and women are forced simply to become men.

One painting showed a woman sitting outside the door to a traditional house that had no interior. Inside there was nothing—only another house, another blue sky above its roof, another cloud to one side. As I studied it Kato said, "There is no unconscious in the Japanese anymore, no heart, no mind. Only the outside. The exterior is all there is."

It is strange to begin a chapter on Japanese culture in a Brooklyn loft, with an account of an artist who has gone unrecognized, deservedly or not, since the shock value of his street performances wore off many years ago. But Japan has produced many artists in exile since 1868. When I asked

Kato why we had come to America he replied, "People can't discover who they are while looking at others and not at themselves. And you can't see yourself when you live in Japan."

*   *   *

TO SEE ONESELF may seem to be a simple thing, but it has been the artist's endeavor the whole of the modern era. As such it began with all the other stirrings of Meiji—in education and politics, in the social customs of a country trying to make itself modern. But one could not apply specious measures of success to the idea of seeing oneself. It could not produce distortions of the original intent or badly borrowed institutions, as occurred in schools, for instance, and in politics. Painters and writers required an authentic revolution; anything less was failure. They had to explore the autonomy ordinary people glimpsed briefly but never grasped. Otherwise they would not be artists; their productions would be mere poses, falsehoods. This is evident even today, for to see oneself remains, with important exceptions, an unachieved ambition. Look at the paintings, sculpture, novels, and films of the Japanese: How often are they derivative of Western fashions, devoid of any revelatory aspect—and therefore dead, like the poetry that scholars obsessed with mimicking China wrote many centuries ago?

In 1876 Tokyo recruited an Italian academician named Antonio Fontanesi to instruct Japan's first oil painters. Fontenesi worked in the Barbizon style, favoring landscapes rendered directly from nature. He once sent his students into the city to sketch, and they returned to their painting master the next day with blank sketchbooks. They found nothing appropriate to draw, they said—no temples, no scholar's retreats, no blossoming boughs, no flocks of geese against snow. This story was related by a painter named Chu Asai, who became an important Meiji-era artist. Asai must have seen in it his own essential shortcoming, the thing without which he could not go on. And he must have known that it was something Fontanesi could not teach, for that was the point of the story. Tokyo was rich, the master admonished his students. But they were unable to see its richness, because to see the world they first had to see themselves, to understand where they stood within it.

Chu Asai and his fellow students studied Western technique as architects did cast iron and doctors Western hygiene. They worked on mechanical problems (stiff brushes, stretched canvas, the properties of oils) and formal questions (internal light, the portrayal of volume in space). But the toughest task reached deeper within. An engineer might build a cast iron bridge according to the Meiji precept "Japanese spirit, Western thing." The oligarchs did the same in erecting their political system. But *wakon yosai* could not apply in the arts; an artist's endeavor placed him squarely in opposition to such a dictum. That is not to say a painter, poet, or novelist had to abandon his Japaneseness. Not at all. But he would have to discover something other than the tradition implicit in the term "Japanese spirit." He had to be an artist before he was anything else. This is why culture has been partly a political question ever since the restoration, and why the ordinary act of seeing has been in a certain way a transgression.

What was the tradition? What did the arts consist of before the beginning of the modern era? To put a complex answer simply, only form, form exquisitely empty of content. True, by the end of Edo, a lively popular culture had developed, familiar to us today in the ukiyo-e prints of Utamaro, Hiroshige, and Hokusai. But woodblock prints and the demotic theater drew from everyday life; they were part of the little tradition, not the great. Tea ceremony and the other samurai arts were the essential examples—one mastered only the movements of the past. Painting meant joining a school and learning from that school's *sensei,* its master, how to reproduce formal scenes derived from Chinese tradition. The same was true of poetry. The perfect haiku, seventeen syllables in a sea of silence, was like an abstract design woven into the silk of an elegant kimono. Noh drama was made of masked faces, stilted speech, and movements so stylized as to be scarcely human. Japanese fiction traces its roots to the eleventh-century *Genji Monogatari,* the *Tale of Genji,* the world's first novel. But *monogatari* (the telling of things) were made of two-dimensional characters, casts of many, and repeated conventions rather than plots. As the critic Kojin Karatani points out, "*Monogatari* is pattern, nothing more, nothing less."

But for the fact that the conventions lingered so late in history, they had much in common with premodern art elsewhere. They reflected no point of view, no transforming individual experience. In painterly terms, missing from the tradition was perspective—not only perspective as a draftsman's device, a method of representation, but perspective as a psychological discovery. A brush-and-ink painting was a flat rendering. It did not say, implicitly, "I am standing here, and this is what I see," because it did not matter where the painter was: He was merely copying. He could paint a goose in snow and be honored for his mastery without ever having seen a goose. His work lacked not only perspective; also absent was the modern painter's reference to the world around him.

It is astonishing how quickly Meiji artists began their passage toward the modern, a passage that required centuries to complete in the West. Poets began to "sketch" from nature and wrote about factory workers and dank city streets. Chu Asai and others among Fontanesi's students went off to French art colonies and returned to paint toiling rice farmers and women reading newspapers in the style that best expressed their new excitement, plein air. What could be more antithetical, more directly challenging to the tradition, than a landscape rendered as the artist saw it, produced *in* that very landscape?

We can write the script for what happened as the cultural scene exploded. The new artists posed, more acutely than anyone else, the questions at the core of the era: Who were the modern Japanese going to be? What sort of individuality would they possess? Would they celebrate it or suppress it? Since we have already explored how these questions were answered, the cultural xenophobia that followed the initial enthusiasm for the nineteenth-century modern is hardly a surprise. The reaction even had its Western exponent. Two years after Antonio Fontanesi arrived in Tokyo, Ernest Fenollosa, a young Harvard graduate, went to teach philosophy. Fenollosa became a sort of art impresario and did much to promote the *japonisme* that gripped the West toward the century's end. Fenollosa advocated a closed door to "the curse of Western art," for nothing should disturb the Japanese as they went on producing art and artifacts as they always had.

Fenollosa asserted that the "true painting" of Japanese tradition had to be preserved so that, from the encounter of East and West, a new synthesis would emerge to make an art of the future. "The greatest central genius of Meiji," Fenollosa declared, was a forgotten scroll painter who was tending silkworms and daubing pottery when Fenollosa rehabilitated him. To find value in a tradition the Japanese were rushing to discard was a fine thing. But to posit that Japanese artists must be segregated was preposterous. An Orientalist in the fullest sense of the term, Fenollosa later built and curated the still-famous Japanese collection at the Boston Museum. With ink sticks and silk, he preached, must Japan go forward.

Fenollosa made Japanese art conscious of itself. *Nihon-ga,* Japanese painting, was a term coined only after the arrival of Western influences. The shriveled fruit of Fenollosa's synthesis was called "new *nihon-ga,*" which combined traditional art with cautiously chosen Western techniques. If the style is obscure outside Japan, that is because it was stillborn, mismatching medium and theme while managing to avoid even a whiff of innovation. The new *nihon-ga* led nowhere in any case, for Fenollosa and his disciples were soon swept aside by nativist reactionaries alarmed that the Japanese would lose touch with their spirit and the *kokutai,* the national soul. Western influences never disappeared. But the artists who explored them were cast in opposition to "official" culture for most of the modern era. There was no middle road for the nationalists. Art and culture went along with ideology, implements of the state.

The reaction against Western culture was to some extent provoked. The Meiji writers and painters pricked the nationalists' pride. They made one of the era's essential mistakes: They assumed that whatever happened in the West was superior to what happened in Japan. Once that was accepted, once everything in the past was thrown out as invalid, culture became another import. But to adopt the objectivity of Flaubert or Zola did not make one a realist or a naturalist. Few artists saw that what they were searching for in the landscape, the portrait, the plot, or the character was no more or less than themselves. They missed the ultimate lesson of the West: that the end of all the learning lay finally in an act of creative rejection.

Fiction is a good lens through which to view the evolution of culture in the modern era, for the narrative of fiction reveals the narrative of Japanese thinking in some detail. Fiction written by Japanese became immensely popular after the restoration. The first crop of novels were not much more than political tracts by intellectuals close to the movement that advocated civil and democratic rights. Filled with stick figures who delivered leaden monologues on the virtues of democracy, these books would be judged a terrible bore today. But they offer a starting point: the writer's concern with the individual in society, even if the portrayal of the individual was an unpracticed one.

In 1886 a serialized novel appeared that changed everything. *Drifting Clouds* concerned a young civil servant named Bunzo. Bunzo was a brooding sort, another rustic in from the prefectures, lost in the new Japan but pleased to have exited the old one. He is indifferent to the old social conventions. He spends much of the novel withdrawn in his room, which is by far the most important room in Meiji-era writing, for Bunzo's time alone there was something quite new. "He entered the third house from the corner, a two-story building with a lattice door," the narrator says. "Shall we go in too?" And then we do—a momentous passage. In *Drifting Clouds,* Shimei Futabatei wrote what is considered Japan's first modern novel. It was rendered in colloquial language. And it gave readers a first taste of interiority—psychological depth. A Japanese critic put it perfectly at the time: "The characters in most novels these days resemble figures in woodblock prints. The characters in *Drifting Clouds,* however, are people in oil paintings."

Drifting Clouds was completed in 1889, the year the emperor Meiji gave Japan its constitution, a year before his Imperial Rescript on Education, which declared the samurai virtues supreme. Japan was starting its long march to the sound of ideology. And as the martial cadences gathered momentum, the artists of the age became ever more isolated. At odds with the mainstream, they turned inward. The ideal of the individual was no longer expressed in political novels, however unreadable. Naturalism was the great literary movement of late Meiji and after. But if its influence lingered, its time was brief. In its place came confessional novels and the "I" novel, so named for its relentless, hermetic depiction of the author's psyche. The "I" novel was made entirely of the writer's innermost thoughts, a claustrophobic exaggeration of individual perspective. An "I" novel's success depended on whether it convinced readers that the "I" of the story was congruent with the "I" who was the author.

The first "I" novel appeared in 1913. Placed alongside the concurrent emergence of modernism in the West, the "I" novel was an authentically Japanese reaction against the conventions of nineteenth-century narrative realism, conventions Japanese writers had only just learned. But events elsewhere afford only one way to look at the "I" novel. Placed against a Japanese backdrop, it looks like a regression. The self had always been a private matter, driven inward and expressed only in such contexts as the diary. So the "I" novel can be cast as a fictional account of withdrawal—a record of one's retreat into private individuality.

There were other writers whose portrayals of the individual survive today: Mori Ogai, whose isolation produced a pronounced objectivity in his narrative voice; Nagai Kafu, whose characters were pushed to the margins of the new Japan, stunned and repulsed by it. But no novelist still looms so large as Soseki Natsume. In both life and art, Soseki looked like a classic case of Meiji-era ambivalence toward the modern. An avid student of English, he famously decided after years of study that the literature of Wordsworth and Whitman, Fielding and Dickens had betrayed him— that the promise it seemed to hold let him down. In later life Soseki wrote fiction in the morning and poetry in the classical manner after lunch—a partial retreat from the modern endeavor, it seemed.

But the bare facts must be properly understood. Soseki broke the mold. He is the towering figure of early modern writing in Japan, and a great novelist by anybody's measure, precisely because he let himself be cheated: Anyone could love English literature, he found, but it was still English. The Japanese could not, as he put it, ask someone else to drink their liquor, then take the other person's opinion as theirs. The Japanese had to learn to taste and see for themselves. In the end, Soseki saw no alternative for the Japanese but to make something of their own.

It is almost as if Soseki were cut out from birth to arrive at such realizations. Shuffled between households as a child, he seemed to be rehearsing the displacement between East and West that haunted him all his adult life. He studied in England for two gruesomely lonely years and vowed afterward never to return—only to find himself uncomfortable back in Japan. He replaced Lafcadio Hearn, the noted American writer, as professor of English at Tokyo University. But the higher he rose in modern Japan, the more he hated it. In 1904, at thirty-eight, he started writing fiction.

Soseki created many memorable characters who, like him, were caught in the desolate terrain between tradition and the modern. Botchan, the antic title character of his second novel, is a classic late-Meiji type—a brash, selfish upstart who considers himself much in the modern mold. He is impatient with the old ways but entirely unconscious of his dependence on them. Confronted with others making their way in a changing social order, Botchan innocently concludes, "The world seemed to be composed solely of imposters and schemers who were ever trying to scheme against, and impose upon, one another." Botchan finds comfort in his family's aging maid, an early example of the many women in modern Japanese fiction to represent the past preserved.

Botchan made readers laugh when it was published, in 1906—and still does. There is a comic unawareness in its first-person narrative that betrays the essential Japanese confusion between selfishness and individuality. This is what comes of mindlessly aping the West, Soseki all but stated. *Botchan* introduced most of Soseki's themes, but it gave only a sadness-of-the-clown hint of the depression its author would display in *Kokoro,* his penultimate work and arguably his finest. *Kokoro* concerns an innocent student and a wiser man known only as Sensei, master. Although Sensei is attached to the past, Tokyo has allowed him to shed the old village values. Like Botchan, he distrusts his confused compatriots while holding himself above them. But he, too, has mistaken selfishness for individuality—a mistake that leaves him tragically isolated.

The student first sees Sensei at a summer resort, where on most days "the sea, like a public bath, would be covered with a mass of black heads." One day, the student recounts, he followed Sensei into the water

> and swam after him. When we had gone more than a couple of hundred yards out, Sensei turned and spoke to me. The sea stretched all around us, and there seemed to be no one near. The bright sun shone on the water and the mountains, as far as the eye could see. My whole body seemed to be filled with a sense of freedom and joy, and I splashed about wildly in the sea. Sensei had stopped moving, and was floating quietly on his back. I then imitated him. The dazzling blue of the sky beat against my face, and I felt as though little, bright darts were being thrown into my eyes. And I cried out, "What fun this is!"
>
> After a while, Sensei moved to an upright position and said, "Shall we go back?"

Beneath the apparently innocuous description an important question is addressed. Sensei has led the student beyond the communal mass of bobbing black heads to a place where one is alone. The student eagerly enters a world of pure seeing and feeling where there are no relationships, only individuals. For him, as for the early modern painters, sight and sensation are the portals to selfhood. He does not understand this, for at the first chance he falls to imitating his teacher.

In the last third of the novel, Sensei tells the student the story at the center of the book. It was Sensei who had a friend named K during his university years—the true believer in "Japanese spirit, Western things," the updated samurai. Sensei is not unsympathetic. "You must understand that to K, his own past seemed too sacred to be thrown away like an old suit of clothes." But K's rigors leave him incomplete—"inhuman." He is capable of love, Sensei surmises, but incapable of acting upon it. When Sensei discovers that he and K love the same woman, he schemes to win her hand. K commits suicide, and Sensei is forced to accept himself as no more than another weak human being, neither above nor below anyone else. Love has led Sensei into loneliness, for love is self-assertion.

There is something of Conrad's Kurtz in Sensei. As the explorer in Africa found at the heart of things "the horror, the horror," Sensei found "moral darkness." There is peril in swimming out beyond the crowd. Becoming a modern individual did not require a wholesale rejection of the past. But it meant leaving behind the certainties of community and dictated morality, the samurai code and the Confucian virtues. In their place there was freedom—and the responsibility that arrives with choice. There are no bad men, Sensei told the student once. "Under normal conditions, everyone is more or less good, or, at least, ordinary." There were only men capable of being bad, and they included oneself.

Soseki had the confidence never to retreat from the insight his varied life gave him. He rejected the prevalent version of the world as a collection of superior/inferior opposites: the village and the city, the traditional and the modern, the foreign and the Japanese. Nothing could more obscure the challenge simply to be oneself—which meant to see oneself. But few Japanese since Soseki have shared his confidence. Only in our own time do they seem prepared to live up to the truth Soseki put before them.

IN THE 1920s and 1930s there was a lively avant-garde in Japan, at least until the dictatorship extinguished it. It took up Surrealism and Dada and all the other currents of European and American art. Among these movements, another appeared. It began to ask, What had Japan made of itself with all its copying from the West? In 1942 a group of thinkers met in Kyoto to discuss this question. They named their subject "overcoming the modern." The conference is still considered an important moment in Japan's cultural history. But there was a familiar problem: Overcoming the modern seemed to mean looking backward, not ahead. It assumed that Japan could still be understood as distinct from the rest of the world, which was to assume that the clock could be turned back. Overcoming the modern might be an interesting idea—except that it could never be anything more than an idea. There was no taking back the previous seven decades. As leading thinkers discussed overcoming the modern, the imperial army occupied Southeast Asia and was spreading the war across central China.

Beneath the impulse to overcome the modern there lay sentimental regret. No one expressed this more artfully than the novelist Junichiro Tanizaki. Tanizaki was an extraordinary writer, but he never transcended the idea of a world made of opposites. Instead, he swerved wildly from one side to the other and back again—a familiar pattern by his time.

Raised on Kabuki and Chinese classics, the young Tanizaki took little interest in the West. Then, in his thirties, he became a fanatic worshipper of the foreign. He moved to the Bluff in Yokohama, the heart of the gaijin community. He took dancing lessons, studied English, and made himself a Jazz Age grandee. Nothing Japanese satisfied him. When the earthquake of 1923 leveled Tokyo, Tanizaki thought it was "marvelous." He conceived of a rebuilt city with no place for the kimono or the primitive tatami, "where champagne glasses floated like jellyfish among the evening dresses, tailcoats, and tuxedos":

> Orderly thoroughfares, shiny new paved streets, a flood of cars, blocks of flats rising floor on floor, level on level in geometric beauty. . . . And the excitement at night of a great city, a city with all the amusements of Paris or New York. . . .

Tanizaki's first reaction to the earthquake was typical. Many Japanese made the destruction of Tokyo into a metaphor of psychological and cultural transformation. The old, once wiped out, would be replaced by the new, the modern, the advanced, and the nation would never be the same. Tanizaki was not the only one to applaud.

Then he turned abruptly back. He moved to Kyoto, the ancient capital, where he fell in love with the regional accent and became a passionate devotee of traditional culture. *A Fool's Love,* the first thing he wrote after his move, satirized his own follies among foreigners. *Some Prefer Nettles* followed, another novel in which the protagonist must choose between East and West. In the former book the protagonist never escapes the buffoonery of imitation; in the latter he divorces his stylish, modern wife and sinks gently into a life of traditional ease in an old Kyoto house.

In Praise of Shadows, written at around this time, is not among Tanizaki's great works. It is of interest because it distills the traditional aesthetic at war with the modern with startling (if idiosyncratic) clarity. Against the brightly illuminated world imported from the West he posits the dimly lit, the obscure, the recessive, and passes through these poles of light and dark an astounding variety of subjects: architecture, toilets, hospitals, hotels, teeth, soup, lacquerware, gold—and, of course, women:

> We Orientals tend to seek our satisfactions in whatever surroundings we find ourselves, to content ourselves with things as they are; and so darkness causes us no discontent. . . . But the Westerner is determined always to better his lot. From candle to oil lamp, oil lamp to gaslight, gaslight to electric light—his quest for a brighter light never ceases, he spares no pains to eradicate even the minutest shadow.

From here he enters a blunt commentary on skin color:

> From ancient times we have considered white skin more elegant, more beautiful than dark skin, and yet somehow this whiteness of ours differs from that of the white races. Taken individually there are Japanese who are whiter than Westerners and Westerners who are darker than Japanese, but their whiteness and darkness is not the same. . . . For the Japanese complexion, no matter how white, is tinged by a slight cloudiness. . . . But the skin of Westerners, even those of a darker complexion, [has] a limpid glow. Thus it is that when one of us goes among a group of Westerners it is like a grimy stain on a sheet of white paper. . . . And so we see how profound is the relationship between shadows and the yellow races.

It is difficult to read Tanizaki without concluding that he was, at last, a tourist in his own country. If his West was an imagined West of champagne and tuxedos, so was his Japan a fantasy. One of the most telling passages of *In Praise* concerns traffic signals and busy intersections:

> It seemed to me the end of everything when the traffic policeman came to Kyoto. Now one must travel to such small cities as Nishinomiya, Sakai, Wakayama, or Fukuyama for the feel of Japan.

This is package-tour Orientalism. Tanizaki's detachment from the world around him is woven into every page of his work. He is often criticized for his characters' lack of depth, but this absence of interiority cannot be surprising. As the critic Kojin Karatani pointed out, Tanizaki's novels "constitute a series of repetitive rituals," new versions of the old tales called *monogatari*.

Tanizaki defined an important aspect of Japan's encounter with the modern. One characteristic of prewar Japanese writing was its pervasive sense of shock. The Japanese were the only Asians to adopt the scientific and industrial achievements of another civilization—and so assume the imperative of consciously locating their Asianness in a new context. And in Tanizaki "culture" was finally severed from modern Japan; it was instead cast as a refuge. The scholar Tetsuo Najita distilled this to the poles of culture and technology, an oil-and-water equation toward which Japan had been moving since the restoration. It is an apt description of the failure of Japanese artists, the prison most of them constructed for themselves: If it was modern it was not Japanese; if it was Japanese it could not be modern.

With Tanizaki the flight to tradition became the tradition. His successors, though his writing life overlapped with theirs, were Yasunari Kawabata and Kawabata's famous protégé, Yukio Mishima. Neither was untouched by Western influence and contemporary trends. Both were writers of immense originality, though they were vastly different in temperament and style. And both shared Tanizaki's distaste for modern Japan and his view of culture as a matter not to be mixed with it. Not coincidentally, Kawabata and Mishima shared one other thing: Both were suicides—Mishima in his spectacular seppuku, in 1970; Kawabata more prosaically (he gassed himself in his writing studio) two years later.

Kawabata's stance toward the modern was passive acceptance. His characters are exhausted—trapped in claustrophobic shelters of their own devising, tiny empires of solitude where they savor anguish, impotence, loss, and "a certain sad purity" *(Of Birds and Beasts).* The reflex to keep everyday life at the barely visible periphery is a feature of all his important writing. *Of Birds and Beasts,* a small but essential part of the whole, is set in Tokyo, but the city appears as if in a distant fog. Isolation and distance run through everything Kawabata wrote. Love, he said in an early autobiographical sketch, was his lifeline. "But I have the feeling that I have never taken a woman's hand in mine with romantic intentions. . . . And it is not only women I have never taken in hand—I wonder if it isn't true of life itself as far as I am concerned."

Passivity gave Kawabata an active appreciation of *bitai,* unfulfilled allure, a recurrent motif in Japanese aesthetic tradition. Love was his lifeline, but he never loved. He was deeply nostalgic—in part, one suspects, because nostalgia can never be satisfied. In life and art Kawabata was much given to young virgins. *House of the Sleeping Beauties,* a 1960 novella, concerns an old man who frequents a brothel where the prostitutes are, paradoxically, virgins and cannot be touched. As Mishima noted in an appreciation of his early sponsor, "Because a virgin ceases to be a virgin once she is assaulted, impossibility of attainment is a necessary premise. . . ."

Mishima's first efforts suggested that he might follow Kawabata into a mode of passivity and distance. His early characters are frail outsiders, aesthetes with furtive desires and secret selves. But, still in his twenties, Mishima abruptly left behind the notion of life as an essentially hermetic exercise. He later called this his turn from darkness toward a lifelong worship of the sun. His output changed radically. *The Sound of Waves,* set in a fishing village far from the modern world, is a stripped-down, Hemingway-simple retelling of the ancient Greek *Daphnis and Chloe.* In 1956 came *The Temple of the Golden Pavilion,* a masterful treatise on creativity and destruction, the beauty of the past and the freedom of the living. As he published it Mishima was engaged in his own conflict between reverence and creativity; he later described "the destruction of classical perfection" as a lifelong impulse. With *Pavilion* Mishima appeared set to break the mold—to leave behind the flight to tradition. But instead the mold broke him.

Pavilion is the story of a young monk who destroys the temple in which he studies, for its beauty oppresses him. Mishima never matched this novel. In quality or clarity of vision, nothing he wrote afterward came up to it because he lost his willingness to destroy as part of the creative act. Mishima became a public figure, and as he did he, too, sought "culture" as a retreat. Frail and short, he found in bodybuilding a "language of the flesh." In 1960, he reacted to the AMPO protests much as Tanizaki did to the earthquake in 1923: He turned inward and backward, revealing himself as an emperor worshipper and an extroverted exponent of the samurai ideal. He loved the shouts that punctuated his training in kendo. "This sound is the cry of Nippon itself buried deep within me," he wrote, "a cry that present-day Japan is ashamed of and desperately tries to suppress."

After a time he approached buffoonery. For photographers Mishima struck poses that would have pleased the masturbating aesthetes who peopled his early work. In 1967 he began raising a private army. No one who knew him wanted to believe these embarrassments were anything other than jokes—public farces quite separate from his writing. This was pure denial: Mishima's life was notable for its internal logic. The anthem he wrote for his army read in part:

> We must hide our great sorrow
> And conceal our great dream—
> In our land so low fallen
> We all frown with dismay.

Mishima died mourning a half-imagined Japan. The end came, famously and tragically, when he led his "troops" into a defense agency building in Tokyo and disemboweled himself with a favorite sword. The Japanese were shocked and saddened. But something he said a few months before his final act will probably outlast his lesser work, of which there was much. "I come out on the stage determined to make the audience weep," he remarked in conversation with another novelist, "and instead they burst out laughing."

In Kawabata's novella *House of the Sleeping Beauties,* the main character's thoughts return many times to the others who frequent the untouchable virgins. He wonders: "Was not the longing of the sad old men for the unfinished dream . . . concealed in the secret of this house?" What was the unfinished dream? In the same elegant sentence Kawabata explains it as "the regret for days lost without ever being had."

That dream, the dream of the past as protection against the present, died with Mishima and Kawabata. No one would write like them again. But what about the other unfinished dream: the dream of seeing clearly, the depiction of Japan as it was, the silent past combined with the cacophonous present? The failure to address this project was the reason Japan's most gifted novelists were not necessarily its best.

THERE IS A photograph taken in the 1950s showing a Japanese artist throwing bottles of paint on a canvas laid out on a Tokyo rooftop. The bottles break, the paint splatters, an abstract composition is made. Another, taken at the same time, shows a painter applying oils to an unstretched canvas with his feet. What do these photographs represent? Japanese "action painting," as this sort of thing was called in New York at the time? Or is it fairer to say the Japanese had still not learned to see for themselves—that they were still asking others to drink their liquor for them?

In *A Cultural History of Postwar Japan,* the scholar Shunsuke Tsurumi offers us another photograph. Although it appears to be nothing more than a random snapshot, it tells us something important about the climate in which artists worked after the war. A man and a woman are crossing a Tokyo street. They are walking side by side instead of the customary man in front, woman behind. "The photograph . . . will not strike you as anything noteworthy," Tsurumi wrote, "but to the photographer himself it must have given the impression that a new age had arrived."

It would be difficult to exaggerate how eagerly the Japanese anticipated the arrival of a new age after the war. This was as evident among artists as it was among ordinary people—as true as a cultural and aesthetic stance as it was in law, education, politics, and social customs as commonplace as the way couples walked. In the age of *shutai-sei,* autonomous selfhood, the pendulum swung radically away from the notion of culture as a refuge from the modern. If it had to do with "the feudal legacy"—a phrase on everyone's lips after the war—it had to be uprooted.

Considering where the feudal legacy had led, one can understand this. But people alienated from their past can lose themselves further by adopting someone else's past. And that is what the Japanese did after 1945: They cut themselves adrift, so producing in very short order the confusion and vacancy still characteristic of Japan. All that was traditional was simply abandoned to the realm of "official culture"—to traveling exhibitions sponsored by the government, and to the lingering ultranationalist fringe.

The consequences are evident to any visitor to Tokyo today. American films, music, and customs did not merely transform Japanese popular culture—they more or less obliterated it. Culture became again what it had been for the clumsy experimenters of the early Meiji period: another import. A new sort of nostalgia eventually appeared—an ersatz nostalgia for the icons and artifacts of other people (Mickey Mouse, James Dean, old Chevrolets and Fords with fins). This notion—of culture as an imported commodity—reached an extreme during the 1980s, when a fad for theme parks inspired reproduction Dutch villages, German villages, Canadian villages, Danish villages, and so on. An unintended air of sadness hung over such places. Culture was what others had, and for the price of an admission ticket one could go to see it.

In the postwar setting there was also a burst of artistic production. Painters, writers, filmmakers, and architects still sought an authentic art of their own. The prewar avant-garde left behind a record of difficult struggle as a more or less permanent cultural opposition, but it made little art that was really its own. The postwar avant-garde wanted to paint on empty canvases and write on blank sheets. Theorists exhorted artists to "create what has never existed before." And with the weight of ideology lifted, they also wanted to avoid the prewar mistake of taking "Japanist" work for Japanese work.

But like the producers and consumers of popular culture, artists ignored the opposite danger, the danger of mistaking everything Japanese as Japanist and discarding all of it. And to judge by the compassless activity of many postwar artists, and how little of their work is memorable, this is frequently what happened. Artists traveled less to Paris and more to New York, the art world's new capital. But the familiar problems soon reappeared. Action painting in Tokyo resembled action painting in lower Manhattan and the studios of eastern Long Island. Not surprising, the art of the postwar period became extremely diffuse. Artists addressed the problems of Europeans and Americans without following the path that led to those problems. Their work was either directionless or pointed in infinite directions at once, and from our vantage point today, it is hard to tell which.

In 1994 a large exhibition of postwar Japanese art was mounted in Yokohama and later traveled to New York and San Francisco. It was interesting partly for its failures, purely derivative pieces that displayed no hint of self-reference. One could detect in paint and canvas, or in wood and metal, the very fibers of the struggle to see clearly and authentically. Yet it was impossible to conclude, as some Japanese thinkers did after the war, that Japan was doomed to eternal imitation, empty at its core, ready for the imprint of any other arriving culture. For amid all the failed attempts were a few works of high quality, with an identifiably Japanese vocabulary in terms of form, color, line, or materials. These few works suggested that a new door was opening after the war and that Japan was doomed neither to the abject imitation of America then apparent on any city street nor to the reproduction of its own past as a prison with no possibility of escape.

Where did this work come from? In 1963 a painter and critic named Taro Okamoto offered an eloquent answer in an essay called "What Is Tradition?" In it he laid out the dilemma of postwar artists as clearly as anyone before or since. He attacked the official idea of culture since the restoration. For a century Japan had advanced tradition as a collection of dead, remote objects, things to be kept in glass cases. The Meiji oligarchs had even invented the term *dento,* tradition, to denote its highly selective catalogue of ideologically useful fragments of the past. "Then tradition is naturally perceived as something antiquated," Okamoto wrote. Older people valued it while the young despised it. Yet tradition "should always be vibrant and pulsating," Okamoto asserted. His argument is worth quoting. It was catalytic, a moment of recognition:

> I want to believe that "tradition" is the driving force that can tear down the old framework, open up the field for new ideas, and allow new possibilities for human life to emerge. I use the word "tradition" in such a radical way.
>
> . . . I must reexamine Japan with my new eyes. Then I can truly be free. My task is rediscovering Japan. This is my last resort in order to create new art. . . .
>
> . . . We somehow lack confidence in the past and the present, and we also lack the energy that will propel us into the future. . . .
>
> The present does not exist because of the past. On the contrary, we must regard the past as a premise of the

present. . . . All of us must discover the past in our own vitality and passion and view it from our own perspective in the present. That is what I mean by tradition.

Okamoto could have written "What Is Tradition?" twenty-five years later and still made a valuable contribution to Japan's thinking about itself. He addressed not only the prewar problem—"the heavy shell of the past," as he put it—but the postwar problem, too: the rejection of all tradition. Okamoto's imperative went beyond the arts; it was to locate the self amid the past and the present, the indigenous and the foreign. This should not have been difficult for people who had, since the sixth century, borrowed from abroad and then transformed what they borrowed. But Okamoto noted a decisive feature of the postwar era when he noted the lack of confidence the Japanese had in themselves.

As a painter Okamoto found inspiration in prehistoric earthenware somewhat the way Picasso took up African masks before painting *Les Demoiselles d'Avignon.* But if art was to disrupt received notions of the past (and reflect the reality of postwar Japan), he insisted that it also had to be unaesthetic, even ugly. Apart from ancient pots, Okamoto also liked pinball parlors. He was a better critic than he was an artist. But there are moving examples of his ideas in practice. Among the most graphic, the easiest to understand, is the Sogetsu school of ikebana, which turned flower arrangement into the kind of "vibrant and pulsating" art Okamoto wanted.

Sogetsu was founded in 1927 by an ikebana master named Sofu Teshigahara. Sofu's problem was merely a variation on everyone else's: He wanted to make flower arrangements that could accommodate Western architecture. From this premise Sogetsu developed into an important artistic presence in the 1950s. This is apparent today in the work of Sofu's son, Hiroshi, who assumed control of Sogetsu in 1980. Much influenced by Taro Okamoto, Hiroshi began as a painter. He then became an internationally noted film director before turning back to ikebana.

Sogetsu is unusual because it incorporates the modern into a traditional art, instead of the other way around. The risks are obvious: With a five-hundred-year history behind it, ikebana could lead straight to the nostalgic or, displayed abroad, ordinary Orientalism. But Hiroshi Teshigahara's work—large, environmental pieces in bamboo and other natural materials—is palpably alive and powerful. It transcends everything commonly associated with ikebana, forcing the viewer beyond any lingering idea of Western art as a standard to be applied anywhere. "Tradition is not something to stick to, but something to break," Teshigahara once told me. "We have maintained a succession of breaks up to the present."

Sogetsu now operates from an imposing building in the Aoyama district of central Tokyo. All of the stonework (impeccably modern, impeccably Japanese) was done by Isamu Noguchi, the Japanese-American sculptor, who was long associated with the Teshigaharas' experiments. Along with Noguchi's stones are a number of large works by Hiroshi Teshigahara. It is impossible to enter this building without feeling its creators' confidence that they have made a synthesis that is both new and faithful to the culture it grew from.

I once asked Hiroshi Teshigahara whether his work ever ceased to be ikebana and became contemporary sculpture. He was in his seventies when I met him, with silvery hair and a glib, impatient manner. "I don't see the point," he replied. "Labels don't interest me."

"But when I see your work I see it as contemporary art," I persisted. "Apart from the materials, I'm not sure there's any ikebana left in it. How does that make you feel?"

"It doesn't matter at all."

TARO OKAMOTO'S INFLUENCE is not so quickly evident among postwar novelists. There is nothing so graphic among their books as a modern installation made of weeping willow, bamboo, sunflowers, pomegranate, hydrangea, pine, or Chinese pear. But it is through Okamoto that Sogetsu ikebana can be connected to the writers who produced Japan's greatest postwar literature. The link is best expressed in this passage, also from "What Is Tradition?":

> The most urgent task of contemporary art is to synthesize the global and the particular; to understand the particular in a global perspective; and to achieve a global perspective that is based on the particular.

This was Okamoto's simplest assertion of how authentic culture is made. Nothing better refuted the lingering idea that culture was something impresarios purchased from abroad, or bureaucrats selected from the native past and sent through the country as if it were so much rice after a bad growing season. The imperative lay in seeing the strangeness of the familiar—in recognizing that contributions to the world's art and literature were made by "gulping the dailiness of life" in the ancestors' village, the shabby quarter of the city, or the cramped suburban apartment.

The novelists who best accomplished this are Kobo Abe and Kenzaburo Oe. It would be hard to find two writers less alike, at least on the surface. "I dislike locality as a device," Abe once told me. "It's not necessary to write specifically about Japan." Abe's Japan was Beckett's Ireland or Kafka's Prague—everywhere in the work but nowhere described. Oe thought just the opposite. From the first scene of his first recognized work, the 1958 novella *The Catch,* Oe signaled the rootedness and specificity of everything he has since written:

> Our village had been forced to begin cremating out of doors by an extended rainy season. . . . When a landslide crushed the suspension bridge that was the shortest route to the town, the elementary school annex in our village was closed, mail delivery stopped, and our adults, when a trip was unavoidable, reached the town by walking the narrow, crumbly path along the mountain ridge. Transporting the dead to the crematorium in the town was out of the question.

This is more than a rendering of a geographic site, the village where Oe grew up. It is a doorway to the marginal, peripheral Japan, the little tradition, the Japan that official culture blotted out. It is well known that much of Oe's work, including *A Personal Matter* and *The Silent Cry,* his best novels, revolve around his beloved eldest son, Hikari, who has suffered a slight brain disorder from birth. Hikari proved a gift (in life and work), for he led Oe out to the margin he wanted to depict: Hikari was the self from which there is no escape. "As a novelist I am concerned with the periphery, where ordinary people live," Oe once said. "I want to write about the inner selves of the Japanese, but the Japanese in this periphery, where real Japanese culture has evolved alongside the other."

Abe's work is by comparison stripped bare. His characters are urban misfits and lost souls: an errant husband, a divorced detective, a man who lives in a box, another who lives behind a mask of bandages. In *The Ark Sakura,* his last major novel, the main character occupies an urban cave stuffed with the objects of our age. Abe loved things. "I'm attracted to objects themselves, not ideas," he once said. His novels are famously cluttered, and through the detritus littering his work we can trace his (and Japan's) progress: from the straw mats, wooden buckets, and cheap cotton clothes of *The Woman in the Dunes,* his 1962 masterpiece, to the steel doors, Belgian weapons, surveillance gear, and computers of *Ark.* Abe explored his themes—human isolation, identity, the individual's worth in society—while consciously eschewing locale. But he still wrote unmistakably about Japan—the Japan, one might say, in which all of us can recognize something of our world.

Neither Abe nor Oe, it is fair to say, had the native gifts of Japan's other noted novelists; they were not masters of style. But their Japan was neither imagined nor lost, only Japan as it was. As Oe put it somewhat stiffly later on, they provided "a total, comprehensive contemporary age and a human model that lived it." Along with others of their generation, they made Japanese art "contemporaneous" (a favorite word among postwar painters) with the West. To borrow from Yoshiro Kato in his Brooklyn loft, they were able "to see themselves." And in so doing they made something of universal value.

In a certain way the story ought to end there, at the moment Japanese artists broke through all the conundrums and complexes and learned to see. Yet it does not. For the postwar moment of Teshigahara and Abe and Oe, as we have seen in other ways, was only that—a moment, a glimmer before the darkness resumed.

When Kenzaburo Oe won the Nobel Prize for Literature, in 1994, it suggested that the rest of the world, too, had finally come to see Japan and the Japanese as they really were. It was refreshing to see new translations of his novels, and reprints of work previously brought out. But at home things were different. Oe's Nobel revealed more clearly than anything else the distance that had grown up between his generation and the rest of Japan. By the time Oe went to Stockholm, he and Abe (who had died in 1990) were literary dinosaurs in their own country. Afterward, as if to cover the country's embarrassment, Emperor Akihito hastily offered Oe an imperial prize. But Akihito merely threw into awkward relief the alienation he intended to disguise, Japan's alienation from its best writers, for Oe refused an award that symbolized the very culture he wrote to overcome.

Just as the explorations of the 1950s began to bear fruit in the 1960s, Japan took its dramatic economic and political turn. The catharsis of the AMPO protests and the Ikeda plan that followed produced a society that could neither nourish its artists nor be nourished by them. And it was then that the artistic champions of the 1950s began to take on the characteristics they bear today: They began to resemble statues erected in a desert.

Hayato Ikeda used a new language when he launched his Income-Doubling Plan. He avoided assertions of Japaneseness or national pride, or references to Japan as a sovereign nation. Instead he employed the terminology of technocrats and managers. This marked a change in the idea of culture. If, before the war, culture and technology were understood as opposed poles, the one a hiding place from the other, they became one after 1960. Sonys, Toyotas, and Nikon cameras were advanced (and accepted, by and large) as the emblems of modern Japanese culture. They were what the Japanese produced to represent themselves, tokens of what the rest of us could learn from Japan. "After the war we had two cultures to display before foreigners—the imperial culture of Mishima and the culture of industry," Kenzaburo Oe once said in conversation. "Our authentic local culture was still submerged."

Oe is quite specific as to when Japan's postwar artistic energies began to collapse. He relates this sad reversal not to the Ikeda plan (which could not have suffocated the cultural scene instantly, after all) but to Mishima's death, in 1970. Until then, he has said, literature was uniquely able "to enlighten Japan and the Japanese to reality and culture." This is accurate, so far as what happened. But it is puzzling that Oe would single out Mishima to date the decline of postwar culture, because he detested Mishima's glorification of the sword-bearing samurai. For all Mishima's apparent pride, Oe believed, Mishima's Japaneseness was calculated to win the acceptance of foreigners. "Mishima concocted a version of Japan for export," Oe once told me. "This was his great betrayal of Japanese people and their culture."

Even Mishima at his most pessimistic could not have foretold the cultural wasteland Japan became during its "miracle" years. Culture was turned into a product fabricated by corporations—directly, in the case of popular culture; indirectly, by way of funding and sponsorships in the arts. We know little of Japan Inc.'s art, the culture of GNPism, for little of it is worth bothering with. Apart from "all those Hondas," as Oe said, culture was infantilized. The 1950s and 1960s had been "the springtime of

Japanese filmmaking," as Akira Kurosawa put it, but that season gave way to "the dark ages": genre films featuring furry animals, *yakuza* crime gangs, or hapless *sararimen*. There were no major novelists or poets. Painters and sculptors, still organized into schools, had the single, grim alternative of seeking corporate commissions—which hardly afforded them independence. Galleries were either controlled by the schools or rented out to anyone who could afford them. Amid this sad scene, ordinary people lost themselves in pinball parlors, *manga* comics, Tokyo Disneyland, and then the new theme parks. "Virtual reality" arrived in the 1990s, though by then Japan was already a kind of dreamscape.

Much as Americans did in their moments of new prosperity—at the turn of the century and again after the war—the Japanese imported billions of dollars worth of art in the late 1980s. The Yasuda Fire & Marine Insurance Company's purchase of van Gogh's *Sunflowers* in 1987, for a record $47 million, was merely the most publicized of many ostentatious acquisitions. By decade's end, six of the world's ten most expensive paintings belonged to Japanese. But this famous spree consisted mostly of corporate trophy collecting and investment purchases kept in vaults. Museums dedicated to both Western and Japanese art proliferated in Japan during this period; only after they were built did bureaucrats, governors, mayors, and curators realize there was nothing to put in them. So they stood empty, unintended metaphors of the age.

THE JAPANESE ART scene today must in some ways resemble that of the immediate postwar years. There is much ferment. The atmosphere is one of healthy experiment. Yet there is little suggestion of a renaissance among Japanese artists—not yet, anyway. There is only "a little seed," as Kenzaburo Oe put it. Though generalizations are always imperfect, one finds mostly the residue of GNPism, which obliterated the essential connection Taro Okamoto wrote about, the living connection between people and their past. The task of rebuilding such a broken connection is immense; in the end it is political as well as cultural. Rather than face it, most young artists have chosen to ignore the break—to pretend that one can live and create without history, with no connection to the past and not much of one to the present. They describe themselves with a convenient term, a term that can mean almost anything (or almost nothing). They call themselves postmodernists.

The best known of the postmoderns, the quintessential "new species" novelist, is Haruki Murakami. Popular at home and well published in the West—*A Wild Sheep Chase; Norwegian Wood; Dance, Dance, Dance*—he is advanced as Mishima's heir. This is a gaijin marketing manager's crude ploy, a fleck of latter-day Orientalism, for all Murakami shares with Mishima are his nationality and his foreign-language sales figures. Murakami has not, by his own admission, even read Mishima. He is indifferent to the past. His solution to the Japanese artist's task—to see oneself, to escape both imitation and dead tradition—is to opt out of his Japaneseness altogether. He craves, above all, distance from the world around him, from Japan as a problematic society—the distance, at last, of the foreigner. "I would like to write about Japan from the outside," he has said. "You might call it the Japanese nature that remains after you have thrown out, one after another, all those parts that are altogether too 'Japanese.'" This is perfect nonsense, an insupportable paradox. Too Japanese? One suspects another round of the felt inferiority that is as old as the modern era. In a decade, one also suspects, Murakami will be a sentimental nationalist.

Donald Richie, the noted critic of Japanese cinema, once described the fascination early Japanese directors had for Western technique. They would use flashbacks and pans without understanding the emotional and psychological impact of such devices. A camera moves in for a close-up of, say, a man reading a newspaper at a bus stop. The shot frames a moment of narrative intensity, but the man is an extra and the moment is of no importance. Form without content was a brief phase: Japanese directors went on to produce classics even during the silent era. But the effect of the early mistakes was telling of the point from which they began.

The books of the postmoderns share this odd quality. To read them is a bit like watching a child play with matches. Murakami's novels are cluttered with detail. Conversations are reported, apartments lived in, houses burned down, walks taken. Brand names proliferate. *A Wild Sheep Chase* revolves around an elaborate search for a mysterious sheep. There are ghosts, girlfriends, long journeys, fast food, sex scenes, and cheap hotels. But they are no more than ghosts, girlfriends, and trips to the countryside. The dialogue is pointless and the sheep is simply an unusual sheep. Like the early film directors' incongruous camera work, no meaning attaches to the technique, the device.

The common thread among the postmoderns is willed blindness: a prideful ignorance of history. Murakami describes himself as "an original," he has explained, "because I had to create, all on my own, a new Japanese language for my novels." Does authentic originality need to declare itself? He is offhandedly dismissive of all those he does not read, as if the giants of the generation before him were no more than waiters who brought the wrong wine. "Yes, the old gatekeepers. They are just like the leaders of the Communist Party in Eastern Europe," Murakami has said of Kenzaburo Oe's generation. "The older writers live in a very closed world. They really don't know what's going on." This is not an acceptable assertion from a writer who refuses to depict the conditions of his characters' lives, who purports to write about Japan but who keeps Japan as it is out of his work. "On arriving in Tokyo," the narrator of *Norwegian Wood* says, "I hadn't a clue what to do. Only not to take things too seriously and not to let things get too close." This is a telling passage. What is it if not a resolute refusal to "know what's going on"?

Among the other acclaimed productions of Murakami's generation is *Kitchen,* a 1988 novella by Banana Yoshimoto. It concerns a young woman who has lost her family. She is another postmodern character: an enervated postadolescent, "drifting, listless," with no past and not the dimmest notion of the world around her. The first-person narrator loves her kitchen, shrine to consumer gadgetry since the "electric boom," the place of blenders, fridges, and automatic rice cookers. She would like to live there—even die there. In the opening scene, Yoshimoto captures faultlessly (though almost certainly without intending to) the fate of a profoundly privatized generation—stupified by affluence and starved of spiritual nourishment:

> Now only the kitchen and I are left. It's just a little nicer than being alone. . . . I pulled my futon into the deathly silent, gleaming kitchen. Wrapped in a blanket, like Linus, I slept. The hum of the refrigerator kept me from thinking of my loneliness.

It seems odd that writers, the inheritors of a Soseki, an Abe, or an Oe, have so little to contribute as Japan finds its way forward. Odder still when writers are placed against the work of contemporary Japanese architects—some of whom are young enough to know Japan as Haruki Murakami and

Banana Yoshimoto know it. Perhaps it is among these architects that Oe's seed of re-creation is taking root, for their buildings are a radical challenge to the postmodern novelists. They suggest what the little seed might eventually produce in other arts. The best of them are determinedly contemporary, so tough and informed as to declare nostalgia a ridiculous waste of time. Yet they are exuberantly aware of their Japaneseness, a quality evident in their surfaces and spaces, lights and shadows, their allusions to the past and their occasional lyricism. To visit them and think of *Kitchen* or *Dance, Dance, Dance* forces a point (another) that is unflattering to the postmodern writers: Amid desolation there is also fertility.

Kisho Kurokawa, the noted architect of the first generation to mature after the war, once recalled returning to his native Nagoya a few days after the surrender, in 1945. His family had evacuated, and when they went home it was to discover that the allied bombing had turned the city into smoldering ruins. His father took him walking through neighborhoods they no longer recognized. "He was an architect. Together we looked for a site to build a new firm. He said, 'We have nothing, but an architect can create a new city.' To a small boy this looked impossible. How can a city be built from nothing? But at that moment I decided to follow in his footsteps."

The story says something important about architecture in Japan. Like fashion and interior design—other fields in which the Japanese now distinguish themselves—it is a response to material circumstances. To create new cities has been an imperative the whole of the modern era. Urban growth before the war (along with the 1923 earthquake) inspired recognized stars among architects, notably Kunio Maekawa, a student of Le Corbusier. After the war, when growth resumed (and public-works budgets grew huge) architects again derived immense power from the sheer drive to build. Architects can get along in a world of patronage politics and commerce in a way novelists and painters cannot. But their privileged place goes deeper than this. Art has always been more closely joined to life in Japan than in the West: Think of tea ceremony, swordsmanship, or gardening. Architecture is, like these only more so, lived in: a practical art for practical people.

Modern Japanese architects never severed their essential connection with the past, as so many others did. Visiting practitioners, Frank Lloyd Wright among them, were quick to recognize that the vocabulary even of a traditional Japanese house could teach things to modernists everywhere: the use of asymmetry and of empty space, the blurring of all defining lines.

These suggest the distinguishing quality of Japanese architecture: its ambiguity, its refusal to commit, to pose the man-made against the natural or the internal against the external. Consider one of the old houses Wright admired: Slide a *fusuma* door open, and private space becomes public; slide open another, and an interior room becomes an adjunct to the garden. Space is neutral—"ambiguous," Kurokawa calls it. It is a good word, for this concept of space is rather like the Japanese themselves.

It is arguable whether Maekawa or his most renowned protégé, Kenzo Tange, got far enough beyond their admiration of Le Corbusier and (in Tange's case) Mies van der Rohe to produce anything authentically Japanese. But Tange's students, Kurokawa among them, were decisive on this point. They mounted a direct assault on Western assumptions about urban design and architecture. And when they attacked Western standards they began to address the long, deep ambivalence the Japanese have felt about their cities: places of unassailable modernity but monuments to separateness and duality, places where people dwell in unprecedented densities but where nature is nonexistent.

In our time the originality of Japanese architects is on display from Los Angeles and New York to Paris and Seville. It is an architecture of unity. Kurokawa labels his theories "symbiosis," an architectural system verging on a philosophy. Along with other Japanese masters—notably Arata Isozaki and Tadao Ando—he combines in "a new internationalism" things modern culture views dualistically: humanity and nature, science and religion, East and West, past and future, logic and intuition. It is at once universal and particular—authentically postmodern and authentically Japanese.

When I first met Tadao Ando, he climbed interior stairs to the third floor of his Osaka studio, exited the building to cross an exterior catwalk, and then reentered through a glass door to reach the room I sat in. Intentionally or not, he had already asked, Did I really exit the building, or was I all the while within it? What is inside and what outside? What is our truest relationship with the elements, the natural world? Ando is an ex-boxer, self-taught in architecture. His buildings are full of exposed entry halls and roofless interior passages. His breakthrough project, a row house of raw concrete and glass built in 1976, has an open courtyard at its center with a suspended first-floor walkway across it. Twelve years later he built a church in Hokkaido with three walls, giving onto meadows and trees. The altar is surrounded by sky and a shallow pool of water.

We talked for several hours. There was something Brando-like in Ando's rough voice and boxer's nose. In a certain way he reminded me of Yoshiro Kato in his Brooklyn loft, though their work is very different. Ando, too, regrets what postwar Japan has made of itself—"an artificial, rational environment," as he put it, "that canceled any dialogue with nature." But he is adamantly unsentimental. He feels no nostalgia for an old, irretrievable Japan. He wants to express Japaneseness—he uses the word often—but not by letting the elements into all of his buildings, or by filling them with straw tatami or rice-paper shoji. He means Japaneseness as it really is—now. He uses steel, glass, and his signature raw concrete just as Kato used bright acrylics and canvas. These are "universal materials." And to be a Japanese architect is to negotiate with them, between the artificial and the natural world.

In a corner of the room, under a skylight, there was a 1:100 model of a museum Ando had completed a few years earlier along the Inland Sea near Kobe. He once wrote of it:

> To be at once public and private. To be open and closed at the same time. To be unified even while being fragmented: the antagonism of the multiple contradictions that architecture cannot escape.

I had seen the building. It was quintessentially Ando: massive but light, severe but at home in its surroundings. To meet Ando was to understand that the contradictions he named expressed those he felt as a modern Japanese. And to look at the museum was to understand that Ando had resolved his antagonism, as he put it, just as he had resolved it in the building. It was to see that he was able to see himself.

Ando glanced at the model. "How do we Japanese think?" he asked abruptly. "This was the question I posed to myself when I began. I thought, If I can answer that in my work, I can make something Japanese."

10

THE OTHER
WITHIN

"You know what, Sada, the baby's naked. . . . And it's got no name."

"Ha, ha, ha! You are funny, Ko. Everybody's like that when they're born."

"Yes. Everybody's got no name and everybody's naked when they're born, even the Emperor, even eta."

—SUE SUMII
The River with No Bridge, 1961

IN TOKYO I knew a Korean-Japanese woman named Akemi Matsuura. Stylish, intelligent, multilingual, Matsuura was somewhere in her mid-twenties and worked for a French fashion company. Like many other Korean-Japanese, she had changed her name from its original Korean. She was born and raised in Osaka and had then attended university in Seoul. That was Matsuura's first trip to Korea. She was eighteen.

Korea changed Matsuura. She found that she was not really Korean. And when she returned home after her studies, she saw Japan differently, too. "When I came back, I discovered little by little a very sad and cold part of the Japanese. There is a big gap between who they say they are and who they are. You can never be close to a Japanese. To be Japanese means to be alone."

Matsuura felt the separateness of the Japanese from both sides (as subject and object) because, paradoxically, she was and was not Japanese herself. When she went to Korea it was she who decided that, apart from her ancestry, she was not Korean. At home it was the opposite: She was Japanese, for better or worse, by any measure other than her family tree; but the Japanese decided that she was not Japanese.

Matsuura's peculiar position in life gave her a clear sight of things. Implicit in her explanation of the Japanese (and of herself) was the separation the Japanese suffer not just from others, but also from themselves. Loneliness is pervasive in Japan. It is one of the first things one notices after settling there. To be Japanese means to be alone: separation from "others," separation from one another, separation within each - individual—a gap, as Matsuura said, between how they present themselves and how they are. It is possible to make such a sweeping assertion because the Japanese have so thoroughly made an "other" of themselves.

The Japanese do not customarily think of themselves this way, of course. Instead they have been relentlessly prejudicial toward others for as long as they have recorded their own history. They have made an obsession of the strangeness of outsiders. We know this about them as well as we know they make efficient cars. We put it down to the ordinary xenophobia of island people, or the xenophobia whipped up by Japanese rulers at moments of political insecurity: when Westerners spread firearms and Christianity in the sixteenth century, or when the Meiji ideologues wanted to unite a nation that seemed set to go in all directions at once. But it is not so simple. The xenophobia of the Japanese is intimately related to their history as borrowers from others. And it reflects the way they see themselves—or, to put it in the terms of the previous chapter, their inability to see themselves clearly.

Who are the "others" of the Japanese? There are Westerners, of course, and everyone else who lives beyond the sea. Then there are the "others" among the Japanese. There is an untouchable caste known as *burakumin*, and there are the indigenous people of the Japanese islands, the Ainu in the north and the Okinawans in the south. There are also ethnic Koreans and Chinese who live in Japan. The economic bubble of the 1980s brought a wave of Japanese from Brazil, home to the largest settlement of Japanese outside the islands. Japanese-Brazilians proved to be an other, too, for they were considered to be no longer purely Japanese. The bubble also drew many thousands of laborers from Southeast Asia, the subcontinent, and the Middle East—the first such population Japan has ever had: others, obviously.

This is an extraordinary list. Apart from Westerners and the laborers arriving from underdeveloped countries, they are all others within—invented others to one degree or another. The *burakumin* are utterly indistinguishable from other Japanese, which makes the national prejudice against them awkward and unwieldy to the point that it becomes ridiculous. Japan makes a fetish of the minor physical characteristics that differentiate the Ainu and Okinawans. The Chinese and Koreans, it is fair to say, have made the Japanese much of what they are—culturally, materially, and (more directly, in the case of the Koreans) genetically. Though the Japanese exclude these groups, they are part of the makeup of the Japanese, who are not a race, as they often pretend, but an ethnic group within the Mongoloid race.

A certain self-loathing must surely lie buried somewhere in the way Japan treats its invented others. The place of the Chinese in Japan's past, for instance, is not a scholarly abstraction. The Japanese are reminded of it every time they read a sign or pick up chopsticks. Language betrays the Japanese on this point. One of the many disparaging terms for the *burakumin* is *ningai,* literally "outside of humanity"—other than human. Why would the Japanese so classify people who are not merely like them, but who are them, down to the most minute findings of DNA analysis? The term "gaijin" is never applied to Koreans or Chinese. Not even the arriving foreign workers are gaijin—and certainly the *burakumin* or the indigenous peoples are not—for the word connotes a certain privilege, which seems to reside in both the first character (*gai,* outside) and the second (*jin,* person).

"We will always feel inferior when we look toward the West, and always superior when we look to Asia," a Tokyo friend once told me. One could easily accept this as true. Many Japanese certainly do. Since the restoration they have not even been sure whether they are Asians or some murky concoction, such as "the Europeans of Asia." But the idea that the Japanese will always bow diffidently toward gaijin while looking with contempt upon those with whom they share a long history does not stand up. In the end it repeats the notion of the unchanging East—it is a shard of "Oriental fatalism." Prejudices do not change easily or quickly. But there are many signs that the Japanese are restless with their separateness from themselves and the rest of us.

At the end of the 1980s the psychoanalyst Julia Kristeva wrote a book called *Strangers to Ourselves.* In it she asserted that we learn to accept others by recognizing

> our own disturbing otherness, for that indeed is what bursts in to confront that "demon," that threat, that apprehension generated by the projected apparition of the other at the heart of what we persist in maintaining as a proper, solid "us." By recognizing *our* uncanny strangeness we shall neither suffer from it nor enjoy it from the outside. The foreigner is within me, hence we are all foreigners. If I am a foreigner, there are no foreigners.

Kristeva writes partly from personal experience. She is a Bulgarian Jew whose family resettled in France. She never mentions the Japanese in *Strangers to Ourselves,* but her book has much to say to people who have, by a succession of historical turns, become complete strangers to themselves. To say that the Japanese are learning to see clearly who they are is to say precisely that they are discovering their own "disturbing otherness." It is to say that they are finding the foreigner within the "proper, solid 'us'" that the word "Japanese" has always signified.

BETWEEN 1868 AND 1945 the Japanese oligarchy considered the possession of "others" essential to Japan's arrival as a great nation. The restoration occurred amid the age of empire, after all, and what the Japanese learned of empire they learned from the West. It would be comical, were it not so tragic, how closely modern Japan made its initial adventures according to Western designs, which it considered "the public law of the whole world." After the restoration Korea refused to recognize the new Japanese government. The argument was immediately made that Tokyo should forcibly open Korean ports, the way the West had just opened Japan's. This idea was rejected only because Japan was not strong enough to pursue it. But in 1875 Japan sent naval vessels to linger along the Korean coast in imitation of Perry's "black ships." A year later Japan and Korea signed a treaty: Three Korean ports would be opened to Japanese trade; Japanese could reside in Korea under the principle of extraterritoriality.

Japan had an on-and-off history of territorial ambition in Korea that went back many centuries. But its conquest of Korea in 1910—it had taken Taiwan fifteen years earlier and would soon advance upon China—was filled with irony. Tokyo's initial impulse was partly to recruit Korea in an alliance against the West. This is an idea nationalists still advance to defend the imperial cause. Yet as occupiers the Japanese were hideously cruel toward Koreans. The savagery of the Japanese would not be acceptable in Japan, officials allowed, but it was all right in Korea, for Koreans were uncivilized.

We customarily reject the excuses Japanese nationalists give for overrunning Asia and fighting the Pacific war, as we should: The idea that imperial Japan began a war against the West on behalf of all Asians is preposterous considering Japan's behavior. But we must recognize in the obnoxious dissembling of ultrarightists another of the contradictions Japan failed to resolve as it made itself modern. Japan responded to contact with the West by making an other of people whose past was inseparable from its own past. So Koreans were at once other and familiar, which may be why Korea was annexed, not colonized. Japan wanted to obliterate Korean identity, to destroy "Koreanness," in order to assimilate Koreans into the lower ranks of Japanese society. So annexation was two contradictory things at once. Opening to the "superior" West caused the Japanese to seek their own inferiors and treat them cruelly. At the same time, Japan proposed taking Koreans along as it went forward into the modern age.

The Chinese, historically familiar to the Japanese as merchants and traders, never developed a presence in Japan beyond enclaves in Japanese ports. Apart from a small population of laborers, this remains true today, and the Chinese are generally left to themselves. For the Koreans, who were farmers, factory workers, and finally subjects, the pattern was different. A decade after the annexation there were forty thousand Koreans in Japan, and ten times that number ten years later. By 1940 there were one and a quarter million, and that figure nearly doubled during the war.

Assimilation has always been official policy toward Japan's Korean minority, but there is considerable distance between the official policy and the unofficial reality. Today there are about seven hundred thousand ethnic Koreans in Japan, almost all of them born there. Like Akemi Matsuura, the fashion executive I met in Tokyo, most of them speak Japanese in their homes and have taken Japanese names. But assimilation is a complicated matter in Japan. The psychoanalyst Julia Kristeva is a naturalized French citizen, but that does not make her background any the less Bulgarian, and she is no more or less a Jew. Nothing is erased. And that cannot be said of Koreans invited to become Japanese.

Akemi Matsuura's father came from Korea to work during the war. Afterward he started his own construction company. There was never any question as to the identity of Matsuura *père:* He was a Korean by birth, he had married a Korean, and he raised a Korean family. Akemi's father never hesitated to remind his children that they were Korean, even as they lost the language. "I believed I thought like a Korean," Akemi said as she explained her family. But in Korea she found she was not Korean, and then in Japan that she was not Japanese. I was not surprised when she told me she had spent the first few years of her professional life accepting and then quitting jobs—one in Tokyo, the next in Seoul, the next back in Tokyo, and so on.

Each year a small number of Koreans become citizens, but it is a forbidding experience. While the legal requirements of citizenship are straightforward enough, "to become Japanese" is a phrase freighted with meaning. Citizenship strips Koreans of their otherness in the eyes of the Japanese, but that is to say it strips them of their selves. They must become, as the Japanese have, others to themselves. They must give up not just their names but their culture, dress, quite often their neighborhoods, and so on. It is because citizenship entails such an encompassing loss of identity that most Koreans prefer the precarious status of resident alien.

One of the two most famous incidents involving Koreans in Japan occurred after the earthquake of 1923. Between Tokyo and Yokohama eighty thousand people died in the tremors and the ensuing "sea of fire." Rumors immediately spread that Koreans were setting the fires, poisoning wells, throwing bombs, raping Japanese women, and looting Japanese shops. Nothing ever came of these rumors; not one was ever substantiated. But neighborhood vigilante groups, along with police and army units, nonetheless began a rampage of executions. The earthquake coincided with Japan's version of the red scare that gripped America after World War I. And after the anti-Korean riots subsided Tokyo spread the false information (at home and abroad) that the Korean victims were "reds" bent on fomenting violence.

The events of 1923 remain a controversial matter in Japan and Korea. There are many estimates of the number of slayings—a subject scholars still pursue through the historical records. The numbers range from 231 (the official 1923 police report) to six thousand (Japanese and Korean scholars writing in recent years). It is now safe to assume that the number of executed Koreans lies somewhere above four thousand. And it is safe to assume that the post-earthquake slaughter left a deep mark upon relations between Japanese and Koreans residing in Japan.

The other noted incident involving Koreans took place during the war but erupted as a public issue only a half century later. This was the use of what official Japan called during the war (and calls even now) "comfort women"—a tidy euphemism for girls and young women forced to serve as prostitutes for imperial army troops. Camp followers, officially sanctioned or not, have been around as long as there have been wars. But in scale and efficiency—and therefore barbarity—the Japanese perfected the practice as if it were a better way to make transistors. The army ran its platoons of prostitutes like corporate subsidiaries, fixing prices, working hours, refund policies, time alloted each customer, and so on. The first comfort women were shipped to Shanghai in 1938 as "war supplies." There are no reliable numbers as to how many others were coerced into service. The evidence suggests there may have been as many as 139,000 comfort women over the next seven years. Most were Korean.

The existence of comfort women was obscured until 1962, when a Japanese journalist rummaging through old photo files found a censored picture of two Korean women shin deep in a shallow stretch of the Huang He (Yellow) River in China. It took twenty-six more years for Korean women to bring the issue into the open. Silenced by shame, the first comfort woman testified publicly only in 1991, when a lawsuit was filed against the Japanese government. Since then, comfort women have come to haunt Japan "like a vengeful ghost," as a Tokyo politician put it. In 1993, after official documentation was uncovered and publicized, Tokyo finally acknowledged that the imperial army and the wartime government had recruited, tricked, and forced women into an officially sanctioned system. In 1995, Tokyo finally set up a fund to aid the tens of thousands of surviving comfort women of numerous nationalities. But then the fund began to unravel: It failed to raise enough money, and the prime minister elected afterward was reluctant to offer the official apologies that were to accompany compensation awards.

The accounts of comfort women, many of which were collected in a book published in 1995, make moving evidence of the inadequacy of court verdicts and financial awards in any case. Legal resolutions cannot make up for the troubled lives many comfort women led after the war and the unhealed sorrow common to all of them. Nor do they have much to do with Japanese attitudes toward others. Sex tours to Seoul, Manila, Bangkok, and elsewhere are highly popular among Japanese men today. In provincial Japanese cities one finds groups of Thais, Koreans, Chinese, Filipinas, or Brazilians recruited as nightclub "entertainers," whose employers often take away their passports and routinely withhold wages. It is difficult to view these practices as distinct from the imperial conscript's one-hour visit to the house of comfort women.

In many ways the lives of Koreans in Japan resemble those of the outcast *burakumin.* Many are haunted by the social pressure to hide their background—to pass, as a *burakumin* might. There are Koreans with their own businesses, such as Akemi Matsuura's father. There are others who have taken advantage of business connections in Seoul, or who have made good in show business or sports. But most Koreans live on the margins of society. They were traditionally thought to have an affinity for dirt, as if squalor were the preferred condition. This idea is reflected today in the low-paying jobs and poor housing available to them: They like it that way, the Japanese tell themselves. Like abused minorities anywhere, Koreans are not strangers to crime—most of it petty but some not so. They own many of Japan's eighteen thousand *pachinko* parlors, the pinball halls closely tied to the *yakuza* underworld.

There is a long list of things the Koreans cannot do in Japan. They cannot expect to attend a major university or work at a leading corporation. They pay taxes as if they were citizens, but they cannot partake of many of the social benefits their taxes help finance—public housing, for instance, and government health-care programs. They cannot vote, stand for public office, or support a political party. Nor can a Korean, even a third- or fourth-generation Korean who has never been to Korea, carry a Japanese passport. They travel on Korean documents and cannot leave Japan without a reentry visa. In effect, Koreans must have an official permit to make a journey outside Japan.

For many years Koreans were periodically fingerprinted as aliens, even though they were resident in Japan. This was long considered among the most offensive of official policies toward Koreans, but a movement of "fingerprint refusers" appeared only in the 1980s. It spread rapidly and had the evident support of many ordinary Japanese. In 1993 the movement of refusers forced the government to relax the system, though it has not been eliminated.

Among the first fingerprint refusers was a pianist named Choi Sun-Ae, a second-generation Korean from the city of Kitakyushu, in western Japan. Choi's father, like Akemi's, was born in Korea and married a Korean. In Kitakyushu he became a pastor of a congregation of Christian Koreans. I met Choi (which Koreans pronounce *Cheh*) at a coffee shop near her apartment in Tokyo. She was quiet, unassuming, dedicated to her work. As soon as I sat down across from her I wondered why such a person would become embroiled in an issue such as fingerprinting. She had the demeanor of an earnest graduate student. Yet Choi had been in and out of Japanese courtrooms since refusing in 1981, when she was twenty-two.

Choi had been fingerprinted several times before she decided to refuse. Her inspiration was her younger sister, who, at fifteen, was to be finger-printed for the first time. The sister became Japan's first refuser. She refused for the disarming reason that none of her chums at school had to go through such a routine. At this time Choi was a university student. One day without warning her roommate told her she was a *burakumin*. It was the first time she had mentioned it to anyone. Choi was shocked. "Why does that remain a problem?" she recalled asking herself. "My sister and my roommate taught me that if one does nothing, history repeats itself. Watching the two of them, I decided to refuse."

Choi and her sister both went to court. As a minor Choi's sister was simply sent home, but Choi's case became national news. After her first court case she was invited to study piano in America and waited a year for Tokyo to issue a reentry permit. Then she left Japan without one. By the time Choi finished her studies it was clear the government was skittish. Twenty thousand Koreans had refused. When Choi flew from Los Angeles to Tokyo in the spring of 1988, she was permitted reentry without the required documents.

When I met Choi many years later she was married to a Japanese and the mother of a one-year-old, born in Japan. She was still certain of her Japaneseness—a certainty she traced, like Akemi, to her visits to Korea, of which there were only two. In one of her court appearances Choi made these remarks:

When I was in the sixth grade, my mother and I went to Seoul to attend a piano concert. It was my first visit to Korea. I remember the sultry smell of humanity there, and I recall wanting to go back to Japan as soon as possible. I went to Korea again during the spring vacation . . . in 1980. I went expecting to feel that Korea was really my ancestral country, but I had to face the fact that, deep inside, my feeling of being Japanese was stronger than any sentiments I may have had about Korea.

An odd note is sounded in these words. From her reference to sultry smells one may suspect that Choi was trying to pass by sharing a widespread Japanese prejudice. Yet she had acknowledged her background her entire life and had paid heavily for it. Japanese or not, she decided as a child to keep her Korean name even as her teachers badgered her to change it. Perhaps it was then that the collision course was set. By the time I met her Choi had lost even her status as a permanent resident and was living tenuously on a visitor's visa in the only country she knew.

Choi seemed to have as little interest in politics as she had at the outset of her travails thirteen years earlier. She said, "The fingerprinting isn't the issue. It's the pain. Koreans have no chance to show pain. They are always trying to show they are Japanese—hiding, always frightened. Somehow, the refusing made Korean people change. It made them less afraid to reveal themselves, to show their feelings openly in front of Japanese society."

Choi and other refusers often mention the many ordinary Japanese, especially younger Japanese of their generation, who urge them to keep challenging the legal and social conventions. It is no longer a question of whether they will succeed—only of when. Japan's embrace of Asia is already evident in the economic interdependence it has developed with Korea, Taiwan, and the rest of the region. In time, the economic embrace will become broader and deeper, and discrimination will simply become too expensive—politically, diplomatically, commercially. Then the Japanese will at last have to recognize themselves in the others they have kept away. But the "when" of this agreeable narrative is not near. It will arrive so gradually that there will probably never be a moment of which we can say, "When Koreans were finally accepted in Japan . . ."

Among the other things Koreans cannot do in Japan is teach. They can earn teaching credentials, but they are barred from the profession by a law requiring teachers to be Japanese nationals. In the late 1980s an aspiring teacher named Shu In-Shik challenged the nationality clause in court. In his opening statement Shu used the term *zainichi,* the Japanese for Koreans born in Japan:

> It took me twenty-one years to be able to use my Korean name in society. I want to create a society where the next generation of Koreans can use their real names as a matter of course. If I become a teacher it will be good for Korean children: They will see hope in their future. For Japanese children, having a teacher with different ethnicity will help change the deep-rooted prejudice against Koreans. . . . It will be truly worthwhile . . . for all children if we, *zainichi,* become school teachers.

In 1991 the question of teachers became a diplomatic matter between Tokyo and Seoul. And it provides some insight into the grudging, reluctant manner by which Tokyo—the Japanese government, not the Japanese people—will allow the pretense of sameness to dissolve. Japanese and Korean officials met to consider the case of Korean teachers such as Shu. Afterward, Tokyo announced that it would eliminate the nationality clause, but there was a catch. Koreans would be hired at lower wages and in a lower status. They would be *koshi,* instructors, and serve under the *kyoyu,* the teachers, who would be Japanese.

OF JAPAN'S INTERNAL others, the *burakumin* are the least strange and yet the strangest. Scientists have tested their blood and measured their faces and heads to find some evidence of difference, something to make a physiological fact of their separateness. They have tried to demonstrate that the *burakumin* are genetically Korean, though it is not clear just what that would have proven, or that they are related to an aboriginal race from Sakhalin, the Russian island to Japan's north. Before the war there was even a theory that the *burakumin* were descendants of the lost tribe of

Israel. None of this has led anywhere, needless to say. The *burakumin* remain an invisible other.

In Osaka, where many of the 3 million *burakumin* live, I went to a *buraku* neighborhood at the edge of the mountains behind the city. After walking some distance past neat rows of apartments and well-tended gardens, I began to wonder when I would arrive. Surely there would be a wall or some other demarcation, or an abrupt decline in the condition of the houses and shops. Then I saw a sign, characters painted on a cloth hung across the front of a building. REVERE THE RIGHTS OF ALL HUMAN BEINGS, it said. I had reached the center of the community.

The *burakumin* live in a kind of gulag archipelago centered around the Inland Sea. This is an accident of history, for the Inland Sea was for many centuries the center of Japanese commerce. There are forty-four *buraku* neighborhoods in Osaka and roughly two hundred tiny ones in Hiroshima. Altogether in Japan there are six thousand. The urban quarter below the mountains is one small part of this community of islands.

Until the mid-1970s the Osaka neighborhood was surrounded by wasteland. Then the taboo was broken, a practical matter of land pressure. A local railway operator began buying plots for company housing. The rest of the land sold instantly. The only things that separate the *burakumin* from their neighbors now are a stream, an old wire fence along one edge of the quarter, and bits of a crumbling cinder-block wall—things you would not notice unless you were looking for such signs. The subway stop serving the *buraku* quarter is called Mino-o and was, for a long time, among the least used in Osaka. People who lived near Mino-o preferred to get off one stop either side of it so the other passengers would not mistake them for *burakumin*. But that practice, like the perimeter around the neighborhood, has disappeared.

The ancient ancestors of the *burakumin* were associated with animals and the human dead. They slaughtered stock, tanned leather, and dug graves. Their status is said to have reflected the Shinto emphasis on symbolic pollution. So they were called *eta,* an old word meaning "abundant filth." But the *eta* prospered. The feudal estates competed for them, for the samurai depended on the *eta* for armor, saddlery, and weapons made of bone and gut. Only under the Tokugawa did the status of the *eta* become a legal matter. In a society obsessed with rank they were rankless. The *eta* must have made it slightly easier for the peasants to accept lives of brutality and deprivation. Hence *ningai,* other than human. Edo-era edicts required the *eta* to wear patches of leather on their clothes and banned them from the houses of *ryomin,* acceptable people.

It stands to reason that those off the human map were doomed eternally, for such a condition was by definition hereditary (as everything was during Edo). In 1871 the Meiji government abolished the old discrimination and made the *eta* "new commoners." But *tatemae* and *honne,* the announced situation and the reality, never matched after the restoration. Having declared the equality of all, the oligarchs instituted an open census register that listed everyone's previous place in the feudal castes. The *eta* became known as *burakumin,* hamlet dwellers, and lived in identified communities. This was the era of the imperial restoration, after all. To place the emperor atop the new society would have no meaning unless there was also a bottom.

In 1922, during the period known as Taisho democracy, the *burakumin* organized for the first time. They were much influenced by Christian socialists and what they read of the radical republicans of the English Civil War. They started a group called the Levelers Association and flew a flag that featured a crown of thorns, symbolizing the suffering of the oppressed. Their founding manifesto began, "*Burakumin* throughout the country, unite!" But the true political arrival of the *burakumin* had to wait until after the war. In the 1947 elections ten *burakumin* won Diet seats. That was a high-water mark, as it was for women. Jiichiro Matsumoto, a prewar activist and the great hero of the *burakumin,* was voted vice president of the Diet's upper house and so became the first *burakumin* permitted to enter Fukiage Palace for an imperial audience. He refused the honor.

The neighborhood I visited had once been nicknamed Apache City because it consisted of families who lived in tents. There are still places in Osaka and elsewhere with houses of corrugated tin, no plumbing, and poor sanitation. But the redevelopment of Apache City was not unusual. Since the 1960s the government—Tokyo as well as the municipalities—has spent heavily in *buraku* areas. By 1993 this money had come to more than $30 billion. That is why prosperous Osakans can live next to a *buraku* quarter with nothing but a stream between them. But the less evident problems persist. *Burakumin* children do less well than others in school, and go less far. There is a good chance they will grow up to join *yakuza* crime syndicates, become alcoholics, or become refuse collectors, septic cleaners, or junkyard operators—modern-day equivalents of the old professions.

Subsidies have lulled many ordinary Japanese, perhaps a majority, into thinking of the *burakumin* question, when they think of it at all, as a feudal hangover that will disappear on its own. They can no longer be bothered, it would seem. But that is only part of the story. Subsidies have also commuted prejudice into resentment. And there are many Japanese who still go to remarkable lengths to avoid the indistinguishable other. It is still routine for the families of engaged couples to hire private investigators to research each other's ancestral backgrounds. Large corporations— Nissan, Mitsubishi, Mobil Oil of Japan, and others—have been found screening job applicants with lists based on genealogies and census data compiled as far back as the 1930s. Such lists have been good business. At one time there were nine of them in circulation, produced and sold at high prices by the same investigators who handle marital matters.

The successor of the Levelers Association, formed only a few months after the surrender, is called the Buraku Liberation League. It has fought hard, and not always attractively, to combat discrimination and keep government money flowing into *buraku* communities. Among other things, the league has intimidated corporations using the lists into setting up departments to educate employees about the *burakumin*. But the fundamental problems linger, like the *burakumin* themselves, invisibly: ignorance, fear, and denial.

Curiously, the Buraku Liberation League does not want the *buraku* people simply to become ordinary Japanese. Absorption into a society cleansed of discrimination is not the point. It is to achieve equality as an identifiable group. Perhaps this is a question of power for the *burakumin* leadership: Complete assimilation, of course, would mean there would be no more liberation league. For many years the league has appealed to the United Nations for recognition as a legitimate minority. So the league encourages *burakumin* to declare themselves—to come out, as we would say—by revealing their ancestry. To do this, it is often enough for a *burakumin* simply to let others know where he or she lives.

Until recently coming out was more or less the rule among schoolchildren. They were encouraged to write out declarations and read them in front of their teachers and classmates. But coming out soon caused controversy among the *burakumin*. What does such a declaration mean, students and parents began to ask, if it is written and read only because others in the community expect it? This question reflects the other tendency evident among *burakumin:* the desire of many, especially those few who have a chance to get a decent education and a secure job, to solve the problem by passing among other Japanese, the way some Koreans pass.

Whether to pass or come out is now a source of deep anguish. What is the way to authentic self-acceptance? To pass is to leave behind an empty distinction—or does passing, with all the effort involved, mean accepting the prevailing prejudice? To pass requires one to live in a strange neighborhood with a constant fear of discovery; it also produces feelings of guilt about abandoning the community.

But coming out is not an easy alternative. It is difficult, for one thing, especially when children move from local schools to high schools outside of the neighborhood. That first step into the wider world gives the first taste of the real price to be paid. For another, what does it mean to declare oneself *burakumin* if that has no real meaning? The *burakumin* share no distinguishing ethnic characteristics. In the end they are bound only by their understanding of suffering—and (no small matter) their well-developed understanding of Japan.

In Osaka I met a woman in her sixties who strongly favored coming out. Her name was Kimio Kobayashi and she had a son and daughter, both grown. "It's sad to put them through an experience like that. It's painful, but we want to raise kids who can stand up against discrimination, name calling, and the graffiti on the walls." Another woman, much younger than Kobayashi, interrupted as she said this. "The problem begins and ends with education. The power of self-expression, the ability to realize yourself, to act in the world—these things come from education. But they are not encouraged in Japan. It is the biggest problem of all."

In the early 1960s a writer named Sue Sumii, who was not *burakumin,* began publishing a six-volume novel titled *The River with No Bridge,* about the life of the *burakumin* in the first quarter of our century. In the first volume the hero, Koji, is a small boy slowly awakening to his separateness from other Japanese. He learns it first in school, not at home, and from the gradual accretion of cruelties others direct toward him. The realization that he is different is followed by the realization that he is no different at all. These are Koji's twin epiphanies.

Kimio Kobayashi's life was the same. She had a happy childhood in a village near Kyoto, unaware that she was anything but ordinary. She still had great fondness for the village, which sat by a river and "seemed to float when you saw it in the evening from the other side." Kobayashi learned about the *burakumin* in school before discovering by accident, at fourteen or so, that she was one. In her twenties she took a factory job near Osaka and became a production manager. "One day the boss told me, 'One of your girls is from a *buraku* neighborhood. You'd better stay away from her.'" Kobayashi became friendly with the girl without revealing herself. Many years later she was living near Mino-o when the tent houses were razed and apartments went up. She had still not declared herself. Then she moved into one of the new flats and began working openly in the *buraku* community center.

I met Kobayashi and a few others in the community center's lobby. We were sitting on sofas when we were joined by a nervous, middle-aged woman named Nobuko Aoki. Everyone wanted me to meet her. She was heavily made up and sat behind a thick cloud of cigarette smoke. The others urged her to tell her story, which was quite simple. Nobuko Aoki had only recently revealed her background. She had been working at the Osaka City Hall when, four years earlier, an anonymous letter arrived. It was "terrible to look at," she said, still evidently in awe of the moment it came. The letter read simply: "You should work as a shoemaker." Aoki held on at City Hall for three more years before quitting and moving to the neighborhood near the mountains. "I wanted a work situation where I hid nothing. So I declared myself."

Among the striking features of the *burakumin* I met was the complete-ness of their humanity. They would leave a powerful impression anywhere, but they are especially striking in Japan, where the ordinary personality is notable precisely for its incompleteness. Among themselves, at least, the *burakumin* have bridged the divide that separates other Japanese from one another. They are whole, comfortable in their skins. There is a closeness in their communities, a strength and even a joy, that is unlike the rest of Japan, where one finds only an enforced closeness between profoundly private beings. The explanation for this is easily evident: The *burakumin* have accepted the simple matter of difference.

Perhaps only the past can explain the persistence of the prejudice against the *burakumin*. It was under the Tokugawa, who feared the "superior" gaijin and shut Japan off from them, that the Japanese isolated an internal "other" to whom they could feel superior. These are facts of history. Taken together they suggest that the *burakumin* are a mirror of ordinary Japanese. The anxi-eties they are forced to carry within are the anxieties the Japanese feel in front of gaijin. I know of no way to determine if the historical facts are related, but it would be well if they were. For it would suggest that the Japanese, as they put behind them their feelings of inferiority toward Westerners, can put the superiority they assume over others behind them, too.

But we encounter again the distance between people who are prepared to change and those who govern them. The *burakumin* problem is fading, however slowly. Nearly three-quarters of young *burakumin* now marry outside their communities. And Tokyo has spent generously on the *burakumin*. But the subsidies are best understood as an effort to avoid an explosive social problem. The government has refused to pass laws against *burakumin* discrimination, so the *burakumin* question remains as a psychological problem even as it is reduced as an economic issue. This is almost certainly by design. Modern Japanese leaders, no less than the Tokugawa, have cultivated the illusion that the Japanese are all the same. And the illusion of homogeneity is reinforced when there are islands of difference in the sea of sameness.

In Osaka, where the Buraku Liberation League has its headquarters, I once asked an official whether he was hopeful about change in the *buraku* situation. His name was Seiji Nakamura, and he worked in the league's research department. Yes, he said, he was very optimistic, but not because of any domestic policy, and not even because the Japanese, apart from the government, seemed to make less and less of a fuss over the *burakumin*. He thought the fate of the *burakumin* rested with the changing place Japan occupied in the world.

I told Nakamura I did not understand the connection. He was tall and well built and dressed casually, like a scholar. He said, "Japan wants to be very 'international.' The government in Tokyo wants to cooperate in world affairs, and Japanese companies want to operate overseas. It comes down to a basic human rights issue, national behavior. To be accepted among others, Japan will have to accept us at home."

MINAMOTO NO YORITOMO* became the first shogun (barbarian-slaying generalissimo) in 1192. Yoritomo represented the Yamato, the rice-cultivating people who came to prominence in central Japan during the

---

* Rendered in Japanese order.

first few centuries A.D. Extreme nationalists still invoke the spirit of Yamato, as we have noted previously, for its smell of blood-and-soil belonging. The barbarians Yoritomo was to suppress once lived in central Japan, too, but were driven northward over the centuries and occupied, in his time, only northern Honshu and Hokkaido. These were the Ainu. They were hunters, not farmers; Caucasian, not Mongoloid.

Today the Ainu number twenty-five thousand. They live in isolated villages in Hokkaido, though a few of them drift down to the industrial cities to work as day laborers and live in neighborhoods such as Sanya, the derelicts' quarter of Tokyo. Bleak, often riven with alcohol problems, and surviving on subsidies and trade in carvings, furs, and folk artifacts, the Ainu communities in Hokkaido resemble Native American reservations in the United States. The same desolation pervades them. No matter where they are, they give the feeling of being in a forgotten corner.

In their villages the Ainu struggle to preserve their customs and language. The remnants of a rich oral tradition survive, but there is no written literature. In this struggle they will succeed, but there is little chance that the Ainu and their traditions will survive as anything other than folkloric curiosities. Sometime after the Meiji government set about settling the Hokkaido frontier, the living spirit of the Ainu was fatally injured. Though there are thoughtful Ainu leaders struggling to preserve the identity of their people, one does not find much in the way of a vibrant will to survive among the Ainu. They will live only by disappearing into the Yamato majority.

Ordinary Japanese think of the Ainu, when they think of them at all, as something like theme-park attractions. They are especially preoccupied with the physical characteristics of the Ainu, who are hairy, whose features are distinctively chiseled, and who sometimes have blue eyes. Scholars have been known to dig up Ainu graves to measure the heads of corpses. Of all Japan's internal others, only the Ainu are occasionally called gaijin. Shigeru Yosano, the Ainu leader, is bitter about the way his people are treated. He wants a treaty between Japan and the Ainu that would recognize Hokkaido as their native land. But there is little chance of it, as even Yosano must realize. He spent twenty years trying to stop construction of a dam near his village that would destroy a river sacred to the Ainu. Yet when he brought the government to court it refused to acknowledge that there was such a thing as the Ainu people.

For a long time the Japanese felt roughly the same about Okinawans as they did about the Ainu. Cultivators and traders, the Okinawans presented no threat with their way of life or with attacks on the Yamato majority. But they must have threatened the Japanese nonetheless, with a gentle but unshakable certainty about themselves that remains apparent even today. In the sixteenth century the Chinese emperor officially named the tiny Okinawan kingdom Liu-chu, the Land of Propriety. In the 1960s an American civil-rights activist concluded a tour of Japan and famously described it as a country divided between Okinawans and non-Okinawans.

Okinawans are no clearer about their origins than the Japanese. The Ryukyu chain, where they live, was probably settled from the main Japanese islands, possibly by people who mixed with Ainu on the way, but it is not certain. Over centuries of trading with China, Korea, and Southeast Asia as far as present-day Thailand, the Okinawans absorbed numerous cultural influences. It is partly from the earliest of these contacts that the southern-origin theory of the Japanese has arisen. For a long time the Okinawans paid tribute to China, but if they learned anything from the varied human currents bathing their shores, it was an almost infinite flexibility that allowed them to keep a measure of independence even from their most imposing neighbor.

In 1609 Ieyasu, the first Tokugawa shogun, ended Okinawa's ease among others when he commissioned a warrior clan from Kyushu to invade the Ryukyu Islands. These were the Satsuma, later to distinguish themselves as leaders of the restoration. Kidnapping the Okinawan king, the Satsuma spirited him back to Kyushu and forced him to acknowledge Japanese supremacy before sending him home. After Japan was closed to the outside world in 1639, the Satsuma used the Ryukyus as a back door for Edo Japan's surreptitious trade with the mainland.

Four dates define official Japan's attitude toward Okinawa in the modern era. In 1879 the restoration government replaced the Okinawan king with a prefectural governor sent from Tokyo. In 1945 Okinawa became the only home territory on which the Japanese fought the Western allies. In 1952 Tokyo agreed to let the Americans extend their occupation of Okinawa for twenty years. The last date is the most eloquent of all, though the event it marks remains officially unconfirmed: Before the islands reverted back to Japan, in 1972, Hirohito casually offered to let President Nixon keep them.

Okinawans carry these dates within themselves. After the governor arrived and the last Liu-chu king was exiled to Tokyo (and then made a marquis in the new peerage), Okinawa went from kingdom to periphery overnight. Everything was Japanized; by the Second World War, to speak Okinawan or to observe local customs were punishable acts of subversion. Today Okinawans struggle, like the Ainu, to preserve their language and customs from oblivion. But while the Ainu will have to accept a glass museum case that encloses their past, the Okinawans will keep a living culture alive. "The Ainu insist on their identity. So do Okinawans," an Okinawan intellectual once told me. "But we have no possibility of losing ours, partly because we still have our land."

Time is unlikely ever to wear smooth the Battle of Okinawa, a ghastly scar in relations between Okinawans and the "mainland," as they call the principal Japanese islands. Three hundred thousand were killed, half of them civilians, and of those civilians, many died by suicide at the encouragement of Japanese troops—or at their hands. What did this three-month atrocity reveal if not the imperial army's willingness to throw innocent Okinawans in the path of the invaders to slow their progress toward Fukiage Palace? In 1993 the recently enthroned Akihito became the first emperor in history to visit Okinawa. Two decades after the islands reverted to Japanese control, it was more momentous a journey than most of those he took to other countries.

Okinawa was the only prefecture Hirohito skipped in his postwar rounds of Japan for a simple reason: The Okinawans, having died en masse for him, felt none of the mainland's confusion as to his responsibility for the war. Today Okinawa is still treated as a kind of peripheral dumping ground. Three-quarters of the American military bases in Japan are located there—out of sight from Tokyo's perspective, if not Okinawa's. The Americans occupy a fifth of Okinawa's scarce land, including a fair amount of Naha, the capital.

Tokyo's betrayals continued after the war. For evident reasons, keeping Japan free of nuclear weapons is a near obsession among all Japanese. But Okinawans have long suspected that Tokyo allows the Americans to keep them covertly in Okinawa. Always a plausible suspicion, it now borders on certainty. When I was in Naha in 1994, the governor had just jetted to Washington in search of Henry Kissinger. New details of the negotiations prior to reversion had just emerged: According to a former Japanese emissary,

Nixon (through Kissinger) won a secret agreement from Tokyo in 1969 that the Americans could, in emergencies, import nuclear weapons into Okinawa after reversion three years later. Neither Tokyo nor Washington has ever confirmed the agreement, but it would be in keeping with the way both treat Okinawa. Okinawan opinion is never more than a footnote, as the rape incident in 1995—another betrayal, another date to remember—demonstrated.

In most Okinawans one finds animosity toward the mainland, subdued by a pragmatic appreciation of the benefits of belonging to it. They did not share much in the postwar miracle because there were better places for corporations to invest than an atoll whose capital is eleven feet above sea level. The economy became an awkward creature with three unenviable legs: handouts from Tokyo, the American military bases, and tourism. For a long time, the bases were the Okinawans' most important source of employment and income, but mainland visitors have overtaken G.I.'s as the American century wanes. Today more than half Okinawa's income is from official subsidies, not quite a quarter is from tourism, and about 10 percent is from the American occupiers.

Naha today is a mix of tropical beachhead, palms, and flat, sixties-style office buildings of five or six stories. There is no hinterland—no plantations, mines, or forests to feed it. Naha resembles Manila during the Marcos days, or any of the laconic towns in Southeast Asia that grew up around American military installations. Along Sunshine Avenue the bars are called Buffalo, Sugar Boys, Moonstone, the Peacock. Mixed among them are army surplus stores and gift shops selling coral jewelry, hand-embroidered textiles, and Okinawan sake. When I arrived my flight was forced to circle for half an hour, because American fighter jets have right-of-way over all commercial flights at the airfield.

Naha is where Japan and America hide the unattractive mechanics of the postwar relationship. To see it is to confront the vestiges of camp-follower subservience that began in 1945 and that the Japanese try to obscure in Tokyo. Okinawans dislike the American presence—the governor they elected in 1992 ran on his opposition to the bases—but this is a practical matter now as much as it is one of dignity and principle. The bases simply take up too much space, hindering economic development.

Americans did Okinawa one favor after the war. After sixty years of Japanization, they encouraged Okinawans to think again about themselves. There was nothing altruistic about this, nothing ennobling:

Americans wanted only to demolish another aspect of the enemy's prewar nationalism. But it benefited Okinawans anyway. They revived their language and culture. Their young intellectuals—the generation of graduates who now run Okinawa—were able to go off to earn doctorates in Ohio and Illinois. Okinawans rediscovered themselves at a time mainland Japanese were still reeling from the defeat and turning themselves into a society of lost, rootless city dwellers.

In 1960 a famous folklorist named Kunio Yanagita published a book called *By Way of the Sea.* Yanagita advanced the southern-origin theory and postulated that in Okinawans the Japanese could find an authentic version of themselves, the earlier culture they buried when they sinicized and samuraized and later westernized. The Okinawan language, called Shuri in its purest form, is an older and consequently softer dialect than those spoken on the mainland. It did not harden into a "respect language," as mainland Japanese did. ("It's difficult to argue in Shuri," an Okinawan once told me. "It's too nice.") Traces of a matriarchal system remain evident in the place of women in the family and in society at large. There is less *tatemae* among Okinawans, who prefer to live by *honne*—which is to say they like to live without masks.

Yanagita struck a chord in the Japanese. Many have since begun to look upon Okinawans with something like envy. Mainland Japanese do not easily articulate this, but they find in the south a self-confidence they lack, reflected most superficially in an ease of manner and a physicality especially attractive to younger Japanese. In the early 1990s there was a pop-culture *bumu* in Okinawan music. The southern origin of the Japanese is nothing more than an attractive hypothesis. But the past, of course, is not really the point. It is the search through the past for a way forward—a familiar Japanese habit. "In Okinawa we may find clues not only for the reconstruction of past Japan, but also for the construction of future Japan," the scholar Shunsuke Tsurumi said at the turn of the 1980s. "The culture of Okinawa, where women play a central role in religious rituals and in the formation of basic social values, may contribute to a reformation of the male-centered society of the other islands, which . . . failed with the loss of the war."

FIFTY YEARS AFTER the failure of the Greater East Asia Co-Prosperity Sphere, Tokyo's wartime design for the region, Japan became a metropole.

The flood of Japanese capital into neighboring countries began to turn Japan's edge of the Pacific into a single, complex economy. All over East Asia, Japanese corporations were loosening traditional ties to land and family and creating a new class of uprooted urban dwellers—unskilled or semiskilled, people seeking livelihoods at the wellspring of wealth. The French had done this, and the English, over long periods of time. Almost every country in Europe thus created the problem of workers migrating from South to North. Once again, the Japanese merely speeded up the process.

In the late 1980s, the economy at fever pitch, Japan began importing labor on a large scale for the first time since Koreans arrived in numbers before the war. By the 1990s, even after the bubble economy burst, it maintained a population of roughly three hundred thousand foreign workers. These were not, by and large, assimilable—not by Japanese standards. Hamlets of plywood houses began to spring up in and around large cities. As time went on foreign workers appeared more or less everywhere. In the mid-1990s the most reliable profile I found looked like this: forty-four thousand Thais, forty thousand Iranians, thirty-eight thousand Malaysians, thirty-one thousand Filipinos, and so on down to eight thousand Pakistanis and seven thousand Taiwan Chinese.

What did these new arrivals do? The women among them were usually "entertainers" or maids. The male majority worked primarily in construction and in the vast sea of small and medium-sized companies. Imported workers were essential to these sections of the economy. But Japan was wholly unprepared even to acknowledge their presence. Virtually all of these new workers were in Japan illegally. Eighty-five percent had arrived on tourist visas and overstayed.

Traveling once along the coast south of Tokyo, my train stopped at a local station. Two foreigners waited amid the crowd of Japanese on the platform. They were Middle Eastern, and in appearance everything the Japanese were not: a bit careless of their clothing, a couple of days' stubbly growth apparent on their faces. No Japanese stood near them. Those at some distance seemed to stare past them, or avoided looking in their direction. When the train doors opened, those boarding walked straight through the pair. It was as if they were invisible—as if I, another foreigner, were the only one who saw them.

This is precisely how Tokyo treated those arriving en masse to work in the very economy that had, in a sense, created them. The government guarded its right to prosecute, but for a long time it prosecuted almost no one. In June of 1990 it announced the first rules governing workers without visas. Employers using illegals who arrived after June 1 faced fines of 2 million yen and up to three years in prison. But of workers themselves the law said nothing. By publicizing only the punishment to employers—and refusing, incredibly, to provide any translations of the rules—Tokyo maintained an apparently desired terror quotient at a comfortably intense level.

"There is no basic law. There is no labor law. There is no immigration law. All that can be said is that Japan has officially acknowledged that foreign workers are here." Katsuo Yoshinari spoke in the shabby offices of a group called the Asian People's Friendship Society. He had been a union official when the flood of foreigners began. Oyama, his neighborhood at the northern edge of Tokyo, began to fill with Filipinos and Bangladeshi in need of advice. Yoshinari offered it informally. As the problem worsened, he helped found the society and took up arriving foreigners as full-time work.

The workers I met through Yoshinari offered an unending litany of problems: unpaid wages, confiscated passports, untreated injuries, hospital bills, evictions, court appearances, marital disputes. There was an Iranian in the society's office who was very insistent. "The Japanese can't understand," he kept telling me. "Everywhere I go they say, 'You have a different face, a different culture. You are Iranian.' Japan is an Asian country. I'm an Asian. But they can't understand." But they did understand, as Yoshinari agreed. "The official stance is to keep them insecure so that their numbers can be controlled according to economic conditions."

Not long after I had these conversations one of Japan's most thoughtful economists spread the choices out before his country. "What kind of nation do we want to be?" he asked. Then he offered four alternatives. Japan could continue to let foreign workers in and discriminate against them; it could close the door to them; it could allow them in and integrate them. The last alternative he called "sophisticated discrimination": Make foreign workers legal but segregate them socially. He himself favored a combination of the middle two options: close the door partially so that labor scarcity would improve the vast, poor end of the economy, but integrate those allowed past a partially closed door.

The economist's question is the right one: What Japan does about its new foreign population will determine much about its future character. But his underlying assumption is troubling: that Japan is in perfect control of itself, with a precisely calibrated future before it. Missing from this intelligent, technocratic account is the proper sense of inevitability. The foreign workers prying Japan open represent unavoidable economic demand. And that is why belonging in Japan on the basis of rights and not of blood or ancestry is also inevitable. In this I preferred the remark of an old man I once met in Tokyo. He traced Japan's progress by recalling his walks through Ueno Park, a large tract of hills and meadows at the capital's edge. Before the war he had seen only men there. After the war, men and women. And then it was men, women, and Iranians.

In Niigata Prefecture I once met a Bangladeshi named Elahi Mohamed Nurul. He came from a family of physicians in Dhaka and arrived in Japan to study computer science. When that dream died he went to language school, and at night studied *enka*, a slightly old-fashioned kind of popular song. Then came work in a fast-food restaurant, a threatened arrest, unemployment, a job in a silver-plating factory, more unemployment, another brush with the law. When I met him he was making plastic molds for a small company in a nothing-special industrial town called Mitsuka, near the Sea of Japan. The hours were long—thirteen a day—but he was learning the technology.

Nurul was dark and stocky, with handsome, fine features. He was twenty-six when I met him, illegal but unbothered. Nurul was happy. Five years earlier he had married a nurse named Misako. He found himself in the peculiar position of being legally recognized as a husband and wanted as an illegal resident. But his employer liked him and would wait patiently for his visa to come through. Yes, he said, he and Misako would have children, as soon as things were settled.

I considered Mitsuka as we spoke: a section of old shop-houses, nearly moribund; a busy, soulless thoroughfare lined with car lots, electronics outlets, chrome-and-glass "family restaurants." We sat in one, talking over coffee. The city lay amid a flat, treeless landscape. Nurul knew of five Sri Lankans in the area, the only foreigners. I said, "You must feel as if you're walking on the moon."

Nurul smiled. "It's very strange. Whenever we go out, everyone looks at me as if I'm an animal. They say, *'Oka-san! Gaijin!'*—Mother! A foreigner! Sometimes people say, 'You look the way Japanese people used to look.' Or they say, 'You don't look Asian.' I don't know what they all mean. My wife says, 'You're a Muslim. Teach them. Teach them that you're just human, and they will change.' I don't know. But Mitsuka is home. Yes. Yes, it's home."

Nurul's smile was unforced and more or less constant. When we got up to leave, he insisted on taking the bill. "You've come all the way from Tokyo. This is my city." So I agreed—but only on the condition that Nurul would sing an *enka* while I drove him home.

In the car Nurul turned shy. He still sang *enka* a couple of nights a week in a local karaoke bar, but that was probably after many drinks. *Enka* are swooning laments about bad love and hard lives, favored now by middle-aged housewives and slightly past-it *sararimen*.

Finally Nurul relented:

> Tears have many memories.
> The heart has many wounds,
> I drink alone,
> Pouring my sake myself,
> Listening to enka.
>
> Sake, O sake, do you understand?
> I will drink a lot of sake,
> As if I could drown myself in sake.

Sad words. Tuneless voice. But Nurul's Japanese was excellent.

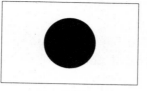

11

A FUGITIVE
VIRTUE

The paradox is irresoluble: The less one culture communi-
cates with another, the less likely they are to be corrupted, the
one by the other; but, on the other hand, the less likely it
is . . . that the respective emissaries of these cultures will be
able to seize the richness and significance of their diversity.

—CLAUDE LÉVI-STRAUSS,
Tristes Tropiques, 1955

"TUCKED AWAY THERE in the north Pacific," Douglas MacArthur once
said of the Japanese, "they had little or no realization of how the rest of the
world lived."

It was May 5, 1951. The occupation would end in less than a year.
President Truman had already removed MacArthur as S.C.A.P., supreme
commander for the allied powers. Home from Tokyo, the general was
called to explain the Japanese to the Senate, which was then considering
the security treaty that would bind Japan to America.

MacArthur, by any measure, was an Orientalist. And like the observations of Orientalists throughout history, the things he said that day were
not devoid of truth, only of history—and therefore of understanding. The

Japanese remember MacArthur's speech today for what came next. It is a remark that most of them, whether alive at the time or not, can cite more or less as the general uttered it:

> Measured by the standards of modern civilization, they would
> be like a boy of twelve as compared with our development of
> forty-five years.

The American legacy in Japan is complex. But in his Senate speech MacArthur captured one of the lasting and least fortunate parts of it: the Japanese as marginal beings, as understudies to the rest of us. The imagery stuck—among the Japanese about themselves, and among the rest of us. In 1958 Khrushchev remarked that they had nothing to offer but volcanoes and earthquakes. De Gaulle soon matched him: Japan is a nation of transistor salesmen, he famously noted after the Japanese premier called upon him in Paris.

How did the Japanese respond? Not with diplomatic protests, as one might expect today. They had only two alternatives after the war: They could become "internationalists," as Edwin Reischauer and others urged, or they could become (or remain) nationalists. This was really no choice at all. Nationalism was a proven danger: Everyone, or nearly everyone, believed that. The nationalist impulse meant righteous denunciations of the West, justifications of the war, or the odd declaration of racial superiority—the embarrassing messages of the fanatical few. Most Japanese took the obvious path. To be an internationalist meant to support the constitution Americans gave Japan, the peace constitution that barred Japan from war except in self-defense. And it meant accepting the opinions of Americans and others as to who the Japanese were and what they had to do to improve themselves.

In postwar Japan you risked your job and your family's reputation if you got mixed up with the nationalists. This is still true. Whatever one's political opinions, whatever one's misgivings about the Americans and the security arrangements that still put Japan under United States military protection, one does not draw too close to those who linger at the far-right fringe.

But things are not so simple anymore. They never were as simple as most Japanese and most Americans wanted them to be.

THREE NEIGHBORHOODS IN Tokyo tell the complex story MacArthur left unmentioned. They are unrelated, but taken together they complete the picture of what Americans left behind when the occupation formally ended in April of 1952. All of them were within walking distance of the wooden house I lived in during my final year in Japan.

Not far above the ceramic roofs along my street sporadic helicopter traffic used to begin early each morning. Sometimes it did not end until ten or eleven at night. The helicopters were American. They served a small military facility at the edge of the Roppongi district. Coming in to land, they disappeared behind a mishmash of residential blocks, office towers, and multistory buildings full of bars. I often walked past the old base, a set of gray, flat-roofed buildings marked off by a gate and a guard-house. Late at night a few lights burned: *Stars and Stripes,* the military daily, was still edited there.

If I walked in the other direction I passed through the fashion district and arrived in a quarter called Harajuku. For some years Harajuku has enjoyed a certain fame as the venue of cutting-edge trends. My favorite feature in the neighborhood, added in the 1990s, was called Hooptown Harajuku, which was just what its name implied: an asphalt basketball court, complete with messy graffiti (applied by the owner) and a chain-link fence. The going game was three-on-three; a group of six paid roughly $60 an hour to pretend they were in inner-city America.

Harajuku was a weekend phenomenon: On Sundays its main avenue was sealed to traffic and taken over by rock bands and dancers. The most curious of these celebrants were the Elvis impersonators, of whom there were dozens. "It's just history," a media executive once told me. "The Elvis thing has no social significance." He was partly right: American popular culture is now a global phenomenon. But the Harajuku Elvises were too young to remember Elvis Presley. Their act was better understood not as "just history" but as a parody of history and memory, an obliteration. "It's not nostalgic," a young friend told me as we walked through Harajuku once, "but a 'virtual reality' Elvis that is even more authentic to us than the 'real time' Elvis."

The third neighborhood, farthest from my house, is near the imperial palace. It is marked by the towering torii at the entrance to Yasukuni

Shrine. In the geography of the extreme right this bit of Tokyo is the most hallowed real estate in Japan. Yasukuni is dedicated to the dead of Japan's modern wars: the Sino-Japanese conflict of 1894–95, the Russo-Japanese War a decade later, and the Pacific war. Four million souls, including those of convicted war criminals, reside at Yasukuni as Shinto gods. It is a place of simple, straight lines. Beyond the torii is a graveled walk lined with cherry and pine trees. Usually the branches are covered with strips of paper or tiny wooden plaques—offerings to the deities. When there are enough of them, the strips suggest long rows of Christmas trees. The shrine is of plain wood in the traditional style. But for displays of flowers and sticks of incense, it is empty. People bow in prayer, clapping twice when they are finished. Apart from the crunch of gravel underfoot, the only sound is of coins dropped into a worn wooden chest.

Rightists like to say the shrine is their Arlington or their Flanders Field. But Yasukuni is more complicated than its appearance, or any such analogy, implies. After the war the American authorities judged state Shinto to be a primary source of the ultranationalist impulse. They discouraged worship at Yasukuni. The postwar constitution, by separating religion from the state, barred those in government from visiting the shrine in an official capacity. Today many Japanese go to Yasukuni to honor their ancestors. But the shrine still wears a slight taint of the forbidden.

On a landscaped patch behind Yasukuni sits a museum. It contains the artifacts of various adventures: officers' uniforms, artillery shells, a kamikaze plane. Its plaques and testimonials are cast in the language one expects in such a place. They invoke "we" in their gratitude toward the dead; they speak of "the nation." But these terms are complicated, too, for Japanese rightists have appropriated Yasukuni and its museum. It is their "we," not the "we" of the internationalist majority.

What do these three places tell us? The common thread is abandonment, vacated ground. At the old base near Roppongi we see Japan's abandonment of its responsibility to the rest of the world: If it does not have to do with trade, the Americans will take care of it. In Harajuku there is the abandonment of identity: Let us celebrate the figures and icons of our postwar instructors, let us even pretend to a nostalgia for them, for our own have been discredited. And at Yasukuni we see the abandonment of the past: History and sentiment as the provinces of the ultraright.

There is another way to describe this long morning's walk through parts of central Tokyo: It is the narrative trail of "internationalism," an internationalism that requires quotation marks because it is a variant of an admirable idea—a corruption peculiar to the postwar Japanese.

"We should not be cultivating any form of patriotism or nationalism. Rather, our aim should be to become international citizens." This remark belongs to Hitoshi Motoshima, the mayor of Nagasaki, whom I visited one weekend not long before I left Japan. Motoshima had good reason to make such an observation: As we previously noted, he was shot by right-wing extremists in 1990 after observing that Hirohito, along with the rest of the Japanese, bore responsibility for the war. Aging, frail, and easily tired, Motoshima lived with round-the-clock bodyguards. But his was scarcely a voice in the wilderness. His "we" was authentic. In the matter of nationalism and internationalism he spoke for many Japanese—a majority, if newspaper polls are to be credited.

Mayor Motoshima was a firm supporter of the peace constitution. From the constitution flows the internationalist ideal, at least as the Japanese understand it. That is why it is considered a document of near-sacred immutability. The Japanese value many things in the constitution—universal education, female suffrage, civil rights—even if, in practice, some of these principles were bent or restricted after the reverse course. But the truly revered part of the constitution is Article 9, which bars Japan from raising an army or making war. Article 9 was also bent, of course: Japan does have a standing army, even if it is called the Self-Defense Force. Nonetheless, Article 9 is considered an essential protection, one of the two ways America protected the Japanese: The security treaty protected them from others, and Article 9 protected them from themselves.

The constitution's 103 articles make peculiar reading. In tone they are a lengthy scolding. They are full of "shall not's," like a set of commandments. "Children shall not be exploited." "Freedom of thought and conscience shall not be violated." "Peers and peerage shall not be recognized." "There shall be no discrimination in political, economic or social relations . . ." The peace constitution calls to mind generals who prepare to fight the last war, which is not surprising, as it was given to the Japanese by American military men. It is not a document upon which a nation can be built. It is essentially a ban against prewar Japan. And it is amid all the "shall not's" that "the Japanese people forever renounce war as a sovereign right of the nation"—the wording of Article 9.

It is difficult to exaggerate the stupidity of the rules circumscribing the Self-Defense Force. Article 9 bans the S.D.F. from any activity not named in law. When Japan sent an observer ship to Antarctica in the early 1960s, statutes governing naval missions had to be rewritten first. When Tokyo hosted the summer Olympics a few years later, the law had to be rewritten again so that S.D.F. vehicles could assist in traffic control. After the Kobe earthquake in 1995, the S.D.F. waited two days before aiding victims, while bureaucrats and politicians debated the precise wording of the military's orders. Above all, of course, there was Japan's flubbed response to the Gulf War crisis, which bred resentment around the world.

There is also a language problem. The constitution was originally written in English, and as rightists are forever complaining, it reads like a translation. To illustrate this they sometimes seize upon Article 12:

> The freedoms and rights guaranteed to the people by this constitution shall be maintained by the constant endeavor of the people. . . .

Too Jeffersonian, the nationalists assert.

The preamble gives this account of Japan's security arrangements:

> . . . we have determined to preserve our security and existence, trusting in the justice and faith of the peace-loving peoples of the world.

The justice and faith of whom? One does not have to be a rampant nationalist to find something strange in this notion. It is impossible to imagine a country writing itself into such a defenseless corner, simply because no nation ever has. And it is impossible to imagine another country that defines itself so thoroughly by what it will not do. But that is internationalism, Japanese style.

For a long time there was not much substance to the internationalist ideal. Then in the late 1980s, with the yen rising and the Cold War about to end, the internationalists came upon an idea they thought could carry the weight of global influence. In the coming century, economic power—capital and technology, the things Japan was prepared to give the rest of the world—would replace the old notion of power as a function of military strength and territorial dominion. "It may seem that Japan is abnormal," a thoughtful politician said to me as this idea began to circulate, "but when we succeed in restructuring the international community, countries like Japan will become the normal nations and those that maintain military power and dispatch it abroad will be abnormal." The French call this kind of talk *angélisme*. But many Japanese cling to the idea of a Japan that stands for something new on the planet, an unarmed evangelist for diplomacy and reason.

Where has internationalism really led the Japanese? What has it taught them? With the last half century as testament, the lesson is easily discerned. With the constitution as their tablet the internationalists have taught the Japanese that their proper role in world affairs is to stay clear of them. This is the "internationalism" that lies at the core of the confusion the Japanese feel as to who they are, what they stand for, what their purpose is in the global order. Internationalism is what the Japanese propose instead of Japaneseness, which they abandon to the far right. It is no wonder that here, now, in the unappealing final years of our century, the Japanese are precisely nowhere—ill at ease with themselves as well as with the rest of us. Understood properly, Japan's internationalism is essentially a doctrine of shame that sends a simple message: Do not trust us, for we do not trust ourselves.

Mayor Motoshima was a gentle man with a lively sense of humor. He was also a Christian, which put him in a minority of a million or so in all of Japan. Like other Japanese Christians, he was able to view his own society with something of an outsider's distance. He was at once self-deprecating, as the Japanese so often are, and blunt as to Japan's frailties and failures. In Japan an overprotected schoolgirl is called *hako iri musume*, literally "girl in a box," he said. "This is how Japan is, too. We are innocent of the outside world. Sometimes we are selfish. Japan wants to contribute to international society, but it doesn't know how."

Motoshima was right. Japan has "a very difficult time coping with the rest of humanity," as he put it at another point. This was as true as anything Douglas MacArthur told the Senate in 1951. But the mayor made the same mistake as the general: He failed to consider the reasons for Japan's predicament. He did not see that the internationalism he urged the Japanese to cultivate contributes to their isolation. He did not see that one cannot be an internationalist without first being a nationalist of one kind or another—a truth so evident it is hard to understand how anyone could miss it.

AMONG THE SINGULAR features of life in Tokyo are the sound trucks that cruise the main thoroughfares in nationalism's name. These are extraordinarily disruptive contraptions. Long, boxlike, and dark, their window slots covered with wire mesh, sound vans are much like Japanese police transports, except for the right-wing slogans daubed across their sides and the din of the megaphones on their roofs. Many sound trucks fly the flag of the old imperial army, with the emanating sun rays MacArthur removed a half century ago.

The sound trucks wage a war of shouted words on many fronts. In the early 1990s, as Japanese markets opened to imported beef and oranges, the farmer was a running theme: America was destroying the mythic man so central to the traditional idea of Japan. Over the years there have been many other subjects: high-school history texts, a territorial dispute with Moscow, the impurities of foreign rice. The postwar constitution has been an especially deep grudge. To the ultraright it is a symbol of Japan's fall from greatness at the hands of foreigners, its lost sovereignty and defeated spirit. It is an excrescence that must be eliminated if Japan is ever to be Japan again. But to talk of the constitution in such a way, or even to expand upon where it came from, is not done outside of nationalist circles. There have been other postwar taboos, but with the possible exception of the emperor's true role during the war, the peace constitution has been the most carefully observed.

After a time one takes no notice of the sound vans. I minded them only when their megaphones defeated a conversation I would be having with a Japanese. We would both fall silent, and my companion would turn visibly embarrassed. And then I became embarrassed for him. It was at such moments that the meaning of the sound trucks became clear. They are like the politicians who occasionally make ridiculous claims about the justness of the war. With each passing tirade the Japanese are reminded of the ever-present danger of revived militarism. The more the sound vans blared on about the constitution they so detested, the more all of its "shall not's" seemed a necessary thing.

Westerners assume the truth of this danger more or less without question. Even now there are occasional reports in respected newspapers suggesting darkly that an old, barely tamed passion for the sword lurks just below the surface of the unfathomable ocean that is the Japanese soul. A few years ago an American reporter interviewed a senior American officer in Okinawa. Why do the Americans remain in Japan? the correspondent asked. It was a simple question, for the spoken reason, the *tatemae,* was well known: They were there to protect Japan from potentially hostile neighbors—the North Koreans, say, or the Russians, or the Chinese. But the American officer offered a different reply and briefly stunned all of Japan. "Nobody wants a rearmed, resurgent Japan," he said. "So we are a cap in the bottle if you will."

This is a preposterous assertion, a gross and silly exaggeration that is widely believed out of sheer intellectual sloth. We cannot accept it until we ask whom Japan would attack, and why, once it was fully "resurgent." Then we find that there are no sensible answers, not if we consider how the world, and Japan along with it, has evolved over the past five decades.

What do we mean, in any case, when we speak of the frightening right?

A few years ago I was told that the Australian intelligence service had estimated the size of the extreme right in Japan at twenty-three thousand. I never saw the report, and it would be difficult to confirm even its existence. My source was reliable, though, a respected scholar, and the number seemed about right. Right, that is, if we include unreconstructed war veterans in their seventies and eighties, tactless politicians, a proliferation of bizarrely named microsects, sound-truck drivers, *yakuza* bagmen, and the paid-by-the-hour noisemakers who shout through megaphones. These, after all, are the stuff of which the menace is made.

There is also a large, loose group of commentators who represent the spectrum of far-right opinion. Mishima, had he lived, might have fallen into this group. Their writings fascinate the Japanese, partly because they are daring and partly because they say things ordinary people, as good internationalists, have been taught not to think. The upper echelon of the Self-Defense Force includes, along with scholars versed in international affairs, a few officers still willing to rattle their swords from time to time. They resonate with the public, too, because they confirm the popular fear that Japan has never developed sufficient civilian control over the military.

Control over the military? Japan has roughly 150,000 ground troops in uniform—all of them voluntary. In an economy so large that it requires imported labor, who is going to join a force with nothing to do, no role in domestic, regional, or global affairs? Although foreigners are barred by law from defense force bases, a Diet member once secreted me into a camp to watch a dress parade. The experience was eye opening. There before us was an assembly of Beetle Baileys who had evident trouble marching in unison and who simply could not keep their tank turrets straight. Any officer—Japanese or American—willing to dispense with the pretense of defense readiness will confirm this impression.

The ultranationalists can be considered in another light. They may deny both history and their responsibilities in it, but it has always struck me that they deserve a more careful hearing. The gray old war horses have kept alive the ideas of self-respect and sovereignty and Japaneseness, even if they do so in a form that appeals to no one but themselves. They alone stand for these things, and make caricatures of them, for the simple reason that internationalists have surrendered the ground.

Japan as a tightly coiled jack-in-the-box waiting to be sprung endures as a version of reality—among gaijin and among the Japanese themselves. But if we dispense with this anachronistic notion we arrive at obvious conclusions. The rightists are correct: Japan should shred the constitution the Americans gave it and begin again with one of its own. Then it should decide whether it wants to rearm itself without restriction and, if it so chooses, begin to do so at the earliest possible moment.

I know of few Japanese who will easily accept such assertions. They will be taken as a kind of blasphemy—the ideas of a gaijin who must be either reckless or an ultrarightist himself. But I have met few Japanese who are not restless, in some way, with the constraints under which they have lived since the war—and who have not come to believe that this restlessness must somehow be addressed. It is almost as if, amid the professions of pacifism and cosmopolitan purpose, the detested far right voiced, in perverse form, the disavowed desires of the entire country.

THE POSTWAR TABOOS, those forbidden zones of political and historical discourse, work in strange ways. Hirohito's wartime responsibility was, to make an apt reference, a matter of the emperor having no clothes. Until he died and people such as Mayor Motoshima spoke out, many people knew the truth but no one spoke it. It is somewhat the same with the other important taboo, the constitution. Everyone knows the Americans imposed it upon the Japanese without so much as a nod to democratic process. But the polite way to put it is that it was written under American supervision, or tutelage—so avoiding the nature of the document as a relic of foreign occupation.

When the Liberal Democrats were born, in 1955, they merged two conservative parties: the followers of Shigeru Yoshida, who wanted to prosper while America minded security matters, and a group of "Gaullists," who opposed the Yoshida deal in favor of rearmament and a new constitution without the antagonizing Article 9. This is why the L.D.P., though it ruled Japan without interruption for nearly four decades and remains influential today, has always been a tippy ship. The well-worn cliché in Tokyo, only too true, has it that the L.D.P. is neither liberal nor democratic nor a party. It survived on one of the paradoxes peculiar to postwar Japanese politics. A new constitution was a plank in the L.D.P. platform from the beginning—an overt, explicitly stated goal. Every Japanese knew that. But no Liberal Democratic premier ever went near the issue.

The one exception was Yasuhiro Nakasone, who held office from 1982 until 1987. Nakasone was one of the two most important prime ministers of the postwar era. Not even Kakuei Tanaka—the corrupt kingmaker who helped put Nakasone in office—can be counted a contender. The only premier whose vision rivaled Nakasone's was Yoshida. Yoshida shaped the postwar system. Under him, Japan rechanneled its energy into its economy, and the power of the central bureaucracy was restored to oversee it. But if Yoshida was architect of the machine later known as Japan Inc., Nakasone was the first premier to propose destroying the circumstances that brought it into being.

Nakasone's project had many dimensions. In politics he was presidential. He remains the only premier to address the trade problem with any seriousness. Nakasone made *kokusaika,* internationalization, the new Japanese ambition. Under him Japan signed the Plaza Accord, which made the yen a world currency. Nakasone was a committed cold warrior. He vigorously favored a place for Japan in the American security system—but not the place assigned after the war. Nakasone insisted that Tokyo should be Washington's equal partner in securing the Pacific. We must open ourselves to the world, join it, Nakasone often told his audiences. Japan has achieved its long-standing ambition: We have caught up. Now we must set ourselves new goals.

The Japanese liked Nakasone for the stature he gave them. Tall, handsome, impeccably dressed, he was wholly at ease conversing in English with the world's most powerful politicians. At home and abroad, he understood the grand gesture. The 1983 summit of industrial nations, in Williamsburg, Virginia, was the quintessential display of Nakasonian imagery. The Japanese were used to seeing their premier looking small, distracted, and beside the point at the edge of the post-summit photograph. At Williamsburg Nakasone was in the center, flanked by Ronald Reagan and Margaret Thatcher. The picture electrified the Japanese when it appeared in the next day's national dailies. In a photographic album of postwar Japan the Williamsburg shot would rank alongside the old image of Hirohito standing next to MacArthur; each told the story of its time.

No one in the postwar era had ever asked the Japanese to look at the world as more than a market and themselves as more than merchants—no one but the ultranationalist fringe. But did the Japanese know where Nakasone was leading them when he swept into office full of new ideas? Gaijin knew Nakasone as an internationalist, but that was only half the story. He was certainly not an internationalist of the postwar Japanese type. Nakasone had no sympathy for the peace constitution pacifists. He was a nationalist-turned-internationalist. And when we term Nakasone a nationalist, we meant it without reservation, for he was a nationalist of the deepest hue.

In August of 1945 Nakasone was a naval officer of twenty-seven based at Takamatsu, on the Inland Sea. From there he had watched the mushroom cloud ascend over Hiroshima. Much later, Nakasone presented an almost cinematic image of himself after the surrender: wandering aimlessly through Tokyo's ruins, his sword given up to the occupying army, his officer's stripes ripped from his uniform. Defeat, he wrote in his memoirs, "left a stain on Japanese history." The only course was to rebuild Japan as much as possible as it had been—its soul, its pride, its family-state; its purity, its tradition, its unity under the emperor.

As a politician Nakasone swam against the tide. When he first ran for the Diet, in 1947, he won handily on an unfashionably nationalistic platform. As soon as he was elected he began attacking Yoshida for selling Japan's independence to the occupying army—a true enough charge. The Tokyo administration, he said, was a subcontractor for MacArthur's grunt work—true again. Shortly before Truman recalled MacArthur in 1951, Nakasone went to the general with a petition calling for a security treaty between equal partners and the early departure of American troops. By Nakasone's account MacArthur binned the document without even a browse, but the effort earned the brash nationalist deep respect among his fellows.

Nakasone detested all the postwar taboos. He saw no reason for Japan to huddle defenselessly behind the Americans. Devoted to the emperor, he had no intention of giving up displays of patriotism because of his political status. When he campaigned in 1947, he rode a bicycle with a rising-sun flag on the handlebars. Elected prime minister thirty-five years later, he wasted no time raising the self-defense budget beyond customary limits. In 1985, when he visited Yasukuni Shrine on August 15 to mark the surrender, he made it unambiguously clear that his visit was official—so setting off a controversy over the separation of religion and government that has been repeated most years since.

Nakasone's deepest ambition, logically enough in view of his policies and political gestures, was to revise the postwar constitution. He had been premier only a few months when he put this item on the table at a gathering of Liberal Democrats. Predictably, a wall of popular and political opposition arose. At that Nakasone stood down, but only to avoid what he later called "a wasteful social upheaval."

He was a hawk, an archconservative, a nationalist: Whether one takes these as compliments or criticisms is beside the point. Nakasone eventually aroused grave concern among the internationalist majority. He was deeply unpopular by the time he left office. Japan must never again revisit the past, the internationalists asserted. That was scarcely Nakasone's plan, of course. His critics missed the larger issue. His constitutional proposal created a moment when the Japanese could have looked beyond the postwar equation toward a new definition of who they were. The pacifists would never have agreed with Nakasone on this point. The debate would have been ferocious. But that was not the issue, either.

The Japanese needed another decade to address the question he raised. At that missed moment, who was stuck in the past and who looked forward—Nakasone, or his "internationalist" adversaries? Who was retrograde and who had cultivated a picture of the Japan that was to come?

JAPAN SHRANK FROM Nakasone's vision after he left office, in 1987. At the moment of its deliverance from the task set at the restoration, at the moment it could logically confront once again the arrangements fixed after the war, it retreated into old habits. Bureaucrats ruled, as they do today. Prime ministers—with the exception of Morihiro Hosokawa, who broke the Liberal Democrats' hold on power in 1993, and of a Social Democrat who held office briefly—were again drawn from the usual collection of ineffectual party hacks. Political corruption was rampant (through Nakasone had hardly been a stranger to it). Trade problems festered. In short, Japan again embraced the cult of irresponsibility fostered by the postwar equation.

Nothing else changed because nothing else was resolved. Where Nakasone left off, a new generation of shrill neonationalists took over. The best known was Shintaro Ishihara, author in his youth of *Season in the Sun,* a novel that defined the 1950s generation. He was an outspoken Liberal Democrat in the Diet. But in his spiteful, provocative criticism of all things American he was an impetuous child. In 1989 Ishihara and Akio Morita, the worldly chairman of the Sony Corporation, published *The Japan That Can Say No.* At home the book was an instant sensation. Then it sent shock waves through Washington. Pirated translations appeared; the Pentagon summarized it for controlled circulation; Congress read it into the record—all as if this were a document so astonishing that its existence might otherwise be doubted. But news that the Americans were reading *The Japan That Can Say No* embarrassed the Japanese; Morita all but disowned his part in the book.

Stripped of bluster, Ishihara's basic argument was that Tokyo has the right to address Washington as an equal, that Japan should recognize its destiny as a world power—that Japan should, in short, reclaim the sovereignty it surrendered after the war. "We Japanese now face choices as to whether we can boldly proceed or stand back quietly," Ishihara wrote. "The lingering dregs of the postwar period are too prominent in the Japanese consciousness." This was no more than jumped-up Nakasonianism. But once again nothing seemed to come of the essential challenge. On both sides of the Pacific, most readers seem to have done everything but consider the thesis carefully. An unfettered, sovereign Japan was still not quite imaginable.

The Gulf War changed that. Saddam Hussein's invasion of Kuwait created another critical moment for the Japanese. The Gulf crisis did not alter the discourse on the constitution—it more or less created it. After the

Gulf incident it became permissible for the first time to discuss amendments to MacArthur's basic law. At first this occurred in the most circumspect of terms. Perhaps, many Diet members said, we could tinker with Article 9 to allow Japan some minimal role in international security matters. Or perhaps, they said, we could simply reinterpret the constitution—that is, bend it, as it had been bent in the past. In 1993 Tokyo sent a hundred unarmed volunteers to Cambodia by bending the law. But as that operation showed, the reinterpretation route led only to unresolvable conundrums as to whether a handgun is different from a field weapon and whether a plane or ship can perform this or that function inside or outside a security zone.

A few years after the Gulf incident I met a writer and television commentator named Yukio Okamoto. Okamoto had been a diplomat for twenty-two years. He had strong views about the United States. He spoke at length about how the two countries complemented each other: Even their differences—cultural, economic—could bind them together. But I often sensed that the turn of our conversation had something to do with the fact that I am American. So I asked Okamoto bluntly whether he thought the machinery of our relations—the peace constitution and its companion text, the security treaty signed in 1951 and since updated—needed no reconsideration.

Okamoto shifted uneasily, gazing at me for a long moment. When he spoke again it was as if a curtain hung between us had suddenly been swept aside. "Maybe MacArthur was right: 'The Japanese are twelve-year-olds. So we take away the guns and we provide security.' Maybe this was inevitable in that historical situation. But the notion hasn't changed. And the moment you raise this fact you're a 'rightist.' You lose the respect of moderate intellectuals and the entire mainstream community. Here we have to say . . ."

Okamoto stopped abruptly before continuing in a calmer tone. "This inflexibility has pulled Japan further and further from international reality. 'Don't fight. Harmony is important.' When the Gulf War broke out, the media and the intellectuals started in. 'There should be a dialogue. Bush and Hussein must have a dialogue.' We advance this cheap notion of pacifism when we have no idea what our values are. In postwar Japan, we must have dialogue—dialogue for the sake of dialogue. . . . Our relations with the world could be much more normal."

"Normal" was a charged word when I met Okamoto. Ichiro Ozawa had given it wide currency in the book he published at the time, *Blueprint for a New Japan.* "What is a normal nation?" he asked. It is one that takes its share of responsibility and one that cooperates with others, Ozawa argued. Then he observed:

> It does not refuse such burdens on account of domestic politi-cal difficulties. Nor does it take action unwillingly as a result of "international pressure." . . . But when we consider the burden that individual nations must bear in international society, it is questionable whether Japan has functioned fully enough to be called a "nation" at all.

Were the Japanese finally ready for these sorts of ideas? It became evident as time went on that the Gulf conflict had begun to change everything—that is to say, to change people's minds. To take a small example, let us consider a *manga* called *The Silent Service* that was published not long after the Gulf War. *Manga,* the ubiquitous comic books the Japanese lose them-selves in, are full of violence, sex, and derring-do of all varieties. They are a prevalent addiction because they are an outlet for people whose social codes are rigid and confining. This makes them a kind of inverse image of the Japanese, a way to gather and explore the collective wishful thinking, and *The Silent Service* was much in the mold.

The plot is easily summarized: A submarine built by Japan and the United States is taken over by a Japanese crew, which declares the vessel a nation called Yamato, Japan's ancient and still-evocative name. The submarine-nation Yamato allies with the high-tech Japan of today and enters a war against the Americans. This *manga* sold some 7 million copies, as the story line was elaborated through volume after volume—twenty by the time I left Japan.

Fanciful but superbly to the point, *The Silent Service* was taken widely as a sign of change astir among the Japanese. Many *manga* with similar themes afterward enjoyed success. But we need not limit ourselves to comic books. While *The Silent Service* was published, the same drift emerged everywhere—in culture, sports, politics, diplomacy. In 1993 Morihiro Hosokawa, then the prime minister, visited Washington to deliver a blunt rejection of President Clinton's "results-oriented" trade proposals. At home, even Hosokawa's enemies hailed this as the first Japanese "No!" of the sort urged by Ishihara and other neonationalists. A few months later, when Japan was eliminated from World Cup soccer competition, the nation shocked itself with the depth of its spirited regret.

At the end of 1994 the *Yomiuri Shimbun,* the largest of the four national dailies, took a remarkable step. "In hope of stirring national debate," as it said in a headline, the paper published a draft of a proposed new constitution. The event received little attention abroad. Yet it was a profound departure for the Japanese. The taboo was broken—not by another band of nationalists or their offspring, but by legal scholars and others the *Yomiuri* recruited. "Life in the present age is so multifaceted," the newspaper said, "that we should seek to design a new model to deal with our new, multifaceted society." This meant "a new constitution proceeding from a new point of view."

Among its 108 articles, the *Yomiuri* document declared the armed forces constitutionally legal, allowed the country to fulfill international security obligations without encumbrance, and (not least) simplified procedures for future amendments. It was not necessary for the paper to state the most important feature of this extraordinary exercise: It was written by Japanese in their own language. "Freedom of thought and conscience shall not be violated" became "The right to freedom of thought and conscience shall be inviolable." "The people shall not be prevented from enjoying any of the fundamental human rights" became "The people possess all fundamental human rights."

Semantic adjustments? It was much more. The Japanese had begun to recognize that the fundamental question was not Article 9, but the constitution in its entirety. They had begun to see the failings of their internationalism and to explore what a constructive notion of nationalism might look like once taken beyond *manga* comics—and out of the hands of ultraright xenophobes. All the "shall not's" had been erased so that Japan could finally say what it was, and what it would do.

For a long time, to mention constitutional reform of any kind was taken as a calculated affront or a macabre breach of manners. That is how taboos work in Japan, and it was remarkable how readily gaijin participated in this one. At lunch once with a high Foreign Ministry official and a colleague from a well-known newspaper, I asked how long Japan expected to keep the postwar constitution. The official changed the subject, and when he excused himself briefly my colleague whispered, "It's not a matter we raise here." Much later I asked the American ambassador the same question. "For the foreseeable future," he replied curtly.

I never agreed. Discussions of a new constitution, including the elimination of the no-war Article 9, are the only cure for Japan's neurosis of history. A new document is the only way Japan will be able to assume the responsibilities that must accompany its economic prominence. Over time Japan may choose the same constitution it now possesses; it may choose to rearm fully, or not at all. But this is less important than the choice it makes after an open national debate—the more contentious the better. Required to answer for itself and suffer the consequences, Japan would no doubt be more responsive in matters such as trade and the global environment. Its psychologically fraught relations with the rest of Asia would suddenly have more to do with the future than the past.

Nothing better expresses the reigning neurosis than Japan's tortured struggle with the need to apologize for its aggression during the war. Most Japanese, as Mayor Motoshima suggested so effectively after Hirohito's death, are quite prepared to take this not very daunting step. It is only the persistence in power of the prewar political lineage that has made it impossible. To apologize or not: Here we have the perfect diagram of the postwar fault line between pacifists and nationalists. And, as they are by now expected to do, the Koreans and Chinese play their part by censuring the Japanese as if on cue, parsing each of Tokyo's short-of-the-mark apologies as if it were bad poetry.

This is a shadow play. Who cares how deeply the Japanese grieve? What does it matter how long are their crocodile tears? Mincing language has become a grotesque memorial to the violated. The real issues are trust, maturity, and clear sight. And it is imperative that the Japanese be allowed to give themselves the room to demonstrate that they are worthy of the trust of others, that they are mature and clearsighted about both the past and the future. "I cannot praise a fugitive and cloistered virtue, unexercised and unbreathed," Milton wrote three and a half centuries ago. The passage describes the Japanese dilemma perfectly. Who can praise a nation that is only allowed to say "Yes"? Who can trust a nation that does not trust itself?

"THERE'S SOME RISK involved in this," Yukio Okamoto said the last time I saw him.

We had been talking about the paths a confident Japan might take. It was not the best moment to consider the idea of a renewed, energetic Japan. The previous autumn a senior officer in the S.D.F. had wondered publicly whether a military coup was not the proper solution to the long-running scandals in Nagatacho. Then an aging rightist shot himself in a meeting with the editors of the *Asahi Shimbun,* the most fervent supporter of the peace constitution among the national dailies. Then a newly appointed justice minister asserted that the Nanking Massacre really had not happened the way the world believed it had.

Why do such events still exert a mesmerizing hold upon the Japanese? I counted members of the extreme right among my regular contacts, and a few as friends, since I first arrived in Japan: not because I accepted their point of view, but because until the very end of my years there they were the only ones willing to discuss the pithy questions—sovereignty, self-respect, the constitution. But I never awarded these gentlemen, with their bristly gray crew cuts and suits worn shiny with age, the status of a national threat. The more I got to know them, the more I thought the assumption must have seemed ridiculous even to them.

The appearance of risk serves a useful purpose. The mythical menace of the right has been an important prop in Tokyo's postwar arrangements with Washington. The ultraright's intimate connections with the political elite are well documented; the Liberal Democrats, indeed, can still turn sound trucks on and off like faucets. This has served Tokyo well by quelling any questions as to the presence of American troops and Washington's power to dictate foreign policy in all but a few instances. The United States, for its part, does not wish to give up these privileges. Japanese politicians, meantime, are left with little to do—and so get on with the corruption and pork-barreling that are their only serious business.

The sadly obscured irony is that the postwar orthodoxy is the only shield behind which the old militarists have continued to haunt the collective memory at home as well as abroad. Push their ideas into the light and air of national debate and they will disintegrate like mummified remains once unwound. The Japanese are gradually learning this, as they make their way toward a new idea of internationalism—which is to say, a new nationalism.

Tokyo spent many years preparing for 1995, the fiftieth anniversary of the war's end. Among its plans was a new library and historical center dedicated to war research. A $120 million project, a decade in gestation, it was to be housed not a hundred yards from Yasukuni Shrine. In 1994, just before construction was to begin, the government suddenly shifted. There would be no research institute; instead there would be a prayer hall and a museum of war memorabilia, much like the museum at Yasukuni. In an ironic nod to the 1990s, the exhibits would consist of reproductions—virtual-reality war relics.

A smoldering dispute quickly caught fire. Nearby residents protested that the proposed building would look like something out of Nazi Germany. The rightists at Yasukuni protested, too, for their franchise was clearly threatened. Most important were the scholars, who wanted a place to nourish a clear, dispassionate version of history. "An objective institute, combined with a prayer hall, is impossible. It would always have a political point, an ideology," one of them told me. "We planned a library that could collect everything about the war—from the left, the right, progressives, liberals, conservatives: all of it. But the government got nervous."

In the end there was no monument in time for the 1995 commemoration. Nor would the government go forward until everyone—the neighbors, the rightists, the historians—was in agreement as to what should be built. To me, this seemed a superb denouement, the most accurate expression of its time one could imagine. The absence of such a monument fifty years after the surrender was a kind of monument in itself—an antimonument, perhaps—for to resist the version of history sanctioned at Yasukuni, the official version, was in no small measure to begin reclaiming the whole of the Japanese past.

The last sound truck I saw before leaving Japan—in Harajuku, of all places—declared in bold characters across its side, GET RID OF FOREIGN WORKERS, WHO WILL DISRUPT OUR CULTURE, TRADITION, AND HISTORY. Immigrant labor was a new complaint; foreign workers had been arriving in significant numbers for only a few years. As a sound-van theme, it erupted at about the same time as the dispute at Yasukuni. Copying down this particular slogan, I was perversely pleased to see it for the implicit connection it made. The ultranationalists had it upside down, as usual, but the Japanese, now that they are learning to challenge such crude displays, will eventually right it. The presence of foreigners will disrupt "culture," "tradition," and "history"—that is, the ultranationalist version of these things—because the Japanese are coming to recognize that the embrace of otherness, like the embrace of their own past, is also essential to an authentic internationalism. And they are slowly discovering among themselves enough individual and collective self-confidence finally to dismiss the self-hatred one always finds at the bottom of the far right's well.

HOW WILL THE Japanese realize themselves in a new way—as arrogant nationalists, generous internationalists, Swiss-style neutralists, or in some fashion not yet thought of? This question is not unrelated to others posed in this book—about schools and workplaces, men and women, cities and villages, culture and identity. The essential question, binding all of these, is a change in psychology—a change we have considered from these various perspectives.

But any such change must also be viewed from a political point of view. It is politics—not "culture," not "spirit" or "tradition"—that has kept the Japanese from resolving these various questions long after they might have. And it is politics that will enable the Japanese to overcome them. The Japanese stand poised to rid themselves of the psychology of dependence that has haunted them for many more years than it would have, if only those who led Japan over the centuries had made history differently. But this will not happen automatically, without engagement, without a civic life.

Japan also still bears the mark of a foreign occupier—an influence that weighs heavily, for we cannot talk about politics in Japan without talking about America. This book began with the assertion that the Americans must stand aside and see the Japanese as they really are. Let us conclude by considering just how this might be done.

To an extraordinary extent, Americans have fooled themselves about the Japanese. Seduced by the appearance of democratic procedure and the popularity of their films, food, music, clothing, and so on, Americans accepted the standard conceit that the Japanese wanted no more than to be just like them—that Japan was somehow caught in a permanent state of aspiration. But Americans ignored history, as they often do. They failed to see that Japan, as the world's premier learning culture, can absorb anything and still go on being Japan. Nothing the Japanese import—not chopsticks, not constitutional law—remains quite the same once they adopt it. A millennium before the Americans arrived, the Japanese were awash in Chinese culture and civilization. But they never became Chinese.

What did the Japanese really think about the occupying Americans? What did they feel, to take one obvious instance, when they looked at the famous photograph of MacArthur with Hirohito? "That was a great shock to all of us," Yoshikazu Sakamoto, a prominent postwar intellectual and a fervent supporter of the peace constitution, once remarked. "Here was a large American in casual dress, and the small emperor in a morning suit next to him. We saw this enormous gap in power, culture, physique." For half a century the image has been fixed. But the feelings of the Japanese were always more complicated than Americans thought. In Sakamoto's words, "admiration of things American—democracy, large automobiles, refrigerators. But admiration coupled with inferiority and envy, which together easily generate a sense of hatred."

Americans fooled themselves about themselves, too—an equally important point—and they continue to do so today. Having reinstalled the prewar political elite fifty years ago, having excused the emperor of war crimes, Americans are to blame in no small way for the palsied political system that has plagued Japan ever since. Far from helping the Japanese cultivate a working democracy, Americans rely upon the absence of democratic practice—as, for example, in Okinawa. They prefer the psychology of dependence fostered by the political elite. The result is "Japanese democracy," but that is a cover, for there is no such thing.

Okinawa offers a perfect expression of America's relations with Japan. After the rape of a twelve-year-old schoolchild in 1995, massive protests erupted. Masahide Ota, the prefecture's strong-minded governor, refused to sign leases that were due to be renewed for American-occupied land. Then what happened? The prime minister in Tokyo signed the leases in Ota's stead. And to defuse the protests Tokyo announced that a few bases would be moved—to localities whose mayors learned of Tokyo's plans when they read of them in the newspapers. The mayors then refused the honor of American bases in their jurisdictions. In the end, the Japanese Supreme Court effectively ruled that in the matter of American bases, Japanese citizens have no property rights.

In the last century it was the oligarchy's hatred of the unequal treaties signed after Perry's arrival that drove the modernization project. To repudiate them, the oligarchs reasoned, Japan first had to prove itself the West's equal. So began the long endeavor that produced, among much else, an industrial economy, an attempt at empire, and the Elvis Presleys who inhabit Harajuku. The first thing Americans (and by implication its friends in the West) must recognize, if we are to understand the Japanese, is that today the equation is reversed. The Japanese have caught up to the West. Now they must prove themselves by revealing who they are. The West no longer holds the mirror; the mirror has turned around, and in it the Japanese see themselves.

If admiration is not to turn to hatred, it is time for America to understand this—to allow the Japanese to gaze in the mirror for as long as they require. It is time to break the cycle of dependence in all its guises: their dependence on undemocratic authority, America's dependence on theirs. I know of few Japanese, perhaps none, who propose a break in Japan's close ties to the United States. But almost everyone recognizes that things as they are have reached their logical conclusion—if they have not gone beyond it. A healthy relationship with America will inevitably be a more distant one.

The fear of change of this sort is great on both sides. That is inevitable after so many years of no change at all. Yet there can be no restraints other than those the Japanese choose themselves. America cannot cut the Japanese loose only on the condition that the kind of nation they make of themselves is the kind America wants it to be. What is it that has so concerned Americans that they still station nearly fifty thousand troops in Japan? Not the militarist genie in the bottle—no one can believe that any longer. What worries them, now as before, is indifference (and its companion, competition), a Japan that has its own map of the Pacific and is uninterested in Washington's. That, it must be said, is a more realistic fear. A neutralist Japan was Washington's Cold War nightmare. Now it is a competitive Japan—powerful, economically uncontained. Given Japan's vast interests abroad, an indifferent Japan may prove no more realistic today than a newly militarist Japan. But whether it is or not, American troops will have nothing to do with it. In any case, Americans cannot continue to claim the question is theirs to decide.

None of this is reflected in America's current policy toward Japan. The Cold War over, it advances numerous new reasons for leaving everything just as it is. Japan lives in a bad neighborhood—a true enough point.

Problems in the region will not disappear overnight. As I write, Pyongyang has unilaterally repudiated the demilitarized zone established between North and South Korea. China is accumulating enough economic and military power to turn the rest of the region into the world's liveliest arms market. But which of these problems has anything to do with maintaining a force of fifty thousand in Japan? It is unlikely we would ever engage China on the ground; any conflict that involved ground troops would by definition involve many hundreds of thousands of Chinese soldiers, if not a million or more. South Korea has an army of its own—650,000 strong—and an economy sixteen times larger than the North's.

There is only one way to justify a continued American presence in Japan—for a time. It is to ease the disintegration of its historic relationship—to end it properly, so to say, the way the British liked to think they always did when leaving their colonies. It is only a matter of time before the pillars of U.S.-Japanese ties—the constitution, the security treaty—are gone. This may lead Japan to rearm—which it probably should—or it may lead in some other direction entirely. The process of renewal will produce political and diplomatic earthquakes and cannot come immediately. But however much Japan's neighbors protest—some will, others will not—the process cannot be avoided forever. And it is entirely possible that nervous neighbors will eventually applaud a rearmed Japan, for Japan and China are the Germany and France of East Asia: Until they find a way to address each other in a balanced relationship, the region will not be settled.

America has its own *tatemae* with the Japanese, its own spoken truth, and must now get beyond it to the *honne*, the reality of the relationship. It can begin by acknowledging that the peace constitution was written by the Americans, a fact every Japanese knows but one Washington has not yet stated openly. A point of history, yes. But it is obvious, given how frequently this question arises, that such an admission would make easier the task of renewal.

Then comes the security treaty. At this point, to rely upon it is Japan's worst nightmare, for as every thoughtful Japanese knows, the pact is good only as long as it is not implemented in a crisis. Once it is—once American soldiers and pilots begin dying for Japan's protection somewhere in the Pacific while the Japanese simply continue producing Walkmans and Hondas for export—the security pact would very probably damage relations with America beyond immediate repair. The treaty has become, in this sense, a dangerous anachronism.

Beneath these practical questions lies another, the one with which this book began and the hardest to address. We can call it Orientalism, though of course there are blunter terms. Would Washington speak to London, Paris, or Bonn the way it speaks to Tokyo? It is unthinkable. Does it negotiate diplomatic and security questions in Europe, or does it simply send orders across the Atlantic as it does, more or less, to Tokyo? In Japan you do not wonder whether American policy and American attitudes have been colored with the tint of race for the entire postwar period: This is perfectly obvious from the Western end of the Pacific.

If we consider America's two centuries of experience in Asia, the current attitude of Americans cannot be a surprise. These centuries began in 1784, when the first Americans sailed to China eager to exploit its markets (including that for opium) and carried on through Perry's opening of Japan, possession of the Philippines, the defeat and occupation of Japan, and the war with Vietnam. Where in any of these events have Americans displayed a convincing break from their initial presumption of superiority—that is, from the Orientalism we assumed by way of European colonizers? Today such a break turns on the question of power and the West's willingness to acknowledge that Japan and the rest of Asia have entered upon their century as Americans have had theirs. Policy planners in Washington now scratch their heads, asking why things have begun turning slightly sour in East Asia just as the region rises in strength and importance. Americans face the same predicament as the Japanese with regard to their apologies: The only useful response requires not words but action of a new kind.

The Japanese explain away this dimension of things in many tolerant ways. "There are still many Americans who remember us when we were at the bottom," a forgiving Diet member with much experience in Washington once told me. Within their own set of complexes, the Japanese are only too prone to share judgments such as De Gaulle's as to what they have become. It is America's place to recognize the ways in which Japan remains underdeveloped; the awkward aspect of MacArthur's blunt *mot*, after all, was the truth of it. But it is not America's place to inhibit Japan's effort to grow out of old truths. That stance dignifies no one.

But let us not limit this discussion to considerations as remote as sovereignty and democratic principle, for the question goes far beyond mere decency. Ultimately at stake is the quality of America's future relations in Asia. Already in Japan there is a new vocabulary to describe changing

Japanese attitudes toward America: There is *hanbei*, antagonism toward America; *kenbei*, dislike of America; and *bubei*, looking down on America. The latter two terms became current in response to Washington's rough treatment of Tokyo during the Persian Gulf crisis. They do not describe bureaucratic positions, obviously. In bureaucratic form the equivalent view is called Asianism, a policy calling for a decisive tilt away from America (and the West). While most Japanese still favor close ties with America, Asianism does not lack a following—even within the Foreign Ministry. Asianism is an old, recurrent theme in Japanese thinking. In its present guise it is partly a reflection of the region's growing economic interdependence. But it is rooted in the ethnic and cultural facts of history. And like *kenbei* and *bubei*, Asianism also arises partly in response to America's condescension toward Japan and partly out of a perception that America is in decline.

Whenever I visit Japan I try to see a man named Reizo Utagawa, a friend of some years. He is a jolly, relaxed man near the end of his career. Now in his sixties, Utagawa is a researcher at a conservative think tank headed by Yasuhiro Nakasone, the former premier. He knows America well. For many years he was a correspondent abroad, including a long tour in Washington for *Mainichi Shimbun*, one of the four national dailies. We do not agree on much except (as with my ultranationalist acquaintances) what the questions are.

When I saw Utagawa last, late in the summer of 1994, he greeted me with his ready smile and showed me into Nakasone's office, which is otherwise rarely used. Surrounded by the memorabilia of Nakasone's premiership, we discussed the upheavals occurring beneath the surface in Japan—upheavals that, Utagawa was sure, would eventually change the nation and so change its relations with America and the rest of the world.

What do the Japanese want from Americans at such a moment? I wondered.

Utagawa hardly hesitated. "Silence and respect," he replied.

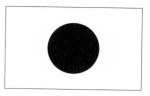

EPILOGUE

It is useless to maintain that social progress takes place of itself. . . . It is really a leap forward which is taken when the society has made up its mind to try an experiment . . . and it is no use maintaining that this leap forward does not imply a creative effort. . . . That would be to forget that most great reforms appeared at first sight impracticable, as in fact they were.

—HENRI BERGSON,
The Two Sources of Morality and Religion, 1932

IN THE RICH rice country of Niigata, a house once occupied by Japan's largest landowners is hidden behind high walls and a weathered wooden gate. The compound is now a museum of family possessions, among them two screens dating to about 1600. They are called *namban hyobu,* literally "south barbarian screens," because they depict the first Westerners to arrive on Japanese soil—sailors, traders, and clerics who came by way of the southern seas.

Across one screen Europeans disembark from a black ship. Many wear the black habits of Jesuits. They have long noses and chalk white faces. The lands beyond are painted without shape or features, like clouds, and the land where they arrive is signified by a single bonsai pine, trained in the traditional manner. On the other screen the Jesuits cross an arched wooden bridge to a place rendered in more detail. They are clearly disoriented. They do not connect with the crowd of Japanese, who are less afraid than curious and amused, and who keep themselves half hidden: A man peaks out from behind a curtain, a woman's eye smiles above a fan.

I keep a postcard copy of the screens in a notebook. I have seen nothing that better captures the primal encounter long ago between Japan and the West. Nor can I think of a more bluntly revealing expression of what it means to be either "outside" or "inside." When we emerged from the wooden gate at the compound, I asked my assistant what he thought the old screens meant.

"That you have to cross a bridge to understand Japan."

WE HAVE BEEN required to cross a bridge (and the Japanese to cross it in our direction, too) for all of the four and a half centuries since the first Westerners arrived in Japan. Will this still be necessary in the future? It is an imaginary bridge, of course, constructed partly by Westerners and partly by the Japanese. But that does not really help us. For Japan has been an imaginary country—imagined by foreigners and the Japanese alike—ever since it took the name Nippon from Chinese characters. There is nothing to say it cannot go on being an act of the imagination, a place where change seems constant but at the same time evanescent, like the flow of a river and the spray above it.

Yet Japan seems now to be preparing to dispense with both the bridge and the nonexistent country on the far side of it—the image of themselves they hold up to the West. They seem ready to reinterpret themselves—an act of far greater importance than any reinterpretation an outside person can offer.

The architect Kisho Kurokawa keeps a map of Tokyo on his studio wall. It is his redesign of the capital. It shows man-made islands in Tokyo Bay that do not yet exist and an extensive system of canals that was filled in, lost, during the modern era. So it is at once a map of a past and future city. Most of all, it is a place where the world will want to come, Kurokawa says, as it has by turns been drawn to Vienna, London, Paris, Berlin, New York. "Cities are societies. If societies change, cities will change. It's not a strange idea."

Another vision of the future: Japan will take the world into a healthier ecological balance, back toward humanity's true relationship with nature. Considering Japan's environmental record, this seems preposterous. Yet it was only when Japan modernized (and therefore westernized) that it learned the ambition of conquering nature—an ambition none of us can any longer afford to entertain. "Japan is therefore particularly suited to leading the way in global environmental recovery," Ichiro Ozawa wrote in *Blueprint for a New Japan*. "We must take the initiative in this area."

Two dreams, two imaginary Japans. There are others, shared by many Japanese. In all of them there is an implicit act of recovery—a retrieval of history, or part of it, of another way of living and thinking. Yet each idea asserts that a new and entirely tangible Japan has something to contribute to the world. And each expresses the notion that Japan is prepared to advance beyond the old assumption that the modern is by definition the Western.

Predictions are useless as well as treacherous, especially in our "globalizing" world—where, it is asserted, there is no alternative to the loss of autonomy at every level, from the individual to the national. At the same time, there seems to be something inexorable about the sometimes imperceptible process the Japanese have begun.

At home the Japanese must accept diversity; abroad, that they are the same as the rest of us. The paradox is apparent, not real. When Japan at last manages these things it will have found the national purpose that has so far eluded it. But no one can say how long this turn in thinking will take. Against the acceptance of diversity and sameness is posed the notion of Asian values—that Japan (or China, or Malaysia, or Singapore) is different, that its people do not esteem the principles held highest elsewhere, chiefly the rights of the individual. Of course, it is only the Asian elite that asserts such things—the ruling, never the ruled. This, of course, is the fundamental falsehood the Japanese must reject. The modern can no longer be taken as the Western, but that is not to say there is any such thing as "Eastern morality," or a "Japanese spirit." There is only the human spirit, just as there is only a universal morality.

We in the West urge these truths upon Japan in countless ways, small and large. And we have no small stake in the triumph of what is human and universal over what is particular. Do we (any more than an ordinary Japanese, Chinese, Malaysian, or Singaporean) want to live in a world where a small undemocratic elite with immense and still accumulating power defends itself with assertions of difference? Yet the West is unprepared for the Japan that is emerging. We want the Japanese to dispense with their bridges and come out from behind their curtains and fans—to "do more," to take a "global role." At the same time we inhibit them. Japan has always been the follower, the imitator. The last time it asserted itself it was a fifteen-year tragedy. We do not welcome their influence. At this point we accept only their money; then we accuse them, variously, of trying to buy responsibility, or buy their way out of it.

Our ambivalence is matched by the ambivalence of the Japanese themselves. They will join the world slowly after living so long a time apart from it. But some event will shake us all awake, some entirely practical development—Japan's assumption of a seat in the U.N. Security Council, say, or its initiative in this or that critical situation, or its adoption of a new constitution, or the emergence of a new political order. Then we will realize that the imaginary Japanese have begun to become real, the representation the thing represented, the imitator authentically itself.

CHRONOLOGY

50,000–30,000 B.C.	**PALEOLITHIC PERIOD** Probable period of settlement, primarily from the Asian mainland.
10,000–300 B.C.	**JOMON PERIOD** Hunting-and-gathering culture. Evidence of a matrilineal clan culture.
300 B.C.–A.D. 300	**YAYOI PERIOD** Wet rice cultivation, weaving, bronze objects, and weaponry. Tribes in the Yamato region of central Honshu extend their power. Contacts with China begin.
CA. 297	First written account of the Japanese, by visiting Chinese, describes thirty countries united under a shaman-queen named Himiko.
300–CA. 600	**KOFUN PERIOD** Final stage of prehistory, marked by large burial mounds. Yamato sovereigns further extend power.
405	Chinese script introduced via Korea.
552	Buddhism arrives from the mainland.
592–622	Shotoku reigns as prince regent beginning Japan's great borrowing from China.
604	Japan's first constitution, of seventeen articles.

645–701	Taika reforms consolidate imperial rule.
710–794	**NARA PERIOD** Capital is fixed for the first time, at Nara, laid out according to Chinese design.
712	The *Kojiki (Record of Ancient Matters)*, the oldest Japanese text, is compiled. The *Nihongi (Chronicles of Japan)* follows in 720.
794–1185	**HEIAN PERIOD** Classical Japanese culture reaches its height amid reaction against mainland influences.
794	Heian, now Kyoto, becomes capital.
858	The Fujiwara become a family of hereditary regents, establishing a civilian dictatorship.
1020	Shikibu Murasaki, a lady-in-waiting at the Heian court, completes *Genji Monogatari,* the *Tale of Genji.*
1185–1333	**KAMAKURA PERIOD** Military rule begins. The culture of daimyo (literally "great names," feudal lords) takes its place as the "great tradition."
1185	The Minamoto clan defeat the Taira clan and become the enforcers of imperial authority.
1191	The Ch'an school of Buddhism, to be known in Japan as Zen, introduced.
1192	Yoritomo Minamoto becomes the first shogun, establishes administrative seat at Kamakura, south of present-day Tokyo.
1232	Kamakura issues first legal warrior code.
1274, 1281	Mongols invade twice across the Japan Sea.
1333–1336	Brief period of direct imperial rule. Two imperial courts, northern and southern, claim legitimacy.

1338–1568	**WARRING STATES PERIOD** Also called the Muromachi period. The Ashikaga shogun rule. The military administration is moved to Kyoto.
1363–1443	Life of Ze-ami, Noh drama's greatest master.
1392	Shogun Yoshimitsu Ashikaga reunifies the northern and southern courts.
1467–1477	The Onin War, between rival daimyo, begins more than a century of military conflict.
1542	First Europeans reach the Japanese coast, off Kyushu.
1549	Saint Francis Xavier arrives from Goa.
1568–1600	**MOMOYAMA PERIOD** Japan absorbs impact of European missionaries and merchants. Three unifying forces contend for power.
1568	Nobunaga Oda, a daimyo general, conquers Kyoto, ending the Ashikaga shogunate and uniting Japan.
1571	Nagasaki begins operating as a foreign-trade port.
1582	Nobunaga Oda is assassinated. One of his commanders, Hideyoshi Toyotomi, succeeds.
1587	Persecution of Christians begins. Samurai are formally separated from peasants. A sword hunt strips the peasantry of arms.
1592	Failed invasion of Korean peninsula.
1598	Hideyoshi dies.
1600	Ieyasu Tokugawa, a general charged with supporting the succession of Hideyoshi's son, reneges, crushes opposition, and seizes power.
1603–1867	**TOKUGAWA PERIOD** Japan's late-feudal period. A commercial economy germinates. A popular urban culture appears in merchant quarters. Peasant revolts grow in frequency as the era proceeds.

1603	Ieyasu establishes the military government at Edo, present-day Tokyo.
1616	Ieyasu dies. Successors revive persecution of Christians.
1639	*Sakoku* edicts expel foreigners and close Japan.
1644–1694	Life of Matsuo Basho,* the greatest of haiku poets.
1645(?)	Sogoro Sakura, a legendary village headman, is executed after leading a peasant protest. He becomes a popular symbol of resistance to official authority.
1649	The Keian edict, Edo's best known, instructs officials on the proper treatment of peasants.
1653–1724	Life of Monzaemon Chikamatsu, the celebrated dramatist of the feudal era.
1656	Soko Yamaga, a Confucianist scholar and military instructor, begins to codify the Bushido, "way of the warrior."
1672	The Confucianist scholar Ekken Kaibara publishes *Onna Daigaku* (*Greater Learning for Women*).
1701–1703	Forty-seven *ronin* (masterless warriors), led by a disciple of Soko Yamaga, avenge their daimyo's death, beginning official Japan's most enduring legends of samurai loyalty.
1721	Villages are organized into five-man groups that constitute a societywide system of spying.
1753–1806	Life of Kitagawa Utamaro,* first of the great ukiyo-e printmakers.
1760–1849	Life of Katsuhika Hokusai.*
1767–1858	Life of Ando Hiroshige.*
1853	The American commodore Matthew Perry arrives at Uraga, south of Tokyo. The shogunate is in a state of advanced decay.

---

* Names rendered in Japanese order. These artists are customarily known by their given or chosen names.

1858	Edo signs unequal treaties with the United States, Britain, Holland, Russia, and France.

MEIJI PERIOD

1868–1912

Japan begins its modern era, constructing a centralized state, a modern military, and an industrial economy.

1867–1868

The Meiji Restoration. Two provincial clans, the Satsuma and the Choshu, topple the last Tokugawa shogun and return the emperor to power.

The new emperor issues the Charter Oath. The imperial court moves to Edo, now Tokyo.

1870

Commoners are permitted surnames.

1871

The Iwakura Embassy, best known of the missions sent abroad to study the West, departs for America and Europe. The *han,* the feudal domains, are declared prefectures. John Stuart Mill's *On Liberty* is translated.

1873

Meiji Six Society encourages learning from the West and experiment in political and social affairs.

Land taxes are switched from rice to currency. Military conscription begins.

1874

The Society to Establish One's Ambitions is founded, forerunner of modern political parties.

1875

People's Rights Movement opposes the growing authority of the Sat-Cho elite. A press law imposes political censorship.

1877

Satsuma rebellion. Conservative forces turn against the Sat-Cho's adoption of Western practices.

1880—

Law of Public Meetings requires police approval of all political gatherings.

1881

Liberal Party is formed. Others follow. The Liberals and the Constitutional Progressive Party are the ancestors of the postwar Liberal Democrats.

---

* Names rendered in Japanese order. These artists are customarily known by their given or chosen names.

The emperor promises a national assembly.

1882   Hirobumi Ito, a Sat-Cho leader, travels to Europe, chiefly Berlin and Vienna, to study constitutional law. Emperor issues the Injunction to Soldiers and Sailors.

1884   Peerage system begins, after the German model.

1885   Cabinet government. Ito is the first premier.

1889   Emperor hands down the imperial constitution.

1890   The imperial Diet convenes. Emperor issues the Imperial Rescript on Education.

1894–1895   Sino-Japanese war. Japan acquires Formosa (Taiwan).

1899   Unequal treaties are succeeded.

1904–1905   Russo-Japanese War. Imperial navy's victory marks Japan's arrival as a world military power.

1906   South Manchuria Railway is begun.

1910   Japan annexes Korea. Agreement is reached with Russia on mainland spheres of influence.

1912   Emperor Meiji dies.

1912–1926   **TAISHO PERIOD**
The period is marked by an openness to the West that will not be equaled again until the postwar era. European modernism influences art and culture, as do socialist and democratic currents in politics and social affairs. An urban middle class takes shape. The first feminist movement emerges. Industrial unrest accompanies the evolution of the economy.

1912   Yuaikai, the Friendly Society, is formed. It becomes the first national trade union.

1918   Inflation prompts nationwide rice riots, and the cabinet resigns. Takashi Hara, the first commoner to become premier, begins brief period of party government, recalled today as "Taisho democracy."

1921	Hara is assassinated. Elder statesmen of the Meiji era are dying off, increasing tension between elected politicians and the nonelected elite. Tension between government and military over China also mounts. Crown Prince Hirohito visits Europe. On return he is named prince regent.
1923	Tokyo earthquake.
1924	A new government reflects the increasing influence of industrial and commercial interests.
1925	Universal Manhood Suffrage Act expands the electorate from 3 million to 13 million. Peace Preservation Law limits political activity.
1926–1989	**SHOWA ERA** Hirohito's reign will see Japan through sixty-two years: militarization, war, defeat, reconstruction, and affluence.
192	Imperial army intervenes in Chinese civil war.
1928	First elections under universal suffrage law are followed by mass arrests. Imperial army assassinates a Manchurian warlord, Chang Tao-lin.
1929	Depression prompts unrest in armed services.
1931	The Manchuria Incident: Army attacks and occupies northern China, beginning "Fifteen-Year War."
1932	Emperor Pu Yi declares government of Manchukuo independent of China. In Tokyo young army officers assassinate premier.
1936	The 2-26 Incident, named for its date: Army officers occupy central Tokyo. Several senior officials are assassinated before coup collapses.
1937	Marco Polo Bridge Incident: Fighting near Beijing begins full-scale war. Nanjing, site of Pacific war's worst atrocities, is captured.

1938	Sanpo, Industrial Patriotic Society, formed. Labor unions formally dissolved following year.
1939	War in Europe, September 1.
1940	Political parties dissolve into the Imperial Rule Assistance Association. Army invades French Indochina.
1941	Japanese assets in America frozen. General Hideki Tojo becomes premier. Pearl Harbor attacked, December 7.
1941–1945	The Pacific war.
1945	Atomic bombings of Hiroshima and Nagasaki. Japan surrenders. Douglas MacArthur arrives as supreme commander for the allied powers. American occupation begins.
1946	Emperor renounces his status as a divine being. First postwar elections; women vote for the first time. Postwar reforms begin. Purges of military, bureaucracy, and political elite begin.
1947	New constitution made law. MacArthur bans a general strike, an early signal of reversal of initial reform agenda.
1948	Reverse course" becomes policy. Shigeru Yoshida is elected premier (for a second term).
1949	Chinese revolution.
1950–1953	Korean War. Japan's role as military supplier provides an important economic boost.
1951	Peace treaty and U.S.-Japan Security Treaty signed at San Francisco.
1952	Occupation ends.
1955	Socialists reunite, prompting merger of conservatives into Liberal Democratic Party: The "1955 system" is formed.
1956	Government white paper declares postwar era over.

1959–1960	Miners at Miike, the nation's largest coal mine, strike. Settlement is a permanent setback for organized labor.
1960	Renewal of security treaty prompts nationwide protests. Hayato Ikeda declares Income-Doubling Plan.
1964	Tokyo hosts summer Olympics. Japan admitted to Organization for Economic Cooperation and Development.
1968	Yasunari Kawabata wins Nobel Prize.
1973	Kakuei Tanaka, kingmaker of postwar Japanese politics, becomes premier.
1982–1987	Yasuhiro Nakasone is premier. Proposes equal partnership with America.
1985	Plaza Accord, signed in New York, begins revaluation of the yen as a world currency.
1986–1990	Economy begins longest postwar boom, the bubble economy. Total capital investment is largest in human history.
1989	Hirohito dies.
1989–	**HEISEI ERA** From its inception the era marks a fundamental reordering of Japanese society.
1989	Scandals force Noboru Takeshita and successor to resign premiership. Berlin Wall is torn down. The 1955 political system begins to crumble.
1990	Saddam Hussein invades Kuwait. Liberal Democrats lose their majority in the Diet's upper house. Women enter legislature in numbers not seen since 1946. Economy begins a slide into worst postwar recession.

1991	Akihito accedes to throne.
1993	Morihiro Hosokawa is elected premier, ending thirty-eight years of Liberal Democratic rule.
1994	Kenzaburo Oe wins Nobel Prize.
1995	Earthquake in Kobe.
1996	General elections return Liberal Democrats to power.

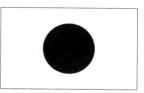

An

Acknowledgment

FAMILY, FRIENDS, COLLEAGUES, and acquaintances in numerous places have helped with this book. I cannot name them all. But each knows the part he or she took, and I trust each knows how grateful I am.

There is an unwavering core. Caroline Matthews, to whom this book is dedicated, has run on faith for a very long time. As guides, critics, facilitators and friends, Sheila and Chalmers Johnson have done more than one could ever reasonably expect. Sarah Chalfant at the Wylie Agency, and her colleague Jeffrey Posternak, have been allies and advisors in many matters, professional and occasionally non-. Dan Frank at Pantheon displayed exemplary patience, even as he gave form to the sometimes formless. Terry McCarthy has been a generous friend, critic, and Nishi-Azabu neighbor. And there is *mia famiglia italiana:* Marco and Francesca Panara, in Rome; Miriam Verrini and Patrizio di Marco, in New York. Their friendship and succor during our years in Tokyo made many things possible.

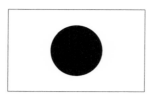

NOTES

AN ATTENTIVE CORRESPONDENT is to an extent a professional student with many masters. I have mine, and I hope I have applied their lessons well. Here I wish to note my debts to them with gratitude—and to excuse them, certainly, from any errors of fact or interpretation I have made.

This is not a scholarly book, and the notes below follow scholarly practice neither in form nor extent. The number of high school dropouts and Shimane Prefecture's 1949 population are not footnoted. Documents and facts of this kind are readily available. I have elaborated on certain passages and named the sources of facts that may be disputed. But these notes are intended primarily to acknowledge scholars and writers whose work has informed my perspective on Japan, especially my perspective on its past.

Western scholarship on Japan has been deeply divided since the war. It is badly in need of its own restoration. This is a tragedy—not just an intellectual calamity, a squabble in the upper reaches of the ivory tower, but a tragedy that touches all of us. Our misunderstanding of Japan is also a misunderstanding of ourselves. Just as the Japanese do not exist as we think they do, neither do we. This concern, noted in Chapter 1, took root while I was still reporting from Tokyo for the Paris *Herald Tribune* and the *New Yorker,* and then grew along with the book over the years of research and writing. The Japan that I saw—"seething within," as Robert Jay Lifton has since put it—was simply not the country I went home at night to read about in the standard books purporting to describe Japan and the Japanese.

My view of this sorry situation is evident enough in the text. Western thinking about Japan is still shot through with Cold War politics. Deep thinkers in Washington now talk about America's need to extend a "benevolent hegemony" across the Pacific and all the other oceans. If there has been a less appropriate moment to float such an idea, I cannot think when it might have been. It is an oxymoron the match of any concocted over the past half century. So the fog machine rolls on, turning the simple matter of impartial scholarship into questions of politics, ideology, and patriotism.

The best to be said now about our study of Japan is that a stream of scholarship, confronted by those who dispense with detachment and objectivity, is toughened in its rigor and its resolve to stay the course. For me this stream begins with Hugh Borton and E. H. Norman before the war and runs through many distinguished names after it: through Norman's postwar work and on to Masao Maruyama, Chalmers Johnson, Tetsuo Najita, John Dower, Herbert Bix, Ivan Hall, George Wilson, Victor Koschmann, and several of the scholars, from Shunsuke Tsurumi forward, who have written books for Kegan Paul International under the editorship of Yoshio Sugimoto.

There are others, noted in the bibliography. These may be surprised to find themselves in the same sentence, to say nothing of the idea that they swim in the same stream. But I stand on the bank and salute them all.

PROLOGUE

1 The lines by Boncho are from a *renku,* a form in which two or more poets amuse themselves by taking turns composing stanzas. Boncho was a student of Matsuo Basho, the great wandering master of the seventeenth century, the greatest of haiku poets. Basho led Boncho and Kyorai, another of his students, in composing *The Summer Moon* in Kyoto, where he rested after the famous journey he made around Japan and recorded in *Narrow Road to the Interior.* From Ueda, *Matsuo Basho,* pp. 102–3.

1 A newspaper account of the robotic puppets appeared in the *Japan Times,* November 17, 1992, and was carried the previous day on the Kyodo wire.

1 The Levenson quotation from *Confucian China and Its Modern Fate* is from the trilogy's first volume, *The Problem of Intellectual Continuity,* p. xxi.

1 The awkward relationship between the traditional and the modern after 1868 is briefly considered in Masao Maruyama, "Japanese Thought," *Journal of Social and Political Ideas in Japan* (April 1964), pp. 41–42. Maruyama found this odd juxtaposition throughout history: "It is extremely difficult to grasp what organic relationship existed between a specific idea of a particular thinker and other ideas current during the period in which that thinker lived. It is likewise difficult to determine how specific ideas of a given period of history were integrated with the ideas of a subsequent period." This is an oddity in the Japanese tradition, which Maruyama explains in various ways. I consider it one factor in Japan's nature as a country imagined and reimagined at various points in the past, and in Japan's habit (noted in Chapters 1 and 2) of producing Orientalists the match of any in the West.

3 Bitai was explored by the philosopher Shuzo Kuki in his 1930 book, *"Iki" no Kozo* (The structure of Edo aesthetic style). Both Kuki and his ideas are dexterously illuminated in Pincus, *Authenticating Culture in Imperial Japan,* and "In a Labyrinth of Western Desire," in Miyoshi and Harootunian's *Japan in the World,* pp. 222–36.

4 Images of cresting waves are plentiful in the ukiyo-e-tradition—enough to prompt analysis as to their meaning apart from their ubiquitous presence in the Japanese seascape. There are interpretations other than mine—all more widely accepted, I might add. Even the nineteenth-century Europeans adopted the motif during their enthusiasm for the recently opened Japan, the phenomenon we call *japonisme.* The best known of Japan's wave makers was Hokusai.

ONE: THE INVISIBLE JAPANESE

7 The Enchi quotation is on p. 30 of *Masks.*

7 "In fact the whole of Japan": cited in Ellmann's edition of Wilde's essays, *The Artist As Critic,* p. 315. Wilde's subject was artistic styles, not the psychology of empire.

7 Le japonisme was documented in the art exhibition of that name mounted in Paris and Tokyo from May to December 1988.

8 "The actual people who live in Japan": Wilde, *The Artist,* p. 315.

8 Orientalism was named and explored in Edward Said's book of that title and later in his "Orientalism Revisited," *Times Literary Supplement,* February 3, 1995, from both of which this account draws.

8 The Jesuit was Alessandro Valignano, Francis Xavier's successor in Japan, who is quoted in Cooper, *They Came to Japan,* p. vii. This passage is also informed by Wilkinson, *Japan Versus Europe.*

8 "The people are incredibly resigned": Valignano, cited in Cooper, *They Came to Japan,* p. 44.

8 "in our way": Francis Xavier, cited in Cooper, p. 180.

9 Japan as a vertical society, a notion much admired in the West, is explored in Nakane, *Japanese Society,* which contrives to explain the whole of the Japanese hierarchy with no recourse to political history. Democracy in the Japanese context, Nakane writes, is nothing more than "a negative reaction against the operation of the prewar system" (p. 148).

9 "an antipodean New York with more sushi": Nicholas Kristof, "A People Tremble in Harmony with the Land," *New York Times,* January 22, 1995.

9 "the Japanese of Kobe are ideal": Again, Kristof in the *Times,* January 22, 1995.

9 "the deliberate self-conscious creation": Wilde, *The Artist,* p. 315.

11 Oe's observations in Stockholm were recorded in David Remnick, "Reading Japan," *New Yorker,* February 6, 1995.

12 Pocket billiards and square dancing are noted in Cohen, *Remaking Japan,* p. 9. Big-band jazz comes from my reporting on the Tokyo jazz scene. During my years at the *Herald Tribune*'s bureau a dance hall in Yokosuka, a town south of Tokyo that still hosts an American navy base, was torn down. It was there during the occupation that many Japanese first heard jazz. When the wrecking ball arrived, the building was given a long sentimental stretch of the national evening news broadcast.

12 "One trembles": Cohen, p. 6

14 Maruyama's view of democracy as a fiction is cited in Koschmann's paper "Intellectuals and Politics in Postwar Japanese History," in Gordon, *Postwar Japan As History,* p. 403. As Koschmann explains, the remark came in a debate as to whether communism was a threat to Japanese democracy: "Maruyama insisted that Japanese democracy was still an unrealized 'fiction' and that cries to defend the actual state of Japanese politics would actually have the effect of strengthening its premodern and undemocratic elements"—a prescient observation, for that is precisely what happened in the ensuing years.

14 "Considering what it might have been": Ellen L. Frost, *For Richer, For Poorer,* p. 3.

15 I owe the phrase "the Yoshida deal" to Richard Nations, formerly the diplomatic correspondent of the *Far Eastern Economic Review,* who used it in conversation often but in print only once, in "Japan: Practice Democracy Instead of Imitating It?" in the *International Herald Tribune,* December 10, 1988.

16 The "1955 system" was named by Junnosuke Masumi and is well dissected in his *Contemporary Politics in Japan.*

16 Japan's first postwar foreign policy decision to run counter to Washington's wishes occurred during the Arab oil embargo, in November 1973. The cabinet of Kakuei Tanaka backed the Organization of Petroleum Exporting Countries, so handing the second Nixon administration, with Henry Kissinger at the foreign policy helm, an unexpected reversal.

17 "C.I.A. Spent Millions to Support Japanese Right in 50's and 60's," by Tim Weiner, Stephen Engelberg, and James Sterngold, *New York Times,* October 9, 1994. See also Jim Mann's piece in the *Los Angeles Times,* March 20, 1995, "CIA Keeping Historians in the Dark About Its Cold War Role in Japan." These stories were drawn from a few declassified State Department and C.I.A. documents, but since they were published there has been dead silence. The agency refuses to release even those files the State Department deems clear of national security concerns.

The reference to hundreds of millions of dollars is speculative but cannot be dismissed. There is much to suggest that various secret funds, accumulated by the occupation from black market activities, confiscated property, and sales of military stockpiles, congealed at the occupation's end into a so-called M Fund, which was jointly and secretly operated by Japanese and Americans for a time and eventually turned over to the corrupt inner core of the Liberal Democratic Party as political slush—not a puddle, it would seem, but an ocean today worth $500 billion. The case for the fund is put in Working Paper No. 11, July 1995, of the Japan Policy Research Institute, by Chalmers Johnson, "The 1955 System and the American Connection," and by Norbert A. Schlei's piece in the same paper, "Japan's 'M-Fund.'"

18 For the phrase "desire without hope" I am indebted to Kay Itoi, my colleague at the *Herald Tribune*'s Tokyo bureau, who used it in conversation one evening without realizing how aptly she had described all of Japanese society for a considerable period of its history.

18 "unsinkable aircraft carrier": one of Yasuhiro Nakasone's best-known descriptions of Japan's role in the security alliance, used often during his premiership.

20 "a slight readjustment of the rules": Reischauer, *The United States and Japan*, p. 283.

20 "propaganda work," "very profound practical results": Reischauer, quoted in Dower's introduction to E. H. Norman, *Origins of the Modern Japanese State: Selected Writings*, pp. 49, 44. The former remark was made at a State Department conference held in October 1949: "If we exploit the special prestige position of the scholar [in Asian societies], the intellectual group in that area, it would seem to me that propaganda work, information aimed primarily at them would be the most effective kind of information work." The latter comment was made at a 1958 conference of scholars: Countering the "historical illusions behind Marxism" with an alternate version of history, Reischauer said, "could have very profound practical results."

21 "retrenchment": Reischauer, *Japan: Past and Present*, p. 212.

21 "What was now needed": Reischauer, *Past and Present*, p. 212.

21 "On the surface Japan gives": Reischauer, *The Japanese Today*, p. 174.

21 "Political corruption is not widespread": Reischauer, *The Japanese*, p. 309. In *The Japanese Today* this passage was altered to read: "Political corruption is less widespread in Japan than in many other countries and is probably much less than in local government in the United States." The assertion is no more defensible in modified form, and the comparison with local government a nonsense entirely beside the point.

21 "cries of corruption": Reischauser, *The Japanese Today*, p. 283.

23 "satisfied with the way things are going": Reischauer, *The Japanese Today*, p. 282.

23 Suzuki's notion of "self-revolution" is described in Andrew Gordon, *The Evolution of Labor Relations in Japan*, p. 71, and at greater length in Stephen Large, *The Rise of Labor in Japan: The Yuaikai, 1912–1919*.

23 "the pledge of a Sunday school club": Ayusawa Iwao, *A History of Labor in Modern Japan* (Honolulu, 1966), p. 99, cited in John Crump, *The Origins of Socialist Thought in Japan*, p. 172.

24 The number of workers fired in 1949–50 is from Halliday, *A Political History of Japanese Capitalism*, p. 218. The number labeled communist or sympathetic to communism is from Gordon, *Evolution*, p. 333.

Throughout the 1950s and into the 1960s some of those accused of plotting political subversion fought their cases in Japanese courts; some became national causes célèbres. Years on, the charges against most were quietly dropped.

25 E. H. Norman's case is movingly described in Dower's introduction to the *Selected Writings*. He was, as Dower puts it, "sympathetic to some of the insights of Marxist analysis"—scarcely a distinguishing characteristic among twentieth-century scholars—but his ideas were at bottom "close to traditional liberalism, couched in the concept of 'self-government.'" He was denounced as a communist before the Senate in 1951 by Karl Wittfogel, a scholar best known for his book *Oriental Despotism* and his equally perverse denunciation of Owen Lattimore, the China scholar and diplomat. The rest of Norman's persecution was hung loosely upon scholarly associations and publications.

26 The man at the center: The scholar Michael Schaller supplied much of the background on Kishi in Working Paper No. 11 of the Japan Policy Research Institute, "America's

Favorite War Criminal: Kishi Nobusuke and the Transformation of U.S.–Japan Relations," July 1995.

28 Johnson's comparison between the AMPO incident and the Hungarian revolt of 1956 was made in private conversation.

30 "deeply entrenched Marxist concepts": Reischauer, *My Life Between Japan and America,* p. 155.

30 "Many Japanese . . . felt helpless": Reischauer, *My Life,* pp. 164–65.

30 "all these distorted concepts": Reischauer, *My Life,* p. 165.

31 "We now know": Reischauer helped plan the funneling of funds to the Liberal Democrats to influence elections held in Okinawa in the summer of 1965. The documents detailing this plan are dated July 16, 1965, and were obtained, via the Freedom of Information Act, from the State Department in September 1996 by Robert Wampler, of the National Security Archive.

31 "Thus, the Japanese": Reischauer, *Japan: Past and Present,* p. 225.

34 "power without purpose": The phrase was coined by Tag Murphy, who first used it as the title to a paper, "Power Without Purpose: The Crisis of Japan's Global Financial Dominance," *Harvard Business Review,* March–April 1989, pp. 71–83.

34 "a normal nation": Ichiro Ozawa, *Blueprint for a New Japan,* pp. 91ff..

35 At the brink of the Cold War's end: The term "revisionism" was first applied in this context by Bob Neff in "Rethinking Japan: The New, Harder Line Toward Tokyo," in *Business Week,* August 7, 1989.

36 Chalmers Johnson has traced the origins of the term "Japan bashing" to the Japan Economic Institute and its former president Bob Angel, who coined the phrase in the early 1980s. The J.E.I. was created in 1957 as the U.S.-Japan Trade Council. In 1992 Johnson wrote in correspondence to associates: "For many years it posed as an independent trade association with dues-paying members. But in fact the J.E.I. was fully funded by the Japanese government." See John Judis's piece, "Trade," in the *Columbia Journalism Review,* November–December 1992, pp. 38–39. "I looked around for a phrase to use to discredit Japan's critics," Angel is quoted as saying, "and I hoped to be able to discredit those most effective critics by lumping them together with people who weren't informed and who as critics were an embarrassment to everybody else."

37 The "yellow peril" theme extends back to the turn of the century and picked up momentum after the Japanese victory over Russia in 1905. From World War I onward it was a favorite of William Randolph Hearst and his shrill editorialists.

37 "beasts"—Harry Truman's judgment: Truman in a letter dated August 11, 1945: "When you have to deal with a beast you have to treat him as a beast." Cited in Dower, *Japan in War and Peace,* p. 155. Dower cites Barton J. Bernstein, ed., *The Atomic Bomb: The Critical Issues,* Boston: Little, Brown, 1976.

37 An account of M.I.T.I.'s postwar revival (as the Ministry of Commerce and Industry) appears in Johnson, *MITI and the Japanese Miracle,* p. 172. Targeted industries, "priority production," and the Americans' dislike of the term are described on pp. 182ff.

38 The distinction between center and periphery is a central theme in Oe's work and conversation. In "Japan's Dual Identity," in Miyoshi and Harootunian, *Postmodernism in*

Japan, Oe traces the theme to *Periphery and Center,* an untranslated work by the anthropologist Masao Yamaguchi.

Herb Bix also uses the term "little tradition" in his *Peasant Protest in Japan, 1590–1884,* as do other scholars, including James W. White, who explicates the chasm between little and great in his "Dynamics of Political Opposition," in Gordon, *Postwar Japan As History.*

Kunio Yanagita, the founder of Japanese folkloric studies, invented the term *jomin,* common people, ordinary people, and it is in this sense I use the term "ordinary Japanese" throughout this book.

TWO: HIDDEN HISTORY

42 The Futabatei quotation from *Drifting Clouds* is on p. 199 of the translation of the Japanese, *Ukigumo.*

43 "a false one in their mouths": Rodrigues, quoted in Cooper, *They Came to Japan,* p. 45.

44 "Eight clouds arise": Translations of the poem appear in de Bary et al., *Sources of Japanese Tradition,* vol. 1, p. 30, and in Singer, *Mirror, Sword, and Jewel,* p. 44. They differ in word order and English prosody. I have used William de Bary's order but broken the lines according to Singer.

47 "ura of the ura*":* Doi, *The Anatomy of Self,* Ch. 1, 7, 8, 9.

47 "What is concealed": The phrase appears in *On the Art of the No Drama: The Major Treatises of Ze-ami* (Princeton, 1983) and is quoted in Doi, *The Anatomy of Self,* p. 110. An alternative translation is given in the Sumiya-Shinobe edition of *Kadensho,* p. 91.

47 "The ideal condition of the mind": Doi, *The Anatomy of Self,* p. 114.

49 My treatment of *shutai-sei* draws from Koschmann, Kersten, Kazuko Tsurumi (in Takayanagi and Miwa, *Postwar Trends in Japan*), Lifton ("Youth and History: Individual Change in Postwar Japan," in Erikson, *The Challenge of Youth*), and numerous interviews with Japanese variously familiar with the 1950s, 1960s, and 1970s.

49 A blanket of ideology is suggested by Masao Maruyama's well-known phrase. See the note to p. 65 below.

51 My treatment of the Japanese virtues has benefited from Michio Morishima's analysis, p. 3 and following, in *Why Has Japan 'Succeeded'?*

53 The number of peasant uprisings in the Edo period has been analyzed many times, beginning with Borton, *Peasant Uprisings in Japan of the Tokugawa Period.* My figures derive from Bix, whose statistical study is the most thorough I have seen (*Peasant Protest in Japan, 1590–1884,* pp. xx–xxi. Bix cites three key Japanese scholars on this subject, Koji Aoki, Toshio Yokoyama, and Kiyotaka Yamanaka. Mita, *Social Psychology of Modern Japan,* p. 148, also provides figures for the years 1848–77.

For my overall account of the true nature of the Edo era I have relied upon Borton, *Peasant Uprisings,* and Norman, *Japan's Emergence As a Modern State* and *Feudal Background of Japanese Politics.*

54 "The prolonged, complete peace": Reischauer's picture of the Tokugawa period is laid out in *Japan: Past and Present,* ch. 8, p. 96ff.

55 *"They all depended on the government"*: Fukuzawa is cited in Maruyama, *Studies in the Intellectual History of Tokugawa Japan*, p. 334.

56 *"True shame cultures"*: Benedict, *The Chrysanthemum and the Sword*, p. 223.

57 *"warfare in peacetime"*: This phrase, from Kunitake Kune's account of the most important of the early Meiji missions to the West, the Iwakura Embassy, is cited by Eugene Soviak, "On the Nature of Western Progress: The Journal of the Iwakura Embassy," in Shively, *Tradition and Modernization in Japanese Culture*, p. 15. My treatment draws also upon *The Diary of Kido Takayoshi*, vol. II, 1871–74. Kido also was a member of the Iwakura Embassy, and his diary entries for the mission's nineteen months in the West are superb for the impression they convey of the blank-slate innocence of these Japanese abroad. Like many Japanese before him, Kido was fascinated above all with Western objects—everything from air conditioners, steam laundries, and deep-sea diving gear to naval vessels, railroads, and threshers.

58 *Japan was about to get:* Wilson, in *Patriots and Redeemers*, casts much interpretive light on Japan's state at the moment of the restoration.

59 For the account of the *ee ja nai ka* interlude I have drawn from Wilson, *Patriots and Redeemers*, Norman's *Feudal Background of Japanese Politics*, Bix's *Peasant Protest*, Mita's *Social Psychology*, and Shohei Imamura's 1981 film, *Ee ja nai ka* (Shochiku Studios, Tokyo; subtitled version, Kino International, New York, 1990).

60 The scholar responsible for the vulgar translation is Wilson; see *Patriots and Redeemers*, p. 98.

60 The Charter Oath is translated variously, all versions in fairly close conformity. I have used Mita's, in *Social Psychology*, p. 196, with a few words altered according to the version in Scalapino, *Democracy and the Party Movement in Prewar Japan*, p. 52.

62 *"When the people of a nation"*: The quotations are from pp. 16–17 of the translation of Fukuzawa, *An Encouragement of Learning*.

63 The comparison with Germany is suggested in Hobsbawm and Ranger, *The Invention of Tradition*.

64 *"The major task facing us today"*: Ito is quoted in Horio, *Educational Thought and Ideology in Modern Japan*, p. 44.

65 *"The old, beautiful customs"*: Juichi Soeda, a ranking finance ministry official, quoted in Andrew Gordon, *The Evolution of Labor Relations in Japan*, p. 68.

65 *"a many-layered though invisible net"*: Maruyama, "Theory and Psychology of Ultra-Nationalism," in *Thought and Behavior in Modern Japanese Politics*, p. 1.

65 *"An enormous black box"*: Daikichi Jrokawa, cited in Gluck, *Modern Myths*, p. 6. Gluck's note tells us Jrokawa alluded to "Marx's *camera obscura*, the device of optical inversion here enlarged to its original sense of a chamber large enough to enter (hence to be unaware of the ideological distortion within)."

66 *"You make peace with yourself"*: Soseki Natsume, "My Individualism," p. 37. The insight into Soseki's probable state of mind is suggested by the translator in his introduction, pp. 21–25.

66 *"I urge you to accomplish this"*: Soseki Natsume, p. 36.

66 *"Individual liberty is indispensable"*: Soseki Natsume, p. 41.

67 "As I see it, individualism": Soseki Natsume, p. 42.

68 "Conductors are having difficulty": Gayn, *Japan Diary*, p. 13.

69 "I exhort you to do": Osaragi, *The Journey*, p. 76.

69 "The real point is that": Osaragi, p. 77.

70 "Apart from the process of growing up": Osaragi, p. 139.

70 Lifton describes his interview in "Youth and History," in Erikson, *The Challenge of Youth*, pp. 264–67.

74 "It is not true that we refuse": cited in Takashi Nemoto, *Shinjinrui vs. Kanrisha*. The translation is by Nobunaga Honma, whose work as guide, translator, and interpreter during my final year of research was a valued contribution to this book.

THREE: BECOMING *NIHONJIN*

77 The Mori quotation appears in Horio, *Educational Thought and Ideology in Modern Japan*, p. 100. Horio's translator is Steven Platzer. I acknowledge here my debt to him not only as a scholar and translator, but as a generous guide and interpreter during the autumn of 1988 and the early months of 1989, a crucial period, when Hirohito passed away and Japan reached what was soon evident as a historic turning point.

82 "Our educational ideals are better realized": Bennett, *Japanese Education Today*, cited by Platzer in Horio, *Educational Thought*, p. xvi.

82 "It is the American belief": Bennett, in Horio, p. xvi.

83 "In Japan the care of children": White, *The Japanese Educational Challenge*, p. 11.

86 When I met Masao Miyamoto he handed me a series of his speeches, which were later published in books. The account of the Health Ministry, and the citations, are from the speeches.

86 "a sadistic impulse which seeks": Miyamoto, "Structural Corruption: The Result of Envy and Masochism," paper delivered before the Kaisha Society and the Canadian Chamber of Commerce in Japan, September 22, 1993.

86 "You are allowed to have divergent thoughts": Miyamoto, "Self-Sacrifice and Conformity," paper delivered before a meeting of the Harvard Business School, Keio Plaza Hotel, Tokyo, March 14, 1994.

86 My account of the *otaku* draws from a few published news accounts and numerous interviews, but notably from conversations with Masachi Ohsawa, associate professor of sociology at Chiba University.

88 Mori's English-language biographer is Ivan Hall, who drew upon several earlier biographies by Japanese scholars. I am much indebted to Hall, and indirectly to his predecessors, for the following account, which also draws from Horio, Lehmann, Mita, Gluck, and others. The photograph of Mori in 1872 appears as the frontispiece to Hall's biography.

89 "our meager language": from Mori's introduction to *Education in Japan* (1873), cited in Ivan Hall, *Mori Arinori*, p. 189.

89 Spencer, as numerous scholars make clear, was among the most influential Westerners to advise the Japanese during the Meiji period, but his counsel cut two ways. The early liberals liked the English sociologist for his liberalism, and the elite for his social Darwinism. Spencer preferred the latter when it came to Japan. He advised a succession of Japanese sojourners to London that the past had left them a gift. Do not tinker much with the old hierarchical values, Spencer urged; individualism will only produce the West's unenviable social ills. "You have, I believe, in Japan still surviving the ancient system of family organization. This organization should be made use of in your new political form." By the time he wrote that, in 1892, Spencer the liberal was embarrassed enough to ask his Japanese correspondent to keep his counsel private.

89 "a Westerner born in Japan": Ito, cited by Hall, *Mori Arinori,* p. 64.

90 "dual structure of the spirit": Kakichi Omura, cited in Hall, p. 15.

91 "It was not originally the intention": Mori, cited on p. 367 of William Braisted, *Meiroku Zasshi, Journal of the Japanese Enlightenment,* a translation of the Meiji Six Society's monthly periodical.

92 "When doing research and making judgments": cited in Horio, *Educational Thought,* p. 77.

92 "It is a big mistake": from Horio, p. 47.

93 The other prewar document of indisputable importance was the Injunction to Soldiers and Sailors, issued in 1882. The Imperial Rescript on Education suggests the cadence and intent of both:

Know Ye, Our Subjects:

Our Imperial Ancestors have founded Our Empire on a basis broad and everlasting and have deeply and firmly implanted virtue; Our subjects ever united in loyalty and filial piety have from generation to generation illustrated the beauty thereof. This is the glory of the fundamental character of Our Empire, and herein also lies the source of Our education. Ye, Our subjects, be filial to your parents, affectionate to your brothers and sisters; as husbands and wives be harmonious, as friends true; bear yourselves in modesty and moderation; extend your benevolence to all; pursue learning and cultivate arts, and thereby develop intellectual faculties and perfect moral powers; furthermore advance public good and promote common interests; always respect the Constitution and observe the laws; should emergency arise, offer yourselves courageously to the State; and thus guard and maintain the prosperity of Our Imperial Throne coeval with heaven and earth. So shall ye not only be Our good and faithful subjects, but render illustrious the best traditions of your forefathers.

The Way here set forth is indeed the teaching bequeathed by Our Imperial Ancestors, to be observed alike by Their Descendants and the subjects, infallible for all ages and true in all places. It is Our wish to lay it to heart in all reverence, in common with you, Our subjects, that we may all thus attain to the same virtue.

The 30th day of the 10th month of the 23rd year of Meiji.

94 Successism is well explained in Mita, *Social Psychology in Modern Japan,* ch. 15, pp. 268 and following, and in Gluck, *Japan's Modern Myths,* pp. 204–12.

99 The Image of the Desired Japanese, available in the original from the Diet Library, was translated informally in my Tokyo office by Nobunaga Honma. I am grateful to Steven Platzer for drawing my attention to this document.

100 "Nowadays, as a result of too much emphasis": Teiyu Amano, cited in Horio, *Educational Thought,* p. 151.

102 "While there is no one who cannot read": Hatoyama, quoted on the Kyodo wire from Washington on August 7, 1992.

FOUR: FENCES IN THE HEART

109 Soseki Natsume's line is on pp. 189–90, of *Kokoro.*

111 The term "high collar" and its many associations are explained in Seidensticker, *Low City, High City,* pp. 93 and following.

112 The figure on industrial output is from Nigel Holloway, "Time to Tame the Monster of the Capital," *Far Eastern Economic Review,* June 16, 1988, p. 53.

113 "'Even in the town you will find'": quoted in Singer, *Mirror, Sword and Jewel: The Geometry of Japanese Life,* p. 70.

117 "It is the accumulation of inefficiency": Miyamoto, "Self-Sacrifice and Conformity," speech delivered before a meeting of the Harvard Business School, Keio Plaza Hotel, Tokyo, March 14, 1994.

117 The terms "window sitter" and "industrial waste" are not quoted in the government's book.

118 "Salarymen in their 50s": Japan Travel Bureau Inc., *"Salaryman" in Japan,* p. 105.

119 "No more shall we have to live": cited in Roberts, *Mitsui,* p. 12. See his note on this speech, p. 535.

123 "Let's think about slavery": National Defense Council, *Karoshi: When the Corporate Warrior Dies,* p. 4.

128 The switch of modernization from a means to an end is often considered, and cast in many ways. I have drawn here from Kosai Yutaka, *The Era of High-Speed Growth,* especially ch. 12. "Before the war the ultimate values were traditional," Yutaka writes on p. 199. "Modernization was no more than a means of protecting what was traditional. After the war, however, modernization itself became a value, a goal. . . . Japan's traditional values were banished from consciousness into the world of the unconscious, but they survived in Japanese groupism as methods of goal attainment."

129 Apart from my own interviews, the account of the electric boom and the consumption fads that followed draw from Michitaro Tada, "The Glory and Misery of 'My Home,'" in Koschmann, *Authority and the Individual in Japan,* and from David W. Plath, "My-Car-isma: Motorizing the Showa Self," in Gluck and Graubard, *Showa: The Japan of Hirohito.*

132 "Individuals have to be liberated": Ozawa, *Blueprint for a New Japan,* p. 173.

133 The employment figures are from Gavan McCormack, "Afterbubble: Fizz and Concrete in Japan's Political Economy," Working Paper No. 21, Japan Policy Research Institute. McCormack quotes Robbie Feldman, the Salomon Brothers economist in Tokyo.

133 "Japan's most pressing need": Ozawa, *Blueprint,* p. 12.

134 "Branches were assessed according to": Akio Koiso, *Record of a Fuji Bank Man,* pp. 47–50 of the original. The translation is unofficial.

135 "This kind of contradiction": Koiso, *Record,* pp. 4–5.

141 The Tanizaki quote is from p. 33 of *In Praise of Shadows.*

144 *"As she attempted to keep off"*: Chinatsu Nakayama, *Star Time,* in *Behind the Waterfall: Three Novellas,* p. 4.

145 The figure for unemployed women graduates is from Sheryl WuDunn, "In Japan, Still Getting Tea and No Sympathy," *New York Times,* August 27, 1995.

145 The mission's best known girl was named Umeko Tsuda, whose life is explored in Rose, *Tsuda Umeko and Women's Education in Japan.*

145 The reception given *A Doll's House* is described in Laura Rodd, "Yosano Akiko and the Taisho Debate over the 'New Woman,'" in Gail Lee Bernstein, *Recreating Japanese Women, 1600–1945.*

147 *Dansei joi, josei yui* is invoked extensively in the arguments advanced by Sumiko Iwao, *The Japanese Woman: Traditional Image and Changing Reality.*

149 *"You'd better go after dawn"*: translation from Yoko Akiyama, "The Hidden Sun: Women in Japan," a paper delivered to a N.O.W. conference in Cambridge, Mass., in 1973, printed in the *International Socialist Review,* March 1974.

150 Miyamoto's account of *anshin* is in "Narcissism and Illusion in Japanese Society," a paper presented at the Tokyo Foreign Correspondents' Club, May 13, 1993.

150 *"Take no naps," "never write," "don't go"*: translations from Akiyama's essay "The Hidden Sun," cited above.

151 *"Women have five defects"*: from Akiyama's translation.

152 *the call of the crane:* a phrase usually associated with the emperor but used several times in my conversations with Japanese women.

152 *"The home is a public place"*: from the Education Ministry's *Meiji Greater Learning for Women,* issued in 1887, cited in Nolte and Hastings's essay "The Meiji State Policy Toward Women," in Bernstein's *Recreating,* p. 156.

154 The *moga* and her companion, the *modaan boy,* or *mobo,* along with the *Marx boy,* nickname for those captivated by *Kapital,* are much-chronicled characters from the period of Taisho liberalism. This passage benefited especially from Miriam Silverberg, "The Modern Girl As Militant," in Bernstein, *Recreating.*

155 *"Sometimes our public involvement"*: The quotation and information about the writing group are from Kazuko Tsurumi, *Social Change and the Individual,* ch. 8, "The Family: The Changing Roles of Women as Mothers and Wives," pp. 277 ff.

156 *"The day the mountains move has come"*: There are several translations. This one is quoted in Rodd, "Yosano Akiko," in Bernstein, *Recreating,* p. 180.

161 *"CROWN PRINCE WON OWADA'S HEART"*: *Asahi Shimbun,* January 20, 1993.

161 *"It was as though his heart"*: Soseki Natsume, *Kokoro,* p. 188.

164 *"The salary man is essentially free"*: Vogel, *Japan's New Middle Class,* p. 37.

165 *"on such a thing as individual"*: *Kokutai no Hongi,* ed. Robert King Hall, p. 87.

165 *"reverence and affection"*: *Kokutai no Hongi,* p. 87.

168 The Soseki passage appears on p. 72 of Norma Field's translation of *And Then.*

168 The photograph of the Tokaido was taken in 1867 or 1868 by Felix Beato, a celebrated Italian photographer who recorded many scenes from the final years of Edo and the first of the Meiji era. Beato kept a studio in Yokohama. The reproduction was published in *Japan Digest,* January 1991.

170 "*The train came out*": Kawabata, *Snow Country,* p. 3.

171 "*But if the truth be known*": Murakami, *A Wild Sheep Chase,* p. 208.

175 an arresting response to the city's rise: The boycott of cities was proposed by Tokiyoshi Yokoi, an instructor at a government agricultural college in Tokyo. Cited in Gluck, *Japan's Modern Myths,* p. 180.

180 The painting of the Hokkaido countryside, called *Kayabemine District,* was painted by Togai Kawakami, who journeyed to Hokkaido in August 1876 with, among others, Hirobumi Ito, the first prime minister, and Aritomo Yamagata, the prime mover behind Japan's modern military. The painting is reproduced and discussed in John M. Rosenfeld, "Western-Style Painting in the Early Meiji Period and Its Critics," in Shively, *Tradition and Modernization in Japanese Culture.*

181 The odd understanding of iron beds and telegraph poles is described in Mita, *Social Psychology of Modern Japan,* pp. 176–77.

183 "*After the execution of all these*": *Report of the 1964 Mission on Urbanization and Regional Planning,* U.N. Commissioner for Technical Assistance, Department of Economic and Social Affairs, p. 13. The report number is TAO/JAP/2, dated August 15, 1965.

183 Tanaka's singing at the I.M.F. meeting is noted in Johnson, *Japan: Who Governs?,* ch. 9, "Tanaka Kakuei, Structural Corruption, and the Advent of Machine Politics in Japan," p. 186.

183 "*Rapid urbanization has bred*": Tanaka, *Building a New Japan,* p. iii.

184 "*rebuild the home of the Japanese*": Tanaka, p. 218.

184 My analysis of the construction state rests on many pieces of journalism and many political and economic texts, but most explicitly on McCormack, *The Emptiness of Japanese Affluence.* The statistics on public spending appear on p. 33 of McCormack's book.

185 Tanaka's public works budget is discussed in Curtis, *The Japanese Way of Politics,* p. 64.

187 "*Having come this far*": Tanizaki, *In Praise of Shadows,* pp. 8–9.

188 Ienaga's discussion of nature is delineated and analyzed in Robert Bellah, "Ienaga Saburo and the Search for Meaning in Modern Japan," ch. 11 of Jansen, *Changing Japanese Attitudes Toward Modernization.* Ienaga also touches on the theme in his *Japanese Art: A Cultural Appreciation.*

189 "Little politics," "big politics," "a revolt from the periphery," and "abolish the prefectures" were ideas Hosokawa discussed often and eventually published in "Toward a New Party: Action Program for a 'Third Opening' of Japan," *Bungei shunju,* June 1992. The translation is courtesy of the Center for Intercultural Communication, Tokyo.

NOTES

190 A "United States of Japan" is now cited often as an alternative to Japan's centralized structure. My own exposure to the idea was through Hosokawa and his counterpart in neighboring Oita Prefecture, Morihiko Hiramatsu, whose generosity of spirit and insights on numerous trips to Oita were valuable aids.

SEVEN: THE SPIRIT THAT RUNS THROUGH HISTORY

195 The chapter title is from *Kokutai no Hongi*, ed. R. K. Hall, pp. 105 and following.

195 The Mishima quotation appears on p. 257 of the translation of *The Temple of the Golden Pavilion*.

197 The correspondent was Michel Random, who visited Mishima in December 1968. Random recounted the episode on p. 14 of his *Japan: Strategy of the Unseen*. The description of Mishima's house is drawn from Random, from photographs, and from Henry Scott-Stokes's biography, *The Life and Death of Yukio Mishima*. Recounting a visit to Mishima's house in May 1968, Scott-Stokes identifies the statue as one of Apollo, and I assume it is the same one Random saw seven months later.

201 *The Tale of the Forty-Seven Ronin* is discussed in Benedict, *The Chrysanthemum and the Sword*, pp. 199ff., and, with more nuance, in ch. 11, "The Vendetta of the Forty-Seven Samurai," of Eiko Ikegamai, *The Taming of the Samurai*. Details of the tale's fortunes through history are drawn from the latter work.

202 "*Seppuku has its origin*": This and the two following quotations are from Algernon Bertram Mitford, who served in the British Embassy from 1866 through the restoration. Mitford published his record of these remarks, made in 1869 during debates in an early-Meiji government council, in *Tales of Old Japan* (London, 1871). They are quoted in Catharina Blomberg, *The Heart of the Warrior*, p. 190.

203 Hearn's essay appears as ch. 26 of *Glimpses of Unfamiliar Japan*, pp. 656–83.

204 Kinjiro Ninomiya is described in Mita, *Social Psychology of Modern Japan*, pp. 271–72, and in Gluck, *Japan's Modern Myths*, pp. 158–59.

205 I have drawn from Gluck, *Japan's Modern Myths*, to describe the various conceptions of *kokutai*. She quotes Fukuzawa on p. 144.

205 "*and shines resplendent throughout our history*": *Kokutai no Hongi*, ed. R. K. Hall, p. 59.

205 "*The atmosphere was tense, panicked*": Kurosawa, *Something Like an Autobiography*, p. 145.

205 "*When I walked the same route back home*": Kurosawa, p. 145.

206 "*Something huge had just cracked*": Robert Guillain, *I Saw Tokyo Burning* (London: John Murray, 1981), cited in Behr, p. 318.

206 "*dismiss it as the propaganda*": Lifton, "Youth and History," in Erikson, *The Challenge of Youth*, p. 270.

207 "*the polarizing tendencies that still haunt*": Lifton, p. 270.

207 The Sogoro story is probably the best known of the many surviving peasant legends. This rendering is from Anne Walthall's *Peasant Uprisings in Japan: A Critical Anthology of Peasant Histories*, ch. 1, "The Sakura Sogoro Story."

209 "My findings seem to provide": from Tsunoda's introduction to *The Japanese Brain: Uniqueness and Universality,* p. xx.

214 The poem from the *Manyoshu* comes from book XI, entry no. 2531, p. 198 in H. H. Honda's edition.

214 "I recall those days": Akihito and Michiko, *Light,* entry no. 136 in Michiko's section of the book, p. 144.

215 "precious paradox": The entire Barthes quotation is from "Center-City, Empty Center," in *Empire of Signs,* pp. 30–31.

220 "A young emperor who has broken": Adachi Kinnosuke, "Hirohito, Who Has Shown Himself Ready to Break with Traditions of the Past, Comes to the Throne at the Moment When His Country Appears to Be Entering an Era of Change," *New York Times Magazine,* January 9, 1927.

221 Akihito's tutor, Elizabeth Gray Vining, detailed her work with the imperial heir in *Windows for the Crown Prince.*

223 "Seeing the acacia trees": Akihito and Michiko, *Light,* entry no. 59 in Akihito's portion of the book, p. 35.

223 "Having spent": Light, entry no. 156, p. 74.

224 The most famous speech: The drafting process is discussed in Nakamuka's *The Japanese Monarchy,* pp. 109–12, and in Bix, "Inventing the 'Symbol Monarchy,'" pp. 328–32.

228 The account of the Daijosai draws from many sources, official and scholarly, and for historical background from Emiko Ohnuki-Tierney, *Rice As Self: Japanese Identities Through Time,* pp. 45–51.

230 "a divine event at which the emperor": The questions were submitted to the speaker of the Diet's lower house by Tatsutoshi Komori on November 7, 1990.

234 "idealized amae *and considered a world dominated":* Doi, *The Anatomy of Dependence,* p. 60.

234 "It was not until the emperor himself": Doi, p. 61.

235 "the spirit of resistance to the authority": Doi, pp. 59–60.

237 The account of the documentary film *Hirohito: Behind the Myth* is based on newspaper accounts and interviews.

237 "It's nonsense," "It's entirely wrong": Reischauer, quoted in William H. Honan, "Hirohito's War Guilt Debated in Docudrama," *New York Times,* February 6, 1989. See also Judith Michaelson, "Public-TV's 'Hirohito' Under the Gun," *Los Angeles Times,* February 24, 1989.

237 Hirohito was published by Chelsea House (New York), in 1988.

238 "leaders in action—the leaders described": Hirohito, p. 8.

238 "He was more at ease collecting": Hirohito, p. 70.

238 "Hirohito was kept uninformed": Hirohito, p. 83.

238 *"Hirohito played a minor role":* Hirohito, p. 89.

239 The account of Aristides Lazarus was carried in the *Mainichi Shimbun* of February 21, 1989, and in the English-language *Mainichi Daily News* of the same date under the headline "Truman Saved Emperor, Made Tojo Scapegoat."

239 The *Sugiyama Memoranda* was published in 1967 and almost completely ignored. Bergamini, in *Japan's Imperial Conspiracy,* pp. xxviii–xxix, recalls: "Skillful mythmaking . . . could account for the imprinting of a false image, but I was perplexed by the ease with which the true image had been obliterated. It was difficult for me to believe that an entire people, plus foreign observers, could suffer consistently from mass blindness. Could an Emperor really strut about naked while everyone, including envoys from other nations, admired the quality and refinement of his clothes?"

However grave the errors in Bergamini's book, this was a good question.

240 The *Monologue* recorded by Hidenari Terasaki was published in the December 1990 edition of *Bungei shunju* and received considerably more attention in the Japanese and Western press than previous documents relating to the emperor's responsibility. *Bungei shunju* dedicated its next edition to scholarly comment on the *Monologue.* It was the scholar Herb Bix who made use of the *Monologue,* in the context of all the other documents on Hirohito's wartime role, to draw the entire question to its logical conclusion:

"In his Monologue the emperor (with the assistance of his aides) presents himself as a peace-minded constitutional monarch, who, when his generals and admirals resolved on war, went along because he had no choice. That passive imperial image is unbelievable when contrasted with the image found in the subtext of the Monologue. The subtext emperor is obsessed with fighting and winning battles. . . ." In the end, it was the emperor, more than anyone else, who delayed Japan's surrender."

Bix published his conclusions in "The Showa Emperor's 'Monologue' and the Problem of War Responsibility," *Journal of Japanese Studies* 18, no. 2 (Summer 1992), pp. 295–363. He later used the *Monologue* in reanalyzing the accepted account of the emperor's role in ending the war. See "Japan's Delayed Surrender: A Reinterpretation," *Diplomatic History* 19, no. 2 (Spring 1995). I am grateful to Professor Bix for his guidance in these and other matters.

241 *"Forty-three years have passed":* from the Nagasaki Municipal Assembly Records, quoted in Norma Field, *In the Realm of a Dying Emperor: A Portrait of Japan at Century's End,* p. 178. This account of Motoshima and the letters his shooting precipitated draws from Field, the published letters, newspaper accounts, and my later interviews.

242 *"If you do not do this":* Kido's diaries were used (selectively) as evidence during the Tokyo war-crimes trials and were, as Bix points out, a scholarly breakthrough when they began to be published, in 1966. The quotation is cited in Bix, "The Showa Emperor's 'Monologue.'"

243 *"a tremendous convulsion among the Japanese":* MacArthur, letter to the Joint Chiefs of Staff, January 25, 1946, quoted in Behr, *Hirchito,* p. 346.

NINE: THE UNFINISHED DREAM

248 The anecdote told by Chu Asai regarding Fontanesi's admonition is from Janine Beichman, *Masaoka Shiki* (Boston: Twayne Publishers, 1982), and is quoted on pp. 5–6 of Brett de Bary's introduction to Kojin Karatani, *Origins of Modern Japanese Literature,* from which my account of the evolution of Japanese artistic perceptions draws. Shiki was an influential writer and critic who, as Karatani recounts, was an advocate of poetic "sketching" from life. Fontenesi's influence, as well as Shiki's, is discussed also in Toru Haga, "The Formation of Realism in Meiji Painting: The Artistic Career of Takahashi Yuichi," ch. 6 of Shively, *Tradition and Modernization in Japanese Culture.*

249 "Monogatari *is pattern, nothing more":* Karatani, *Origins,* p. 164.

250 "*the curse of Western art," "true painting":* These phrases are from a well-known speech Fenollosa delivered in Tokyo in May of 1882, "Truth in Fine Arts." It is discussed by both Toru Haga and John M. Rosenfield in their essays in Shively, *Tradition and Modernization.*

250 "*The greatest central genius":* This was Hogai Kano. Fenollosa's remark is quoted in Rosenfield's essay in Shively, *Tradition and Modernization,* p. 206.

252 "*He entered the third house":* Futabatei, *Ukigumo* (*Drifting Clouds*), p. 199.

253 "*The world seemed to be":* Soseki Natsume, *Botchan,* p. 103.

254 "*the sea, like a public bath":* Soseki Natsume, *Kokoro,* p. 2.

254 "*and swam after him":* Kokoro, p. 6.

255 "*You must understand that to K":* Kokoro, p. 218.

255 "*moral darkness":* Kokoro, p. 128.

255 "*Under normal conditions, everyone":* Kokoro, p. 61.

255 "Overcoming the modern" is considered in many contexts. A good summary of the question appears in Alexandra Munroe's catalogue introduction to *Japanese Art Since 1945: Seven Against the Sky,* pp. 23–24.

256 "*where champagne glasses floated like jellyfish":* from Tanizaki's collected works, vol. XXI, pp. 12–13, quoted in translation in Keene, *Dawn to the West,* pp. 750–51.

257 "*We Orientals tend to seek our satisfactions":* Tanizaki, *In Praise of Shadows,* p. 31.

257 "*From ancient times we have considered":* Tanizaki, p. 31.

258 "*It seemed to me the end of everything":* Tanizaki, p. 39.

258 "*constitute a series of repetitive rituals":* Karatani, *Origins,* p. 163.

258 Najita's observation is explained in "On Culture and Technology in Postmodern Japan," in Miyoshi and Harootunian, *Postmodernism and Japan,* pp. 3–20.

259 "*But I have the feeling":* from an autobiographical sketch Kawabata wrote in 1934, quoted in Keene, *Dawn to the West,* p. 795.

259 "*Because a virgin ceases to be a virgin":* from Mishima's introduction to Kawabata, *House of the Sleeping Beauties,* p. 8.

259 "*the destruction of classical perfection":* Mishima, *Sun and Steel,* quoted in Scott-Stokes, *The Life and Death of Yukio Mishima,* p. 222.

260 "*language of the flesh":* Sun and Steel, in Scott-Stokes, p. 218.

260 "*This sound is the cry of Nippon itself":* Mishima, in a piece published in *Sports Illustrated,* December 1970, cited in Scott-Stokes, *Life and Death,* p. 230.

260 "We must hide our great sorrow": The anthem is translated by Scott-Stokes, *Life and Death,* p. 247.

260 "I come out on the stage determined": The conversation was with the novelist Jun Ishikawa during the autumn of 1970. Quoted in Scott-Stokes, p. 312.

260 "Was not the longing of the sad old men": Kawabata, *House of the Sleeping Beauties,* p. 39.

261 The photographs of postwar painters are of Shozo Shimamoto and Kazuo Shiraga respectively and appear on catalogue p. 120 of Munroe, *Japanese Art Since 1945.*

261 asking others to drink: From Soseki's "My Individualism," p. 33: "At long last I saw that I had been no better than a rootless, floating weed, drifting aimlessly and wholly dependent upon others—'dependent' in the sense of an imitator, a man who has someone else drink his liquor for him, who asks the other fellow's opinion of it and makes that opinion his own without question."

261 "The photograph . . . will not strike you": Tsurumi, *A Cultural History of Postwar Japan,* p. 11.

261 The 1994 exhibition was Munroe's *Japanese Art Since 1945,* which began in February 1994 and ran in the cities named until August 1995.

263 "Then tradition is naturally perceived as something": Okamoto's "What is Tradition?" was published in *My Contemporary Art* (Tokyo: Shincho-sha, 1963). The quotations here are from translated portions of the essay in Munroe, pp. 381–82.

265 "The most urgent task": Okamoto, cited in Munroe, p. 381.

266 "the dailiness of life": The phrase, utterly unrelated to Japan, is apt in the context. It is from Randall Jarrell's "Well Water," in *The Collected Poems,* New York: Farrar, Straus & Giroux, fifth printing, 1981, p. 300.

266 "Our village had been forced to begin": Oe, *The Catch,* p. 112 (published in *Teach Us to Outgrow Our Madness* as *Prize Stock*).

Unless otherwise noted, the comments of Oe and Abe are from conversations with the author.

267 "a total, comprehensive contemporary age": Oe, "Japan's Dual Identity," in Miyoshi and Harootunian; *Postmodernism and Japan,* pp. 189–213.

268 "to enlighten Japan and the Japanese": Oe in "Japan's Dual identity."

268 "the springtime of Japanese filmmaking": Kurosawa, originally quoted in Derek Elley, "Kurosawa at the NFT," *Films and Filming,* May 1986; drawn here from Stephen Prince, *The Warrior's Camera: The Cinema of Akira Kurosawa,* p. 8.

270 "I would like to write about Japan": Murakami's remark in a P.E.N.-sponsored discussion with Jay McInerney that was expanded and published in the *New York Times Book Review,* September 27, 1992.

270 Richie's comments were in conversation. He touches on the point in *Japanese Cinema: An Introduction,* pp. 5–6.

271 "an original . . . because I had to create": cited in the *New York Times Book Review,* September 27, 1992.

271 "Yes, the old gatekeepers": *New York Times Book Review,* September 27, 1992.

271 "On arriving in Tokyo": Murakami, *Norwegian Wood,* p. 48.

271 "Now only the kitchen and I are left": Yoshimoto, *Kitchen,* pp. 4–5.

272 "He was an architect": Kurokawa, in conversation.

274 "To be at once public and private": Ando, in the catalogue of *Tadao Ando,* an exhibition at the Centre Georges Pompidou, Paris, March 1993. The translation is mine.

TEN: THE OTHER WITHIN

275 The quotation from Sumii's *The River with No Bridge* is from p. 354.

278 "our own disturbing otherness, for that indeed": Kristeva, *Strangers to Ourselves,* p. 192.

278 "the public law of the whole world": from *Meiji Japan Through Contemporary Sources,* vol. 2 (Tokyo: Center for East Asian Cultural Studies), pp. 69–70, cited in Weiner, *The Origins of the Korean Community in Japan, 1910–1923,* p. 8.

280 The figures for Koreans killed after the 1923 earthquake are based on Weiner's work with various statistics, *Origins,* pp. 181ff. Shunsuke Tsurumi, *An Intellectual History,* puts the figure unequivocally at six thousand.

281 The account of "comfort women" draws primarily from George Hicks's richly detailed book *The Comfort Women* (1995).

284 "When I was in the sixth grade": Choi's first oral statement before the Fukuoka district court, October 17, 1986, printed in *Liberation of the Korean Minority in Japan,* presented to the U.N. Division of Human Rights on June 23, 1990, published by the Association Fighting for the Acquisition of Human Rights of Koreans in Japan (Kitakyushu, 1990).

285 "It took me twenty-one years": Shu In-Shik, quoted in Yumi Lee, *Who Has Heard Japanese-Born Koreans' Voice?: The Myth of Japan's Minority Issue* (privately printed, n.d.).

294 —or at their hands: The question of civilian murder by Japanese military personnel is examined in Norma Field's *In the Realm of a Dying Emperor,* p. 62ff.

296 "In Okinawa we may find clues": Shunsuke Tsurumi, *An Intellectual History of Wartime Japan, 1931–1945,* pp. 108–9. This theme is also considered in (among other works) Kenzaburo Oe "Japan's Dual Identity," in Miyoshi and Harootunian, *Postmodernism and Japan,* and in Karatani, *Origins.*

297 The breakdown of illegal foreign workers is from the Immigration Control Bureau, Justice Ministry, November 1992. Haruo Shimada, in his well-considered *Japan's "Guest Workers": Issues and Public Policies,* supports the estimate of the total number of illegals. The recession of the first half of the 1990s appears only to have slowed the rate of new arrivals.

298 "What kind of nation do we want to be?": from Shimada, *Japan's "Guest Workers,"* pp. 201–13.

ELEVEN: A FUGITIVE VIRTUE

301 The Lévi-Strauss quotation is on p. 45 of *Tristes Tropiques.*

306 Objections to the Jeffersonian nature of Article 12 are spelled out in *The Japan That Can Still Say No,* Shintaro Ishihara's (untranslated) sequel to *The Japan That Can Say No.* Kay Itoi translated this and other portions of the sequel for publication in the *International Herald Tribune,* August 30, 1990.

309 *"Nobody wants a rearmed, resurgent Japan":* Fred Hiatt got the quotation and published it in the *Washington Post,* March 27, 1990, under the headline "Marine General: U.S. Troops Must Remain in Japan."

312 *"left a stain on Japanese history":* Nakasone, *Memoirs: Life and Politics* (1992), p. 88 of the Kodansha edition. The translation, done in my Tokyo office, is unofficial. Details of Nakasone's wartime and early postwar life are also drawn from this book.

316 *"What is a normal nation?"* . . . *"It does not refuse":* Ozawa, *Blueprint for a New Japan,* pp. 94–95.

317 *"In hope of starting national debate":* Yomiuri Shimbun published *A Proposal for the Revision of the Text of the Constitution of Japan* in book form on November 3, 1994. The project was carried out by the Yomiuri Research Institute.

318 *"I cannot praise a fugitive and cloistered virtue":* Milton, *Areopagitica,* pp. 33–34.

320 *"An objective institute, combined with a prayer hall":* Professor Ikuhiko Hata of Chiba University, to whom I am grateful for time spent discussing this issue.

EPILOGUE: THE IMAGINARY JAPANESE

327 The Bergson quotation appears on p. 74. I have combined this translation with Toynbee's, on p. 231 of vol. 3, *A Study of History.*

329 *"Japan is therefore particularly suited":* Ozawa, *Blueprint for a New Japan,* p. 148.

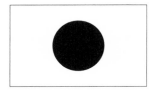

BIBLIOGRAPHY

Where possible, the date of original publication precedes the date of the edition from which I worked, whose publisher is that named.

Abe, Kobo. *Friends.* Tokyo and Rutland: Charles E. Tuttle, 1969, 1986.

———. *Secret Rendezvous.* Tokyo and Rutland: Charles E. Tuttle, 1969, 1986.

———. *The Ark Sakura.* New York: Vintage International, 1988, 1989.

———. *The Box Man.* Tokyo and Rutland: Charles E. Tuttle, 1974, 1986.

———. *The Face of Another.* Tokyo and Rutland: Charles E. Tuttle, 1966, 1986.

———. *The Ruined Map.* Tokyo and Rutland: Charles E. Tuttle, 1969, 1988.

———. *The Woman in the Dunes.* Tokyo and Rutland: Charles E. Tuttle, 1964, 1988.

Adachi, Kenji et al. *Modern Japanese Art: Selected Works from the National Museum of Modern Art.* Tokyo: National Museum, 1984.

Akihito and Michiko, the emperor and empress of Japan. *Light (Tomoshibi): Collected Poetry by Emperor Akihito and Empress Michiko.* Edited by Marie Philomène and Masako Saito. New York and Tokyo: Weatherhill, 1991.

Akiyama, Yoko. *Ribu Shishi Noto (Personal Notes on Women's Lib).* Tokyo: Impakto Shuppansha, 1993.

Amano, Ikuo. *Education and Examination in Modern Japan.* Tokyo: University of Tokyo Press, 1990.

Asahi Shimbun, Sezon Museum of Art et al. *Tadao Ando—Beyond Horizons in Architecture.* Tokyo: Executive Committee for the Exhibition, 1992.

Asano, Toru, Atsushi Tanaka, et al. *An Eye for Minute Details: Realistic Painting in the Taisho Period.* Tokyo: National Museum of Modern Art, 1986.

———. *Development of Western Realism in Japan.* Tokyo: National Museum of Modern Art, 1985.

362

————. *Realistic Representation III: Painting in Japan, 1884–1907.* Tokyo: National Museum of Modern Art, 1988.

Ashihara, Yoshinobu. *The Hidden Order: Tokyo Through the Twentieth Century.* Tokyo and New York: Kodansha International, 1986, 1989.

Bando, Mariko. *Nihon no Josei Databanku (Japanese Women's Databank).* Tokyo: Okurasho Insatsukyoku, 1992.

Barshay, Andrew E., "Imagining Democracy in Modern Japan: Reflections on Maruyama Masao and Modernism." *Journal of Japanese Studies* 18, no. 2 (1992).

————. *State and Intellectual in Imperial Japan: The Public Man in Crisis.* Berkeley, Los Angeles, and London: University of California Press, 1988.

Barthes, Roland. *Empire of Signs.* New York: Hill & Wang, 1982.

Bascou, Marc, Conservateur au Musée d'Orsay, et al. *Le Japonisme.* Paris: Editions de la Reunion des musées Nationaux, 1988.

Basho, Matsuo. *Narrow Road to the Interior.* Boston and London: Shambhala, 1991.

Beasley, W. G. *The Modern History of Japan.* 3d rev. ed. London: Weidenfeld and Nicholson, 1985.

Behr, Edward. *Hirohito: Behind the Myth.* New York: Villard Books, 1989.

Benedict, Ruth. *The Chrysanthemum and the Sword.* Rutland and Tokyo: Charles E. Tuttle, 1946, 1992.

Bergamini, David. *Japan's Imperial Conspiracy.* New York: William Morrow and Co., 1971.

Bergson, Henri. *The Two Sources of Morality and Religion.* Notre Dame: University of Notre Dame Press, 1932, 1986.

Bernstein, Gail, ed. *Recreating Japanese Women, 1600–1945.* Berkeley, Los Angeles, and Oxford: University of California Press, 1991.

Bestor, Theodore C. *Neighborhood Tokyo.* Stanford: Stanford University Press, 1989.

Bix, Herbert P. "Inventing the 'Symbol Monarchy' in Japan, 1945–1952." *Journal of Japanese Studies* 21, no. 2 (1995).

————. "Japan's Delayed Surrender: A Reinterpretation." *Diplomatic History* 19, no. 2 (Spring 1995).

————. *Peasant Protest in Japan, 1590–1884.* New Haven and London: Yale University Press, 1986.

————. "The Showa Emperor's 'Monologue' and the Problem of War Responsibility." *Journal of Japanese Studies* 18, no. 2 (1992).

Blomberg, Catharina. *The Heart of the Warrior: Origins and Religious Background of the Samurai System in Feudal Japan.* Sandgate, Folkstone: Japan Library, 1994.

Borton, Hugh. *Peasant Uprisings in Japan of the Tokugawa Period.* Transactions of the Asiatic Society of Japan, vol. 16, 2d series. Tokyo: 1938.

Boscaro, Adriana, et al., eds. *Rethinking Japan.* 2 vols. Sandgate, Folkstone: Japan Library, 1991.

Braisted, William Reynolds, trans. *Meiroku Zasshi, Journal of the Japanese Enlightenment.* Cambridge, Mass.: Harvard University Press, 1976.

Broadbridge, Seymour. *Industrial Dualism in Japan: A Problem of Economic Growth and Structural Change.* Chicago: Aldine Publishing Co., 1966.

BIBLIOGRAPHY

Buraku Kaiho Kenkyusho (Buraku Liberation Research Institute), ed. *Long-Suffering Brothers and Sisters, Unite!: The Buraku Problem, Universal Human Rights, and Minority Problems in Various Countries.* Osaka: Buraku Liberation Research Institute, 1981.

————. *The Road to a Discrimination-Free Future: The World Struggle and the Buraku Liberation Movement.* Osaka: Buraku Liberation Research Institute, 1983.

————. *The United Nations, Japan and Human Rights.* Osaka: Buraku Liberation Research Institute, 1984.

Buruma, Ian. *A Japanese Mirror: Heroes and Villains of Japanese Culture.* London: Jonathan Cape, 1984.

————. *The Wages of Guilt: Memories of War in Germany and Japan.* New York: Farrar, Straus and Giroux, 1994.

Centre Georges Pompidou and Marina Lewisch, *chargée d'edition. Tadao Ando.* Paris: Editions du Centre Pompidou, 1993.

Chapman, William. *Inventing Japan: The Making of a Postwar Civilization.* New York: Prentice Hall Press, 1991.

Chatterjee, Partha. *Nationalist Thought and the Colonial World.* Minneapolis: University of Minnesota Press, 1986, 1993.

————. *The Nation and Its Fragments: Colonial and Postcolonial Histories.* Princeton: Princeton University Press, 1993.

Chosakyoku, Keizai Kikakucho, Chiiki Keizai Reporuto (Local Economy Report). Tokyo: Okurasho Insatsukyoku, 1992.

Christopher, Robert C. *The Japanese Mind: The Goliath Explained.* New York: Linden Press, Simon and Schuster, 1983.

Coaldrake, William H. *Architecture and Authority in Japan.* London and New York: Routledge, 1996.

Cohen, Theodore. *Remaking Japan: The American Occupation as New Deal,* Herbert Passin, ed. New York: The Free Press, 1987.

Collcutt, Martin, Marius Jansen, and Isao Kumakura, eds. *Cultural Atlas of Japan.* Oxford: Equinox; New York: Facts on File, 1988.

Collingwood, R. G. *The Idea of History,* rev. ed. Edited by Jan van der Dussen. Oxford and New York: Oxford University Press, 1946, 1993.

Cooper, Michael, S.J., ed. *They Came to Japan: An Anthology of European Reports on Japan, 1543–1640.* Berkeley, Los Angeles, and London: University of California Press, 1965, 1981.

Craig, Albert M., and Donald H. Shively, eds. *Personality in Japanese History.* Ann Arbor: Center for Japanese Studies, University of Michigan, 1995.

Crowley, James B., ed. *Modern East Asia: Essays in Interpretation.* New York: Harcourt, Brace & World, 1970.

Crump, John. *The Origins of Socialist Thought in Japan.* London and Canberra: Croom Helm; New York: St. Martin's Press, 1983.

Curtis, Gerald L. *The Japanese Way of Politics.* New York, Columbia University Press, 1988.

Dallmayr, Fred R. *Twilight of Subjectivity: Contributions to a Post-Individualist Theory of Politics.* Amherst: University of Massachusetts Press, 1981.

Danly, Robert Lyons. *In the Shade of Spring Leaves: The Life and Writings of Higuchi Ichiyo, a Woman of Letters in Meiji Japan*. New Haven and London: Yale University Press, 1981.

Dazai, Osamu. *Blue Bamboo*. Tokyo and London: Kodansha, 1993.

———. *Return to Tsugaru, Travels of a Purple Tramp*. Tokyo and New York: Kodansha International, 1944, 1987.

———. *Self Portraits*. Tokyo and New York: Kodansha International, 1991.

de Rougement, Denis. *Love in the Western World*. New York: Harcourt, Brace and Company, 1940.

Deacon, Richard. *A History of the Japanese Secret Service*. London: Frederick Muller Limited, 1982.

Doi, Takeo. *The Anatomy of Dependence*. Tokyo and New York: Kodansha International, 1971, 1988.

———. *The Anatomy of Self: The Individual Versus Society*. Tokyo and New York: Kodansha International, 1986, 1989.

———. "The Japanese Psyche: Myth and Reality." Remarks to the Japan Society, New York, May 2, 1989.

Dower, John W. *Japan in War and Peace: Selected Essays*. New York: New Press, 1993.

———. "The Bombed: Hiroshimas and Nagasakis in Japanese Memory." *Diplomatic History* 19, no. 2 (Spring 1995).

———. *War Without Mercy: Race and Power in the Pacific War*. New York: Pantheon Books, 1986.

Duke, Benjamin C. *Japan's Militant Teachers: A History of the Left-Wing Teachers' Movement*. Honolulu: University Press of Hawaii, 1973.

Embree, John F. *A Japanese Village: Suye Mura*. London: Kegan Paul, Trench, Trubner & Co., 1946.

Emmott, Bill. *Japanophobia: The Myth of the Invincible Japanese*. New York: Times Books, 1992.

———. *The Sun Also Sets: The Limits to Japan's Economic Power*. New York: Times Books, 1989.

Enchi, Fumiko. *Masks*. Tokyo and Rutland: Charles E. Tuttle, 1958, 1984.

Endo, Shusaku. *Deep River*. New York: New Directions, 1994.

———. *Silence*. Tokyo and New York: Kodansha International, 1966, 1989.

———. *Stained Glass Elegies*. London and Washington: Peter Owen, 1984.

———. *The Girl I Left Behind*. London: Peter Owen, 1994.

Engelhardt, Tom. "Fifty Years Under a Cloud: The Uneasy Search for Our Atomic History." *Harper's*, January 1996.

———. *The End of Victory Culture: Cold War America and the Disillusioning of a Generation*. New York: Basic Books, 1995.

Fairbank, John K., Edwin O. Reischauer, and Albert M. Craig, eds. *East Asia: The Modern Transformation*. Modern Asia Edition. Boston: Houghton Mifflin; Tokyo: Charles E. Tuttle, 1965.

Fallows, James. *Looking at the Sun: The Rise of the New East Asian Economic and Political System.* New York: Pantheon Books, 1994.

Feinberg, Walter. *Japan and the Pursuit of a New American Identity: Work and Education in a Multicultural Age.* New York and London: Routledge, 1993.

Field, Norma. *In the Realm of a Dying Emperor: A Portrait of Japan at Century's End.* New York: Pantheon Books, 1991.

Frost, Ellen L. *For Richer, For Poorer: The New U.S.-Japan Relationship.* New York: Council on Foreign Relations, 1987.

Fujii, James A. *Complicit Fictions: The Subject in the Modern Japanese Prose Narrative.* Berkeley, Los Angeles, and London: University of California Press, 1993.

Fujita, Juniko, and Richard Child Hill, eds. *Japanese Cities in the World Economy.* Philadelphia: Temple University Press, 1993.

Fukutake, Tadashi. *The Japanese Social Structure: Its Evolution in the Modern Century.* 2d ed. Tokyo: University of Tokyo Press, 1989.

Fukuyama, Francis. *The End of History and the Last Man.* New York: Free Press, 1992.

Fukuzawa, Yukichi. *An Encouragement of Learning.* Tokyo: Sophia University, 1969.

———. *The Autobiography of Yukichi Fukuzawa.* Tokyo: Hokuseido Press, 1981.

Futabatei, Shimei. *Japan's First Modern Novel:* Ukigumo *of Futabatei Shimei.* Ann Arbor: Center for Japanese Studies, University of Michigan, 1990.

Gayn, Mark. *Japan Diary.* Rutland and Tokyo: Charles E. Tuttle, 1981, 1984.

Gessel, Van C. *Three Modern Novelists: Soseki, Tanizaki, Kawabata.* Tokyo and New York: Kodansha International, 1993.

Gibney, Frank. *Five Gentlemen of Japan: The Portrait of a Nation's Character.* Rutland and Tokyo: Charles E. Tuttle, 1953, 1984.

———. *Japan: The Fragile Superpower.* Rev. ed. New York: New American Library, 1979, 1980.

———, ed. *Senso: The Japanese Remember the Pacific War, Letters to the Editor of* Asahi Shimbun. Armonk and London: M. E. Sharpe, 1995.

Gluck, Carol. *Japan's Modern Myths: Ideology in the Late-Meiji Period.* Princeton: Princeton University Press, 1985.

Gluck, Carol, and Stephen R. Graubard, eds. *Showa: The Japan of Hirohito.* New York: W. W. Norton, 1992.

Gordon, Andrew. *The Evolution of Labor Relations in Japan: Heavy Industry, 1853–1955.* Cambridge, Mass., and London: Council on East Asian Studies, Harvard University, 1988.

———, ed. *Postwar Japan As History.* Berkeley, Los Angeles, and Oxford: University of California Press, 1993.

Goto, Takanori. *Japan's Dark Side to Progress: The Struggle for Justice for the Pharmaceutical Victims of Japan's Postwar Economic Boom.* Chiba: Manbousha Publications, 1991.

Gray, John. *Enlightenment's Wake: Politics and Culture at the Close of the Modern Age.* London and New York: Routledge, 1995.

Greenbie, Sydney. *Japan Real and Imaginary, with Many Illustrations and Photographs.* New York and London: Harper & Brothers Publishers, 1920.

Hall, Ivan Parker. *Mori Arinori*. Cambridge, Mass.: Harvard University Press, 1973.

Hall, John Whitney. *Japan from Prehistory to Modern Times*. New York: Delacorte Press, 1970.

Hall, Robert King, ed. *Kokutai no Hongi: Cardinal Principles of the National Entity of Japan*. Newton, Mass.: Crofton Publishing, 1974.

Halliday, Jon. *A Political History of Japanese Capitalism*. New York: Pantheon Books, 1976.

Halloran, Richard. *Japan: Images and Realities*. Rutland and Tokyo: Charles E. Tuttle, 1970, 1989.

Harvey, David. *The Condition of Postmodernity: An Enquiry into the Origins of Cultural Change*. Cambridge, Mass., and Oxford: Blackwell, 1990, 1995.

Hearn, Lafcadio. *Glimpses of Unfamiliar Japan*. Rutland and Tokyo: Charles E. Tuttle, 1894, 1991.

———. *Japan: An Interpretation*. New York and London: MacMillan Company, 1907.

———. *Kokoro: Hints and Echoes of Japanese Inner Life*. Tokyo and Rutland: Charles E. Tuttle, 1896, 1991.

———. *Writings From Japan*. Edited by Francis King. Hammondsworth: Penguin Books, 1984.

Heilbroner, Robert. *21st Century Capitalism*. New York and London: W. W. Norton, 1993.

Hendry, Joy. *Wrapping Culture: Politeness, Presentation, and Power in Japan and Other Societies*. Oxford: Clarendon Press, 1993.

Hersey, John. *Hiroshima*. New York: Alfred A. Knopf, 1946.

Hicks, George. *The Comfort Women: Sex Slaves of the Japanese Imperial Forces*. London: Souvenir Press, 1995.

Hiramatsu, Morihiko. *Chiho kara no Haso (Ideas from the Provinces)*. Tokyo: Iwanami Shoten, 1990.

———. *Globaru ni Kangei, Lokaru ni Kodoseiyo (Thinking Internationally, Acting Locally)*. Tokyo: Toyokeizai Shimposha, 1990.

Hirschmeier, Johannes, and Hyoe Murakami, eds. *Politics and Economics in Contemporary Japan*. Tokyo: Kodansha International, 1979, 1987.

Hobsbawm, Eric. *The Age of Extremes: A History of the World, 1914–1991*. New York: Pantheon Books, 1994.

Hobsbawm, Eric, and Terence Ranger, eds. *The Invention of Tradition*. Cambridge: Cambridge University Press, 1983, 1992.

Hofheinz, Roy, Jr., and Kent E. Calder. *The Eastasia Edge*. New York: Basic Books, Inc., 1982.

Holstein, William J. *The Japanese Power Game: What It Means for America*. New York: Charles Scribner's Sons, 1990.

Honda, H. H., trans. *The Manyoshu: A New and Complete Translation*. Tokyo: The Hokuseido Press, 1967.

Honda, Katsuichi. *The Impoverished Spirit: Selected Essays*. New York: Monthly Review Press, 1993.

Horio, Teruhisa. *Educational Thought and Ideology in Modern Japan: State Authority and Intellectual Freedom*. Tokyo: University of Tokyo Press, 1988.

Hosokawa, Morihiro. *The Time to Act Is Now: Thoughts for a New Japan*. Tokyo: NTT Mediascope, 1993.

Hunt, Morton. *The Natural History of Love,* rev. ed. New York: Doubleday, 1959, 1994.

Huntington, Samuel P., et al. *The Clash of Civilizations?: The Debate*. New York: Council on Foreign Relations, 1993.

Ibuse, Masuji. *Black Rain*. Tokyo and New York: Kodansha International, 1969, 1988.

Ienaga, Saburo. *Japanese Art: A Cultural Appreciation*. New York: Weatherhill; Tokyo: Heibonsha, 1979.

———. *The Pacific War, 1931–1945: A Critical Perspective on Japan's Role in World War II*. New York: Pantheon Books, 1978.

Iijima, Takehisa, and James M. Vardaman, Jr., eds. *The World of Natsume Soseki*. Tokyo: Kinseido, 1987.

Ikegamai, Eiko. *The Taming of the Samurai: Honorific Individualism and the Making of Modern Japan*. Cambridge, Mass., and London: Harvard University Press, 1995.

Ikku, Jippensha. *Shank's Mare, Being a Translation of the Tokaido Volumes of* Hizakurige. Tokyo and Rutland: 1960, 1988.

Imamura, Anne E. *Urban Japanese Housewives: At Home and in the Community*. Honolulu: University of Hawaii Press, 1987.

Irokawa, Daikichi. *The Age of Hirohito: In Search of Modern Japan*. New York: Free Press, 1995.

Ishihara, Shintaro. *The Japan That Can Say No: Why Japan Will Be First Among Equals*. New York: Simon and Schuster, 1989, 1991.

Isozaki, Arata. *The Island Nation Aesthetic*. London: Academy Editions, 1996.

Ivy, Marilyn. *Discourses of the Vanishing: Modernity, Phantasm, Japan*. Chicago and London: University of Chicago Press, 1995.

Iwakuni, Tetsundo. *Izumakara no Chosen (Challenge from Izumo)*. Tokyo: Nihon Hosso Shuppan Kyokai, 1991.

———. and Hosokawa, Morihiro. *Hina no Ronri (The Logic of the Countryside)*. Tokyo: Kobunsha, 1991.

Iwao, Sumiko. *The Japanese Woman: Traditional Image and Changing Reality*. New York: Free Press, 1993.

Jameson, Frederic. *Postmodernism: or, The Cultural Logic of Late Capitalism*. Durham: Duke University Press, 1991, 1995.

Jansen, Marius B., ed. *Changing Japanese Attitudes Toward Modernization*. Rutland and Tokyo: Charles E. Tuttle, 1982, 1985.

Japan Architect, ed. *A Guide to Japanese Architecture*. Tokyo: Shinkenchiku-sha Co., 1984.

Japan Travel Bureau Inc. *"Salaryman" in Japan*. Tokyo: J.T.B., 1986, 1991.

Japanese Folk Craft Museum, ed. *Mingei: The Living Tradition in Japanese Arts*. Tokyo: Kodansha International, 1991.

Johnson, Chalmers. *Conspiracy at Matsukawa.* Berkeley, Los Angeles, and London: University of California Press, 1972.

———. *Japan: Who Governs? The Rise of the Developmental State.* New York and London: W. W. Norton, 1995.

———. *MITI and the Japanese Miracle: The Growth of Industrial Policy, 1925–1975.* Stanford: Stanford University Press, 1982.

Johnson, Sheila. *The Japanese Through American Eyes.* Stanford: Stanford University Press, 1988, 1991.

Jung, C. G. *The Basic Writings of C. G. Jung.* New York: Modern Library, 1993.

Kaiko, Takeshi. *Darkness in Summer.* Tokyo and Rutland: Charles E. Tuttle, 1973, 1984.

Kamata, Satoshi. *Japan's Underground Empire: The Triangle of the L.D.P., Corporations, and Crime Syndicates.* Tokyo: Daisan Shokan: 1993.

Kampani, Masako. *Mitsui Mariko no Shiten 1 (The Perspective of Mariko Mitsui),* 2 vols. Tokyo: Josei to Seijikenkyo Senta, 1989, 1991.

Kano, Yoshikazu, Yukio Noguchi, Seichiro Saito, and Haruo Shimada. *The Japanese Economy in the 1990s: Problems and Prognoses.* Tokyo: Foreign Press Center, 1993.

Kaplan, David E., and Alec Dubro. *Yakuza: The Explosive Account of Japan's Criminal Underworld.* London: Futura, 1987.

Karatani, Kojin. *Origins of Modern Japanese Literature.* Durham and London: Duke University Press, 1993.

Kataoka, Tetsuya, ed. *Creating Single-Party Democracy: Japan's Postwar Political System.* Stanford: Hoover Institution Press, 1992.

———. *The Price of a Constitution: The Origin of Japan's Postwar Politics.* New York, Philadelphia, Washington, and London: Crane Russak, 1991.

Kawabata, Yasunari. *House of the Sleeping Beauties and Other Stories.* Tokyo and New York: Kodansha International, 1969, 1980.

———. *Palm-of-the-Hand Stories.* New York: North Point Press, Farrar, Straus and Giroux, 1988, 1996.

———. *Snow Country.* Tokyo and Rutland: Charles E. Tuttle, 1956, 1985.

Kawabe, Nobuo, and Eisuke Daito, eds. *Education and Training in the Development of Modern Corporations.* Tokyo: University of Tokyo Press, 1993.

Kawamura, Nozomu. *Sociology and Society of Japan.* London and New York: Kegan Paul International, 1994.

Kayano, Shigeru. *Our Land Was a Forest: An Ainu Memoir.* Boulder, San Francisco, and Oxford: Westview Press, 1980, 1994.

Keene, Donald. *Dawn to the West: Japanese Literature in the Modern Era.* 2 vols. New York: Henry Holt and Co., 1984.

———. *Japanese Literature: An Introduction for Western Readers.* Tokyo and Rutland: Charles E. Tuttle, 1955, 1987.

———. *Seeds in the Heart: Japanese Literature from Earliest Times to the Late Sixteenth Century.* New York, 1993.

———. *Some Japanese Portraits.* Tokyo and New York: Kodansha International, 1978, 1983.

———. *The Pleasures of Japanese Literature*. New York: Columbia University Press, 1988.

Kennedy, Paul. *The Rise and Fall of the Great Powers: Economic Change and Military Conflict from 1500 to 2000*. New York: Vintage Books, 1987.

Kersten, Rikki. *Democracy in Postwar Japan: Maruyama Masao and the Search for Autonomy*. London and New York: Routledge, 1996.

Kido, Takayoshi. *The Diary of Kido Takayoshi*. 3 vols. Tokyo: University of Tokyo Press, 1983.

King, Winston L. *Zen and the Way of the Sword: Arming the Samurai Psyche*. New York and Oxford: Oxford University Press, 1993.

Kishimoto, Koichi. *Politics in Modern Japan: Development and Organization*. 3d ed. Tokyo: Japan Echo, 1988.

Kitamura, Hiroshi. *Choices for the Japanese Economy*. London: Royal Institute for International Affairs, 1976.

Koiso, Akio. *Fujiginko Koin no Kiroku (Record of a Fuji Bank Man)*. Tokyo: Banseisha, 1991.

———. *Ginko wa do natte iru no ka (What Happened to the Banks?)*. Tokyo: Banseisha, 1991.

Komiya, Ryutaro, Masahiro Okuno, and Kotaro Suzumura, eds. *Industrial Policy of Japan*. Tokyo, San Diego, and New York: Academic Press, 1988.

Koschmann, J. Victor, ed. *Authority and the Individual in Japan: Citizen Protest in Historical Perspective*. Tokyo: University of Tokyo Press, 1978.

———. *Revolution and Subjectivity in Postwar Japan*. Chicago: University of Chicago Press, 1996.

———. "The Debate on Subjectivity in Postwar Japan: Foundations of Modernism as a Political Critique." *Pacific Affairs* 54, no. 4 (Winter 1981).

Koschmann, J. Victor, Tetsuo Najita, eds. *Conflict in Modern Japanese History: The Neglected Tradition*. Princeton: Princeton University Press, 1982.

Kristeva, Julia. *Nations Without Nationalism*. New York: Columbia University Press, 1993.

———. *Strangers to Ourselves*. New York: Columbia University Press, 1991.

Kurokawa, Kisho. *From Metabolism to Symbiosis*. London: Academy Editions; New York: St. Martin's Press, 1992.

———. *Intercultural Architecture: The Philosophy of Symbiosis*. London: Academy Editions, 1991.

———. *New Wave Japanese Architecture*. London: Academy Editions; Berlin: Ernst & Sohn, 1993.

———. *Recent Works: 1987–1992*. Tokyo: 1993.

———. *Rediscovering Japanese Space*. New York and Tokyo: Weatherhill, 1988.

———. *The Architecture of Symbiosis*. New York: Rizzoli Publications, 1988.

———. *The Philosophy of Symbiosis*. London: Academy Editions; Berlin: Ernst & Sohn, 1994.

Kurosawa, Akira. *Something Like an Autobiography*. New York: Alfred A. Knopf, 1982.

Kuttner, Robert. *The End of Laissez-Faire: National Purpose and the Global Economy After the Cold War.* Philadelphia: University of Pennsylvania Press, 1991.

Kyogoku, Jun-ichi. *The Political Dynamics of Japan.* Tokyo: University of Tokyo Press, 1983, 1987.

Large, Stephen. *The Rise of Labor in Japan: The Yuaikai, 1912–1919.* Tokyo: Sophia University Press, 1972.

Lasch, Christopher. *The Culture of Narcissism: American Life in an Age of Diminishing Expectations.* New York and London: Norton, 1979.

Lebra, Takie Sugiyama. *Japanese Patterns of Behavior.* Honolulu: University of Hawaii Press, 1979.

———, ed. *Japanese Social Organization.* Honolulu: University of Hawaii Press, 1992.

Lehmann, Jean-Pierre. *The Roots of Modern Japan.* London and Basingstoke: MacMillan Press, 1982.

Levenson, Joseph R. *Confucian China and Its Modern Fate: A Trilogy.* Berkeley and Los Angeles: University of California Press, 1958, 1965.

Lévi-Strauss, Claude. *Tristes Tropiques.* New York: Atheneum, 1955, 1970.

Lifton, Robert Jay. "Youth and History: Individual Change in Postwar Japan. In *The Challenge of Youth,* edited by Erik H. Erikson. New York: Doubleday, 1961, 1965.

Lincoln, Edward J. *Japan: Facing Economic Maturity.* Washington: Brookings Institution, 1988.

Lippit, Noriko Mizuta, and Koyko Iriye Selden, eds. *Japanese Women Writers: Twentieth Century Short Fiction.* Armonk and New York: M. E. Sharpe, 1991.

Livingston, Jon, Joe Moore, and Felicia Oldfather. *Imperial Japan: 1800–1945 (The Japan Reader,* no. 1). New York: Pantheon Books, 1973.

———. *Postwar Japan: 1945 to the Present (The Japan Reader,* no. 2). New York: Pantheon Books, 1973.

Locke, John. *An Essay Concerning Human Understanding.* 2 vols. London: Dent; New York: Dutton, 1961, 1972.

Lukes, Steven. *Power: A Radical View.* London and Basingstoke: MacMillan Press, 1974, 1978.

Mariani, Fosco. *Meeting With Japan.* New York: Viking, 1959.

Maruyama, Masao. "Japanese Thought." *Journal of Social and Political Ideas in Japan* (April 1964).

———. *Studies in the Intellectual History of Tokugawa Japan.* Tokyo: University of Tokyo Press, 1974.

———. *Thought and Behavior in Modern Japanese Politics.* Expanded ed. London, Oxford, and New York: Oxford University Press, 1963, 1969.

Masumi, Junnosuke. *Contemporary Politics in Japan.* Berkeley, Los Angeles, and London: University of California Press, 1995.

Matthews, Masayuki Hamabata. *Crested Kimono: Power and Love in the Japanese Family.* Ithaca and London: Cornell University Press, 1990.

McCormack, Gavan, and Yoshio Sugimoto, eds. *Democracy in Contemporary Japan.* Armonk and London: M. E. Sharpe, 1986.

———. *The Emptiness of Japanese Affluence*. Armonk and London: M. E. Sharpe, 1996.

McCune, Shannon. *The Ryukyu Islands*. Newton Abbott: David & Charles; Harrisburg: Stackpole Books, 1975.

McKinstry, John A., and Asako Nakajima McKinstry. *Jinsei Annai, "Life's Guide": Glimpses of Japan Through a Popular Advice Column*. Armonk and London: M. E. Sharpe, 1991.

McNeil, Frank. *Democracy in Japan: The Emerging Global Concern*. New York: Crown Publishers, 1994.

Mill, J.S. *On Liberty*. Indianapolis and New York: Bobbs-Merrill, 1859, 1956.

Miller, Henry. *Reflections on the Death of Mishima*. Santa Barbara: Capra Press, 1972.

Mills, C. Wright. *The Power Elite*. Oxford and New York: Oxford University Press, 1956.

———. *The Sociological Imagination*. Oxford and New York: Oxford University Press, 1959, 1967.

Milton, John. *English Prose Works*, 2 vols. Boston: Bowles and Dearborn, 1826.

Mishima, Yukio. *Confessions of a Mask*. New York: New Directions, 1958.

———. *Death in Midsummer and Other Stories*. New York: New Directions, 1966.

———. *The Sailor Who Fell from Grace to the Sea*. Tokyo and Rutland: Charles E. Tuttle, 1965, 1986.

———. *The Sound of Waves*. Tokyo and Rutland: Charles E. Tuttle, 1956, 1988.

———. *The Temple of the Golden Pavilion*. Tokyo and Rutland: Charles E. Tuttle, 1959, 1989.

Mita, Munesuke. *Social Psychology of Modern Japan*. London and New York: Kegan Paul International, 1992.

Mitsui, Mariko. *Majonna Majoriti Sengen (Witches' Majority Statement)*. Tokyo: Metamoru Shuppan, 1989.

———. *Mitwataseba Arra Otoko Bakari (If you look around there are so many guys)*. Tokyo: Nihonjistugyo Shuppansha, 1988.

———. *Momoiro no Kenryoku (Pink power)*. Tokyo: Sanseido, 1992.

———. *Ochakumi no Seijigaku Jiko Inkai Ochakumi no Seijigaku (The political study of tea serving)*. Tokyo: Peace-Neto Kikaku, 1992.

Miyoshi, Masao, *Accomplices of Silence: The Modern Japanese Novel*. Ann Arbor, Calif.: Center for Japanese Studies, Univ. of Michigan, 1974, 1994.

Miyoshi, Masao, and H. D. Harootunian, eds. *Japan in the World*. Durham and London: Duke University Press, 1993.

———, eds. *Postmodernism in Japan*. Durham and London: Duke University Press, 1989.

Mori, Ogai. *The Wild Goose*. Ann Arbor: Center for Japanese Studies, University of Michigan, 1995.

Morishima, Michio. *Why Has Japan 'Succeeded'?: Western Technology and the Japanese Ethos*. Cambridge: Cambridge University Press, 1982, 1986.

Moriyama, Alan Takeo. *Imingaisha: Japanese Emigration Companies and Hawaii*. Honolulu: University of Hawaii Press, 1985.

Morris, Ivan. *The Nobility of Failure: Tragic Heroes in the History of Japan*. Rutland and Tokyo: Charles E. Tuttle, 1975, 1982.

Morrison, Andrew P., ed. *Essential Papers on Narcissism.* New York and London: New York University Press, 1986.

Morse, Edward S. *Japanese Homes and Their Surroundings.* Tokyo and Rutland: Charles E. Tuttle, 1886, 1992.

Mouer, Ross, and Yoshio Sugimoto. *Images of Japanese Society: A Study in the Social Construction of Reality.* London and New York: Kegan Paul International, 1986, 1990.

Munroe, Alexandra, ed. *Japanese Art After 1945: Scream Against the Sky.* New York: Harry N. Abrams, 1994.

Murakami, Haruki. *A Wild Sheep Chase.* Tokyo and New York: Kodansha International, 1989.

———. *Dance, Dance, Dance.* Tokyo and New York: Kodansha International, 1992.

———. *Norwegian Wood.* 2 vols. Tokyo: Kodansha International, 1989.

Nagata, Seiji, et al. *Katsuhika Hokusai,* 2 vols. Tokyo: Asahi Shimbun, 1993.

Nakamura, Masanori. *The Japanese Monarchy: Ambassador Joseph Grew and the Making of the "Symbol Emperor System," 1931–1991.* Armonk and London, M. E. Sharpe, 1992.

Nakamura, Takafusa. *The Postwar Japanese Economy: Its Development and Structure.* Tokyo: University of Tokyo Press, 1981.

Nakane, Chie. *Japanese Society.* Tokyo and Rutland: Charles E. Tuttle, 1970, 1990.

Nakane, Chie, and Shinzaburo Oishi, eds. *Tokagawa Japan: The Social and Economic Antecedents of Modern Japan.* Tokyo: University of Tokyo Press, 1990.

Nakasone, Yasuhiro. *Seiji to Jinsei (Politics and Life).* Tokyo: Kodansha, 1992.

Nakayama, Chinatsu. *Behind the Waterfall: Three Novellas.* New York: Atheneum, 1990.

National Defense Council for Victims of Karoshi. *Karoshi: When the Corporate Warrior Dies.* Tokyo: Mado-Sha, 1990.

National Museum of Modern Art, ed. *Art of the Showa Period—From the Museum Collection.* Tokyo: National Museum, 1989.

Natsume, Soseki. *And Then.* Baton Rouge: University of Louisiana Press, 1978.

———. *Botchan.* Rutland and Tokyo: Charles E. Tuttle, 1904, 1992.

———. *Kokoro.* Rutland and Tokyo: Charles E. Tuttle, 1914, 1993.

———. "My Individualism." In "Soseki on Individualism," by Jay Rubin. *Monumenta Nipponica* 34, no. 1.

Nemoto, Takashi. *Shinjinrui vs. Kanrisha.* Tokyo: Chuokeizaisha, 1987.

Ninomiya, Shigeaki. *An Inquiry Concerning the Origin, Development, and Present Situation of the* Eta *in Relation to the History of Social Classes in Japan.* Tokyo: Asiatic Society of Japan, 1933.

Nishiyama. Takesuke. *Za Ligu: Shimbun Hodo no Uraomote (The league: newspaper journalism).* Tokyo: Kodansha, 1992.

Nomi, Masahiko. *Ketsuekigata Ningengaku (Bloodtype as human study).* Tokyo: Sankei Shimbunsha Shuppankyoku, 1974.

Nomi, Toshinori. *Ketsuekigata Watchingu (Watching bloodtypes).* Tokyo: Kosaido Shuppan, 1992.

Norman, E. H. *Japan's Emergence As a Modern State: Political and Economic Problems of the Meiji Period.* New York: Institute of Pacific Relations, 1940.

———. *Origins of the Modern Japanese State: Selected Writings of E. H. Norman.* Edited by John W. Dower. New York: Pantheon Books, 1975.

Oe, Kenzaburo. *A Personal Matter.* Tokyo and Rutland: Charles E. Tuttle, 1968, 1988.

———. *Hiroshima Notes.* Tokyo: YMCA Press, 1981.

———. *Teach Us to Outgrow Our Madness: Four Short Novels.* London: Serpent's Tail, 1977, 1989.

———. *The Silent Cry.* Tokyo and New York: Kodansha International, 1967, 1986.

Ohwa, Satsuki. *Kono Hanashigata ga Donna Aitemo Mikatani Kaeru (This way of speaking makes anyone your ally).* Tokyo: Gendai Shorin, 1989.

Ohnuki-Tierney, Emiko. *Rice As Self: Japanese Identities Through Time.* Princeton: Princeton University Press, 1993.

Okimoto, Daniel I., and Thomas P. Rohlen, eds. *Inside the Japanese System: Readings on Contemporary Society and Political Economy.* Stanford: Stanford University Press, 1988.

Okita, Saburo. *Steps to the 21st Century.* Tokyo: Japan Times, 1993.

Osaka Women's Association, ed. *Women Who Open Up "Tomorrow": Over the Discrimination Wall.* Osaka: Buraku Liberation Research Institute, n.d.

Osaragi, Jiro. *The Journey.* Tokyo and Rutland: Charles E. Tuttle, 1960, 1987.

Ozawa, Ichiro. *Blueprint for a New Japan: The Rethinking of a Nation.* Tokyo, New York, and London: Kodansha International, 1994.

Papinot, E. *Historical and Geographical Dictionary of Japan.* 2 vols. New York: Frederick Ungar Publishing Co., 1910, 1964.

Parkes, Graham. *Nietzsche and Asian Thought.* Chicago: University of Chicago Press, 1991, 1996.

Patrick, Hugh, and Henry Rosovsky, eds. *Asia's New Giant: How the Japanese Economy Works.* Washington: Brookings Institution, 1976.

Patrick, Hugh, ed. *Japanese Industrialization and Its Social Consequences.* Berkeley, Los Angeles, and London: University of California Press, 1976.

Pedlar, Neil. *The Imported Pioneers: Westerners Who Helped Build Modern Japan.* Sandgate, Folkstone: Japan Library, 1990.

Pincus, Leslie. *Authenticating Culture in Imperial Japan: Kuki Shuzo and the Rise of National Aesthetics.* Berkeley, Los Angeles, and London: University of California Press, 1996.

Pons, Philippe. *D'Edo à Tokyo, mémoires et modernités.* Paris: NRF, Editions Gallimard, 1988.

Prange, Gordon W. *At Dawn We Slept: The Untold Story of Pearl Harbor.* New York: McGraw-Hill Book Company, 1981.

Prince, Stephen. *The Warrior's Camera: The Cinema of Akira Kurosawa.* Princeton: Princeton University Press, 1991.

Pye, Lucien W. *Asian Power and Politics: The Cultural Dimensions of Authority.* Cambridge, Mass., and London: Belknap Press, Harvard University, 1985.

Random, Michel. *Japan: Strategy of the Unseen*. Wellingborough: Thorsens Publishing, 1987.

Reischauer, Edwin O., *Japan: Past and Present*. Rev. ed. New York: Alfred A. Knopf, 1946, 1958.

———. *My Life Between Japan and America*. Tokyo: John Weatherhill, 1986.

———. *The Japanese*. Cambridge, Mass., and London: Belknap Press, Harvard University, 1977.

———. *The Japanese Today: Change and Continuity*. Cambridge, Mass., and London: Belknap Press, Harvard University, 1988.

———. *The United States and Japan*. Cambridge, Mass.: Harvard University Press, 1965.

Richie, Donald. *A Lateral View, Essays on Contemporary Japan*. Rev. ed. Tokyo: Japan Times, 1987, 1991.

———. *Different People: Pictures of Some Japanese*. Tokyo and New York: Kodansha International, 1987.

———. *The Inland Sea*. London and Melbourne: Century, 1971, 1978.

———. *Japanese Cinema: An Introduction*. Hong Kong, Oxford, and New York: Oxford University Press, 1990.

Riesman, David. *The Lonely Crowd*. New Haven: Yale University Press, 1950.

Rimer, J. Thomas. *A Reader's Guide to Japanese Literature, from the Eighth Century to the Present*. Tokyo and New York: Kodansha International, 1988.

Roberts, John G. *Mitsui: Three Centuries of Japanese Business*. New York and Tokyo: Weatherhill, 1973, 1989.

Rose, Barbara. *Tsuda Umeko and Women's Education in Japan*. New Haven and London: Yale University Press, 1992.

Rosenstone, Robert A. *Mirror in the Shrine: American Encounters with Meiji Japan*. Cambridge, Mass.: Harvard University Press, 1988.

Rozman, Gilbert. *Japan's Response to the Gorbachev Era, 1985–1991: A Rising Superpower Views a Declining One*. Princeton: Princeton University Press, 1992.

Sadler, A. L., trans. *The Ten Foot Square Hut and Tales of the Heike, Being Two Thirteenth-Century Japanese Classics, the "Hojoki" and Selections from the "Heike Monogatari."* Tokyo and Rutland: Charles E. Tuttle, 1972, 1990.

Saga, Junichi. *Memories of Silk and Straw: A Self-Portrait of Small-Town Japan*. Tokyo and New York: Kodansha International, 1987.

Said, Edward. *Culture and Imperialism*. New York: Vintage Books, 1993, 1994.

———. *Orientalism*. New York: Pantheon Books, 1978.

Sakakibara, Eisuke. *Beyond Capitalism: The Japanese Model of Market Economics*. Lanham, New York, and London: University Press of America, 1993.

Samuels, Richard J. *The Politics of Regional Policy in Japan: Localities Incorporated?* Princeton: Princeton University Press, 1983.

Sansom, George B. *A History of Japan*. 3 vols. Tokyo and Rutland: Charles E. Tuttle, 1963, 1990.

———. *Japan: A Short Cultural History*. London: Cresset Library, Century Hutchinson, 1931, 1987.

Sasaki, Kuniichi. *Kokuhatsu Sumitomo Seimei (The case against Sumitomo Life)*. Tokyo: Yell Books, 1992.

Saso, Mary. *Women in the Japanese Workplace*. London: Hilary Shipman, 1990.

Sato, Ikuya. *Kamikaze Biker: Parody and Anomy in Affluent Japan*. Chicago and London: University of Chicago Press, 1991.

Sato, Seizaburo, Ken'ichi Koyama, and Shunpei Kumon. *Postwar Politician: The Life of Former Prime Minister Masayoshi Ohira*. Tokyo and New York: Kodansha International, 1990.

Sato, Tadao. *Currents in Japanese Cinema*. Tokyo and New York: Kodansha International, 1982, 1987.

Sawada, Yoshihiro. *Sagawa Kyubin o Naibu Kokuhatsu Suru (Inside the prosecution of Sagawa Kyubin)*. Tokyo: Appuru Shuppansha, 1989.

Scalapino, Robert A. *Democracy and the Party Movement in Prewar Japan: The Failure of the First Attempt*. Berkeley and Los Angeles: University of California Press, 1953.

Schonberger, Howard B. *Aftermath of War: Americans and the Remaking of Japan, 1945–1952*. Kent, Ohio, and London: Kent State University Press, 1989.

Scott-Stokes, Henry. *The Life and Death of Yukio Mishima*. New York: Farrar, Straus and Giroux, 1974.

Seidensticker, Edward. *Low City, High City: Tokyo from Edo to the Earthquake, 1867–1923*. Hammondsworth: Penguin Books, 1983.

————. *Tokyo Rising: The City Since the Great Earthquake*. New York: Alfred A. Knopf, 1990.

Sennett, Richard. *The Fall of Public Man*. New York: Alfred A. Knopf, 1977.

Severns, Karen. *Hirohito*. New York: Chelsea House Publishers, 1988.

Shields, James J., Jr., ed. *Japanese Schooling: Patterns of Socialization, Equality and Political Control*. University Park and London: Pennsylvania State University Press, 1989.

Shikata, Hiroshi. *Kemmuri o Hoshi ni Kaeta Machi (The town that changed smoke into stardust)*. Tokyo: Kodansha, 1991.

Shimada, Haruo. *Japan's "Guest Workers": Issues and Public Policies*. Tokyo: University of Tokyo Press, 1994.

Shimizu, Yoshiaki. *Japan: The Shaping of Daimyo Culture, 1185–1868*. Washington: National Gallery of Art, 1988.

Shively, Donald H., ed. *Tradition and Modernization in Japanese Culture*. Princeton: Princeton University Press, 1971, 1976.

Singer, Kurt. *Mirror, Sword and Jewel: The Geometry of Japanese Life*. Tokyo and New York: Kodansha International, 1973, 1990.

Singleton, John. *Nichu: A Japanese School*. New York: Irvington Publishers, 1967, 1982.

Smith, Thomas C. *Native Sources of Industrialization, 1750–1920*. Berkeley, Los Angeles, and London: University of California Press, 1988.

Stephens, Michael D. *Education and the Future of Japan*. Sandgate, Folkstone: Japan Library, 1991.

Stevens, John. *Three Zen Masters: Ikkyu, Hakuin, Ryokan.* Tokyo and New York: Kodansha International, 1993.

Stewart, David B., ed. *Arata Isozaki: Architecture, 1960/1990.* Tokyo: Executive Committee for the Exhibition, 1991.

―――. *The Making of a Modern Japanese Architecture: 1868 to the Present.* Tokyo and New York: Kodansha International, 1987.

Storry, Richard. *A History of Modern Japan.* Hammondsworth: Penguin Books, 1960, 1985.

Street, Julian. *Mysterious Japan.* Garden City and Toronto: Doubleday, Page & Co., 1921.

Sumii, Sue. *The River with No Bridge.* Tokyo and Rutland: Charles E. Tuttle, 1990.

Takaoka, Akio. *Kokuhatsu Jidosha Gyokai (The case against automobile companies).* Tokyo: Yell Books, 1991.

Takashima, Shuji, and J. Thomas Rimer, with Gerald D. Bolas. *Paris in Japan: The Japanese Encounter with European Painting.* Tokyo: Japan Foundation; St. Louis: Washington University, 1987.

Takayanagi, Shunichi, and Kimitada Miwa, eds. *Postwar Trends in Japan: Studies in Commemoration of Rev. Aloysius Miller, S.J.* Tokyo: University of Tokyo Press, 1975.

Takeuchi, Hiroshi. *Flexible Structure of the Japanese Economy.* Tokyo: Long-Term Credit Bank of Japan, 1986.

Tanaka, Kakuei. *Building a New Japan: A Plan for Remodeling the Japanese Archipelago.* Tokyo: Simul Press, 1972.

Tanaka, Yukiko, ed. *Unmapped Territories: New Women's Fiction From Japan.* Seattle: Women in Translation, 1991.

Tanizaki, Junichiro. *In Praise of Shadows.* Tokyo and Rutland: Charles E. Tuttle, 1977, 1990.

―――. *Naomi.* New York: Alfred A. Knopf, 1985. (Also translated as *A Fool's Love.*) New York: Alfred A. Knopf, 1985.

―――. *Quicksand.* New York: Alfred A. Knopf, 1993.

―――. *Some Prefer Nettles.* New York: Alfred A. Knopf, 1955.

―――. *The Makioka Sisters.* New York: Alfred A. Knopf, 1955.

―――. *The Reed Cutter: Two Novellas.* New York: Alfred A. Knopf, 1994.

Thomson, James C., Jr., Peter W. Stanley, and John Curtis Perry. *Sentimental Imperialists: The American Experience in East Asia.* New York: Harper & Row, 1981.

Thurow, Lester. *Head to Head: The Coming Economic Battle Among Japan, Europe, and America.* New York: William Morrow and Company, 1992.

Toland, John. *The Rising Sun: The Decline and Fall of the Japanese Empire, 1936–1945.* 2 vols. New York: Random House, 1970.

Totman, Conrad. *Early Modern Japan.* Berkeley, Los Angeles, and London: University of California Press, 1993.

Toynbee, Arnold J. *A Study of History.* 12 vols. Oxford and New York: Oxford University Press, Royal Institute of International Affairs, 1934–1961.

Tsunoda, Ryusaku, William Theodore de Bary, and Donald Keene, eds. *Sources of Japanese Tradition*. 2 vols. New York: Columbia University Press, 1964.

Tsunoda, Tadanobu. *The Japanese Brain: Uniqueness and Universality*. Tokyo: Taishukan Publishing, 1985.

Tsuru, Shigeto. *Japan's Capitalism: Creative Defeat and Beyond*. Cambridge: Cambridge University Press, 1993, 1996.

Tsurumi, Kazuko. "Animism and Science." Tokyo: Institute of International Relations, Sophia University, 1992.

———. "Japan and Holy War." Tokyo: Institute of International Relations, Sophia University, 1993.

———. *Social Change and the Individual: Japan Before and After Defeat in World War II*. Princeton: Princeton University Press, 1970.

———. "Women in Japan: A Paradox of Modernization." Tokyo: Institute of International Relations, Sophia University, 1977, 1989.

Tsurumi, Shunsuke. *A Cultural History of Postwar Japan, 1945–1980*. London and New York: Kegan Paul International, 1987.

———. *An Intellectual History of Wartime Japan, 1931–1945*. London: Kegan Paul International, 1982, 1986.

Tsushima, Yuko. *Woman Running in the Mountains*. New York: Pantheon Books, 1991.

Ueda, Makoto. *Matsuo Basho: The Master Haiku Poet*. Tokyo and New York: Kodansha International, 1970, 1982.

Ushida, Shigeru, and Ikuyo Mitsuhashi. *Interiors of Ichida, Mitsuhashi and Studio 80*. Tokyo: Rikuyo-sha, 1987.

van Wolferen, Karel. "Japan in the Age of Uncertainty." *New Left Review*, no. 200 (July–August 1993).

———. "Japan's Non-Revolution." *Foreign Affairs*, September/October 1993.

———. *The Enigma of Japanese Power: People and Politics in a Stateless Nation*. London: MacMillan, 1989.

———. "The Japan Problem." *Foreign Affairs*, Winter 1986/87.

Ventura, Rey. *Underground in Japan*. London: Jonathan Cape, 1992.

Vining, Elizabeth Gray. *Windows for the Crown Prince: Akihito of Japan*. Tokyo and Rutland: Charles E. Tuttle, 1952, 1989.

Vogel, Ezra F. *Japan As No. 1: Lessons for America*. Cambridge, Mass., and London: Harvard University Press, 1979.

———. *Japan's New Middle Class: The Salary Man and His Family in a Tokyo Suburb*. 2d ed. Berkeley, Los Angeles, and London: University of California Press, 1963.

von Laue, Theodore H. *The World Revolution of Westernization: The Twentieth Century in Global Perspective*. New York and Oxford: Oxford University Press, 1987.

Walker, Janet A. *The Japanese Novel of the Meiji Period and the Ideal of Individualism*. Princeton: Princeton University Press, 1979.

Walthall, Anne, ed. *Peasant Uprisings in Japan: A Critical Anthology of Peasant Histories*. Chicago and London: University of Chicago Press, 1991.

Washburn, Dennis C. *The Dilemma of the Modern in Japanese Fiction*. New Haven and London: Yale University Press, 1995.

Watanabe, Shoichi. *The Peasant Soul of Japan*. London and Basingstoke: MacMillan Press, 1989.

Weber, Max. *The Religion of China*. New York: Free Press; London: Collier-MacMillan, 1951.

———. *Sociological Writings*. Edited by Wolf Heydebrand. New York: Continuum Publishing, 1994.

Weiner, Michael. *The Origins of the Korean Community in Japan, 1910–1923*. Atlantic Highlands, N.J.: Humanities Press International, 1989.

White, Merry. *The Japanese Educational Challenge: A Commitment to Children*. Tokyo and New York: Kodansha International, 1987.

Wigen, Karen. *The Making of the Japanese Periphery, 1750–1920*. Berkeley, Los Angeles, and London: University of California Press, 1995.

Wilde, Oscar. *The Artist As Critic: Critical Writings of Oscar Wilde*. Edited by Richard Ellmann. New York: Random House, 1969.

Wilkinson, Endymion. *Japan Versus Europe: A History of Misunderstanding*. Hammondsworth: Penguin Books, 1983.

Williams, David. *Japan: Beyond the End of History*. London and New York: Routledge, 1994.

Wilson, George M. *Patriots and Redeemers: Motives in the Meiji Restoration*. Chicago and London: University of Chicago Press, 1992.

Wood, Christopher. *The Bubble Economy: The Japanese Economic Collapse*. Tokyo: Charles E. Tuttle, 1993.

Yokota, Hamao. *Hamidashi Ginkoman no Kinbanniki (The unusual banker's diary)*. Tokyo: OS Shuppansha, 1992.

Yoshimoto, Banana. *Kitchen*. New York: Grove Press, 1993.

Yoshino, Kosaku. *Cultural Nationalism in Contemporary Japan*. London: Routledge, 1992.

Yutaka, Kosai. *The Era of High-Speed Growth: Notes on the Postwar Japanese Economy*. Tokyo: University of Tokyo Press, 1986.

Ze-ami. *Kadensho, The Secret of No Drama*. Tokyo: Sumiya-Shinobe Publishing Institute, 1968.

INDEX

INDEX

RUSSIA

• Vladivostok

CHINA

NORTH
KOREA

★ Pyongyang

Sea of Japan

★ Seoul

SOUTH
KOREA

Kana
In

• Pusan

Izumo
• • Kakeya

Biwako
Kyoto
Shimane •

Tsushima Strait

Hiroshima

Kobe •Nishino

Kitakyushu•

Osaka •Na

Shimonoseki

Takamatsu•

•Sakai

Oita

Tokushima

•Wakayama

Oguni•

•Kumamoto

Shikoku

Kumamoto

Kyushu

Fukuyama•

East China Sea

J

A

Okinawa

•Naha